CAMPUS COMPACT'S

# Introduction to Service-Learning Toolkit

**READINGS AND RESOURCES FOR FACULTY**

second edition

D0557111

**Campus Compact**

# Table of Contents

# Introduction to the Second Edition

THE CONTENTS OF THIS REVISED EDITION reflect growing interest in—and, consequently, publications about—service-learning since the first *Introduction to Service-Learning Toolkit* was published in 2000. This growth is reflected in the expanded "Recommended Readings" lists that accompany each chapter as well as in the new selections that have been added to this edition. In addition to updated material throughout and expanded chapters on Community Partnerships, Student Development, and Redesigning Curriculum, we have added two new chapters, one exploring the connection between service-learning and civic engagement and the other focusing on community-based research.

The growing body of literature about service-learning can be attributed to several factors. The first is a dramatic increase in the number of faculty who employ service-learning in the classroom. Results from Campus Compact's 2002 member survey revealed that campuses offer an average of 30 service-learning courses each, up from 27 just a year before. A related factor is expansion in the number of campuses committed to the civic purposes of higher education. Colleges and universities across the country are rediscovering their historic missions of preparing students for lives of democratic participation and applying their institutional resources to addressing societal needs. This increased commitment is reflected in the growth of Campus Compact, the only higher education association whose sole purpose is to promote campus-based public and community service. In 2000, when the first edition of the *Toolkit* was published, Campus Compact had just over 650 member campuses and 22 state Compact offices. These figures have grown to more than 900 member campuses served by 30 state Compact offices.

Finally, the increased attention to service-learning is part of a heightened focus on engaged teaching and learning practices in general. Scholars and academic leaders such as Ernest Boyer, John Barr, Robert Tagg, George Kuh, and Terry O'Banion—as well as organizations such as the Carnegie Endowment for Teaching and Learning, the American Association for Higher Education, the American Association of Community Colleges, the Association of American Colleges and Universities, and the League for Innovation—have challenged America's colleges and universities to make student learning central to the academic mission of higher education. Those who have accepted this challenge have found service-learning to be a powerful strategy for engaging their students in mastery of academic skills and content through service to their communities.

It is more evident than ever that service-learning is not a recent phenomenon or an educational fad; it has a rich history rooted in the transformative progressive educational and social ideals of those such as John Dewey and Jane Addams. Like other forms of experiential education, service-learning allows students to test skills and facts learned in the classroom, sharpen problem-solving abilities, and work collaboratively with diverse groups of people. At the same time, service-learning differs from other forms of experiential education in that it focuses on preparing students for practical community-based problem solving rather than for a particular job or career.

Service-learning offers students an opportunity to explore the connections between the theoretical realm of the classroom and the practical needs of the community. It simultaneously reinforces the skills of critical thinking, public discourse, collective activity, and community building. The educational context for the service activity requires students to reflect upon their service experiences in relation to community principles, civic ideals, and universal virtues, as well as course content. Perhaps the most important long-term benefit of service-learning is the opportunity for students to connect to a community and identify their civic roles in that community.

This revised toolkit is designed to provide an introduction to some of the fundamental issues surrounding teaching and learning that lie at the core of service-learning. The essays and bibliographies in the toolkit examine both the research underpinning service-learning as a pedagogy and the practicalities of implementing service-learning on campus and in the classroom. Chapters address a spectrum of topics from the principles and theory of service-learning to model programs to promotion and tenure guidelines:

- Definitions and principles
- Learning theory
- Pedagogy
- Reflection
- Redesigning curriculum
- Model programs
- Student development
- Civic engagement
- Community partnerships
- Community-based research
- Assessment
- Academic culture
- Promotion and tenure

Each section begins with a series of questions; reflecting upon these questions can help the reader gain insight into where he or she falls on the continuum of service-learning—from beginner to advanced practitioner. Answers to the questions will assist in the development of individual and/or institutional action plans for incorporating service-learning into the curriculum.

In addition to helping faculty work through "nuts and bolts" issues related to service-learning, this toolkit has another goal: to encourage faculty to reconceptualize not only their curricula, but also their disciplinary training and their roles as educators. Faculty are increasingly defined by narrow disciplinary boundaries. This constriction has resulted in departmental fragmentation, reward structures that are heavily biased toward scholarship, and an insular culture of academic professionalism. Many faculty express a sense of powerlessness on campus and a lack of clarity about their institutional role. This response comes in part from the isolation of privatized work, the disengagement of expertise, and a culture of discourse built on argument.

Part of reconceptualizing the role of faculty in a manner that can address these issues is to think about how to move the fragmented and insular work of the academy toward greater connection and agency. This requires faculty and administrators to examine strategies for shifting from a culture of privatized work to one of collective work, both within the department and across the institution. It also requires connecting professional expertise to public discourse for wider civic engagement and as a way of approaching the construction of knowledge. Finally, allowing faculty, students, and community partners to become part of the process of constructing knowledge requires shifting from a culture of argument to one of dialogue. Moving toward a reflective pedagogy that is student-centered, community-based, and experiential fundamentally redefines the faculty role on campus.

As empowering as service-learning can be in redefining faculty roles, many faculty find it difficult to relinquish the comfortable and predictable nature of classroom work, particularly at the beginning of the process. Service-learning is inevitably unpredictable and often uncomfortable. It challenges faculty and students on many levels as it incorporates shifting dialogues and actively engages participants in issues such as equity, difference, inclusion, tolerance, justice, and power.

In addition to taking faculty out of their comfort zones with respect to how to teach (pedagogy), adopting service-learning often raises issues related to what to teach (epistemology). This is because service-learning shifts the authority of knowledge in the classroom and intentionally places community in the center of the learning process. Such a shift requires acknowledgement that educational design is critical to engagement and that the construction of knowledge is directly related to how we utilize knowledge in reasoning. Furthermore, service as academic work assumes that cognitive, affective, and moral growth are inseparable, and that a student's ability to analyze situations and material is critical to his or her ability to make responsible decisions outside of the classroom. These skills and experiences are critical to participatory citizenship. In both civic and intellectual life one must consistently reflect on one's position, reconcile one's preconceptions with the lived experiences of others, and uphold an ethic of personal accountability and social responsibility.

The readings and questions in the Introduction to Service-Learning Toolkit are intended not only to raise these pedagogical and epistemological issues, but also to help the reader, either alone or with campus colleagues, work through these issues to broaden and deepen teaching and learning. Of course, the manner in which service-learning develops on your campus will differ in many respects from how it emerges on another campus. Its qualities will be shaped in large part by institutional identity and the degree to which that identity is tied to a wider sense of social responsibility. It will develop according to the characteristics of the academic culture on your campus and the degree to which your campus values community-based education, redefinitions of scholarship, and professional service aimed toward outreach and public purpose.

In some cases, institutional adoption of service-learning will be determined by a few faculty who act as agents for transformation. The tools provided here are intended both to assist faculty in thinking about teaching and learning and to encourage faculty to consider their roles as change agents on campus. As educator Parker Palmer has noted, "People seldom think their way into new ways of acting; more often they act their way into new ways of thinking."

**STEVEN JONES**
Project Associate,
Integrating Service with Academic Study
Campus Compact
2003

# SECTION 1

# Definitions and Principles

## TITLES IN THIS SECTION

## QUESTIONS FOR REFLECTION AND PLANNING

How would you define service-learning in the context of your disciplinary training?

What working definition of service-learning can you embrace? (What elements of service-learning concern you? Rigor? Assessment? Pedagogy?)

How does your institution define service-learning? Is this a definition you can embrace? Why or why not?

How do your personal and institutional definitions of service-learning coincide with those contained in these selections? Have these definitions caused you to rethink your understanding of service-learning? In what ways?

# Service-Learning Definitions and Principles of Good Practice

## DEFINITIONS

The methodology of service-learning dictates that a clear link exist between the service experience and the academic objectives of the course. In a service-learning experience, students learn not only about social issues, but also how to apply the new knowledge to action that addresses real problems in their own communities. Service-learning students are assigned challenging community tasks, which take into account the community's assessment of its own needs, strengths, and resources to be leveraged. Students receive academic credit for demonstrated knowledge in connecting their service experience with course content.

> Jan Torres and Ruth Sinton, Eds. (2000). *Establishing and Sustaining an Office of Community Service.* Providence, RI: Campus Compact.

Service-learning means a method under which students learn and develop through thoughtfully organized service that: is conducted in and meets the needs of a community and is coordinated with an institution of higher education, and with the community; helps foster civic responsibility; is integrated into and enhances the academic curriculum of the students enrolled; and includes structured time for students to reflect on the service experience.

> American Association for Higher Education (AAHE): Series on Service-Learning in the Disciplines (adapted from the National and Community Service Trust Act of 1993).

Service-learning means a method under which students or participants learn and develop through active participation in thoughtfully organized service that: is conducted in and meets the needs of a community and is coordinated with an elementary school, secondary school, institution of higher education, [and] or community service program, and with the community; helps foster civic responsibility; is integrated into and enhances the academic curriculum of the students or the educational components of the community service program in which the participants are enrolled; and includes structured time for the students and participants to reflect on the service experience.

> National and Community Service Trust Act of 1993

Service-learning is a method through which citizenship, academic subjects, skills, and values are taught. It involves active learning—drawing lessons from the experience of performing service work. Though service-learning is most often discussed in the context of elementary and secondary or higher education, it is a useful strategy as well for programs not based in schools.

There are three basic components to effective service-learning:

- The first is sufficient preparation, which includes setting objectives for skills to be learned or issues to consider, and includes planning projects so they contribute to learning at the same time work gets done.

- The second component is simply performing service.

- Third, the participant attempts to analyze the experience and draw lessons, through such means as discussion with others and reflection on the work. Thinking about the service creates a greater understanding of the experience and the way service addresses the needs of the community. It promotes a concern about community issues and a commitment to being involved that mark an active citizen. At the same time the analysis and thought allow the participants to identify and absorb what they have learned.

Learning and practicing citizenship are lifelong activities which extend far beyond the conclusion of formal education. Service-learning can be used to increase the citizenship skills of participants of any age or background. For this reason service-learning can be a tool to achieve the desired results of programs, even those involving older, highly educated participants. For example, service-learning can be part of the training of participants to prepare them to do high quality service that has real community impact.

Some service-learning occurs just from doing the work: after a month working alongside police, a participant has surely learned some important lessons about how to increase public safety, and something about what it means to be a good citizen. However, programs that encourage active learning from service experience may have an even greater impact.

> Developed by the Corporation for National and Community Service as part of its briefing materials for national community service.

Service is a process of integrating intention with action in a context of movement toward a just relationship.

Community service is the application of one's gifts, skills, and resources to provide something of value, to enhance the quality of life of people who articulate a need or desire for service.

Community service is a space to practice here and now small scale models of a shared utopian vision.

Service-learning is a form or subset of experiential education and community service.

In service-learning, service is the experiential component of experiential education.

Service-learning is an intentionally designed (course, program, activity, etc.), and is a process of learning through reflection on the experience of doing service.

> Nadinne Cruz, Former Director, Haas Center for Public Service, Stanford University

Service-learning appears to be an approach to experiential learning, an expression of values—service to others, which determines the purpose, nature and process of social and educational exchange between learners (students) and the people they serve, and between experiential education programs and the community organizations with which they work.

> Timothy Stanton, Director, Haas Center for Public Service, Stanford University

Service-learning is the [name for the] various pedagogies that link community service and academic study so that each strengthens the other. The basic theory of service-learning is Dewey's: the interaction of knowledge and skills with experience is key to learning. Students learn best not by reading the Great Books in a closed room but by opening the doors and windows of experience. Learning starts with a problem and continues with the application of increasingly complex ideas and increasingly sophisticated skills to increasingly complicated problems.

> Thomas Ehrlich, in Barbara Jacoby and Associates (1996). *Service-Learning in Higher Education: Concepts and Practices*. San Francisco, CA: Jossey-Bass.

A service-learning program provides educational experiences:

- Under which students learn and develop through active participation in thoughtfully organized service experiences that meet actual community needs and that are coordinated in collaboration with school and community;

- That are integrated into the students' academic curriculum or provide structured time for a student to think, talk, or write about what the student did and saw during the actual service activity;

- That provide a student with opportunities to use newly-acquired skills and knowledge in real-life situations in their own communities; and

- That enhance what is taught by extending student learning beyond the classroom and into the community and helps to foster the development of a sense of caring for others.

From the Commission on National and Community Service (now the Corporation for National and Community Service). In Richard J. Kraft and James Krug (1994). "Review of Research and Evaluation on Service Learning in Public and Higher Education," Richard J. Kraft and Marc Swadener (Eds.) *Building Community: Service Learning in the Academic Disciplines.* Denver, CO: Colorado Campus Compact.

Service-learning is:

...A connection of theory and practice that puts concepts into concrete form and provides a context for understanding abstract matter. This provides an opportunity to test and refine theories as well as to introduce new theories.

...A use of knowledge with a historical understanding or appreciation of social, economic and environmental implications as well as moral and ethical ramifications of people's actions. This involves a strong use of communication and interpersonal skills including literacy (writing, reading, speaking and listening) and various technical skills.

...An opportunity to learn how to learn—to collect and evaluate data, to relate seemingly unrelated matters and ideas, and investigate a self-directed learning including inquiry, logical thinking and a relation of ideas and experience. A transference of learning from one context to another will allow for the opportunity to reflect, conceptualize and apply experience-based knowledge.

...An emphasis on diversity and pluralism that leads to empowerment in the face of social problems; experience that helps people understand and appreciate traditions of volunteerism; and a consideration of and experimentation with democratic citizenship responsibilities.

At their best, service-learning experiences are reciprocally beneficial for both the community and students. For many community organizations, students augment service delivery, meet crucial human needs, and provide a basis for future citizen support. For students, community service is an opportunity to enrich and apply classroom knowledge; explore careers or majors: develop civic and cultural literacy; improve citizenship, develop occupational skills; enhance personal growth and self-image; establish job links; and foster a concern for social problems, which leads to a sense of social responsibility and commitment to public/human service.

From Brevard Community College, *The Power.* July, 1994.

Service-learning is a teaching method which combines community service with academic instruction as it focuses on critical, reflective thinking and civic responsibility. Service-learning programs involve students in organized community service that addresses local needs, while developing their academic skills, sense of civic responsibility, and commitment to the community.

Community College National Center for Community Engagement

Service Learning is a process through which students are involved in community work that contributes significantly: 1) to positive change in individuals, organizations, neighborhoods and/or larger systems in a community; and 2) to students' academic understanding, civic development, personal or career growth, and/or understanding of larger social issues.

This process always includes an intentional and structured educational/developmental component for students, and may be employed in curricular or co-curricular settings. Even with an expanded vision for the field, service-learning will undoubtedly continue to play a critical role in campus-community collaboration..

From *Charity to Change.* Minnesota Campus Compact, 1999.

Service learning is a credit-bearing, educational, experience in which students participate in an organized service activity that meets identified community needs and reflect on the service activity in such a way as to gain further understanding of course content, a broader appreciation of the discipline, and an enhanced sense of civic responsibility.

Robert Bringle and Julie Hatcher, "A Service Learning Curriculum for Faculty." *Michigan Journal of Community Service Learning,* Fall 1995, pp.112-122.

## PRINCIPLES OF GOOD PRACTICE IN COMBINING SERVICE AND LEARNING

### An effective and sustained program:

- Engages people in responsible and challenging actions for the common good.

- Provides structured opportunities for people to reflect critically on their service experience.

- Articulates clear service and learning goals for everyone involved.

- Allows for those with needs to define those needs.

- Clarifies the responsibilities of each person and organization involved.

- Matches service providers and service needs through a process that recognizes changing circumstances.

- Expects genuine, active, and sustained organizational commitment.

- Includes training, supervision, monitoring, support, recognition, and evaluation to meet service and learning goals.

- Ensures that the time commitment for service and learning is flexible, appropriate, and in the best interest of all involved.

- Is committed to program participation by and with diverse populations.

Jane Kendall & Associates (1990). *Combining Service and Learning.* Raleigh, NC: National Society for Internships and Experiential Education (Now National Society for Experiential Education).

## PRINCIPLES OF GOOD PRACTICE IN COMMUNITY SERVICE-LEARNING PEDAGOGY

- Academic credit is for learning, not for service.

- Do not compromise academic rigor.

- Set learning goals for students.

- Establish criteria for the selection of community service placements.

- Provide educationally sound mechanisms to harvest the community learning.

- Provide supports for students to learn how to harvest the community learning.

- Minimize the distinction between the student's community learning role and the classroom learning role.

- Re-think the faculty instructional role.

- Be prepared for uncertainty and variation in student learning outcomes.

- Maximize the community responsibility orientation of the course.

Jeffrey Howard, Ed. (1993). *Praxis I: A Faculty Casebook on Community Service Learning.* Ann Arbor, MI: Office of Community Service Learning Press, University of Michigan.

# Service-Learning:
## A Balanced Approach to Experiential Education

by Andrew Furco

## THE SERVICE-LEARNING STRUGGLE

For over a quarter of a century, education researchers and practitioners have struggled to determine how to best characterize service-learning. In 1979, Robert Sigmon defined service-learning as an experiential education approach that is premised on "reciprocal learning" (Sigmon, 1979). He suggested that because learning flows from service activities, both those who provide service and those who receive it "learn" from the experience. In Sigmon's view, service-learning occurs only when both the providers and recipients of service benefit from the activities.

Today, however, the term "service-learning" has been used to characterize a wide array of experiential education endeavors, from volunteer and community service projects to field studies and internship programs. By perusing schools' service program brochures, one realizes that the definitions for service-learning are as varied as the schools in which they operate. While some educators view "service-learning" as a new term that reveals a rich, innovative, pedagogical approach for more effective teaching, others view it as simply another term for well-established experiential education programs. As Timothy Stanton of the Haas Center for Public Service at Stanford University once asked, "What is service-learning anyway?... How do we distinguish service-learning from cooperative education, internship programs, field study and other forms of experiential education?" (Stanton, 1987). The National Society for Experiential Education, which for years has focused on various types of experiential education programs, broadly defines service-learning as "any carefully monitored service experience in which a student has intentional learning goals and reflects actively on what he or she is learning throughout the experience." (National Society for Experiential Education, 1994).

The Corporation for National Service provides a narrower definition that sees service-learning as a "method under which students learn and develop through active participation in thoughtfully organized service experiences that meet actual community needs...that are integrated into the students' academic curriculum or provide structured time for [reflection],...and that enhance what is taught in school by extending student learning beyond the classroom and into the community" (Corporation for National and Community Service, 1990). The confounding use of the service-learning term may be one reason why research on the impacts of service-learning has been difficult to conduct.

In 1989, Honnet and Poulsen developed the Wingspread Principles of Good Practice for Combining Service and Learning (Honnet & Poulsen, 1989, Appendix B). While these guidelines offer a useful set of best practices for service oriented educational programs, they are not solely germane to service-learning and could easily serve as best practices for other types of experiential education programs (e.g., internships or apprenticeships). Similarly, the Association for Service-Learning in Education Reform (ASLER) has compiled a set of common characteristics of service-learning that help program directors determine whether their programs are meeting the overarching service-learning goals (ASLER, 1994, Appendix A). Again, while these characteristics are very useful in helping practitioners develop effective service-learning programs, they do not provide a definitive characterization of service-learning. ASLER characterizes service-learning as method of learning that enables school-based and community-based professionals "to employ a variety of effective teaching strategies that emphasize student-centered [sic] or youth centered [sic], interactive, experiential education... Service learning places curric-

**Figure 1: A Service-Leaning Typology** (Sigmon, 1994)

| | |
|---|---|
| service-LEARNING | Learning goals primarily; service outcomes secondary |
| SERVICE-learning | Service outcomes primary; learning goals secondary |
| service learning | Service and learning goals completely separate |
| SERVICE-LEARNING | Service and learning goals of equal weight and each enhances the other for all participants |

ular concepts in the context of real-life situations... Service-learning connects young people to the community, placing them in challenging situations ... (ASLER, 1994). One could easily contend that other approaches to experiential education (e.g., internships or field education) purport to do the same. So then, how is service-learning different from other approaches to experiential education?

## DEVELOPING A DEFINITION

According to Sigmon, "If we are to establish clear goals [for service-learning] and work efficiently to meet them, we need to move toward a precise definition" (Sigmon, 1979). Recently, Sigmon attempted to provide a more precise definition of service-learning through a typology that compares different programs that combine service and learning. This typology broadened his earlier "reciprocal learning" definition to include the notion that "service-learning" occurs when there is a balance between learning goals and service outcomes. Herein lies the key to establishing a universal definition for service-learning (see Figure 1).

In this comparative form, the typology is helpful not only in establishing criteria for distinguishing service-learning from other types of service programs but also in providing a basis for clarifying distinctions among different types of service-oriented experiential

education programs (e.g., school volunteer, community service, field education, and internship programs).

## DISTINGUISHING AMONG SERVICE PROGRAMS

To represent the distinctions among various types of service programs, a pictorial is offered that presents an experiential education continuum upon which various service programs might lie. The pictorial is based on both Sigmon's earlier "reciprocal learning" principles and his most recent typology. Where each service program lies on the continuum is determined by its primary intended beneficiary and its overall balance between service and learning (see Figure 2).

As the pictorial suggests, different types of service programs can be distinguished by their primary intended purpose and focus. Each program type is defined by the intended beneficiary of the service activity and its degree of emphasis on service and/or learning. Rather than being located at a single point, each program type occupies a range of points on the continuum. Where one type begins and another ends is not as important as the idea that each service program type has unique characteristics that distinguish it from other types. It is that ability to distinguish among these service program types that allows us to move closer toward a universal definition of service-learning.

## Figure 2: Distinctions Among Service Programs

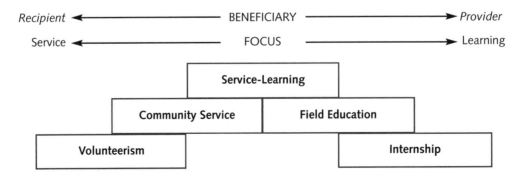

Using the pictorial as a foundation, the following definitions are offered for five types of service programs.

## VOLUNTEERISM

*Volunteerism is the engagement of students in activities where the primary emphasis is on the service being provided and the primary intended beneficiary is clearly the service recipient.*

According to James and Pamela Toole, the term volunteerism refers to "people who perform some service or good work of their own free will and without pay" (Toole & Toole, 1992). The inherent altruistic nature of volunteer programs renders them as service focused, designed to benefit the service recipient. A prime example is a school-based program in which student-volunteers occasionally or regularly visit the local hospital to sit with Alzheimer's patients who need some company. The primary intended beneficiaries of the service are the Alzheimer's patients (the service recipients), and the focus of the activity is on providing a service to them. Although the student-volunteers may receive some benefits from the experience (e.g., feeling pleased with themselves) as well as learn something in the process, these outcomes are clearly serendipitous and unintentional. As the hospital visits of the student volunteers become more regular, and as the students begin focusing more on learning about Alzheimer's disease, the program moves toward the center of the continuum to become more like community service (or even service-learning).

## COMMUNITY SERVICE

*Community service is the engagement of students in activities that primarily focus on the service being provided as well as the benefits the service activities have on the recipients (e.g., providing food to the homeless during the holidays). The students receive some benefits by learning more about how their service makes a difference in the lives of the service recipients.*

As with volunteer programs, community service programs imply altruism and charity. However, community service programs involve more structure and student commitment than do volunteer programs. School-based community service programs might include semester-long or year-long activities in which students dedicate themselves to addressing a cause that meets a local community (or global) need. Recycling, hunger awareness, and environmental improvement are all forms of community service causes around which students have formed organizations to formally and actively address the issue. While the students' primary purpose for engaging in the service activity is to advance the cause, their engagement allows them to learn more about the cause and what is needed to be done to ensure the cause is dealt with effectively. As the service activities become more integrated with the academic course work of the students, and as the students begin to engage in formal intellectual discourse around the various issues relevant to the cause, the community service program moves closer to the center of the continuum to become more like service-learning.

On the opposite side of the continuum lie internship programs.

## INTERNSHIPS

*Internship programs engage students in service activities primarily for the purpose of providing students with hands-on experiences that enhance their learning or understanding of issues relevant to a particular area of study.*

Clearly, in internship programs, the students are the primary intended beneficiary and the focus of the service activity is on student learning. Students are placed in internships to acquire skills and knowledge that will enhance their academic learning and/or vocational development. For many students, internships are performed in addition to regular course work often after a sequence of courses has been taken. Internships may be paid or unpaid and take place in either for-profit or nonprofit organizations. For example, a political science major might engage in an unpaid summer internship at a city hall to learn more about how local government works. Although the student is providing a service to the city hall office, the student engages in the internship primarily for his/her benefit and primarily for learning (rather than service) purposes. Similarly, a legal studies student may have a paid summer internship that allows that student to learn more about how a law firm operates. The student's primary motivations for partaking in the program—to learn legal skills and make some money—are clearly intended to benefit himself/herself. As these students place greater emphasis on the service being provided and the ways in which the service recipients are benefiting, the internship program moves closer to the center of the continuum and becomes more like field education (and service-learning).

## FIELD EDUCATION

*Field education programs provide students with co-curricular service opportunities that are related to, but not fully integrated* with, their formal academic studies. Students perform the service as part of a program that is designed primarily to enhance students' understanding of a field of study, while also providing substantial emphasis on the service being provided.

Field education plays an important role in many service oriented professional programs such as social welfare, education, and public health. In some of the programs, students may spend up to two years providing a service to a social service agency, a school, or health agency. While strong intentions to benefit the recipients of the service are evident, the focus of field education programs tends to be on maximizing the student's learning of a field of study. For example, students in education programs may spend up to one year as student teachers to hone their teaching skills and learn more about the teaching process. Because of their long-term commitment to the service field, students do consciously consider how their service benefits those who receive it. However, the program's primary focus is still on the student teachers' learning and their overall benefit.

## SERVICE-LEARNING

*Service-learning programs are distinguished from other approaches to experiential education by their intention to benefit the provider and the recipient of the service equally, as well as to ensure equal focus on both the service being provided and the learning that is occurring.*

To do this, service-learning programs must have some academic context and be designed in a way that ensures both that the service enhances the learning and that the learning enhances the service. Unlike a field education program in which the service is performed in addition to a student's courses, a service-learning program integrates service into the course(s). For example, a pre-med student in a course on the physiology of the aging might apply the theories and skills learned in that course to providing mobility assistance to seniors at the local senior citizen center. While the program is intended to provide a needed service to the seniors, the program is also intended to help the student better understand how men and women age differently, how the physical aging of the body affects mobility, and how seniors can learn to deal with diminishing range of motion and mobility. In such a program, the focus is both on providing a much-needed service and on student learning. Consequently, the program intentionally benefits both the student who provides the service and the seniors for whom the service is provided. It is this balance that distinguishes service-learning from all other experiential education programs.

## CONCLUSION

While conceptually, this pictorial can assist in bringing us closer to a more precise definition of service-learning, it is obvious that many gray areas still exist. What about the field education program or community service project that is located near the center of the experiential education continuum? How might we distinguish these programs from service-learning? I might argue that no experiential education approach is static; that is, throughout its life, every experiential education program moves, to some degree, along the continuum. Thus, at a particular point in time, a community service program may be farther left of center, appearing to have greater focus on the service and its benefit to the recipient. At another point in time, the same program might appear to have an equal emphasis on service and learning, providing benefits to both the recipients and providers of the service. It is this mobility within program types that suggests that to fully distinguish service-learning programs from other forms of experiential education approaches, one must first determine a program's intended focus(es) and beneficiary(ies). From there, every service program's continuum range can be gauged to determine where it falls among the myriad experiential education endeavors.

## REFERENCES

Alliance for Service Leaning in Education Reform (ASLER). (1994, February). *Standards of Quality for School-Based and Community-Based Service-Learning.*

Corporation for National and Community Service. (1990). *National and Community Service Act of 1990.* Washington, DC: CNCS.

Honnet, E.P., & Poulsen, S.J. (1989). *Principles of Good Practice for Combining Service and Learning.* (Wingspread Special Report.) Racine, WI: The Johnson Foundation, Inc.

National Society for Experiential Education. (1994). *Partial List of Experiential Learning Terms and Their Definitions.* Raleigh, NC: NSEE.

Sigmon, R. L. (1994). *Serving to Learn, Learning to Serve: Linking Service with Learning.* Washington, DC: Council of Independent Colleges.

Sigmon, R. L. (1979, Spring). Service-Learning: Three Principles. *Synergist,* 8(1):9–11.

Stanton, T. (1987). Service Learning: Groping Toward a Definition. *Experiential Education,* 12(1):2–4.

Toole, J. & Toole, P. (1992). *Key Definitions: Commonly Used Terms in the Youth Service Field.* Roseville, MN: National Youth Leadership Council.

# At a Glance:

## What We Know About the Effects of Service-Learning on College Students, Faculty, Institutions, and Communities, 1993–2000, Third Edition

Janet S. Eyler, Dwight E.Giles, Jr., Christine M. Stenson, and Charlene J. Gray, *Vanderbilt University*

*"At a Glance"* summarizes the findings of service-learning research in higher education over the past few years and includes an annotated bibliography. It is designed to provide a quick overview of where we are in the field today and a map to the literature.

## I. WHAT WE KNOW: THE EFFECTS OF SERVICE-LEARNING ON STUDENTS

### A. Personal Outcomes

Service-learning has a positive effect on student personal development such as sense of personal efficacy, personal identity, spiritual growth, and moral development:

Astin & Sax, 1998; Astin, Sax, & Avalos, 1999; Blackwell, 1996 (dissertation); Boss, 1994; Driscoll, Holland, Gelmon, & Kerrigan, 1996; Eyler, Giles, & Braxton, 1997; Eyler & Giles, 1999; Fenzel & Leary, 1997; Freidus, 1997; Giles & Eyler, 1994; Gray, Ondaatje, Fricker, Geschwind, Goldman, Kaganoff, Robyn, Sundt, Vogelgesang, & Klein, 1998; Greene, 1996 (dissertation); Gorman, 1994; Ikeda, 1999 (dissertation); Jordan, 1994 (dissertation); Keen, & Keen, 1998; Kendrick, 1996; Loewen, 1998 (dissertation); Markus, Howard, & King 1993; McMahon, 1998; Ostrow, 1995; Peterson, 1998; Rauner, 1995 (dissertation); Rhoads, 1997; Rockquemore & Schaffer 2000; Schmidt, 2000; Seibold, 1998 (dissertation); Sledge, Shelburne, & Jones, 1993; Vogelgesang & Astin, 2000; VCU, 1997; Wade & Yarborough, 1996; Wang, 2000; Western Washington University, 1994.

Service-learning has a positive effect on interpersonal development, the ability to work well with others, and leadership and communication skills:

Astin & Sax, 1998; Bacon, 1997 (dissertation); Dalton & Petrie, 1997; Driscoll, Holland, Gelmon, & Kerrigan, 1996; Eyler & Giles, 1999; Freidus, 1997; Giles & Eyler, 1994; Gray, et al., 1998; Juhn, Tang, Piessens, Grant, Johnson, & Murray, 1999; Keen, & Keen, 1998; Knee, 1999 (dissertation); Mabry, 1998; McElhaney, 1998 (dissertation); McMahon, 1998; Raskoff, 1997; Rauner, 1995 (dissertation); Rhoads, 1997; Seibold, 1998 (dissertation); Sledge, Shelburne, & Jones, 1993; Peterson, 1998; Tarallo-Falk, 1995 (dissertation); Vogelgesang & Astin, 2000; Wade & Yarborough, 1996; Zawacki, 1997 (dissertation).

### B. Social Outcomes

Service-learning has a positive effect on reducing stereotypes and facilitating cultural and racial understanding:

Astin & Sax, 1998; Astin, Sax, & Avalos, 1999; Balazadeh, 1996; Barber, Higgins, Smith, Ballou, Dedrick, & Downing, 1997; Boyle-Baise, 1998; Boyle-Baise & Kilbane, 2000; Bringle & Kremer, 1993; Driscoll, Holland, Gelmon, & Kerrigan, 1996; Dunlap, 1997; Dunlap, 1998; Eyler, Giles & Braxton, 1997; Eyler & Giles, 1999; Fenzel & Leary, 1997; Giles & Eyler, 1994; Gray, et

August 2001. Funded by the Corporation for National Service, Learn and Serve America subgrant through the National Service Learning Clearinghouse. The full report, including an annotated bibliography, is available on the Campus Compact website at www.compact.org/resource/aag.pdf and on the National Service-Learning Clearinghouse website at www.servicelearning.org.

al. 1998; Greene & Diehm, 1995; Greene, 1996 (dissertation); Hones, 1997; Jordan, 1994 (dissertation); Keen & Keen, 1998; Kendrick, 1996; McElhaney, 1998 (dissertation); Myers-Lipton, 1996a; Myers-Lipton, 1996b; Ostrow, 1995; Pickron-Davis 1999 (dissertation); Potthoff, Dinsmore, Eifler, Stirtz, Walsh, & Ziebarth, 2000; Rauner, 1995 (dissertation); Rhoads, 1997; Vogelgesang & Astin, 2000; Virginia Commonwealth University, 1997; Western Washington University, 1994.

---

*Service-learning may subvert as well as support course goals of reducing stereotyped thinking and facilitating cultural and racial understanding:*

Curran, 1999; Grady, 1998; Pickron-Davis 1999 (dissertation).

---

*Service-learning has a positive effect on sense of social responsibility and citizenship skills:*

Astin & Sax, 1998; Astin, Sax, & Avalos, 1999; Barber, Higgins, Smith, Ballou, Jeffrey, Dedrick, & Downing, 1997; Batchelder & Root, 1994; Dalton & Petrie, 1997; Driscoll, Holland, Gelmon, & Kerrigan, 1996; Eyler & Giles, 1999; Eyler, Giles & Braxton, 1997; Fenzel & Leary, 1997; Giles & Eyler, 1994; Gray, et al. 1998; Johnson & Bozeman, 1998; Keen, & Keen, 1998; Kendrick, 1996; Mabry, 1998; McElhaney, 1998 (dissertation); Myers-Lipton, 1998; Nnakwe, 1999; Ostrow, 1995; Rice & Brown, 1998; Sledge, Shelburne, & Jones, 1993; Rhoads, 1997; VCU, 1997.

---

*Service-learning has a positive effect on commitment to service:*

Astin & Sax, 1998; Astin, Sax, & Avalos, 1999; Blackwell, 1996 (dissertation), Driscoll, Holland, Gelmon, & Kerrigan, 1996; Eklund-Leen, 1994 (dissertation); Eyler & Giles, 1999; Eyler, Giles & Braxton, 1997; Fenzel & Leary, 1997; Giles & Eyler, 1994; Greene, 1996 (dissertation); Keen, & Keen, 1998; Kolcross, 1997 (dissertation); Markus, Howard, King, 1993; McElhaney, 1998 (dissertation); Nnakwe, 1999; Oliver, 1997; Payne, 2000; Payne, & Bennett, 1999; Potthoff, Dinsmore, Eifler, Stirtz, Walsh, & Ziebarth, 2000; Rauner, 1995 (dissertation); Rhoads, 1997; Smedick, 1996 (dissertation); Stukas & Clary, 1998; Tartter, 1996; Western Washington University, 1994; Vogelgesang & Astin, 2000.

*Volunteer service in college is associated with involvement in community service after graduation:*

Astin, Sax, & Avalos, 1999; Smedick, 1996 (dissertation).

## C. Learning Outcomes

*Students and faculty report that service-learning has a positive impact on students' academic learning:*

Astin & Sax, 1998; Balazadeh, 1996; Blackwell, 1996 (dissertation); Boss, 1994; Burr, 1997 (dissertation); Cohen & Kinsey, 1994; Driscoll, Holland, Gelmon, & Kerrigan, 1996; Eyler & Giles, 1999; Eyler, Root, & Giles, 1998; Fenzel & Leary, 1997; Foreman, 1996; Gelmon, Holland, and Shinnamon, 1998; Greene, 1996 (dissertation); Hall, 1996(dissertation); Jordan, 1996 (dissertation); Hesser, 1995; Knee, 1999; Markus, Howard & King, 1993; McElhaney, 1998 (dissertation); McMahon, 1998; Miller, 1994; Oliver, 1997; Schmiede, 1995; Sledge, Shelburne, & Jones, 1993; Soukup, 1999; Strage, 2000; Tarallo-Falk, 1995 (dissertation); Vogelgesang & Astin, 2000; VCU, 1997; Ward, 2000; Western Washington University, 1994.

---

*Students and faculty report that service-learning improves students' ability to apply what they have learned in the "real world":*

Bacon, 1997 (dissertation); Balazadeh, 1996; Cohen & Kinsey 1994; Eyler & Giles, 1999; Fenzel & Leary, 1997; Foreman, 1996; Gelmon, Holland, and Shinnamon, 1998; Gray, et al., 1998; Hall, 1996 (dissertation); Juhn, Tang, Piessens, Grant, Johnson, & Murray, 1999; Kendrick, 1996; Oliver, 1997; Markus, Howard, & King, 1993; McElhaney, 1998 (dissertation); McMahon, 1998; Miller, 1994; Nigro & Wortham, 1998; VCU, 1997.

---

*The impact of service-learning on student academic learning as measured by course grades or GPA is mixed. Some studies have shown a positive impact of community service on academic learning:*

Astin & Sax, 1998; Tartter, 1996; Vogelgesang & Astin, 2000.

*Other studies have shown a positive impact of service-learning on academic learning:*

Gray et al., 1998; Markus, Howard, & King, 1993; Strage, 2000; Vogelgesang & Astin, 2000.

Several studies show differences in academic learning between service-learning and non-service-learning students, but calculate grades differently for these two groups of students:

Balazadah, 1996; Berson & Younkin, 1998; Shastri, 1999.

Some studies show no difference between service-learning and non-service-learning control groups in academic learning:

Boss, 1994; Hudson, 1996; Kendrick, 1996; Miller, 1994; Parker-Gwin & Mabry, 1998.

Service-learning participation has an impact on such academic outcomes as demonstrated complexity of understanding, problem analysis, critical thinking, and cognitive development:

Batchelder & Root, 1994; Eyler & Giles, 1999; Eyler, Root, & Giles, 1998; Osborne, Hammerich, Hensley, 1998.

The impact of service-learning on student cognitive moral development is mixed. Some studies find that service-learning contributes to moral development.

Boss, 1994; Gorman, 1994.

Other studies show no difference in moral development between service-learning and non-service-learning control groups:

Cram, 1998; Fenzel & Leary, 1997; Greene, 1996.

## D. Career Development

Service-learning contributes to career development:

Astin & Sax, 1998; Astin, Sax, & Avalos, 1999; Aultman, 1997 (dissertation); Driscoll, Holland, Gelmon, & Kerrigan, 1996; Fenzel & Leary, 1997; Greene & Diehm, 1995; Juhn, Tang, Piessens, Grant, Johnson, & Murray, 1999; Keen, & Keen, 1998; McElhaney, 1998 (dissertation); Sledge, Shelburne, & Jones, 1993; Smedick, 1996 (dissertation); Tartter, 1996; Vogelgesang & Astin, 2000; VCU, 1997; Western Washington University, 1994.

## E. Relationship with Institution

Students engaged in service-learning report stronger faculty relationships than those who are not involved in service-learning:

Astin & Sax, 1998; Gray et al, 1998; Eyler & Giles, 1999.

Service-learning improves student satisfaction with college:

Astin & Sax, 1998; Berson & Younkin, 1998; Gray, et al., 1998.

Students engaged in service-learning are more likely to graduate:

Astin & Sax, 1998; Roose, Daphne, Miller, Norris, Peacock, White, & White, 1997.

## F. Processes Examined in Qualitative Studies

There is a growing body of case studies that describe service-learning processes and contexts. Themes explored include:

Citizenship development

Dalton & Petrie, 1997; Smith, 1994.

Dealing with diversity

Boyle-Baise, 1998; Boyle-Baise & Kilbane 2000; Dunlap, 1998a; Hones, 1997; Pickron-Davis, 1999 (dissertation); Rockquemore & Schaffer, 2000; Skilton-Silvester & Erwin, 2000.

Institutional support and cohesion

Ward K., 1996.

Transformations in orientations toward service and community

Bacon, 1997(dissertation); Dunlap 1998b; Ostrow, 1995; Rockquemore & Schaffer 2000; Schmidt, 2000 (dissertation); Tarallo-Falk, 1995 (dissertation); Wade & Yarborough, 1996.

Reflection and instructional processes

Freidus, 1997; Hall, 1996 (dissertation); Hones, 1997; Ikeda, 2000; Ikeda, 1999 (dissertation); Schmiede, 1995.

Self and identity

Dunlap, 1997; Rhoads, 1997; Wang, 2000.

## II. WHAT WE KNOW: THE EFFECTS OF PARTICULAR PROGRAM CHARACTERISTICS ON STUDENTS

### A. Placement Quality

Placement quality has a positive impact on student personal and interpersonal outcomes:

Eyler & Giles, 1999; Mabry, 1998.

### B. Reflection

Quality and quantity of reflective activities have an impact on student learning:

Eyler & Giles, 1999; Gray, et al. 1998; Greene & Diehm, 1995; Ikeda, 1999 (dissertation); Loewen, 1998 (dissertation); Mabry, 1998.

## C. Application of Service

*Application of service to academic content and vice versa has an impact on students, particularly learning outcomes:*

Boss, 1994; Batchelder & Root, 1994; Eyler & Giles, 1999; McElhaney, 1999.

## D. Duration and Intensity of Service

*Duration and intensity of service have an impact on student outcomes:*

Astin & Sax, 1998; Astin, Sax, & Avalos, 1999; Mabry, 1998.

## E. Exposure to Diversity

*Diversity has an impact on students, particularly personal outcomes, such as identity development and cultural understanding:*

Eyler & Giles, 1999; Gray, et al., 1998; Pickron-Davis, 1999 (dissertation).

## F. Community Voice

*Community voice in a service-learning project has an impact on student cultural understanding:*

Eyler & Giles, 1999; Gray, et al., 1998.

## G. Feedback

*Receiving quality feedback from professors or clients has an impact on students' self-reported learning, use of skills taught in courses, and commitment to service:*

Greene, 1996; Greene & Diehm, 1995; Subramony, 2000.

## III. WHAT WE KNOW: THE IMPACT OF SERVICE-LEARNING ON FACULTY

*A. Faculty using service-learning report satisfaction with quality of student learning:*

Balazadeh, 1996; Berson & Younkin, 1998; Cohen & Kinsey, 1994; Fenzel & Leary, 1997; Gelmon, Holland, & Shinnamon, 1998; Hesser, 1995; McMahon, 1998; Sellnow & Oster, 1997; Serow, Calleson, & Parker, 1996; Seibold, 1998 (dissertation); Stanton, 1994; Ward S., 2000.

*B. Faculty using service-learning report commitment to research:*

Driscoll, Holland, Gelmon, & Kerrigan, 1996.

*C. Faculty report lack of resources as barrier to providing service-learning:*

Bergkamp, 1996 (dissertation); Burr, 1997 (dissertation); Gray, et al., 1998; Hammond, 1994; National Association of State Universities and Land Grant Colleges, 1995; Robinson & Barnett, 1996; Siscoe, 1997 (dissertation); Stanton, 1994; Wade & Yarborough, 1997; Ward K., 1996.

*D. Faculty increasingly integrate service-learning into courses:*

Burr, 1997 (dissertation); Campus Contact, 1998; Gray, et al., 1998; Martin, 1994 (dissertation);

Oliver, 1997; Robinson & Barnett, 1996; Sagaria & Burrows, 1995; Siscoe, 1997 (dissertation); Stanton, 1994; Ward K., 1996; Ward S., 2000.

*E. Lack of faculty reward is a barrier to service and service-learning partnerships:*

Berman, 1999 (dissertation); Bergkamp, 1996 (dissertation); Euster and Weinbach, 1994.

## IV. WHAT WE KNOW: THE IMPACT OF SERVICE-LEARNING ON COLLEGES AND UNIVERSITIES

*A. Colleges and universities report institutional commitment to service-learning curriculum:*

Battaglia, 1995 (dissertation); Bergkamp, 1996 (dissertation); Berman 1999 (dissertation); Bringle & Hatcher, 1997; Campus Contact, 1998; Dutton, 1993 (dissertation); Gray et al., 1998; Lelle, 1996 (dissertation); Mandell, 1995 (dissertation); National Association of State Universities and Land Grant Colleges, 1995; Robinson & Barnett, 1996; Sagaria & Burrows, 1995; Oliver, 1997; Scott & Ludwigh, 1995; Sellnow & Oster, 1997; Serow, Calleson, & Parker, 1996; Siscoe, 1997 (dissertation); Waring, 1995 (dissertation).

*B. Colleges and universities report availability of service-learning programs:*

Battaglia, 1995 (dissertation); Bringle & Hatcher, 1997; Campus Contact; 1998; Dutton, 1993 (dissertation),

Gray et al., 1998; Lelle, 1996 (dissertation); Mandell, 1995 (dissertation); National Association of State Universities and Land Grant Colleges, 1995; Robinson & Barnett, 1996; Sagaria & Burrows, 1995; Scott & Ludwigh, 1995; Sellnow & Oster, 1997; Serow, Calleson, & Parker, 1996; Siscoe, 1997 (dissertation).

---

C. *Few colleges and universities require service-learning in the academic core:*

Antonio, Astin, & Cress, 2000; Gray et al., 1998; Sagaria & Burrows, 1995.

---

D. *Community service affects student retention:*

Astin & Sax, 1998; Roose, Daphne, Miller, Norris, Peacock, White, & White, 1997.

---

E. *Institutions report enhanced community relations:*

Battaglia, 1995 (dissertation); Driscoll, Holland, Gelmon, & Kerrigan, 1996; Gray et al., 1998.

---

F. *Lack of faculty reward is a barrier to service and service-learning partnerships:*

Berman, 1999; Bergkamp, 1996; Euster and Weinbach, 1994.

## V. WHAT WE KNOW: THE IMPACT OF SERVICE-LEARNING ON COMMUNITIES

---

A. *Satisfaction with student participation:*

Clarke, 2000 (dissertation); Cohen & Kinsey, 1994; Driscoll, Holland, Gelmon, & Kerrigan, 1996; Ferrari and Worrall, 2000; Foreman, 1996; Gelmon, Holland & Shinnamon, 1998; Gray, et al., 1998; Greene and Diehm, 1995; National Association of State Universities and Land Grant Colleges, 1995; Nigro & Wortham, 1998; Ward & Vernon, 1999.

---

B. *Service-learning provides useful service in communities:*

Clarke, 2000 (dissertation); Cohen & Kinsey, 1994; Bringle & Kremer, 1993; Driscoll, Holland, Gelmon, & Kerrigan, 1996; Gelmon, Holland & Shinnamon, 1998; Gray et al., 1998; Henderson & Brookhart, 1997; Nigro & Wortham, 1998; Ward & Vernon, 1999; Western Washington University, 1994.

---

C. *Communities report enhanced university relations:*

Clarke, 2000 (dissertation); Driscoll, Holland, Gelmon, & Kerrigan, 1996; Gray, et al., 1998.

# Service-Learning Resources on the Web

## Campus Compact
*www.compact.org*

A comprehensive site that includes resources for service-learning practitioners, including faculty, presidents, administrators, and students. Includes model programs and sample syllabi, a calendar of events, extensive links to web resources, job listings, news, information on grants and fellowships, legislation, a special section for community colleges, and much more.

## American Association of Colleges & Universities
*www.aacu-edu.org*

AAC&U's site provides detailed descriptions of its projects, including the Diversity Initiative, in which service-learning and campus-community partnerships play an important role, and the new Center for Liberal Education and Civic Engagement, a joint initiative with Campus Compact. The site also contains general information about membership, meetings, and publications.

## American Association of Community Colleges Service-Learning Page
*www.aacc.nche.edu/Content/NavigationMenu/ResourceCenter/Projects_Partnerships/Current/HorizonsServiceLearning-Project/HorizonsServiceLearningProject.htm*

The site for AACC's service-learning project. Includes links to model programs at various community college campuses, general information about federal initiatives such as America Reads, and practical information about applying service-learning in the community college curriculum. Also includes a listing of workshops and events and links to service-learning organizations.

## American Association of Higher Education Service-Learning Project
*www.aahe.org/service*

A description of AAHE's Service-Learning Project, including coalition-building conferences and the multi-volume monograph series on service-learning in the disciplines. Also includes links to other service-learning resources and to other AAHE programs and partnerships.

## The Big Dummy's Guide to Service-Learning
*www.fiu.edu/~time4chg/Library/bigdummy.html*

This site is organized around frequently asked questions and divided into faculty and programmatic issues. Includes "101 Ideas for Combining Service and Learning" in various disciplines.

## CSU Community Service-Learning Website
*www.calstate.edu/csl*

The CSU community service-learning website provides an overview of programs throughout the CSU system. It includes campus profiles, systemwide initiatives, reports and publications on community service-learning, and more.

## Community-Campus Partnerships for Health
*http://futurehealth.ucsf.edu/ccph/servicelearningres.html*

Community-Campus Partnerships for Health (CCPH) promotes health through partnerships between communities and higher educational institutions, using service-learning, community-based research, community service, and other partnership strategies. This site contains a variety of resources, including syllabi and assessment tools.

## Community College National Center for Community Engagement
*www.mc.maricopa.edu/other/engagement*

Includes listings of events, awards, and publications, as well as detailed descriptions of CCNCCE's mission and major projects.

## The Colorado Service-Learning Home Page
*http://csf.Colorado.EDU/sl/*

A comprehensive site with definitions of service-learning; a thorough listing of undergraduate service-learning programs with online course lists and syllabi; links to college and university homepages; and links to service-learning organizations, networks, and resources. This site also houses a searchable archive of the Colorado Service-Learning listserv.

### Council for Independent Colleges (CIC)

*www.cic.org/projects_services.index.asp*

This site contains information on two CIC projects related to service-learning: Serving to Learn-Learning to Serve, and Engaging Communities and Campuses.

### The Journal of Public Service & Outreach

*www.uga.edu/~jpso*

This site includes the Journal's mission and information about subscribing to the Journal or submitting articles.

### Learn, Serve, & Surf

*www.edb.utexas.edu/servicelearning/index.html*

An "internet resource kit" for service-learning practitioners. Lists model programs and practices, listservs, discussion sites, links, etc. Also contains a definition and description of service-learning and its various components, with a bibliography.

### Learning In Deed

*www.learningindeed.org*

Encourages young people to serve in the community as part of academic life, and is also a tool for becoming informed about and involved in service-learning.

### Michigan Journal of Community Service-Learning

*www.umich.edu/~ocsl/MJCSL*

The MJCSL is a peer-reviewed academic journal containing papers written by faculty and service-learning educators on research, theory, pedagogy, and issues pertinent to the service-learning community. The site contains abstracts of MJCSL articles and information on subscribing and submitting manuscripts.

### The National Service-Learning Clearinghouse

*www.servicelearning.org*

This site contains a searchable database of K-12 and higher education service-learning literature; information about events, listservs, and Learn & Serve America efforts, and links to a variety of service-learning information resources.

### National Society for Experiential Education

*www.nsee.org*

Includes information about various experiential education methods, including service-learning. Also includes membership and conference information, lists of publications and resources, and a description of NSEE's mission and history.

### New England Resource Center for Higher Education

*www.nerche.org*

The site includes descriptions of NERCHE's funded projects, including Faculty Professional Service. Also included are news updates, descriptions of think tanks, and contact information.

### NCTE's Service-Learning in Composition Website

*www.ncte.org/cccc/Service-Learning/index.shtml*

This site is a resource for teachers, researchers, and community partners interested in connecting writing instruction to community action.

### International Partnership for Service-Learning

*www.ipsl.org*

IPS-L coordinates programs that unite academic study and community service, making the two activities more relevant and enriching. This site includes information on undergraduate and graduate programs in 14 countries.

### Peace Corps Service Learning

*www.peacecorps.gov/wws/service*

Gives educators and students the tools and resources to plan, create, perform, and evaluate a service-learning project.

## DISCIPLINE WEBSITES

The following websites contain discipline-specific resources for faculty that are currently using, or are interested in using, service-learning as a methodology.

### American Association of Colleges of Teacher Education

*www.aacte.org/other_professional_issues/service_learning.htm*

### American Chemical Society

*www.chemistry.org/portal/a/c/s/1/acsdisplay.html?id=67 4c48b4378511d7e1dc6ed9fe800100*

### American Philosophical Association

*www.apa.udel.edu/apa/governance/committees/teaching/tor cmain.asp*

### American Political Science Association

*www.apsanet.org/teach/service/*
*www.apsanet.org/CENnet/*

### American Psychological Association

*www.apa.org/ed/slce/home.html*

### National Communication Association

*www.natcom.org/Instruction/sl/home.htm*

### National Council for Teachers of English

*www.ncte.org/groups/cccc/com/service/108736.ht*

# Definitions and Principles:
## Recommended Reading

## BOOKS & CHAPTERS

Albert, G. (Ed.) (1994). *Service-learning reader: Reflections and perspectives on service.* Raleigh, NC: National Society for Experiential Education.

American Association of Higher Education. (1996–2003). AAHE's Service-Learning in the Disciplines monograph series. Washington, DC: AAHE.

Bringle, R.G., Games, R., & Malloy, E.A. (Eds.). (1999). *Colleges and universities as citizens.* Needham, MA: Allyn & Bacon.

Eyler, J. & Giles, D.E. Jr. (1999). *Where's the learning in service-learning?* San Francisco: Jossey-Bass.

Eyler, J., Giles, D.E., Jr., & Schmiede, A. (1996). *A practitioner's guide to reflection in service-learning: Student voices and reflections.* Nashville: Vanderbilt University.

Howard, J. (Ed.). (1993). *Praxis I: A faculty casebook on community service.* Ann Arbor, MI: Office of Community Service Learning, University of Michigan.

Howard, J. (Ed.). (1993). *Praxis II: Service learning resources for university students, staff and faculty.* Ann Arbor, MI: Office of Community Service Learning, University of Michigan.

Jacoby, B. and Associates. (1996) *Service-learning in higher education: Concepts and practices.* San Francisco, CA: Jossey-Bass.

Kendall, J., et al. (1990). *Combining service and learning: A resource book for community and public service.* Vols. I and II. Raleigh: National Society for Internships and Experiential Education.

*Michigan Journal of Community Service Learning*, 3, Fall 1996. Ann Arbor: OCSL Press, The University of Michigan. Available through the Michigan Journal of Community Service Learning website at www.umich.edu/~ocsl/MJCSL.

Stanton, T., Giles, D., Jr., & Cruz, N. (1999). *Service-learning: A movement's pioneers reflect on its origins, practice, and future.* San Francisco: Jossey-Bass.

W. K. Kellogg Foundation. (2000). *Service works: A retrospective evaluation of higher education service programs.* Battle Creek, MI: W. K. Kellogg Foundation.

Zlotkowski, E. (Ed.). *Successful service-learning programs: New models of excellence in higher education.* Bolton, MA: Anker Publishing.

## ARTICLES & REPORTS

Bringle, R.G., & Hatcher, J.A. (1996). Implementing service-learning in higher education. *Journal of Higher Education*, 67 (2), 221–239.

Cauley, K., et al. (2001). Service-learning: Integrating student learning and community service. *Education for Health: Change in Learning and Practice*, 14 (2), 173–182.

Delve, C.I., Mintz, S.D., & Stewart, G.M. (Eds.) (1990). Community service as values education. *New Directions for Teaching and Learning*, No. 50. San Francisco: Jossey-Bass.

Marullo, S. & Edwards, B. (2000). From charity to justice. *American Behavioral Scientist*, 43 (5), 895–913.

Prentice, M. (2000). *Service learning programs on community college campuses.* Eric Digest, October.

Prentice, M. & Garcia, R.M. (2000). Service learning: The next generation in education. *Community College Journal of Research and Practice*, 24 (1), 19–27.

Rhoads, R. A. & Howard , J.P. (Eds.). (1998). Academic service-learning: A pedagogy of action and reflection. *New Directions for Teaching and Learning*, No. 73. San Francisco: Jossey-Bass.

# SECTION 2
# Learning Theory

## TITLES IN THIS SECTION

## QUESTIONS FOR REFLECTION AND PLANNING

Do you approach your discipline from a particular theoretical perspective on teaching and learning?

How is that perspective evidenced in your teaching?

How would you integrate service-learning with that perspective?

# Service-Learning Practice:

## Developing a Theoretical Framework

by Dick Cone and Susan Harris

*Service-learning has dramatically increased its impact on the American educational scene during the past few years, and new practitioners are quickly adopting the methods of integrating traditional classroom-based instruction and community service. As might be expected of practitioners, our practices are strong but our theory is sometimes found to be wanting. We have tinkered with methods to perfect practices without understanding the philosophical, psychological and social mechanisms that undergird our practices. For two decades, we have been drawing largely on Dewey, Kolb and Freire for theoretical support for our work. This paper suggests additional theoretical perspectives drawn largely from cognitive psychology and social theory. A number of constructs will be presented, including concept formation, selective perception, categorization, critical reflection and mediated learning, each of which helps to explain the transformational nature of experiential education, as well as provide intellectual support for what are currently recognized as "best practices."*

**CHERYL GILBERT[1]**
**SOCIOLOGY 101**
**JOURNAL ENTRY - WEEK ONE**

**WEEK ONE -** *The Setting:* What are your most vivid first impressions of the site? Describe settings, people, actions and positive or negative feelings you are having.

Today was my first day as a volunteer for USC's Joint Educational Project at Prairie Avenue Elementary School.[2] Despite the fact that this is my third semester on campus, I have never ventured beyond Exposition Boulevard into South Central Los Angeles, and I must admit that I was scared to death. What had I gotten myself into? I had volunteered to spend two hours a week in riot-ravaged South Central LA?! Riding south on Figueroa St., which borders USC on the east, I was thinking that it didn't look much different than Minneapolis (which is about an hour's drive from where I'm from). However, the further south I traveled, the more run down the houses looked, the more boarded up stores I passed. The cars parked on driveways and along the street appeared very old, often with missing tires or broken windows. The scene changed even more dramatically after I turned onto one of the side streets. Suddenly I was thrust into a scene right out of one of the gangsta videos I've seen. I was very conspicuous as I rode my bike; I felt like

every person I passed stared at me, a 19-year-old white girl on a shiny expensive bike, intruding where she shouldn't be.

Luckily, I arrived at the school safely. As I circled the school trying to find a bicycle rack, my thoughts drifted back to Walnut Road Elementary School in Apple Valley, Minnesota. Prairie Avenue Elementary looks nothing like the spacious, lush campus that I once attended. The building was badly in need of repair and there was graffiti and trash in the neighborhood surrounding the school. How could anyone get used to this? I walked around to the front entrance and was stopped by a security guard who asked me to sign in. Once admitted, I waded through a sea of black and Mexican children to the JEP office, and then to the classroom where I am assigned as a mentor.

When I met my "mentee," my heart sank. Standing in front of me was this little Mexican kid who could barely speak English. Although he was smiling and seemed happy to meet me, I could tell that he was poor and probably neglected. While I feel very strongly for the people who live in this community, I do not understand why it is that they continue to live here, subjecting their children to such unbearable conditions. These children are susceptible to picking up bad habits like stealing, lying and cheating in trying to be like the gangbangers who live in the neighborhood.

Cheryl's journal entry is representative of many students venturing beyond the perimeter of the University of Southern California campus through the Joint Educational Project (JEP), a program that links service-learning courses with community schools and agencies. USC is a wealthy, influential institution[3] located in a predominantly Latino and African-American community in which 39% of all residents live in poverty and the per capita income is $6,108 (U.S. Bureau of the Census, 1990). While the contrast between USC and the surrounding community is stark, it is also true that students' impressions of the community are often exaggerated and ethnocentric, if not racist and intolerant.

Cheryl's response highlights a dilemma which we, as service-learning practitioners, struggle with on a daily basis. As the world shrinks and our contact with a wide range of human experience increases, "multiculturalism" is a reality and no longer simply an ideal. However, multicultural experiences do not necessarily lead to a "multicultural attitude" (i.e. one that is tolerant and understanding); students such as Cheryl often draw on deeply-ingrained stereotypes, media images and previous experiences unless they are encouraged to consider new experiences from a critical, academically-informed perspective. Although experiential education has existed in one form or another for almost a century (Kraft, 1996), never before have we lived in such a diverse society and had to deal with the opportunities and challenges such diversity presents.

Cheryl is one of thousands of college students facing similar dilemmas every day in the growing number of service-learning programs nationwide. As the number of programs has skyrocketed, so too has the number of scholarly articles examining service-learning practice and theory. The journal in which this article appears was created to provide a forum for the growing number of educators interested in reading and writing about the field.

Despite this surge of scholarly interest, the academic component of service-learning has not been a priority for the majority of programs, which tend to focus on the personal benefits to the students (Maybach, 1996; Shumer & Belbas, 1996). This emphasis has resulted in creating programs which do, indeed, increase the self-esteem of service providers (Kraft, 1996). However, it is not clear that they avoid doing so at the expense of

the communities they "serve." Without an academically informed understanding of difference and diversity, service may let students like Cheryl feel good about themselves, but they may leave the community having learned very little. Furthermore, this service-heavy approach may have devastating consequences for the future of service-learning as a pedagogy, which, as Cohen (1994) and Zlotkowski (1995) have suggested, may depend on its ability to prove its academic worth.

We believe that service-learning needs to consider the personal and intellectual growth of both the student and the community. For it to serve as an effective tool that will survive the test of time, careful thought must be given to the pedagogy of service-learning. A model which simply asks students to go into community settings and learn through experience is potentially damaging. As we can see from Cheryl's journal entry, simply experiencing new worlds doesn't necessarily increase understanding and may even serve to confirm stereotyped perspectives. Dewey made a similar point when he wrote:

> The belief that all genuine education comes about through experiences does not mean that all experiences are genuine or equally educative.... Everything depends upon the quality of the experience...(as)...every experience lives on in further experiences (1938, pp. 25–26).

A genuine service-learning pedagogy requires careful thought about how people learn experientially and careful attention to the methods educators can use to shape and structure the quality of student experiences.

## THEORETICAL ROOTS

The model which has guided the development of experiential education for more than a decade is the model proposed by David Kolb (1984). Kolb's model is a variation of the process of experiential logical inquiry set out by pragmatist philosopher John Dewey more than half a century ago. Dewey set out a six-step process of inquiry which involved: 1) encountering a problem, 2) formulating a problem or question to be resolved, 3) gathering information which suggests solutions, 4) making hypotheses, 5) testing hypotheses, and making warranted assertions (1938).

Kolb conceptualizes Dewey's six steps as a four-stage experiential learning cycle involving concrete experiences, reflection, abstract conceptualization, and active experimentation (see Figure 1). Learners are engaged in a cycle in which work in community or work settings

## Figure 1: Kolb's Model of Experiential Learning

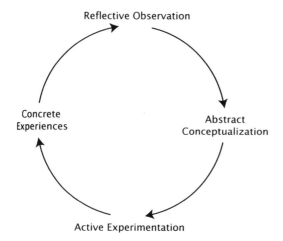

forms the basis for written or oral reflection. Under the guidance of an instructor, reflective work is used to form abstract concepts and hypotheses are generated which then get cycled back into further concrete experiences. It is a student-centered model which Kolb believes allows a variety of students with very different learning styles to develop and integrate their skills.

In 1990, David Moore suggested a post-structuralist approach to experiential learning: a "critical pedagogy ... in which students and teachers conduct an unfettered investigation of social institutions, power relations, and value commitments" (p. 281). He argues that meaning is not centered or fixed and that experiential approaches offer ways for students to examine "shifting systems of meaning." The method requires that students learn to "read" their workplaces as "texts" in which students "examine...the histories, power arrangements, and values underlying their work organizations" (p. 280).

Kolb's model has helped service-learning educators develop an awareness of the role of reflection in relating the world of concrete experiences to abstract theories. The primary thrust of the model, however, has been to suggest that experiential approaches accommodate students with different learning styles better than traditional didactic methodologies. We find Kolb's model is somewhat ambiguous for educators attempting to better understand their role within a service-learning paradigm. As a consequence, many educators continue to send students out to "learn in community settings" and "reflect" on their work without a clear understanding of how experiences instruct or how educators make use of the reflective process. Moore's approach has not, to our knowledge, been

widely adopted, but it falls prey to the same set of instructional ambiguities as Kolb's model.

Service-learning educators also make frequent reference to Brazilian philosopher and educator Paulo Freire. Most often these references are made in describing service approaches that "empower" communities and treat community members with dignity and respect. Less often is Freireian pedagogy applied to our own students. Freire challenges post-secondary education when he opposes a "banking" approach to education and endorses a "[p]roblem-posing education [which] affirms men and women as beings in the process of becoming—as unfinished, uncompleted beings in and with a likewise unfinished reality" (1994, p. 65).

The authors believe that a number of theories evolving from studies of cognition, philosophy, critical pedagogy, and postmodern theory suggest that it may be possible to adapt components of these different strategies into a more comprehensive service-learning model. In proposing this model, we hope to clarify the role of educators, incorporate Freire's ideas, and avoid some of the ambiguity that we find in Kolb's model and Moore's suggested approach.

## A SERVICE-LEARNING MODEL

In this paper, we hope to develop a model of service-learning that bridges the typically expansive gap between theory and practice. A model which best seems to capture both the individual, psychological nature and the interpersonal, socio-cultural nature of service-learning is the six stage lens model which appears in Figure 2.

### A Brief Overview of the Model

Before moving into a detailed analysis of the model, we offer a summary of each of the main components. The model begins with the learner and his or her unique set of characteristics. While it is typically impractical, if not impossible, to coordinate individualized service-learning programs, we nevertheless recognize the significance that individual characteristics have on the service-learning experience. Keeping this in mind, the second component of the model takes a look at the academic and pragmatic issues concerning a service-learning practitioner. The model emphasizes the need for carefully planning the service-learning experience so that the student is intellectually challenged and appropriately placed. This involves providing students with pre-service training and theoretical concepts that the

## Figure 2: A Lens Model for Service-Learning Educators

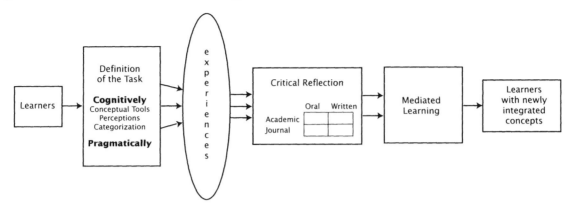

student will be expected to apply and understand in the community.

The third part of the model examines the service experience itself. We argue that it is important to make the experience a "discontinuous" one, distinct from students' everyday experiences, so that students are challenged to broaden their perspectives on the world. Reflection follows the experience, in our model, as in most models of service learning. However, unlike some models, we argue for more a holistic approach to reflection that involves the student's intellectual and emotional capacities, as well as their written and oral skills. As important as individual reflection is, the fifth component of our model proposes that reflection is most effective when guided by an educator or mentor who can facilitate the student's learning process.

In the end, our model returns to the learner, recognizing that service-learning is not simply an abstract pedagogical tool, but an experience that has potentially profound effects on a student's intellectual and personal growth.

### The Beginning—The Learners

Like Kolb, we begin with the assumption that our students come to us not as blank slates but as individuals with different learning styles, skills, histories, philosophies of life, attitudes, values, expectations, and perspectives. Cheryl and her fellow students are products of social forces and their own personal life experiences. Their "knowledge" about the world is a composite of such things as earlier educational experiences, messages from the mass media, influences of home and community, and the reading they have done. Unlike Kolb, we intentionally include students in the model to remind ourselves that the rest of the model is about systematically attempting to help students to use experiences in

the community to better build-upon, critique, and evaluate that knowledge and move to an intellectually "higher ground."

Educational theories of the twentieth century abound with examples of the differences among learners. While an examination of such differences is beyond the scope of this paper, we mention them here in order to emphasize the significance of different learning styles for developing pedagogical tools. In addition to Kolb's work in cognitive learning styles (1984), Bruner (1968) has looked at copers and defenders, Kagan (1964) has examined reflective and impulsive conceptual styles, and Witkin and Goodenough (1977) have looked at issues of field dependence versus field independence. From a sociological standpoint, comparative studies have looked at the effects of class (Heath, 1983), gender (Crockett & Petersen, 1984), and culture (Maehr, 1974) on learning. From the abundance of these focused studies on differences among learners, it is not unreasonable to assume that there are an infinite number of ways that these variables and others could be combined, resulting in what might be thought of as a unique learning mode for each student.

As instructors, we cannot hope to know our students' individual learning styles and custom tailor our work to the wide range of differences. Furthermore, we cannot expect to adapt the curriculum in order to account for the demographic characteristics of each student. Nevertheless, it important to recognize that differences among students exist and factor some of this information in the way we structure and make use of service-learning opportunities. For example, we may assume that Cheryl's small town Midwestern background will not give her the same set of expectations regarding her work in urban Los Angeles as her classmates Jaime, who lives in the barrio in East LA, or Mon-Fan, a student from China. A faculty member creating a service-learning program for a class comprised primarily of students like Cheryl might develop a very different model than a faculty member teaching a class of students like Jaime. In a similar vein, communities in the Midwest will differ from communities in other regions of the country, as will urban, suburban and rural settings have their own unique characteristics. We know from comparing service-learning programs across the country that they vary according to where they are located (Shumer & Belb 1996). Service-learning is particularly well suited to the consideration of differences among students and the communities in which they are placed through the careful use of the mediated learning approach we will examine later.

## DEFINING THE TASK—COGNITIVELY

### Conceptual Tools

Practitioners often describe service-learning as starting with concrete experiences. Moore (1990), for example, starts with "an unfettered investigation of social institutions." However, as noted above, "unfettered"' students enter into a classroom with their own unique ways of looking at the world. Therefore, it is critical that service-learning educators provide assistance and structure for students so they are prepared to learn from experiential opportunities. As Cheryl's journal indicates, without such structure and guidance, each student may simply continue to understand their new experiences in the same ways using the tools of conceptualization that already lie within their grasp. We think Dewey had it right when he talked about encountering a problem, formulating a set of questions to be asked, and gathering information—in other words, approaching experience with a set of conceptual tools. The job of service-learning instructors is to assist students in identifying problems, formulating questions, and knowing how to go about gathering information before they enter the field and as they continue their work in the field.

In our program, students enter the community with a set of clearly explicated theories that have been introduced in the classroom. These offer students a systematic way of looking at the world. Each week students use a single theory or group of concepts in the form of carefully crafted "Academic Questions" as a basis for their observations in the community. In responding to the questions, students are asked to define their terms, cite their observations and describe how their observations support or contradict the theories and concepts presented in class.

In her first week, Cheryl's organizing question is:

> As a community service provider, you play a different role than you do as a USC student. Describe this new role. What specific tasks and behaviors are expected of you? What obligations and rights do you have as a result of being in this role? Compare this new role with your role as student. Are you experiencing any "role strain," "role conflict" or "role distancing?"

Academic Questions ask students to consider their experiences using a new set of conceptual tools. Dr. Sorenson,[4] Cheryl's sociology professor, designed this first set of questions to heighten each student's awareness of his or her various social roles, as well as the potential conflict between the roles of college student and community service provider. In examining this issue, Cheryl must draw upon what she has learned about role theory and relate it to her experiences as a student and a mentor.

The questions force Cheryl to look at and think about those things that are not physically manifested (e.g. role conflict) but that must be understood through analysis and interpretation using ideas which have been introduced in class. Without a somewhat formal structuring of the task, Cheryl's abilities to make observations in the community are limited to the conceptual tools she uses in her daily life. This can be problematic if students, like Cheryl, draw from stereotypes and prejudiced perspectives in their everyday analyses. The task of the instructor is to offer her a new conceptual basis for understanding her experiences.

### Perceptions

Postmodern theorists hold that there is no absolute reality independent of human mental activity (Kincheloe & Steinberg, 1993). Each of us lives in a world created by our own cognition (Goodman, 1986). Another, less technical way of saying the same thing is that no two humans see the world in exactly the same way. Our understanding emerges from worlds that are created by others and transmitted to us. The acquisition of knowledge is not a passive process, however. According to eighteenth century German philosopher Immanuel Kant, the meaning we make of that which we receive and perceive is shaped by an active mind which molds and coordinates ideas with sensations, "transforming the multiplicity of experiences into the orderly unity of thought" (Gardner, 1987, p. 57). Our understanding is shaped by our perceptions and our perceptions by our understanding. Together understanding and perceptions work to create a world that is unique for each of us.

Central to the work of Gardner, Bruner and other cognitive psychologists has been the fundamental questions of the nature of experience. Building on the works of Kant, they hold that no individual can see "the thing in itself" or the actual physical reality. Perception is affected by such things as the amount of material being considered, the conditions under which the perceptions take place, prior knowledge of the perceiver, and the perceiver's beliefs, interpretations, inferences, assumptions, and intentions (Gardner, 1987, p. 309). Faced with trillions of visual and other perceptual possibilities given to us each day, we actually perceive relatively little. Those things we do perceive fit within certain concepts and have meaning at some conceptual level (Bruner, 1996).

If we ask a room full of people to look around and notice everything they see that is blue, then have them close their eyes and name off all of the green objects in the room, the list of items perceived will typically be very short. When then asked to list the blue items, they will generate an extensive list. Clearly their ability to "see" is shaped by the nature of the task. They assumed that our instruction was in some way meaningful and used the concept of "blue" as a filter by which to make their perceptions. The act of seeing is not only physical but mental and psychological (Gardner, 1987, p. 101). More accurately, it is physical, mental, psychological and social. Perceivers sitting in that room are free to "see" whatever they want. Indeed, people who know this game, make it a point to take note of random colors in anticipation of the bait-and-switch nature of the task. But even here, they are not "free" but rather constrained by their own anticipation of a task set within the social interaction. We act in a world we have created, constrained by what we "perfink"—perceive, feel, think (Bruner, 1986, p. 69).

Students venturing into communities perceive those things that they are mentally prepared to see. In her journal, Cheryl makes simplistic, non-critical comparisons between Prairie Avenue Elementary and Walnut Road Elementary and draws upon her experience watching "gangsta" videos because her first journal asked for her "vivid impressions" and offered no other conceptual frame. This initial journal offers a crude baseline of the learner as she or he appears in the first stage of our model. As the semester continues, other journal questions will help learners to focus on different vantage points, helping broaden perceptions and

enabling students to "see" the "same setting in different ways (see Appendix A).

## Categorization

Just as the eyes and mind cannot grasp all of the physical perceptions available to our senses, our brain cannot carry all of the individual bits of information that we take in. Cognitively, we cope by packaging material into working concepts like "blue" or "school" or "sociology." These concepts are formed around discernable attributes or features that have some predictive power (Bruner, 1956). Within our concept of "school" are the attributes of "students," "teachers," "classrooms," and "learning material." Within the culture, the concept of "school" has some common meaning which we, as members of society, use when we are talking about school, complaining about schools, or voting on school funding.

The meaning we make of even insignificant experiences hinges upon the conceptual categories we hold in our heads. Well defined and agreed upon concepts organized into theories form the basis of our academic disciplines and the manner in which knowledge is organized within academic disciplines. With or without formal education, however, the organization of knowledge into conceptual categories is critical to the cognitive process. New information, whether transmitted within the culture or perceived individually, is integrated into our existing concepts, helping us to constantly shape and reshape our concepts.

While we have the power to form original concepts, generally concepts are learned or acquired via social processes. As noted above, we build and reshape acquired concepts to fit a world of our own making. We learned the concept of "school" before we set foot in the schoolhouse door. This conceptual understanding gets modified by our experiences and our concept is "personalized." In presenting relevant theories in class and shaping specific questions using those questions, Dr. Sorenson is offering Cheryl new categories to use. Cheryl's concept of "school" will likely be modified as she integrates her experiences as a college student and as a mentor in urban Los Angeles with her previous experiences as a student in rural Minnesota. Her experience will transform her concepts. If Cheryl's concepts about "school," "education," and "equality" are radically transformed during the course of the semester, her way of understanding the world may be transformed as well.

## DEFINING THE TASK—PRAGMATICALLY

Prior to engaging in community service, students participating in the Joint Educational Project go through a pre-service training session in which they learn more about the nature of the assignment, about the school with which they will be working and the culture of the community and the neighborhood schools. At the conclusion of training students are asked to detail their own expectations for the assignment and include that information in a service-learning "contract."

The purpose of carefully planned pre-service training sessions is to clarify expectations and intentions. Expectancy (our anticipation of what will be encountered) and intention (our tentative plan for what we will do when we encounter that which we expect) are as much a part of the realm of emotion as intellect. Expectations and intentions are shaped by our past experiences and, as a consequence, carry emotional attachments as well as information from the past. Under conditions in which frustration, anxiety and other emotional responses are too high, individuals have difficulty forming clear concepts (Eysenck, 1982). In preparing students for their experiences through pre-service training, efforts are made by the staff at the JEP to shape student expectations in order to minimize frustration and debilitating anxiety. This process calls for the expectations of both the educators and the site to be clarified and for students' own expectancies and intentions to be identified and, as necessary, modified.

It is important to note that what educators tell students to expect in communities will clearly shape what they observe. Educators need to be aware that in providing training on issues such as child abuse, gangs and delinquency, and other problem-focused views of community, students will be more likely to "see" such things, even if these problems are rare or difficult to observe.

### The Experience

Cheryl's assignment involves mentoring a fifth grade immigrant from El Salvador at a nearby elementary school. Her work requires her to enter into the community twice a week during the semester. What she encounters during each week is highly predictable in that the meetings with Miguel are always a combination of academic assistance and relationship-building within a school setting. On the other hand, the quality of that relationship, the responsiveness of the student, Cheryl's skills in working with him, and the events Cheryl has the opportunity to experience are highly unpredictable. In developing experiences which take predictability (continuity) and unpredictability (dis-

continuity) into account, educators can build in factors that promote active learning and minimize those factors which hinder learning.

In our everyday experience, we minimize the demands on our thinking through a process of anticipatory cognition in which we use scraps of input from our perceptions and "read" the rest of the scene from the model that exists in our head. For example, we commute to work daily barely conscious of our surroundings. We do not read signs, notice neighborhoods, or actively think about our route. This process requires that we live in a "continuous world" in which we can fairly accurately predict what we would see if we were to pay attention.

Active cognition is more likely to occur if we encounter the unexpected. There is then a heightened state of arousal (Bruner, 1986, p. 46). Cognitive arousal is most often created when our roles are changed, our concepts challenged, our worlds brought into question. The challenge to existing conceptual frameworks in which our expectations are violated places us in an aroused condition in which we are forced to re-conceptualize (i.e., learn).

In Cheryl's case, the likelihood of active cognition is increased by deliberate thought about the placement of students participating in the service-learning program. JEP attempts to harness the social, cultural and economic discontinuity between the lives of most students at the University of Southern California and the lives of the students in the community with whom they work, in order to promote conceptual challenges. Cheryl is unlikely to have well-formed cognitive models of urban schools, of immigrant life, or of cross-cultural communications. Placing her in this new and different setting challenges existing models and can help her reconceptualize.

Reconceptualization is a process of formulating new hypotheses and testing them (Dewey, 1938). Effective service-learning requires extended experiences and relationship building with members of the community. Cheryl's work requires her to engage in an experiential-reflective cycle on a weekly basis where she can build on her efforts to make meaning of the environment with the help of her instructor, JEP staff members, and members of the community.

### Critical Reflection

Russian psychologist Lev Vygotsky believed that "language (is) an agent for altering the powers of thought—giving thought new means for explicating the world. In turn, language (becomes) the repository for new thoughts once achieved," (Bruner, 1986, p. 143). There is growing evidence that learning in contextual situations not only increases vocabulary but that the improvement in vocabulary increases the ability to learn in contextual situations (Sternberg, 1990). According to Bruner, there are two modes of thought, each of which calls upon a different vocabulary, each "providing distinctive ways of ordering experience, of constructing reality" (1986, p. 11). These are "the well-formed argument" and the "good story." At JEP, we promote both modes of thought by providing students with intellectual stimuli in the form of "Academic Questions" and "Journal Questions."

## Academic Questions

Each week Cheryl is asked to offer a written response to the theoretical or conceptual question described above in "Defining the Task." Drawing upon her observations as well as her conversations with Miguel, Cheryl attempts to define the terms used in the question, cite her observations, and explain how her observations support or contradict the theory. She may also want to explore some secondary sources in the library or in her classroom reading which shed still more light on the topic.

During the second week of her assignment, Cheryl is asked to answer the following set of Academic Questions:

> According to Greenwood, Whyte and Harkavy (1993), participatory research "is a form of action research in which professional social researchers operate as full collaborators with members of organizations in studying and transforming those organizations" (p. 177). How does your work in the community compare to participatory research? How does it compare to other types of sociological research? (Be sure to use examples from your experience in the community that allow you to compare and contrast your work with various research methodologies.) Keeping in mind the Greenwood et al. article, as well as the lecture on research ethics, what might be the ethical issues involved in your work in the community? What precautions might you take to prevent ethical problems from occurring in your assignment?

Reflecting on these questions and their relationship to her experiences challenges Cheryl to compare her work to sociological research and to think about her work in scholarly terms. Furthermore, by asking Cheryl and other students to link their experiences specifically to

"participatory research," Dr. Sorenson encourages students to consider their work from an egalitarian and collaborative perspective.

In response to this question, Cheryl wrote, in part:

> Greenwood et al. challenge us to conduct our observations from the perspective of members of the community, but as careful as I may be, I find myself accepting certain racial and ethnic stereotypes. In my short nineteen years on this earth, I have not been able to interact with many people of other ethnic groups. As a result, much of my understanding of these groups comes from what I see on television. As Professor Sorenson mentioned in class, however, minority groups are typically underrepresented and/or misrepresented in the media. This has left me naive and misinformed when it comes to analyzing my experiences in the community.

Wittgenstein holds that concepts are neither simple mental constructs in the head nor abstract ideas that exist independent of human beings but rather represent a unity of ideas that have utility in the world (Gardner, 1987, p. 346). The more frequently that students use abstract concepts in observing, thinking about, describing, and talking about the world, the more clear those concepts become integrated into the thinking processes of the user. As these analytical methods and organizational concepts are acquired, they move students one step closer to being able to think critically and defend their points of view. As students develop more advanced critical thinking skills, Moore's "critical pedagogy" becomes a more viable alternative. We agree that an instructional approach that invites students to "read" their workplaces in the community as "texts" in which students "examine ... the histories, power arrangements, and values underlying their work organizations" is a worthwhile go. Our disagreement is whether our students are ready to do this without a great deal of mediated skill development.

## Journal Questions

In addition to an Academic Question, Cheryl responds to a reflective question which is designed to help her look at her own personal response to her experiences. Each week a new question helps her look at a new level of the experience or to look at the experience from a different angle to learn more about herself as a participant in the community.

In Cheryl's second week, she is asked to reply to the following Journal Question:

**WEEK TWO** - *Players in the Drama:* Describe who you work with, their lives, their views, their goals in life. Include some personal reaction to the individual or individuals you are working with.

Cheryl offers a lengthy reply which includes the following:

> ... Miguel had a big bandage on his head and several bruises on his legs. Although I didn't ask him, I'm guessing that these are the results of living in an abusive home. Because of the high rates of poverty, crime, gang activity and drug use that plague the community, I assume that the pressures get to be too much, and parents release their frustration on their children...

Academically, in employing Dewey's model of empirical inquiry, we intentionally play down feelings, letting the student play the role of an "objective" observer. We realize, however, that students engaged in service-learning are hardly objective observers. They bring with them beliefs, attitudes, and values which frequently are at odds with the communities in which they work. The discontinuity between student and community, while provoking active learning, also represents a danger in which their "learning" may simply be built upon their prior attitudes and values. When educators and community representatives speak of a "do no harm" policy for service-learning, they are acknowledging that service-learning may have negative consequences. Students who enter into communities and react in racist or patronizing ways may be doing far more harm than the ills they are supposedly addressing (C. Martinez, personal communication, 1995). We believe that this process needs the same sort of mediation that we advocated above and will describe this in more detail in the section on mediated learning.

A second use of these weekly journal questions is to help us identify and resolve problems that hinder student learning. Students engaged in service-learning frequently encounter problems that hinder their ability to learn. A student mistakenly assigned to the school's xerox room or a student assigned to work with an autistic child without the training required for such work can result in high levels of "noise," (Bruner, 1986) or frustration and limited access to new information about the community in which he or she is working (Eysenck, 1982). Many students accept whatever task they are given as they see themselves as "servants" to the community, despite debilitating anxiety produced by the situation. Weekly journals or reflective questions offer them a chance to air their frustrations and, as a consequence, a chance for educators to help establish conditions in which they are more likely to learn.

### Written Reflection

Our efforts to assist students in developing the formal skill of weaving together the two abstract worlds of theory and community-based observations will be most successful if students' responses are in a written form. We believe that written responses are essential for teaching students how to create carefully developed, critical arguments. These written arguments require students to use the more technical vocabulary of the discipline. Our educational institutions expect that students should be achieving this skill as a form of technical literacy (Myers, 1986).

### Oral Reflection

At the same time, we argue that there is an important role for a verbal and interactive reflective process that helps students test their thoughts in a marketplace of ideas. In order to accomplish this goal, Cheryl participates along with her class in a weekly discussion led by her Teaching Assistant on the relationship between the theory and their collective experiences. It is at this level that students must address the consequences of challenging or supporting concepts within a social context. Central to the notion of socially constructed meaning is this process in which students shape and reshape their ideas based upon a larger public discourse. While formal written discourse is the mark of competency in our educational institutions, oral discourse is frequently the mark of an effective figure in the public arena. Whether reflection is written or oral, however, the process of naming and using concepts is central to concept acquisition.

## MEDIATED LEARNING

Students engaged in building bridges between classrooms and communities are engaged in a social process of constructing meaning. The theories they are asked to use in community-based learning are generally significant analytical concepts within the culture of the institution. Student observations, interpretations, questions, and hypotheses are part of the critical discourse about the nature of the world we share (Moore, 1990). Paulo Freire made this same point when he wrote, "Knowledge emerges only through invention and re-invention, through the restless, impatient, continuing, hopeful inquiry human beings pursue in the world, with the world, and with each other" (1994, p. 53).

We take issue, however, with Moore's assertion that this should be a discourse among equals conducting "an unfettered investigation." The discourse is fettered to some degree by what are currently constituted as concepts with some degree of social or cultural "validity." The instructor plays the role of mediator, facilitator, and guide in helping students to develop an understanding of these concepts as a necessary prerequisite to investigating and possibly challenging the concepts. The role of service-learning educators is a delicate one in that, on the one hand, educators act as elders transmitting the concepts of the culture, and, on the other, as agents of change helping students to think critically about the contextual validity of those concepts.

For educators, this process of shaping and refining students' thinking about the world can be greatly improved by applying a concept developed by Lev Vygotsky, which he referred to as the "Zone of Proximal Development," or ZPD. According to Vygotsky, ZPD is "the distance between the actual developmental level as determined by independent problem solving and the level of potential development as determined through problem solving under adult guidance or in collaboration with more capable peers" (Sternberg, 1990).[5] This is a process in which the adult or peer educator mediates between the psychological level of the individual and the complexity of the world in which problems are embedded, helping individuals to progress from the level of understanding they have toward ever more sophisticated understanding.

While Vygotsky's theory has been applied largely to Piaget's pre-adolescent stage of formal operations (1970), others have suggested that many young people in their late teens and early twenties still have very poorly developed skills when it comes to higher level abstractions and systems of abstractions (Fisher & Pipp, 1984). Our work at the University of Southern California during the past twenty years provides support for that theory. It is not uncommon to find university students who have little skill in relating their observations in community settings to the abstract concepts they are encountering in their classrooms, even when we believe that the relationship is self-evident. Lacking these analytical skills, they are unable to critically examine institutional, sociological, cultural, and economic forces at work in the communities and often respond to their experiences within a narrow, ethnocentric framework.

In addition, students often lack the critical self-awareness that is so important for reflecting on themselves and their roles in the community. This is particularly significant for USC students, where there is often considerable discontinuity between their experiences in the community and their experiences as privileged members of society. We believe it is critical to help such students to recognize their privileged status and move from an insular view of the world to a more empathetic, multicultural perspective. Educator and theorist William Tierney (1993) describes this shift as a three-step process of "cultural learning":

1. Step[ping] out of [one's] geographic and temporal spheres of influence and in the spheres of other. Such a step is more complex than it appears, for in doing so, the learner is consciously giving up components of a strategy of power in order to learn about the Other.

2. Developing the desire and ability to listen...We listen to individuals' stories so that we understand their views of the world, and in doing so, we may have to radically transform our own understandings.

3. The internalization of the Other's needs, wants and desires...to understand different people's views of the world so well that we incorporate these views in our own outlook (p. 145).

At JEP, students are asked to reflect on experiences in the community in order to develop abstract analytical skills, increase critical self-awareness, and enhance "cultural learning." Students' written responses to Academic Questions and Journal Questions are read each week by an undergraduate "Program Assistant'" (PA), a student who has had one or more semesters of service-learning courses and has been trained to read student responses and guide students in their thinking and writing. PAs help students to think through any problems they may be encountering, clarify thoughts and feelings, and reduce anxieties. They also extend the discourse, clarify ill-conceived arguments, and direct students to additional sources of information through the use of "Socratic" questions, which challenge student statements with comments like, "How does the observation support or contradict Greenwood's view of participatory research?" or "Might there be other explanations for a child wearing a bandage?"

While Cheryl's PA can often recognize deep-seated fears and prejudices from the very first journal entry, she or he attempts to gradually question and challenge Cheryl's statements using the concepts presented in class, the testimony of those with whom Cheryl interacts in the community, Cheryl's own experiences, as tools to increase her understanding. Through this mediated learning approach, the PA engages Cheryl in a dialogue, questioning her belief system and sources of bias. There is evidence that, during the course of the semester, students such as Cheryl begin to recognize the extent to which they are prisoners of stereotypes and preconceptions, and begin to develop new perspectives. As educators, we believe that carefully guiding the work of students engaged in service-learning is the most effective way of helping students acquire this skill and essential analytical tools.

### The Learner

We conclude our model with the learner as a reminder to ourselves that, as educators, the outcome of our work should not be how much service our students have done, how well they have done that service, or how good they feel about their role in the community. We should judge our success upon the increased ability of students to engage in critical discourse at an abstract and conceptual level and to develop a "meta-perspective" of their experience in the community.

### Discussion

The model can be applied to a single week of a service-learning program, a semester of engagement, or an entire undergraduate approach to service-learning. The goal is to help students constantly critique, evaluate and build on knowledge and move to intellectually "higher ground" and, at the same time, continue to critically examine their roles within our complex and diverse society.

While we have presented the model as a linear one, it is clear that we could have just as easily constructed it as a cyclical model, or, more appropriately, a spiraling model. It is in fact not truly a linear process in that "defining a task" is in itself an "experience" as is reflection and mediation, and each stage of the process can have immediate effects upon the learner and the way he or she sees the world. We elected to present the model in a linear fashion in hopes of improving instructional practices. We think the model can help educators think clearly about their roles in structuring and mediating service-learning.

In short, we believe the role of the service-learning educator is to promote conceptual knowledge by uniting the abstract world of theories from the academy with the unique experiences of students at work in communities. David Lewis (1990) uses a schema that is particularly helpful in understanding this idea. Lewis describes two planes, the plane of intellectual, abstract

**Figure 3: Lewis' Model: Knowledge = the intersection of theory and experience**

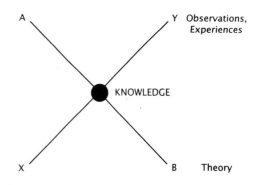

theory (designated by line AB in Figure 3) and the plane of personal observation and experience (designated by line XY). Lewis describes "knowledge"' as the intersection of two planes. This intersection is the line (in our example, the point) toward which the service-learning educator strives. "Knowledge" includes value systems in that these systems color the manner in which we understand the world. Knowledge is, to a degree, a subjective commodity.

Traditionally, the academy has been at the outer extension of the intellectual plane. Non-mediated community service often takes place at the outer extension of the experiential plane. The task of the service-learning educator is to move students as close to that intersecting line of knowledge as possible, given the time and resources available. It is a task which requires careful planning and even more careful instruction, attention to the nature of students' experiences in communities, and constant mediation of the intellectual and personal reflections of students as they try to make meaning of the community they have entered. It is a task where the role of the educator is to be not only a guide for the development of a higher level of intellectual understanding, but also to serve as a guide for the development of more carefully articulated values.

As Bruner says,

> We are living in bewildering times...There are deep problems that stem...from a changing society whose future shape we can not foresee and for which it is difficult to prepare a new generation...[Our] culture is constantly in the process of being recreated as it is interpreted and regenerated by its members...Education is (or should be) one of

the principle forums for performing this function...(1986, pp 121–123).

Our role as educators is to help our students to understand their role as interpreters of the culture who are, in the process, regenerating that culture. As we move toward a multicultural society, the demands on those generating that new culture are indeed bewildering. This educational challenge is not a job for the faint of heart.

## REFERENCES

Bruner, J. S. (1968). *Toward a theory of instruction*. New York: W.W. Norton & Company.

Bruner, J. S. (1986). *Actual minds, possible worlds*. Cambridge, MA: Harvard University Press.

Bruner, J. S., Goodnow, J., & Austin, G. (1956). *A study of thinking*. New York: Wiley.

Cohen, J. (1994). Matching university mission with service motivation: Do the accomplishments of community service match the claims? *Michigan Journal of Community Service Learning*, 1: 1, 98–104.

Crockett, L. J. & Petersen, A. C. (1984). Biology: Its role in gender-related educational experiences. In E. Fennema & M. J. Auer (Eds.), *Women and education* (pp. 85–116). Berkeley: McCutchen Publishing Corporation.

Dewey, J. (1938). *Experience and education*. New York: MacMillan Publishing Company.

Dillon, K. E. & Cooper, D. M. (1996). USC Fall Freshman Survey - 1995 (conducted by the Cooperative Institutional Research Program). *University of Southern California Chronicle*, 15:24, 12–14.

Eysenck, M. W. (1982). *Attention and arousal: Cognition and performance*. New York: Springer-Verlag.

Fisher, K.W. & Pipp, S.L. (1984). Process of cognitive development: Optimal level and skill acquisition. In R. J. Sternberg (Ed.), *Mechanisms of cognitive development* (pp.45–75). New York: Freeman.

Freire, P. (1994, 1970). *Pedagogy of the oppressed*. New York: Continuum Publishing Company.

Gardner, H. (1987). *The mind's new science*. New York: Basic Books.

Goodman, N. (1984). *Of mind and other matters*. Cambridge, MA: Harvard University Press.

Greenwood, D. J., Whyte, W. F., & Harkavy. 1. (1993). Participatory action research as a process and as a goal. *Human Relations*, 46:2, 175–192.

Heath, S. B. (1983). *Ways with words*. Cambridge: Cambridge University Press.

Kagan, J. (1964). Impulsive and reflective children. In J. D. Krumbolz (Ed.), *Learning and the educational process*. Chicago: Rand McNally.

Kincheloe, J. L., & Steinberg, S. R. (1993). A tentative description of post-formal thinking: The critical confrontation with cognitive theory. *Harvard Educational Review*, 63:3, 296–320.

Kolb, D. A. (1984). *Experiential learning: Experience as a source of learning and development*. Inglewood Cliffs, NJ: Prentice-Hall.

Kraft, R. J. (1996). Service learning: An introduction to its theory, practice, and effects. *Education and Urban Society*, 28:2, 131–159.

Lewis, D. (1990). What experience teaches. In W. G Lycan (Ed.), *Mind and cognition*, pp. 499–518. Oxford: Basil Blackwell Ltd.

Maehr, M. L. (1974). *Sociocultural origins of achievement*. Monterey, CA: Brooks/Cole Publishing Company.

Maybach, C.W. (1996). Investigating urban community needs: Service learning from a social justice perspective. *Education and Urban Society*, 28:2, 224–236.

Moore, D. T. (1990). Experiential education as critical discourse. In J. Kendall (Ed.), *Combining service and learning*, pp. 273–283. Raleigh, NC: National Society for Internships and Experiential Education.

Myers, M. (1986). Teaching writing in secondary schools. In K. Rehage (Ed.), *Eighty-fifth yearbook of the National Society for the Study of Education*, pp. 148–169. Chicago: University of Chicago Press.

Piaget, J. (1970). *Science of education and the psychology of the child*. New York: Grossman.

Shumer, R., & Belbas, B. (1996). What we know about service learning. *Education and Urban Society*, 28:2, 208–223.

Sternberg, R. J. (1990). *Metaphors of mind: Conceptions of the nature of intelligence*. Cambridge: Cambridge University Press.

Tierney, W. G. (1993). *Building communities of difference: Higher education in the twenty-first century*. Westport, CT: Bergin & Garvey.

U.S. Bureau of the Census. (1990).

Witkin, H. & Goodenough, D. (1977). Field dependence and interpersonal behavior. *Psychological Bulletin*, 84, 661–689.

Zlotkowski, E. (1995). Does service-learning have a future? *Michigan Journal of Community Service Learning*, 2, 123–133.

## APPENDIX A

Journal Questions:

**WEEK ONE** - *The Setting:* What are your most vivid first impressions of the site? Describe settings, people, actions and positive or negative feelings you are having.

**WEEK TWO** - *Players in the Drama:* Describe who you work with, their lives, their views, their goals in life. Include some personal reaction to the individual or individuals with whom you are working.

**WEEK THREE** - *The Plot:* What activities have you been doing with the person(s) with whom you have been working? Describe your relationship.

**WEEK FOUR** - *The Plot* (continued): How do the student(s) with whom you work react to you? Cite specific examples. How does their reaction make you feel?

**WEEK FIVE** - *The Action:* How do you think your presence in the community impacts the person(s) with whom you work? What impact has this assignment had on you? Illustrate your points with experiences you have had this semester.

**WEEK SIX** - *The Script:* Describe in some detail a JEP session, including bits of conversation or, if you are working in a school, a sample of work in which you and the kids have been involved. Be creative. What is the significance of that which you have described?

**WEEK SEVEN** - *Analysis:* After being in the community for several weeks now, how have your initial impressions been altered? If they have not changed, describe observations that confirmed initial impressions.

**WEEK EIGHT** - *Critique:* Write a summary on your eight weeks. What was learned by both you and the person(s) with whom you worked? Include special experiences or highlights you might have had.

## NOTES

1. While Cheryl is a fictional character, her journal question entries are comprised of direct quotes and paraphrased material from actual JEP students from the past three years.

2. A pseudonym.

3. Although 51% of the 1995 USC freshman class is white/Caucasian, and 27.7% come from families earning over $100,000 annually, USC is one of the most ethnically and economically diverse universities in the country. According to the Cooperative Institutional Research Program, 82% of the 1995 freshman class at universities nationwide was Caucasian. Further, while 23% of freshmen nationwide have families earning more than $100,000, only 8.4% earn less than $20,000 per year, compared with over 13% at USC.

4. JEP often works with professors in constructing Academic Questions for students.

5. The term "more capable peers" is Vygotsky's. We prefer to think of our peer educators as simply "trained."

# Toward a Theory of Engagement:

## A Cognitive Mapping of Service-Learning Experiences

Kerry Ann Rockquemore, *University of Connecticut*
Regan Harwell Schaffer, *Pepperdine University*

*Service-learning in higher education is intended to increase students' civic responsibility and enhance learning. While quantitative assessment of these two outcomes has dominated the existing literature, this article explores the oft-ignored cognitive processes that students undergo during the community service-learning experience. Data from 50 daily reflection journals is used to draw a descriptive map of the social-psychological stages that occur during service-learning. In addition, textual analysis reveals that students progress through three identifiable stages of development: shock, normalization and engagement. To increase the effectiveness of service-learning outcomes, faculty members must understand these specific cognitive processes that accompany community-based learning.*

## SERVICE-LEARNING AND COGNITIVE PROCESSING: OPENING THE 'BLACK BOX'

At most colleges and universities, service-learning has two pedagogical goals: increasing civic responsibility (Myers-Lipton, 1998; Parker-Gwin & Mabry, 1998) and facilitating academic objectives (Astin & Sax, 1998; Claus & Michel, 2000; Eyler & Giles, 1999). Current research on service-learning has focused on these two principle outcomes, using quantitative analysis to measure students' attitudes and substantive knowledge before and after engaging in service-learning (Astin & Sax, 1998; Astin, Sax, & Avalos, in press; Astin, Vogelgesang, Ikeda, & Yee, 2000; Batchelder & Root, 1994; Eyler & Giles, 1999; Eyler, Giles & Braxton, 1997). From these studies, we have learned that service-learning is, in fact, an effective pedagogical technique for meeting these goals. However, little is known about the actual cognitive processes that students undergo during the community learning experience. Students' pre-service and post-service attitudes provide important documentation that learning has occurred over time, yet we are left to wonder what happens to students during this time period. As researchers and educators, we must ask how the learning occurs and how that process is unique to the service-learning experience.

In attempting to answer the process-related questions involved in service-learning, this research project demonstrates, using quantitative data, that learning has occurred for a sample of 120 students at Pepperdine University. Based on the demonstrated attitudinal change, we attempt to unpack the complex social and psychological experiences through which students progress during this learning process. Qualitative data, in the form of daily journals, were used to create a descriptive map of the cognitive stages that occur while students engage in service-learning. Because the integration of service-learning experiences and substantive, disciplinary-specific learning remains the "missing link" for many service-learning courses (Cohen & Kinsey, 1994; Eyler & Giles, 1999), a better understanding of students' cognitive processing is critical to improving the effectiveness of service-learning as a pedagogical tool.

## PROCEDURES

### Sample

Our sample consisted of 120 students enrolled in "service-learning courses" at Pepperdine University in Malibu, California. These courses include Religion 101, Sociology 200 and two freshman seminar courses entitled "The Call of Service." The courses are required as part of the general education curriculum; however, not all sections of these courses utilize service-learning. Consequently, most of the students in our study did not know of the service-learning component of the course until after they were enrolled. Service-learning courses at Pepperdine are those that fulfill the criteria outlined by the National and Community Service Act of 1990.[1]

Within our overall sample, students were 69% female, 31% male, and disproportionately from affluent families: over half were from families with average yearly incomes of at least $75,000, and one fourth were from families with yearly incomes of at least $150,000. All respondents were between 18 and 22 years of age. These students may be considered representative of the student population at Pepperdine University (Fischer, 1999) and of private Christian liberal arts colleges in the U.S. (Sax, Astin, Korn, & Mahoney, 1998). Pepperdine students differ significantly, however, from the general population of college students in that they are more racially homogeneous and higher in parental socio-economic status (Fischer, 1999; Sax et al., 1998).

From this sample, we purposively sub-sampled (Berg, 1995) a group of 50 students for qualitative analysis. The sub-sample was 32% male and 68% female. They were 80% White, 14% Hispanic, 4% Black and 2% Asian. These students were placed in agencies that engaged in the following range of service activities: food delivery, residential geriatric care, youth mentoring, public education, juvenile detention, free health services, free legal aid, shelter for the homeless, and after-school mentoring.[2]

### Analysis

All respondents in our sample completed a 26-item questionnaire (see Appendix A) before and after their service-learning experience. In addition, we required all respondents in our smaller sub-sample to keep a journal that addressed the following questions: 1) What happened today? and What did I do?, 2) What were the effects of what I did?, 3) How did my service today make me feel?, 4) What relationships am I building?, 5) How does what I am observing at my placement relate to the concepts and ideas we are currently learning in class? Students were required to write one journal entry for each day of service. The number of journal entries varied according to the individual student and the frequency of their service, resulting in a range of 10-30 journal entries per student. The journal questions were intended to encourage students to generate three types of data: 1) a descriptive account of the actual events that occurred during the process of respondents' service-learning experience, 2) an ongoing report of their emotional reactions to the events they encountered in their placement agencies, and 3) an unstructured description of the overall integration of the course content and service experiences.

In order to analyze the qualitative data, we took a grounded theory approach (Glaser & Strauss, 1967) and performed content analysis of the daily journals. Specifically, we immersed ourselves in the relatively unstructured data provided in the individual journals in order to identify the common themes that seemed to be meaningful to students' accounts of their service-learning experiences (Abrahamson, 1983). Using this inductive approach to the data, we followed the data analysis procedure outlined by McCracken (1988). This includes five basic stages of analysis: 1) initial sorting of important from unimportant data; 2) examination of the various pieces of data for logical relationships; 3) confirmatory review of the initial documents to assist in recognition of general properties of the data; 4) description of general themes and hierarchical organi-

### Table 1: Percentage of Students Showing Positive Change on Select Items from Pre- to Post-Test

| Survey Question | Positive Change in Post-Test Survey |
| --- | --- |
| In the United States, people basically have equal opportunity to do what they want in life. | 28% |
| I feel that I can have a positive impact on local social problems. | 43% |
| It is important that I work toward equal opportunity for all people. | 44% |
| I feel that I can make a difference in the world. | 48% |

NOTE: N=20

zation of those themes; and 5) determination of how existing themes may be synthesized into theses. The major themes are presented below.

## RESULTS

Using pre-service and post-service questionnaires, we were able to observe student attitudes at two points in time. Our analysis suggests that students made significant changes in their attitudes toward social justice, equality of opportunity, and civic responsibility over the course of the semester. We were most interested in the questions that focused on equality of opportunity as all instructors had, as a basic course goal, for students to understand that inequalities exist within the United States and that they are inherent in the social structures of American society. Table 1 illustrates some of the positive changes that were observed from the pre-service and post-service questionnaires. We interpret this change of attitude in the direction of established course goals to be indicative of the fact that learning took place among our sample of respondents.

### A Stage Theory of Engagement

We are encouraged by the fact that we can empirically demonstrate the fundamental premise that service-learning, as a pedagogical strategy, facilitated student learning in our overall sample of Pepperdine University students. This is consistent with findings in the extant literature (Astin & Sax, 1998; Astin, Vogelgesang, Ikeda, & Yee, 2000; Cohen & Kinsey, 1994; Eyler & Giles, 1999). Our research question, however, is *how* do students learn while they are engaged in service-learning. In other words, what cognitive processing occurs between the pre-service and post-service assessments? Our data suggest that among the students in our sub-sample, individuals progressed through three distinct stages of development: shock, normalization and engagement.

STAGE 1: SHOCK. The first stage articulated in student journals can be described as "shock." As previously stated, the students in our sample came from economically privileged home environments. Many were raised in suburban communities where they attended private schools and were embedded in demographically homogeneous social networks. For middle and upper-middle class students with limited life experience, their first close encounter with poverty is, by their own description, a shocking experience. After one student's first

trip to a maximum-security juvenile detention facility, she wrote:

> On my way to Camp Kilpatrick, my friend and I didn't really know what to expect. We met up with some other volunteers in the parking lot and carpooled there. It went pretty smoothly. When we got there we noticed the fence that was about 25 feet high, with barbwire wrapped around the top and the dirty brick buildings, and I got a little nervous. I guess I just assumed that the boys we would meet would have stolen a candy bar or got in a fight at recess. This looked more like prison to me!...

While most students in the sub-sample expressed shock and disbelief at the social and economic circumstances they were expected to work within, the level of shock, and the articulation of it, varied considerably. Some students expressed awe at the profound similarities and differences between their own neighborhoods and those in which they were expected to serve. The following statement was written by a first year student after her first trip to El Rescate, a free legal clinic in downtown Los Angeles:

> Before going to El Rescate, I had expectations in mind. I thought it would look like any other law office. I was not expecting anything fancy, but I was expecting something clean and professional looking. I was in for a shock. I began to realize that the office would be different from what I imagined when the map we had took us into the ghetto. I thought to myself that we were in the wrong place, but then a sign on the side of a run-down looking red brick building proved me wrong. My first thought was that my dad would kill me if he knew where I was!

This statement is revealing in various ways. The idea that "...my dad would kill me if he knew where I was!" reflects the high level of isolation that is normative among these affluent students. This should not be dismissed, however, as a safety issue. The same student later clarified, "My grandma would die of embarrassment if she knew I was helping 'foreigners' become citizens." Both statements are indicative of deeply rooted negative attitudes about the poor and disenfranchised in our society. These two respondents' experiences in the shock stage revealed both their social isolation and their preconceived ideas about poverty. Another student wrote:

I admit that I live in a bubble settled away from the harsh reality of the world. I heard of what goes on with the rest of the world, but I cannot relate to that part of the world. Before today, I have never gone into a poor minority community. The closest I have been was through movies and television shows. The drive to El Rescate was quite frightening for me. I was beginning to convert my plan of service-learning elsewhere. There were many things that seemed similar to my hometown, but yet, they contained contrary meanings. I saw bars made of iron on every window and door in the ghetto. Those iron bars were there to protect the owners of those stores and houses. The bars underlined the danger, which was always right around the corner. Captiva Island, where I lived in Florida, had gates made of the same material... iron. However, the main purpose of those gates was for decoration. The only protection those gates might give us was preventing tourists from driving onto our private properties.

The shock stage of service-learning is important because it provides a sharp emotional and psychological jolt to students' perceptions of reality. College students, like most humans, tend to generalize their own individual experience to the rest of society. Raised in affluent families with homogeneous social networks, students tend to think that "most people" attend college and "most people's lives" are similar to their own. As the respondent above indicated, she was generally aware that less fortunate people existed, but her perceptions were largely media-derived because of her lifelong geographic separation from low-income housing. The realization that there are many people in American society that have significantly fewer resources than our respondents was, to them, a profound revelation. Evidence of this can be found in the fact that most students expressed a newfound thankfulness for the most basic privileges they had in their own lives. A student working at the legal clinic wrote:

My client was grateful for the possibilities that the U.S. provides. Possibilities that I have taken for granted my entire life. I did not have to grow up in the United States and be blessed with all of these freedoms, but I was. And now I'm thankful for something that I have had access to all my life. I appreciate what I have; I appreciate that the state paid for my high school education, and that I have the opportunity to go to college. I appreciate that I live and go to school in a safe area.

One additional finding that is unique to the context of faith-based institutions is that the shock stage caused many students to offer unsolicited reflections on their faith. At Pepperdine, 60% of students come from an evangelical Christian background and 73% claim "Christian" as their religious self-identification (Fischer, 1999). In this way, our sub-sample is representative of the Pepperdine student population, although drastically different than most institutions of higher education. The shock-induced inquiries about spirituality were most frequent for students who were self-identified Christians working in faith-based organizations. The following excerpt from a student journal provided an illustration of this tension and questioning:

Through my afternoon in L.A. I learned that serving people like that is not without its disappointments, and that lessons can come from unlikely sources; the odd individual who expresses no gratitude . . . or the person we met who loudly objected to our activities. The indignant lady refused to accept a bag of chips, soap and tampons, and she jumped up and chased the student who offered it to her back to our tables. The lady was shouting angrily, expressing her displeasure at our presence, saying that if we really were Christians like we called ourselves then we should experience what she experiences every day. We cannot just go and offer assistance once a week and go back to our own personal lives in Malibu for the rest of the time, she informed us, but we could only be qualified to help if we experienced first hand the kind of life she lived every day. What an interesting thought . . . how many of us who spent our Sunday afternoon feeding the homeless would be willing to dedicate every aspect of the rest of our lives to serving others, to serving the Lord, even if this involved living in an environment, a culture, entirely foreign to us, one which we might possibly consider "below" us?

Experiencing other people living in poverty, students were forced to open themselves up to the realization that their perceptions of the social world may be severely skewed by their affluence and/or Christian worldview. This shock-induced uncertainty, while frightening and upsetting to some students, created in them an ideal state of cognitive openness toward the substantive course material. This stage of shock enabled students to examine the inconsistencies in their lives and in the community around them.

**STAGE 2: NORMALIZATION.** For most of the students in our study, the shock of seeing poverty wears off within the second or third week of their service-learning experience. By the end of week three, the majority of students ceased making comments in their journals that indicated surprise about the circumstances they observed. Students then entered the stage that we have termed "normalization." We use this term because students were quick to adapt to their new circumstances. No matter what level of shock they may have experienced in the first two weeks of their placement, they quickly became accustomed to the sight of poverty and viewed the deprivation of their clients as "normal."

During this period students began to feel comfortable with their role in the community organization. It is here that they began to develop relationships with the staff and regular clients. These relationships were crucial to the learning process because they were based on common human bonds as opposed to pity. In the previous stage, students refer to the poor as "those people" or "them." In the normalization stage, the 'other-ness' gives way to personal description. Three students working as tutors at a juvenile detention facility made the following representative comments:

> After initially being a little intimidated by Joe, I now see he is a normal person just like me. He just had a little tougher upbringing than I did. We relate to a lot of the same things, like how we miss our families, worrying about school and especially our future.

> I'm learning to find common ground with people I thought I had nothing in common with.

> I felt good about today, because I feel that we really bonded and that we are actually like good friends, rather than me just being his tutor. He is even going to come hang out with me when he gets out.

While students began to realize the humanity of their clients in the process of relationship building, they simultaneously started comparing their clients to others in their environment. Comparative assessments were common in this stage and were made to illustrate the similarities between the student and their client. One student favorably compared an "inmate" at the juvenile detention facility to other students he had encountered at Pepperdine: "Eric, on the other hand, wants to learn. He seems to appreciate and respect what all of the Pepperdine volunteers are doing. Eric seems more mature to me than a lot of people I know at Pepperdine."

One final commonality in this stage was for students to express an understanding of the importance of service. Many were surprised that they began to feel committed to the people and the institutions they served. They cared for their clients and began to better comprehend the missions of their community organizations. This sentiment was most commonly expressed among students working with children. Two respondents who tutored homeless children made the following statements:

> When I go home for Thanksgiving I'm going to bring him some of my childhood books, and we can read them together. I think that I will still go to the shelter even after the class requirements are over.

> Throughout the course of my service I realized that I couldn't just stop going when the assignment was over. The kids have become much more than an 'assignment.'

We consider this stage crucial to the learning process because, while students may be shocked into questioning their own perceptions of reality in the first stage of development, they also had the tendency to marginalize those they observed. In the first stage, respondents characterized their clients as fundamentally different from themselves. They consistently described the poor in ways that provided both linguistic and cognitive distance. It was important to the learning process that students developed the capacity to see the poor as human beings, not unlike themselves. In addition, they recognized their preconceived stereotypes and negative perceptions. One respondent described this process as a natural result of her service.

> If there is just one thing that I have learned from typing up numerous itineraries [pre-visa documents], it is that immigrants are hardworking people. I type up employment history, and I have yet to see one lacking a statement of good attendance and excellent work. I think that by placing the stereotype of the 'lazy immigrant' on Latino immigrants, it makes it easier for Californians to pass laws against bilingual education and health care. If people had to wake up and realize that the reason these people are here is just so that they can have a chance at the basic rights we are born with, I bet their views on immigration laws and foreign policy would change. I know mine have.

Acknowledging and facing stereotypes is not a painless process. Students bring a variety of life experiences and psychological baggage to the service-learning experience. Their preconceived, sometimes negative, attitudes may derive from salient personal experiences. For students in our sample, addressing prejudicial ideas about various racial groups provided the greatest challenge to learning. After a disturbing event at the free legal clinic, one respondent wrote the following:

> My hands were shaking and I felt like crying. Some Mexican guys shot my dad last summer, and I thought I was over it, but I guess not. I couldn't quit thinking that maybe I had helped someone like those guys stay here. Part of the reason I wanted to work at El Rescate was to get over my negative feelings towards Hispanic people, because I know it's wrong for me to want to hate an entire group of people for any reason. But I still felt like throwing up.

The normalization stage is critically important to learning because the intensity of our respondents' experiences provoked critical questioning about attribution. They begin asking causal questions because they had developed relationships with people in their organizations and they wanted to know why and how their clients ended up in their current circumstances. The illustrations provided below give a clear idea of how students' questions emerge from their intimate relationships with individuals in their organizations.

> Jeff showed me some new drawing he had done, and sang me a rap song he had just composed. He has a lot of artistic abilities. If he had the right training he could be a phenomenal artist. This made me wonder, how many great would-be doctors, scientists, and artists might have been brushed aside and not given a chance because of their place in the world of social stratification.

> I basically just listened as he shared his family history with me (Mom alcoholic, dad deceased). It was the first time that I actually was able to see how much a person's childhood affects their adult life. Frank believes that he will be in jail for the rest of his life...Tonight was a real eye-opener for me. I came to wonder about how Frank ended up where he is and why he has such a sad view of life.

STAGE 3: ENGAGEMENT. Students began seeking answers to their causal questions in the final stage that we have termed "engagement." In the sixth through eighth weeks of the course, respondents wanted to know why their clients were in poverty and needed the services that their organizations provided. Students became engaged in the learning process because the people and situations they were studying in their course readings were not hypothetical examples, but real people with whom they had developed personal relationships.

Answering these difficult questions requires students to make attributions. The research literature defines attribution as being either individual (internal) or structural (external) (Heider, 1958; Kelley, 1972). Individual explanations attribute economic inequalities to personal characteristics of the poor (i.e., lack of talent, drive, effort, or loose morals). In contrast, structural attributions draw on social factors external to the individual, such as discrepancies in the economic system, lack of political power, educational inequalities, or job discrimination (Kluegel & Smith, 1986). People tend to make individual attributions to explain *other people's* failures, yet make structural attributions to explain their own (Watson, 1982). In addition, existing research illustrates that individuals are likely to make individual attributions to out-groups (groups of which they are not members of), and to make structural attributions for in-group members (Kluegel, 1990; Pettigrew, 1979).

There is a profound tension between the previously described social-psychological patterns for attribution and the course objectives because the stated goals required students to transcend these common ways to explain inequalities in society. In the shock stage, students interacted with people who were different from themselves in every demographic way imaginable. This provided a context of cognitive openness that enabled a reconsideration of their initial construction of reality. In the normalization stage, individuals began to view the poor as individuals like themselves, as opposed to classifying them as an out-group. Relationships were built and adjustments were made in how respondents cognitively classified their clients. Then it was in the final stage that students were forced to reconcile the content of the coursework, which heavily emphasized the size and scope of structural inequalities in American society, with their previous propensity toward individual attributions. If students perceived their clients as similar to themselves, then they began to consider structural attributions. If they viewed their clients as dissimilar, undesirable, or unpleasant, they tended to retain the individual level attributions that they brought with them to the course.

Several examples may help to illustrate this process. Students tutoring juvenile offenders developed strong one-on-one relationships with their tutees throughout the semester. They initially described them as lacking in individual traits that would help them to be successful as an explanation for their current circumstances (i.e., they made individual attributions). Upon entering the engagement stage, they began to focus on external factors in their journal writing. The following comments are illustrative of students questioning family composition, educational inequalities, and political policies (all central elements of the course reading) as causal factors for their tutees' current incarceration and as significant limiting factors in their future mobility.

> I wonder where John's father is or what happened to him. With the guidance of a father I do not think that he would have been led astray...The masculine love and affection that was lacking in his family, he found in his gang. When his mother could not be there, his gang was there for him.

> I know how important the SAT's are and it doesn't look like he has much of a chance at passing...He seems very eager to learn, it is just that he doesn't have the tools given to him in order to learn what he needs to.

> The reading we had about dismantling the welfare state directly affects [the mentee] because the cutbacks that are being proposed will negatively impact him and others in his same position. On the other hand, the things called for to help solve the crisis of poverty in America will help Terry and his family, and give him a chance to exceed any expectations that he has for himself right now. Cost free college would be the only way he could live his dream, which is to attend college.

## DISCUSSION

This article began as an inquiry into the cognitive processes that take place during the service-learning experience. Previous research has illustrated that service-learning is effective in facilitating student learning, yet we know little about how students actually learn. By placing the voices of students at the center of our analysis, we were able to observe their thought processes as they move through a semester of service-learning. This enables us to identify common trends in their cognitive development because the students in our sample progressed through similar stages at clustered times during the semester. In detailing the cognitive map of students' experiences, we have attempted to provide a tentative

theory of engagement. Our findings, however, focused exclusively on the student as the unit of analysis. At this point we state the limitations of our study and then consider how our theoretical model of engagement provides practical applications for faculty using service-learning in liberal arts institutions.

### Limitations

While our findings suggest that important practical applications can be derived from placing the voices of students at the center of developing effective service-learning strategies, there are several important limitations inherent in this study that provide rich avenues for future research. First and foremost, the Pepperdine student population is demographically unique. Our respondents came from affluent backgrounds, were racially homogeneous (i.e., predominately White), and lacked exposure to various ethnic cultures (Fischer, 1999). The stage theory we have presented should be tested in various types of institutions in order to discern what aspects of the process may be unique to affluent White students. What would be the initial reactions of individuals who are socioeconomically diverse, who do not experience shock in the face of poverty? How would their initial experiences be processed in light of their particular biographies? Second, we did not disaggregate the data by race to see if the processes differed between groups. While only 20% of those surveyed were Latino, Black, or Asian, a larger and more diverse sample could have explored potentially interesting racial group differences in the proposed stage theory. If differences do exist, the implications for practitioners designing service-learning courses would also be important. Future research should provide a comparative design between various institutions of higher education and different student populations.

### Practical Applications

In order to improve the service-learning experience, educators should consider both our student-centered perspective and the existing research on organizational effectiveness. Researchers have identified several key organizational elements that facilitate student learning in a service-learning course, including the type of program, the quality of reflection and integration, matching placement agencies and activities with learning goals, and the duration and intensity of the experience (Astin, Vogelgesang, Ikeda, & Yee, 2000; Eyler & Giles, 1997; Waterman, 1997). These organizational elements are consistent with the critical components identified in our analyses, and are particularly salient for faculty members so that they may guide students through the stages from shock to engagement. Because students pass through the cognitive stages we have identified at roughly the same times, the class environment should be structured in such a way as to maximize the learning in each stage. Below, we have identified several organizational elements that emerge from our analysis of student journals.

SHOCK STAGE. In order to absorb initial shock, a baseline of beliefs and feelings must be established and an environment created that fosters a response to those beliefs. Faculty, as part of pre-course preparation, should ensure that activities within the agency not only correspond with the course learning objectives, but also provide meaningful inter-personal experience and learning opportunities that are intellectually challenging for the students. Careful thought should be given to seeking service organizations that place students in situations in which their previous experiences, understanding, and beliefs of society can be challenged and that serve as fertile ground for cognitive growth throughout the semester (Eyler & Giles, 1999). The students in our study entered this stage of shock because of the cognitive dissonance they experienced when placed in a service situation that allowed them interaction with people and situations very different from their own. Because of the importance of student relationships in the learning process, they must have personal interactions with the organization's clients and be engaged in activities that meet the learning objectives of the course (Eyler & Giles, 1997; 1999). The service activities should include tasks that allow student initiative, responsibility, and collaboration with staff and clients so that the students can develop personal relationships. It is essential that the faculty member communicate clear expectations for the learning experience and ensure that service activities are tightly linked to classroom content and reflection. Once expectations are established, the faculty member should design appropriate reflection tools for this stage in the learning process so that baseline feelings can be addressed.

Oral and written communication and application are all reflection tools that promote cognitive development; however, it is the content focus of the reflection activities that enables students to progressively move from shock to engagement (Eyler & Giles, 1999; Welch, 1999). Our analysis suggests that it is not important in the shock stage for students to make connections between their service and the course objectives. More important to the overall learning process is for them to recognize their own beliefs and pre-conceived ideas about the population they will be serving and establishing a foundation from which to grow. Reflection at this time can be purely descriptive, allowing the students to report factual information regarding the service experience while sharing their feelings. During the initial shock stage, students should feel comfortable freely expressing their authentic reactions in a nonjudgmental environment (Welch, 1999). Reflection should be both private, in the form of a journal or paper, and public in a class discussion atmosphere. For many students, this may be the first time articulating their beliefs. At this stage, as we found in our study, it is useful to allow students to recognize that their perceptions of the social world may be skewed. Reflection also enables students to share the shock that they are experiencing with others and create a classroom environment conducive to open dialogue. At this beginning stage, faculty should clarify the link between the service-learning experience and the overall structure of the course. If the placement is not meeting the course objectives, the cognitive thought process will be hindered despite the faculty members' best efforts encourage student reflection (Astin, Vogelgesang, Ikeda, & Yee, 2000; Eyler & Giles, 1999; Welch, 1999). Therefore, program quality is essential to ensure that cognitive growth takes place.

NORMALIZATION STAGE. This stage occurs approximately the second or third week of the service-learning experience. As previously described, students in this stage become more comfortable with their community organization, take on more responsibility, and begin forming relationships with co-workers and clients. In the normalization stage, faculty should move reflection from a descriptive to an integrative format. Reflection should ask the students to draw upon their experiences at their service site and begin connecting their experiences to the classroom content. The reflection content should challenge the students to understand the social problem that the community agency at which they are place is addressing. In addition, the reflection questions, both for written and oral response, should be confrontational and require students to focus on causal questions (Welch, 1999). The students at this stage have more personal relationships with their clients. The reflection questions should take on a more personal nature as well, asking the students to reflect on those people they know by name and humanizing the experience, so that their interactions are not with a nameless "client," but a person similar to themselves. Such reflection questions challenge students to make attributions toward their clients. As time progresses, the students themselves should no longer be dependent on the faculty member to ask the questions, but their experiences should provoke critical questioning on their own.

One cautionary observation is that the faculty member and students can fall into the trap of believing that the normalization stage is where the service-learning experience has reached its full potential. At this stage, students recognize the social problem being addressed and consequently are more aware of social problems. However, it is in the final stage of engagement where students make the cognitive connection between their service-learning experience and the class content. If the students remain in the normalization stage, it is easy for them to become reconciled to the fact that inequalities exist in America and slip into viewing those impacted by these inequalities as an out-group. The faculty member wants to ensure that the learning process continues and may want to integrate class lectures, guest speakers, and specific reflective activities during weeks when the students are in this stage. Otherwise, it is possible that the reflection will remain focused on what the students have learned through the service, devoid of higher level cognitive processing.

ENGAGEMENT STAGE. For faculty using service-learning, the ultimate goal is for students to master course content in a way that meaningfully shapes their understanding of reality and impacts their worldview. This final stage is when students will either reify their original worldview or integrate what they have learned. Reflection at this stage should allow students to question assumptions, gather more extensive information, and then analyze their assumptions using what they have learned through their service and classroom experience. Through this process, the students will be able to reframe their perspectives and beliefs and determine whether their behavior in the future should be modified based upon what they have learned. The amount and quality of class discussion and reflective writing related to the service are all predictors of students' ability to identify social problems from a new vantage point (Blyth, Saito, & Berkas, 1997; Eyler & Giles, 1997; Eyler & Giles, 1999). It is in this stage that the students are able to articulate external attribution and conceptualize social change (Rhoads, 1998). The goal of service-learning is not charity, but increased citizenship and community involvement (Eyler & Giles, 1999). This last stage of cognitive development enables students to move beyond the mere identification of a social problem, beyond "blaming the victim," and toward concrete solutions. Reflection questions no longer should focus on why inequities exist, but on what changes in behavior are needed and what actions should be taken. Even though this last stage may occur in the final weeks of a course, the reflection should be a significant portion of the class assignments and dialogue. These reflection elements need to ensure that students not only reach each stage, but push past the shock and normalization to engagement, which constitutes a change, not only in attitude and understanding, but in behavior.

## NOTES

The authors wish to thank the following individuals for their generous comments and assistance: Lynn Reynolds, Jeanne Heffernan, Robby Schaffer, Joshua Walls, Alison Savage, Brad Dudley, Lorie Goodman, Cynthia Novak and Norm Fischer.

1. The term "service-learning" means a method: a) under which students learn and develop through active participation in thoughtfully organized service experiences that meet actual community needs; b) that is integrated into the students' academic curriculum or provides structured time for a student to think, talk, or write about what the student did and saw during the service activity; c) that provides students with opportunities to use newly acquired skills and knowledge in real-life situations in their own communities; and d) that enhances what is taught in school by extending student learning beyond the classroom and into the community and helps to foster the development of a sense of caring for others (Willits-Cairn & Kielsmeier, 1991, p. 17).

2. Students served in the following non-profit organizations: Camp David Gonzalez, Camp Kilpatrick, El Centro de Amistad, El Rescate, Faith in Christ Ministries—Into the Streets Program, L.A.'s Best—School on Wheels, Meals on Wheels, Organization for the Needs of the Elderly, Point Fermin Elementary School, Salesian Youth Center, Santa Monica Boys and Girls—Club Literacy Program, Union Rescue Mission and the Venice Family Clinic.

## REFERENCES

Abrahamson, M. (1983). *Social research methods.* Englewood Cliffs, NJ: Prentice Hall.

Astin, A. (1985). *Achieving educational excellence: A critical assessment of priorities and practices in higher education.* San Francisco, CA: Jossey-Bass.

Astin, A.W. & Sax, L.J. (1998). How undergraduates are affected by service participation. *Journal of College Student Development, 39* (3), 251–263.

Astin, A.W., Sax, L., & Avalos, J. (forthcoming). Long-term effects of volunteerism during the undergraduate years. *Review of Higher Education.*

Astin, A.W., Vogelgesang, L.J., Ikeda, E.K., & Yee, J.A. (2000). *How service learning affects students.* Executive Summary, Higher Education Research Institute, UCLA.

Berg, B. (1995). *Qualitative research methods for the social sciences.* Boston, MA: Allyn and Bacon.

Blyth, D., Saito, R., & Berkas, T. (1997). A quantitative study of the impact of service-learning programs. In A.S. Waterman (Ed.), *Service-learning: Applications from the research* (pp. 39–56). Mahwah, NJ: Lawrence Erlbaum Associates.

Claus, J. & Michel, T. (2000). Service-learning for social change: The importance of community collaboration and a critically reflective framework (working paper).

Cohen, J. & Kinsey, D. (1994). Doing good and scholarship: A service-learning study. *Journalism Educator, 48* (4), 4–14.

Eyler, J. & Giles, D.E. Jr. (1999). *Where's the learning in service-learning?* San Francisco, CA: Jossey-Bass.

Eyler, J. & Giles, D.E. Jr. (1997). The importance of program quality in service-learning. In A.S. Waterman (Ed.), *Service-learning: Applications from the research* (pp. 57–76). Mahwah, NJ: Lawrence Erlbaum Associates.

Eyler, J. , Giles, D.E., Jr., & Braxton, J.(1997). The impact of service-learning on college students. *Michigan Journal of Community Service Learning,* (4), 5–15.

Fischer, N. (1999). *Fall 1998 comparison data: Seaver freshman vs. national data.* Malibu, CA: Pepperdine University Assessment and Institutional Research.

Glaser, B. & A. Strauss. (1967). *The discovery of grounded theory: Strategies for qualitative research.* Chicago: Aldine.

Heider, F. (1958). *The psychology of interpersonal relations.* New York:Wiley.

Kelley, H. (1972). *Causal schemata and the attribution process.* Morristown, NJ: General LearningPress.

Kluegel, J.R. (1990). Trends in whites' explanations of the black-white gap in SES. *American Sociological Review.* 55: 512–525.

Kluegel, J.R. & Smith, E.R., (1986). *Beliefs about inequality: Americans' view of what is and what ought to be.* New York: Aldine de Gruyter.

McCracken, G. (1988). *The long interview* (Sage University Paper Series on Qualitative Research Methods, Vol. 13). Newbury Park, CA: Sage.

Myers-Lipton, S. (1998). Effect of a comprehensive service-learning program on college students' civic responsibility. *Teaching Sociology, 26* (4), 243–258.

Parker-Gwin, R. & Mabry, J.B. (1998). Service learning as pedagogy and civic education: Comparing outcomes for three models. *Teaching Sociology, 26*(4), 276–291.

Pettigrew, T.F. (1979). The ultimate attribution error. *Personality and Social Psychology Bulletin, 5,* 461–476.

Rhoads, R.A. (1998). Critical multiculturalism and service learning. In R.A. Rhoads & J.P.F. Howard (Eds.), *Academic service learning: A pedagogy of action and reflection* (pp. 39–46). San Francisco: Jossey-Bass.

Sax, L.J., Astin, A.W., Korn, W.S., & Mahoney, K.M. (1998). *The American freshman: National norms for fall 1998.* Los Angeles: Higher Education Research Institute, UCLA.

Waterman, A.S. (ed.). (1997). *Service-learning: Applications from the research.* Mahwah, NJ: Laurence Erlbaum Associates.

Watson, D. (1982). The actor and the observer: How are their perceptions of causality divergent. *Psychological Bulletin, 92,* 682–700.

Welch, M. (1999). The ABCs of reflection: A template for students and instructors to implement written reflection in service-learning. *NSEE Quarterly, 25* (2), 1, 23–25.

Willits-Cairn, R. & Kielsmeier, J. (1991). *Growing hope.* Minneapolis, MN: National YouthLeadership Council.

## AUTHORS

**KERRY ANN ROCKQUEMORE** is an Assistant Professor of Human Development and Family Studies at the University of Connecticut. Her research focuses on the social psychological effects of various pedagogical innovations.

**REGAN HARWELL SCHAFFER** is an Instructor of Management for the Business Administration Division at Pepperdine University. Her research focuses on effective institutional models of service-learning in Christian Higher Education. She is currently a doctoral candidate in Institutional Management at Pepperdine University's Graduate School of Education and Psychology.

## Appendix A: Items on the Student Assessment

*Please indicate how strongly you agree or disagree with each statement. Circle the number that best describes your response from 1=strongly disagree, to 6=strongly agree.*

| | strongly agree | | somewhat agree | | strongly disagree | |
|---|---|---|---|---|---|---|
| 1. I have a realistic understanding of the daily responsibilities involved in the jobs (career) in which I am interested. | 1 | 2 | 3 | 4 | 5 | 6 |
| 2. I am motivated by courses that contain hands-on applications of theories to real-life situations. | 1 | 2 | 3 | 4 | 5 | 6 |
| 3. I am uncertain of what's required to succeed in the career that I want to pursue. | 1 | 2 | 3 | 4 | 5 | 6 |
| 4. I feel that I can make a difference in the world. | 1 | 2 | 3 | 4 | 5 | 6 |
| 5. There is little I can do to end racism. | 1 | 2 | 3 | 4 | 5 | 6 |
| 6. I learn course content best when connections to real-life situations are made. | 1 | 2 | 3 | 4 | 5 | 6 |
| 7. It is important to find a career that directly benefits others. | 1 | 2 | 3 | 4 | 5 | 6 |
| 8. I am an active member of my community. | 1 | 2 | 3 | 4 | 5 | 6 |
| 9. It is important that I work toward equal opportunity for all people. | 1 | 2 | 3 | 4 | 5 | 6 |
| 10. I make very few assumptions about others. | 1 | 2 | 3 | 4 | 5 | 6 |
| 11. I think that people should find time to contribute to their community. | 1 | 2 | 3 | 4 | 5 | 6 |
| 12. It is not necessary for me to volunteer my time. | 1 | 2 | 3 | 4 | 5 | 6 |
| 13. There is no relation between my real life experiences and what I learn in school. | 1 | 2 | 3 | 4 | 5 | 6 |
| 14. I have a good understanding of the needs and concerns of the community in which I live. | 1 | 2 | 3 | 4 | 5 | 6 |
| 15. The world would be a better place if differences between people were ignored. | 1 | 2 | 3 | 4 | 5 | 6 |
| 16. I have a good understanding of the strengths and resources of the community in which I live. | 1 | 2 | 3 | 4 | 5 | 6 |
| 17. I possess the necessary personal qualities (e.g. responsibility, consideration, initiative, etc.) to be a successful career person. | 1 | 2 | 3 | 4 | 5 | 6 |

| | strongly agree | | somewhat agree | | strongly disagree | |
|---|---|---|---|---|---|---|
| 18. I feel that I can have a positive impact on local social problems. | 1 | 2 | 3 | 4 | 5 | 6 |
| 19. The things I learn in school are not applicable to my life outside of school. | 1 | 2 | 3 | 4 | 5 | 6 |
| 20. To be effective in the community, all you need is a caring heart. | 1 | 2 | 3 | 4 | 5 | 6 |
| 21. I feel uncomfortable presenting/speaking in front of a group of individuals in positions of authority. | 1 | 2 | 3 | 4 | 5 | 6 |
| 22. Being involved in a program to improve my community is important to me. | 1 | 2 | 3 | 4 | 5 | 6 |
| 23. I do not feel well prepared to embark on my post-graduate plans (e.g. graduate school, employment, etc.). | 1 | 2 | 3 | 4 | 5 | 6 |
| 24. I have very little impact on the community in which I live. | 1 | 2 | 3 | 4 | 5 | 6 |
| 25. In the United States, people basically have equal opportunity to do what they want in life. | 1 | 2 | 3 | 4 | 5 | 6 |
| 26. I learn more when a course curriculum is relevant to my life. | 1 | 2 | 3 | 4 | 5 | 6 |

# Learning Theory:
## Recommended Reading

## BOOKS & CHAPTERS

Barber, B. (1992). *An aristocracy of everyone: The politics of education and the future of America.* Oxford: Oxford University Press.

Belenky, M., Clinchy, B., Goldberger, N. & Tarule, J. (1986). *Women's ways of knowing.* New York: Basic Books.

Bellah, R., Madsen, R., Sullivan, W., Swidler, A. & Tipton, S. (1996). *Habits of the heart* (2d ed) New York: Harper and Row.

Colombo, G., Cullen, R., & Lisle, B. (Eds.) (1992). *Rereading America: Cultural contexts for critical thinking and writing.* Boston: St. Martin's Press.

Dass, R., & Gorman, P. (1985) *How can I help? Stories and reflections on service.* New York: Alfred A. Knopf.

Delve, C., Mintz, S., & Stewart, G. (Eds.). (1990). *Community service as values education, New directions for student services.* San Francisco: Jossey-Bass.

Freire, P. (1973). *Education for critical consciousness.* New York: Continuum.

Gilligan, C. (1982) *In a different voice.* Cambridge, MA: Harvard University Press.

Kolb, D. (1985). *Learning styles inventories.* Boston: McKerr.

Kolb, D. (1984). *Experiential learning: Experience as the source of learning and development.* Engelwood Cliffs, NJ: Prentice Hall.

Proudman, W. (1995). Experiential education as emotionally engaged learning. In K. Warren, M. Sakoff, & J.S. Hunt, Jr. (Eds.), *The theory of experiential education.* (pp. 240–241). Dubuque, IA: Kendall-Hunt.

Reed, E.S. (1996). *The necessity of experience.* New Haven: Yale University Press.

Warren, K., Sakofs, M. & Hunt, J. (Eds.). (1995). *The theory of experiential education.* Dubuque, IA: Kendall/Hunt Publishing.

## ARTICLES & REPORTS

Bickford, D. M. & Reynolds, N. (2002). Activism and service-learning: Reframing volunteerism as acts of dissent. *Pedagogy, 2* (2), 229–252.

Cassidy, K. (2001). Enhancing your experiential program with narrative theory. *The Journal of Experiential Education. 24* (1), 22–26.

Cone, R., & Harris, S. (1996). Service-learning practice: A theoretical framework. *Michigan Journal of Community Service Learning, 3,* 31–43.

Ellsworth, E. (1994). Why doesn't this feel empowering? Working through the repressive myths of critical pedagogy. In L. Stone (Ed.), *The Education Feminism Reader* (pp. 300–327). New York: Routledge.

*Equity and Excellence in Education.* (1993). 26 (2). [Entire issue is devoted to Service-Learning]

Giles, D.E, Jr. & Eyler, J. (1994). The theoretical roots of service-learning in John Dewey: Towards a theory of service-learning. *Michigan Journal of Community Service-Learning, 1,* 77–85.

Honnet, E. & Poulsen, S.J. (1989). *Principles of good practice for combining service and learning: Wingspread special report.* Racine, WI: Johnson Foundation.

Liu, G. (1995). Knowledge, foundations, and discourse: Philosophical support for service-learning. *Michigan Journal of Community Service Learning, 2,* 5–18.

Kezar, A. & Rhoads, R.A. (2001). The dynamic tensions of service-learning in higher education: A philosophical perspective. *The Journal of Higher Education, 72* (2), 148–71.

McVicker C.B. (1989). On critical thinking and connected knowing. *Liberal Educator, 75,* 14–19.

Palmer, P.J. (1987). Community, conflict, and ways of knowing: Ways to deepen our educational agenda. *Change, 5,* 20–25.

Robinson, T. (2000). Dare the school build a new social order? *Michigan Journal of Community Service Learning, 7,* 142–57.

Shumer, R. & Belbas, B. (1996). What we know about service-learning. *Education and Urban Society, 28* (2), 208–223.

Sigmon, R. (1979). Service-learning: Three principles. *Synergist, 1979,* 9–11.

Speck, B.W. (2001). Why service learning? *New Directions for Higher Education, 114,* 3–13.

Stanton, T. (1987). Service learning: Groping towards a definition. *Experiential Education, 12* (1), 2–4.

Taylor, J. (2002). Metaphors we serve by: Investigating the conceptual metaphors framing national and community service and service-learning. *Michigan Journal of Community Service Learning, 9* (1), 45–57.

Voke, H. (2001). Public deliberation, communication across difference, and issues-based service learning. *Philosophy of Education Yearbook,* 361–9.

Weiler, K. (1991). Freire and a feminist pedagogy of difference. *Harvard Educational Review, 61*(4), 449–474.

Westhoff, L. (1995). The popularization of knowledge: John Dewey on experts and American democracy. *History of Education Quarterly, 35,* 27–47.

# Pedagogy

## TITLES IN THIS SECTION

## QUESTIONS FOR REFLECTION AND PLANNING

What is your understanding of engaged teaching and learning? To what extent is service-learning an effective strategy for engaged teaching and learning?

How would using service-learning enhance a student's learning experience in your course?

What are two to three outcomes you think service-learning could provide for students in your course(s)?

Does your institution value a particular mode of teaching? How would service-learning be perceived within that model?

# Academic Service Learning:
## A Counternormative Pedagogy

by Jeffrey P.F. Howard

FACULTY INTEREST IN ACADEMIC service learning has exploded over the last few years. Some see service learning as a way to prepare students for active citizenship. Others perceive it as a means to involve universities in socially responsible action. Still others find in it a panacea for the perceived shortcomings of the information-dissemination model that prevails in higher education.

These are solid reasons for becoming involved in academic service learning. But once the motivation for becoming involved has emerged, questions about implementation necessarily arise. Though the notion of adding community service to an academic course may not be difficult to conceptualize, the practice of integrating service and learning is anything but simple.

Contrary to some interpretations, academic service learning is not merely the addition of a community service option or requirement to an academic course. A clause on a syllabus that directs students to complete community service hours as a course requirement or in lieu of another course assignment does not constitute academic service learning. Rather than serving as a parallel or sidebar activity, the students' community service experiences in academic service learning function as a critical learning complement to the academic goals of the course.

In other words, academic service learning is not about the addition of service to learning, but rather the integration of service with learning. In this contrasting synergistic model, the students' community service experiences are compatible and integrated with the academic learning objectives of the course, in a manner similar to traditional course requirements. Here students' obser-

vations and experiences in the community setting are as pivotal to the students' academic learning as class lectures and library research. In this integrated model, the service and the learning are reciprocally related; the service experiences inform and transform the academic learning, and the academic learning informs and transforms the service experience (Honnet and Poulsen, 1989).

Integrating service with academic learning, however, catalyzes a complexity to the teaching-learning process that is analogous to adding a newborn to a family. Just as the newborn is not merely the addition of one more member to the family, community service is not merely the addition of one more requirement to a course. As the newborn qualitatively changes the norms and relationships in the family constellation, so, too, community service qualitatively changes the norms and relationships in the teaching-learning process.

## A WORKING DEFINITION OF ACADEMIC SERVICE LEARNING

For the purposes of this volume, we are utilizing the working definition, "Academic service learning is a pedagogical model that intentionally integrates academic learning and relevant community service." There are four key components to this definition. First, academic service learning is a pedagogical model; first and foremost it is a teaching methodology, more than a values model, leadership development model, or a social responsibility model. Second, there is an intentional effort made to utilize the community-based learning on behalf of academic learning, and to utilize academic learning to inform the community service. This presupposes that academic service learning will not happen unless a concerted effort is made to harvest community-based learning and strategically bridge it with academic learning. Third, there is an integration of the two kinds of learning, experiential and academic; they work to strengthen one another. Finally, the community service experiences must be relevant to the academic course of study (Howard, 1993). Serving in a soup kitchen is relevant for a course on social issues but probably not for a course on civil engineering. All four components are necessary in the practice of academic service learning.

## CHALLENGES

From this definition, it is apparent that academic service learning creates a host of stimulating pedagogical challenges that are obviated in traditional pedagogy. For example, how can we strengthen student capacity to extract meaning from community experiences? How can we strengthen student capacity to utilize community-based learning on behalf of academic learning? How can we better enable students to apply their academic learning to their community service? These are challenges that those who consider academic service learning will face.

Many of the pedagogical challenges associated with academic service learning result from its counternormative nature. Academic service learning stands, in some significant ways, in contradistinction to traditional pedagogical principles. For example, broadening the learning environment beyond the instructor's purview is clearly contrary to standard pedagogical operating procedures. Involving students in experiential learning breaches traditional practice. Positioning students with the responsibility for discerning important from unimportant "data" in the community is contrary to traditional courses in which relevant knowledge is deciphered for the students by the instructor. The mix of traditional classroom-based theoretical learning and nontraditional community-based experiential learning clearly "raises the pedagogical bar."

## THE TRADITIONAL PEDAGOGICAL MODEL

At the risk of generalization and simplification, let us review some of the salient features of the prevailing information-dissemination model in higher education. The oft-cited advantage of this model, customarily manifested in the lecture, is that it is efficient in transmitting volumes of academic information and theory

to large numbers of students. Through years of elementary and secondary school rehearsal and then higher education reinforcement, classroom roles, relationships, and norms in the traditional model have been powerfully internalized by all parties; before entering the very first meeting of a class, faculty and students alike know that faculty are the knowledge experts and direct the learning activities in the course, and that students begin with knowledge deficits and follow the prescribed learning activities. In this "banking model" (Freire, 1970), faculty are active, depositing and periodically withdrawing intellectual capital from students who are for the most part passive. The course follows a predetermined structure, learning stimuli are uniform for all students, and each class and each assignment follow a familiar routine. Even in courses in which there is a departure from the standard lecture, "discussion usually focuses on a pre-established set of inquiry questions or curricula" (Chesler, 1993, p. 31). In fact, control of the entire range of teaching and learning activity is within the faculty member's knowledge and experience purview and ascribed and perceived jurisdiction.

Furthermore, in the traditional teaching-learning model, learning is individualistic and privatized; students generally learn by themselves and for themselves. When students do contribute in class discussions, often it is for grade-enhancing reasons rather than to advance their peers' learning. Instructor-determined grades reflect individual achievement. The epistemology that under-girds traditional pedagogy is positivistic and in conflict with communal ways of learning (Palmer, 1990).

## INCONGRUENCIES BETWEEN THE TWO PEDAGOGIES

Academic service learning is incongruent with traditional pedagogy in a number of ways:

A CONFLICT OF GOALS. Service learning's goal of advancing students' sense of social responsibility or commitment to the broader good conflicts with the individualistic, self-orientation of the traditional classroom (Howard, 1993). Perhaps the most important way that academic service learning is inconsistent with traditional pedagogy, and even other forms of experiential learning, is in its insistence on advancing students' commitment to the greater good. "The competitive individualism of the classroom ... reflects a pedagogy that stresses the individual as the prime agent of knowing" (Palmer, 1990, p. 111). In the traditional course, with its focus on the individual, an orientation toward others is necessarily discouraged. The dilemma here is that the nature of the traditional classroom encourages individual responsibility rather than social responsibility.

**A CONFLICT ABOUT VALUABLE LEARNING.** In traditional courses, academic learning is valued, whereas in academic service learning, academic learning is valued along with community-based experiential learning. Academic learning is deductively oriented, whereas experiential learning is inductively oriented. The dilemma here is how these very different kinds and ways of learning not only can coexist but can even create a learning synergy for students.

**A CONFLICT ABOUT CONTROL.** In traditional courses there is a high degree of structure and direction vis-á-vis learning; the faculty control what is important for students to learn. This contrasts with an invariably low degree of structure and direction vis-á-vis learning in the community (the exception may be professional practica, in which there is directed learning by a designated field placement supervisor). Therefore, in the community, students are more likely to be in charge of their learning. Even though they may be armed with a learning schema from the instructor, the dilemma is how to bring the level of learning structure and direction in the two learning contexts into greater congruence.

**A CONFLICT ABOUT ACTIVE LEARNING.** A closely related issue is that student passivity contributes to the efficiency of the information-dissemination model, whereas in the community there is a premium on active learning. The high degree of structure and direction provided by the instructor in traditional pedagogy leads to a passive learning posture by students, but the low degree of structure and direction in communities in relation to learning requires that students assume an active learning posture. The dilemma here is how to bring the role of the learner in the classroom into greater congruence with the role of the learner in the community.

**A CONFLICT ABOUT CONTRIBUTIONS FROM STUDENTS.** The orientation toward efficient transmission of information in the traditional model precludes taking advantage of students' learning in the community Student contributions in traditional pedagogy are discouraged because they compromise the efficiency goal. The dilemma here is how to make student learning that is

harvested in the community not only welcome but utilized in the classroom.

**A CONFLICT ABOUT OBJECTIVITY.** Whereas objectivity is valued in the traditional classroom, in academic service learning a subjective engagement, emanating from the philosophy of pragmatism, is also valued (Liu, 1995). The dilemma here is how to integrate subjective and objective ways of knowing.

## A NEW MODEL: THE SYNERGISTIC CLASSROOM

To resolve these tensions, drastic measures are needed. Nothing less than a reconceptualization of the teaching-learning process will do. We need a pedagogical model that:

- Encourages social responsibility
- Values and integrates both academic and experiential learning
- Accommodates both high and low levels of structure and direction
- Embraces the active, participatory student
- Welcomes both subjective and objective ways of knowing.

For many years I have struggled with these dilemmas in a sociology service learning course here at the University of Michigan. I have struggled in my attempts to prompt student participation, to find a balance

**Figure 1: Stages in Tranforming the Classroom**

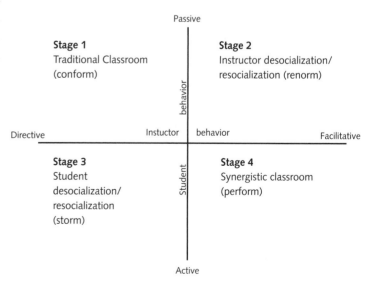

between more structure and less structure, to integrate learning from the community with learning from academic readings, and to encourage social responsibility in the classroom.

Over time I have come to realize that to create a classroom that is consistent with the goals and values of service learning, it is absolutely necessary to deprogram or desocialize students and instructors away from traditional classroom roles, relationships, and norms, and then resocialize them around a new set of classroom behaviors. To accomplish the desocialization and resocialization processes requires that the instructor and the students travel together on a journey to remake the classroom. Figure 1 depicts this journey.

In this matrix, four prototypical stages are identified in moving from a traditional classroom to a synergistic classroom that meets the five criteria enumerated above. The first stage, identified as the conform stage, depicts the traditional classroom model in which the instructor (represented on the horizontal axis) is directive and the students (represented on the vertical axis) are passive. To initiate the transformation process, identified in the model as the second stage, renorm, the instructor must begin to carry out her or his role in an intentionally counternormative way For example, the instructor may ask students what was important in their readings and in their service experiences since the last class, and use their contributions to frame the class discussion. Actions such as this will implicitly communicate to the students that it will not be business as usual.

In this second stage, however, the students, whose schooling has been effective in internalizing a passive, individualistic role in the classroom, resist these change efforts and continue to be primarily passive. This might be manifested in a low participation rate when the instructor seeks contributions from the students. But as the instructor continues to be consistent in her or his new interpretation of the teacher role, and as the students continue to receive the message that their active participation around both academic and community-based learning is encouraged, we arrive at stage 3 in which the students, in fact, become more active and begin to take greater responsibility for the learning in the classroom.

This storm stage, ironically, often becomes problematic for the instructor, who, also schooled for many years to perceive instructors as authorities and students as receptacles, questions the quality of learning under

way. As a result, in this third stage the instructor regresses and retreats to a more directive posture. But over time, the instructor comes to realize that the students are genuinely learning, and returns to a more facilitative approach. As the students continue to assume an active role, the fourth and final stage, the perform stage—the synergistic classroom—is achieved, in which the consistency between the students' and instructor's respective new roles and ways of learning lead to enhanced teaching-learning performance.

Though this diagram illustrates a linear progression from a traditional classroom to a synergistic classroom, the actual movement from one stage to another is not so simple. In fact, faculty can expect a more nonlinear progression, characterized by fits and stops along the way.

## RECOGNIZING THE SYNERGISTIC CLASSROOM

Transforming a classroom from a traditional orientation to one that is consistent with the goals and opportunities associated with academic service learning is not easy. It takes an intentional campaign on the part of the instructor and lots of patience, because change will be far from immediate. If, however, the challenge is accepted and a commitment to experiment is made, how will one know when one has arrived at the synergistic stage?

For the most part, arrival will be self-evident to the faculty member. As Garry Hesser has written, "Every time faculty read students' papers, journals, exams, or listen to the *quality of discussion* [emphasis added] in a seminar, they are responsible for discerning whether learning is taking place" (1995, p. 35). Faculty will know. The most obvious dynamic to change will be the role of the students. An observer in a synergistic classroom will note that the students are actively engaged in discussion, among themselves or with the instructor. Discussion comfortably embraces both the content of academic readings and observations and experiences from the students' community placements. The instructor may be difficult to identify, though she or he might be seen facilitating the conversation to maximize the students' efforts to integrate the community-based and academic learning, contributing her or his own knowledge and relevant experiences to the discussion, or managing the discussion so that there is equal attention paid to the objective and subjective ways that students come to know. We might even see that if the instructor left the room, the level of learning would not be diminished.

In this classroom, discussion about theory and discussion about experiences is embraced by all, and efforts to integrate the two are made by all parties. The lines of distinction between the student role and the instructor role become blurred, so that students are teachers and learners, and instructors are learners as well as teachers. The traditional classroom's orientation toward individual student learning is replaced by a commitment to the learning of the collectivity. Questions and answers are perceived as equally important to the learning process, and ignorance, rather than to be avoided at all costs, is valued as a resource.

Once the synergistic classroom is achieved or at least approached, the new orientation to classroom teaching and learning can fan out to other components of the course. Faculty and students who have achieved the synergistic classroom will find that group academic projects, students reading each other's term papers, and final exams that call for bridging academic and community learning are consistent with the classroom transformation.

## THE COST OF THE SYNERGISTIC CLASSROOM: TIME AWAY FROM TASK?

Inevitably, the question arises: Does this effort to transform the classroom take time away from academic tasks? After all, time is expended in moving through stages 2 and 3 of the model, and, as acknowledged above, time on community learning necessarily takes time away from attention to theoretical learning. How does an instructor committed to student learning about an academic body of knowledge reconcile this dilemma?

The issue at hand has to do with the answer to the question: What is the task at hand in an academic course? If it is to impart as much information as possible, then the information-dissemination model unequivocally receives top honors. But if the task, in addition to learning content, is to excite and motivate students to learn during the course and after, to learn new ways of learning, and to develop a set of overall values in the field of study, then we know that the information-dissemination model is woefully lacking.

For example, one study found that while teachers are lecturing, students are not attending to what is being said 40 percent of the time (Pollio, 1984). Another study found that in the first ten minutes of lecture, students retain 70 percent of the information, but only 20 percent in the last ten minutes (McKeachie, 1986). Still another study found that four months after taking an introductory psychology course, students knew only 8 percent more than a control group who had never taken the course (Rickard, Rogers, Ellis, and Beidelman, 1988).

In contrast, we continually read faculty testimonials about the difference academic service learning has made in students' drive to learn (Bringle and Hatcher, 1996; Hammond, 1994; Hesser, 1995; Hudson, 1996; Kendrick, 1996; Yelsma, 1994). In a study conducted at the University of Michigan, students in sections of a political science class who were involved in community service as part of the course received better grades and reported more enhanced learning than their counterparts who were involved in library research (Markus, Howard, and King, 1993). In addition, they reported a statistically significant difference relative to their library research counterparts when asked about "performing up to my potential in this course," "developing a set of overall values in this field," and "learning to apply principles from this course to new situations."

## A FORMIDABLE CHALLENGE

As a relatively new and dilemma-filled pedagogy, academic service learning is not for the meek. Reformatting classroom norms, roles, and outcomes so that both academic and experiential learning can be joined requires a very deliberate effort around a rather formidable challenge. As a counternormative pedagogy, instructors who accept this challenge can expect initial resistance from students, periodic self-doubt about their own teaching accomplishments, and colleagues' looking askance upon this methodology. But the dividends—renewed motivation for learning by students, enhanced academic learning for students, renewed excitement for teaching by instructors, and better preparation of students for their roles as lifelong citizens and learners—will more than compensate for the effort.

## REFERENCES

Bringle, R. G., and Hatcher, J. A. (1996). Implementing service learning in higher education. *Journal of Higher Education*, 67 (2), 221-239.

Chesler, M. A. (1993). Community service learning as innovation in the university. In J. Howard (ed.), *Praxis I:*

*A Faculty Casebook on Community Service Learning.* Ann Arbor, Mich.: OCSL Press.

Freire, P. (1970). *Pedagogy of the Oppressed* (M. B. Ramos, trans.). New York: Continuum.

Hammond, C. (1994). Integrating service and academic study: Faculty motivation and satisfaction in Michigan higher education. *Michigan Journal of Community Service Learning,* 1, 21-28.

Hesser, G. (1995). An assessment of student learning: Outcomes attributed to service-learning and evidence of changes in faculty attitudes about experiential education. *Michigan Journal of Community Service Learning,* 2, 33-42.

Honnet, E. P., and Poulsen, S. J. (1989). *Principles of Good Practice in Combining Service and Learning.* Wingspread Special Report. Racine, Wis.: The Johnson Foundation.

Howard, J. (1993). Community service learning in the curriculum. In J. Howard (ed.), *Praxis I: A Faculty Casebook on Community Service Learning.* Ann Arbor, Mich.: OCSL Press.

Hudson, W. E. (1996). Combining community service and the study of American public policy. *Michigan Journal of Community Service Learning,* 3, 82-91.

Kendrick, J. R., Jr. (1996). Outcomes of service-learning in an introduction to sociology course. *Michigan Journal of Community Service Learning,* 3, 72-81

Liu, G. (1995). Knowledge, foundations, and discourse: Philosophical support for service-learning. *Michigan Journal of Community Service Learning,* 2, 5-18.

Markus, G., Howard, J. P. F., and King, D. C. (1993). Integrating community service and classroom instruction enhances learning: Results from an experiment. *Educational Evaluation and Policy Analysis,* 15 (4), 410-419.

McKeachie, W. (1986). *Teaching Tips: A Guidebook for the Beginning College Teacher.* (8th ed.) Lexington, Mass.: Heath.

Palmer, P. (1990). Community, conflict, and ways of knowing. In J. Kendall and Associates, *Combining Service and Learning: A Resource Book for Community and Public Service.* Vol. 1. Raleigh, N.C.: National Society for Internships and Experiential Education.

Pollio, H. (1984). *What Students Think About and Do in College Lecture Classes: Teaching-Learning Issues no. 53.* Knoxville: Learning Research Center, University of Tennessee.

Rickard, H., Rogers, R., Ellis, N., and Beidelman, W. (1988). Some retention, but not enough. *Teaching of Psychology,* 15, 151-152.

Yelsma, P. (1994). Combining small group problem solving with service-learning. *Michigan Journal of Community Service Learning,* 1, 62-69

**JEFFREY P.F. HOWARD** is associate director for service learning at the Edward Ginsberg Center for Service and Learning, University of Michigan. He is founder and editor of the *Michigan Journal of Community Service Learning.*

# Pedagogy and Engagement

by Edward Zlotkowski

In a 1994 essay entitled Service on Campus, Arthur Levine (1994) noted that "student volunteer movements tend to be a passing phenomenon in higher education, rising and falling on campuses roughly every 30 years" (p. 4). Are we now riding the crest of such a wave? Several factors suggest we are. Campus Compact, a national association of college and university presidents committed to fostering community service on their campuses, now numbers almost 600 members. New student initiatives such as "Alternative Spring Break" and "Into the Streets" draw thousands of undergraduate participants each year. The number of books, articles, and special issues focused on service-related topics has exploded. What does all this mean for colleges and universities as citizens?

The very cyclicality of this phenomenon may suggest "Not much!" However, unlike earlier waves of interest in community service, the present wave has been characterized not only by a rise in student interest but also by a less visible but no less remarkable rise in faculty interest. Indeed, the late Ernest Boyer (1990) suggested something qualitatively different was taking place this time around:

> The social imperative for service has become so urgent that the university cannot afford to ignore it. I must say that I am worried that right now the university is viewed as a private benefit, not a public good. Unless we recast the university as a publicly engaged institution I think our future is at stake (p. 138).

Hence, without denying the influence of cyclical patterns, we may do well to consider whether the current service phenomenon must not be understood as qualitatively different from its predecessors. For if, as Boyer suggests, community service must now be viewed as an "urgent" "social imperative," it is critically important that those responsible for leading institutions of higher learning understand both its current configuration and its potential to help promote institutional citizenship.

## SERVICE LEARNING DEFINED

If there is any single factor that distinguishes earlier surges of community engagement from the current community service movement, it is a phenomenon already alluded to—namely, the widespread participation not just of students but of faculty. Indeed, on many campuses curriculum-based community service—"service learning," as it is most frequently referred to—rather than traditional cocurricular volunteerism represents the real growth area (Fisher, 1998). The rest of this chapter will focus exclusively on not only what service learning entails but also its potential for helping colleges and universities become more effective participants in civil society. After reviewing a definition of service learning, this chapter will utilize a matrix, structured to reflect key elements of service learning practice, to explore: (1) service learning as a discipline-specific activity, (2) its use of reflection, (3) academic support structures, and (4) considerations that define campus-community partnerships. This chapter will conclude with a glance at some of the larger educational and institutional issues service learning helps to address.

One of the more frequently cited definitions of service learning was offered by Bringle and Hatcher (1996):

> We view service learning as a credit-bearing educational experience in which students participate in an organized service activity that meets identified com-

munity needs and reflect on the service activity in such a way as to gain further understanding of the course content, a broader appreciation of the discipline, and an enhanced sense of civic responsibility. Unlike extracurricular voluntary service, service learning is a course-based service experience that produces the best outcomes when meaningful service activities are related to course material through reflection activities such as directed writings, small group discussions, and class presentations. Unlike practica and internships, the experiential activity in a service learning course is not necessarily skill-based within the context of professional education (p. 222).

The value of this formulation lies not only in its specification of key service learning features but also in its differentiation between service learning and both volunteerism and traditional practica/internships. A clear awareness of these distinctions is essential if one is to understand service learning's potential to shape the academic-civic dialogue.

The first feature Bringle and Hatcher identify is that service learning is a credit-bearing experience, that is, it is a part of the academic curriculum. Not all would agree that this is exhaustive. In *Service Learning in Higher Education* (1996), Barbara Jacoby and Associates work with an approach that includes both curricular and cocurricular practice. However, even those who embrace this broader definition would agree that faculty support and participation make achieving the learning dimension of service learning much more likely. Recognition of the faculty role in sustaining course-based community service first became widespread in the early 1990s, due largely to a report (1990) prepared for Campus Compact by Tim Stanton, then associate director of the Haas Center at Stanford University. Stanton noted that, up until then, "[l]ittle attention [had] been given to the faculty role in supporting student service efforts and in setting an example of civic participation and leadership through their own efforts" (p. 1). This neglect would have to be corrected if course-based community service were to reach its full potential.

As a result of Stanton's report, Campus Compact, with Ford Foundation backing, launched a multiyear initiative aimed at "'Integrating Service with Academic Study.'" This initiative has helped shift the primary focus of service learning from student to faculty affairs. Currently, almost all service learning programs that seek to have a significant institutional as well as community impact also seek to promote faculty involvement and to establish a reliable curricular base.

A second feature found in the Bringle and Hatcher definition lies encoded in its phrase "'identified community needs." One of the most significant ways in which service learning differs from many other community-related campus-based initiatives lies in its insistence that the needs to be met must be defined by the community, not the campus. In other words, service learning deliberately seeks to reverse the long-established academic practice of using the community for the academy's own ends. This, of course, does not mean the academy is expected simply to do the community's bidding. The watchword here is reciprocity: there must be an agreed upon balance of benefits and responsibilities on both sides.

Such a call for reciprocity has far more serious consequences than may at first be apparent. For one, it significantly qualifies the academy's traditional claim to preeminence by virtue of its expertise. In a service learning context, the concept of "expertise" encompasses more than theoretical understanding and technical skill; it also includes the in-depth knowledge that comes from having lived with a problem or set of circumstances over an extended period of time. Thus, the community lays claim to its own kind of expertise—an expertise the academy must acknowledge and respect.

Second, reciprocity implies that all processes and roles are functionally interchangeable. It is no more accurate to identify the academy as "serving" and the community as "being served" than vice versa. If the community benefits and learns from the academy, it is no less true that the academy benefits and learns from the community. If the academy gives the community access to new technical and human resources, the community gives the academy access to new educational opportunities. It is commonplace among service learning practitioners—student and faculty alike—to realize, once a project has been completed and evaluated, that those on campus have gotten back far more than they have given.

If, then, service learning implies that the issues around which projects are organized are to be identified by community partners who are regarded as the academy's equals, the next question must be, What do those involved in service learning mean by the word "community"? Here again, as in the case of "credit-bearing," what prevails is more a tendency than a consensus. Although "community" might well refer to the off-campus community in general or even the on-campus community, the "community service" roots of service learning—still evident in the formulation "community service learning"—point toward a less inclusive understanding. For the most part, the community referred to primarily consists of (1) off-campus populations underserved by our market economy, and (2) organizations whose primary purpose is the common good. To be sure, at institutions where many students come from underserved populations, service activities often include on-campus as well as off-campus activities. However, few programs provide assistance to for-profit enterprises—except in cases in which those enterprises themselves can be regarded as serving more than proprietary interests.

How one understands community is closely related to a third key feature of Bringle and Hatcher's definition; namely, service learning is an experience that includes reflection "on the service activity in such a way as to gain further understanding of the course content, a broader appreciation of the discipline, and an enhanced sense of civic responsibility." Indeed, service learning practitioners place special emphasis on reflection as the key to making community service yield real learning. To be sure, conscientious experiential educators of all kinds have long recognized the importance of reflection as a complement to experience. What is distinctive about reflection in a service learning context is its multilayered quality: what students reflect on results not just in greater technical mastery (i.e., course content) but also in an expanded appreciation of the contextual and social significance of the discipline in question and, most broadly of all, in "an enhanced sense of civic responsibility." Thus, students in a chemistry course may be asked to connect testing for lead in housing projects with what they have learned both in the classroom and in the laboratory while also processing their personal reactions to conditions in the housing projects and their evolving sense of children's rights to a safe environment.

Such a multilayered understanding of reflection is critical to any attempt to differentiate service learning not just from curriculum-based preprofessional field experiences such as internships and practica but also from volunteerism of the kind traditionally associated with student organizations. To the degree that a given community service activity is deliberately tied to structured learning objectives, it can be seen as approaching the functional core of service learning, whether or not it is formally sponsored by a course. However, the very significance of this requirement that structured, in-depth reflection complements the community service experience is what argues most convincingly for service learning as a course-based undertaking. Without such a credit-bearing framework, it is difficult to harvest the learning that community service implies. And without that harvesting, its potential to link private advantage and public good, to facilitate civic as well as more technical kinds of understanding, cannot be realized.

## A SERVICE LEARNING MATRIX

I have proposed elsewhere (Zlotkowski, 1998b) that one useful way to capture the complexity and richness of service learning is to conceive of it as a matrix (Figure 1). Such a conceptualization suggests that service learning can best be seen as a field in which two complementary axes intersect: a horizontal axis ranging from academic expertise to a concern for the common good, and a vertical axis that links the traditional domain of the student (i.e., classroom activities) with that of those who teach and mentor the student in the world beyond the classroom. Through such a utilization of multiple learning sites, service learning also links situations in which student needs dominate (i.e., the academic course) with situations where student needs are subordinate to other concerns (i.e., the delivery of social services and other kinds of practical assistance). In this way, service learning bridges the kind of work characteristic of the classroom—hypothetical, deductive, reflective—with the kind of work most typical outside it—concrete, inductive, results-driven. Or, to appropriate Donald Schon's (1995) memorable image, it connects "the high ground [where] manageable problems lend themselves to solution through the use of research-based theory and technique" with "'the swampy lowlands [where] problems are messy and confusing and incapable of technical solution" (p. 28).

By encompassing this constellation of interests and activities, service learning both complicates and liberates educational practice. No longer can the teaching mission of colleges and universities—as ratified by and articulated in the curriculum—be adequately described in terms of professional and self-contained academic practice. The kind of learning faculty facilitate must now include a broader public dimension. The circle of stakeholders directly involved in the academic enter-

**Figure 1: The Service Learning Conceptual Matrix**

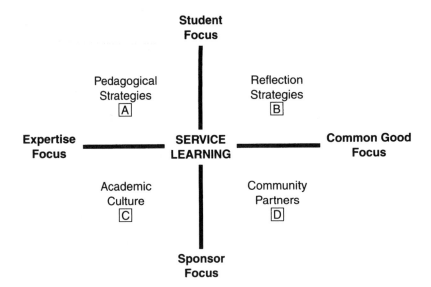

prise must be expanded to include members of the community.

Such imperatives are enough to explain why service learning possesses such enormous potential to move higher education in the direction of civic involvement. It also explains why colleges and universities often find it easier to frame their civic responsibilities in other ways (e.g., in terms of extension services, selectively shared resources, special programs, even purchasing and employment practices). As long as the classroom door can literally and figuratively remain shut, institutions can accommodate a considerable measure of citizenship with little or no challenge to their traditional structures and self understanding. Service learning makes business as usual more difficult.

Boyer himself did not shrink from the consequences of such a challenge. It is fashionable nowadays to cite with approval his vision of a "New American College" (1994). However, if Coye (1997) is correct in asserting that "the New American College was the natural outcome of Boyer's work, the point for him at which all roads met," it behooves us to invoke that vision with special care and attention. For although Boyer does not explicitly refer to service learning in his sketch of such an institution, the kinds of activities and arrangements he recommends leave little doubt as to service learning's central role in it:

This New American College would organize cross-disciplinary institutes around pressing social issues. Undergraduates at the college would participate in field projects, relating ideas to real life. Classrooms and laboratories would be extended to include health clinics, youth centers, schools, and government offices. Faculty members would build partners with practitioners who would, in turn, come to campus as lecturers and student advisers.

The New American College, as a connected institution, would be committed to improving, in a very intentional way, the human condition. As clusters of such colleges formed, a new model of excellence in higher education would emerge, one that would enrich the campus, renew communities, and give new dignity and status to the scholarship of service (p. A48).

Through its institutes and field projects, the New American College can be said to connect different kinds of discipline-specific knowledge and to connect that knowledge to an overt commitment to the common good. By extending the concepts of the classroom and the laboratory to include "health clinics, youth centers, schools, and government offices," it not only links traditional on-campus learning to experiences in the world beyond the campus, but also re-conceptualizes what is appropriate to its curriculum and the ways in which that curriculum should be delivered.

## THE FOUR QUADRANTS OF SERVICE LEARNING PRACTICE

One way to begin unpacking some of the more systemic implications both of Boyer's model and of service learning in general is to explore the four fields of the matrix just introduced. Each quadrant can be said to define a different area of faculty and/or institutional development: A is the design and implementation of course-specific pedagogical strategies; B is the facilitation of course-appropriate reflection strategies; C is the reform of academic culture to recognize community-related professional activities; and D is the creation of community partnerships based on long-term interdependency. Much of the remainder of this essay will explore each of these areas in turn.

### Quadrant A: Pedagogical Strategies

No changes in instructional practice are likely to have greater significance than a shift in basic faculty function from information delivery to learning environment design (Guskin, 1994). As Lee Shulman, president of the Carnegie Foundation for the Advancement of Teaching, remarked (Miller, 1997), working on a "pedagogy of substance" means "assisting teachers to focus on the design aspects of teaching" (p. 6). With regard to service learning, such a focus is essential if the service-related learning process is to have any chance of success. Faculty who practice service learning must begin doing now what Shulman, Guskin, and others see as fundamental to the future of instruction in general.

To many only vaguely familiar with service learning, adopting a service learning pedagogy implies little more than telling students to work at a community site and write a paper on their experiences. The community service activity is generic; the learning—whatever learning there is—is also generic. The entire exercise is justified by the idea that students should be exposed to social problems and encouraged "to give something back."

Indeed, even when such an exercise results in substantive community service, it still may not be service learning. As Benjamin Barber (1997) notes with regard to the propriety of mandatory community service assignments:

> If service learning is about voluntary service, it does not belong in the curriculum, should not be mandatory, and, indeed, when it is mandatory may violate the Constitution. If service learning is about learning, however, then it needs to be directly folded into curricula, it can be made mandatory just as English or Biology can be made mandatory (for pedagogical, not social welfare reasons), and it no more violates the Constitution than does a requirement for freshman math or swimming (p. 228).

If, then, the academic justification of service learning lies primarily in its educational value, faculty are under considerable responsibility to understand how they can most effectively tap that value—and institutions are under equal responsibility to provide the kinds of support faculty need in order to be able to do so. Two kinds of support are at issue, though only the first of these will be discussed in the present section (see Community Partners for the other).

As might be expected, service learning has received an uneven welcome across the disciplinary spectrum. This is explained, most often, as a matter of natural disciplinary fit, but willingness to acknowledge fit is itself reflective of differences in disciplinary cultures. Until recently, service learning in higher education has been championed primarily by faculty from certain liberal arts disciplines (e.g., sociology, psychology, communication, composition, and political science). As I have noted elsewhere (Rama & Zlotkowski, 1996), the interest these faculty have shown has helped reinforce the impression that service learning is best suited to meeting educational goals. And yet, if we look at a document like Porter and McKibbin's *Management Education and Development: Drift or Thrust into the 21st Century?* (1988) that was commissioned by the American Assembly of Collegiate Schools of Business, it is clear that service learning could equally well serve many of the most important self-identified goals of the business disciplines (Zlotkowski, 1996b). A similar argument can be made for the natural sciences.

Thus, to meet adequately the demands of quadrant A, what is needed is a comprehensive faculty development effort to help those working in disciplinary areas across the academic spectrum to both understand and appropriate service learning on their own terms (Zlotkowski, 1995, 1996a). It was, in fact, to help faculty do precisely this, to help them "customize service learning so it supports learning...without sacrificing academic rigor" (AAHE, 1996) that the American Association for Higher Education has supported a new series of books on service learning in the disciplines.

What, then, does such discipline-specific design entail? As a growing number of course models attests, it involves at least three kinds of carefully considered choices: (1) the rationale behind and purpose of the community service activity to be introduced; (2) the kind of community service most appropriate to the goals of the course, the level of student expertise available, and the needs of the community partner; and (3) the course format most appropriate for the learning and the community service goals. Each of these topics challenges the service learning instructor (in consultation with a community partner) to bring to course design a degree of deliberateness many traditional instructional strategies regularly do without.

**RATIONALE AND PURPOSE.** The educational rationale that leads a faculty member to employ service learning may differ widely from discipline to discipline and from course to course, despite the fact that some rationales are more or less universally applicable. Thus, for example, the frequently invoked value of linking practice to theory can take a variety of forms. In a public relations course, it may mean a more or less straightforward application of concepts and practices discussed in class to the issues facing nonprofit agencies serving the off-campus community. In a sociology course, straightforward application may yield to critique because students experience not the utility but the inadequacies of a textbook formulation. In an environmental chemistry course, application may yield to field research whereby students are expected to add to the community's understanding of a local problem.

Still another kind of educational rationale diverges from the theory-practice model altogether: through service learning, students may be challenged to develop more fully their moral imaginations. Courses in literature, Ethics, and religious studies often fall into this category. When, several years ago, I was asked to teach a course on Shakespeare's tragedies, my students spent part of the semester working at a shelter for homeless men. This assignment occurred in conjunction with our discussion of King Lear, and its primary educational purpose was to help the students more successfully appropriate the play's exploration of human blindness and spiritual renewal.

Such an exploration would undoubtedly be irrelevant in the context of a pre-calculus course, but a student's ability to demonstrate a grasp of basic mathematical concepts and procedures would not be. As Lee Shulman (Miller, 1997) once acknowledged: "Indeed, I wouldn't claim that I'd 'learned' something until I had successfully explained or discussed it with someone else, and

seen what they did with what it is I think I know..." (p. 4). Thinking like this underlies the many community service projects that involve students in conveying something they are studying on the college level to the students on lower educational levels. Verbal, cultural, scientific, and financial literacy initiatives all fall into this category.

Still other educational rationales could be adduced, but by now the underlying point should be clear—community service activities must always be grounded in a deliberate, carefully articulated understanding of how such activities advance the specific learning goals of the course in which they are embedded. Students can hardly be expected to do quality community-based work if they are not convinced such work has academic integrity. Nor can they do such work if their instructor has not carefully considered the nature of the community service they can appropriately be expected to provide.

**KINDS OF COMMUNITY SERVICE.** Academics are not the only ones who frequently confuse service learning with traditional volunteer work situated in an academic setting. Those who manage community agencies and public institutions often make a clear distinction. When they do, the care faculty have taken to clarify the educational rationale behind their community service assignments can easily come to naught: instead of creating the donor database that a computer science instructor envisioned, students are busy stacking boxes or standing at a copy machine. Such mis-assignments represent more than a frustration of educational design; they also represent a loss of opportunity for the community partner because the potential contribution of the college student is unrealized.

Indeed, for many faculty, perhaps the single greatest obstacle to sponsoring community-related work is a tendency to see its possibilities solely in terms of some kind of generic busyness. This is especially true at research-oriented universities and highly selective liberal arts colleges. There is, however, no reason why the special strengths and interests of faculty at institutions like these cannot be utilized to create valuable community projects. Courses in research methodology, capstone seminars requiring the production of original work, and courses sufficiently advanced to permit policy analysis and recommendations are at least as suitable for service learning initiatives as are courses that lend themselves to direct kinds of assistance. Undergraduate research and participatory action research represent two established areas of pedagogical practice whose methods and aims lend themselves effortlessly to service learning.

To be sure, not all community service assignments need be of a technical nature. An introductory philosophy course exploring the concept of justice may require—and be able to provide—no more than generic assistance to an agency working with the homeless. In this case, all that will distinguish service learning from traditional volunteerism is the educational framework within which the service experience is set, including the kinds of questions and exercises the instructor provides to help students link their experience to readings and class discussions. In short, whether the service in question is generic or technical, is geared to assist individuals or clarify policy, takes place primarily off or on campus, it is up to the instructor—in conjunction with a community partner—to determine its relevance to the educational objectives. The only constants here are that the activities be designed to address real community issues as well as real educational objectives and that the students be capable of performing the tasks required.

COURSE FORMAT. If the nature of available student expertise helps determine what kinds of community service tasks are appropriate, so also does the instructor's decision as to how those tasks will be weighed in relation to other class assignments. Will the community service component be mandatory or optional? Will it involve a significant or relatively minor time commitment? Will it define or complement core course objectives? Again, there is no single correct answer to any of these questions (Enos & Troppe, 1996). Although some service learning practitioners warn against the dangers of including community service assignments only as a structural add-on, others stress the importance of being sensitive to students' personal circumstances and the dangers of sending unwilling, even resentful students into the community. Community service as a "fourth-credit option" represents an excellent case in point. Some instructors view this arrangement, which allows students to earn four rather than three credits if they complete a set of field-based activities as well as all of a course's regular requirements, as a useful way of making service learning available across the curriculum. However, others see it as reducing community service to an afterthought, a signal to students that the work that really matters still lies in the traditional classroom.

Regardless of the individual choices faculty make with regard to the educational rationale, the kind of community service, and the course format, service learning requires instructors—no less than their students—to become "reflective practitioners" (Schon, 1983, 1987). Because few faculty have been trained to teach in this way, it also requires a serious institutional commitment to faculty development.

### Quadrant B: Reflection Strategies

Most of what has been said up to this point might apply not only to service learning but also to other, more traditional forms of experiential education. Granted, service learning occurs not just in special academic units such as practica and internships but also in standard classroom-based courses. In addition, service learning stresses the importance of reciprocity, of fully taking into account the goals of non-academic partners. Nevertheless, such features could be regarded as differences in degree rather than in kind. Quadrant B, however, fundamentally distinguishes service learning from other forms of experiential education. For as Bringle and Hatcher (1996) note, "Unlike practica and internships, the experiential activity in a service learning course is not necessarily skill-based within the context of professional education" (p. 222). In other words, the purpose of service learning assignments is not just to improve the technical, discipline-specific effectiveness of student skills. It is also "to gain…a broader appreciation of the discipline, and an enhanced sense of civic responsibility" (p. 222). In this regard, service learning shifts attention away from an exclusive preoccupation with education as private gain and seeks to balance that concern with a focus on the common good.

Such a balance clearly pivots on the concept of reflection. As Eyler, Giles, and Schmiede (1996) point out in *A Practitioner's Guide to Reflection in Service Learning*, no less an advocate of experiential education than John Dewey insisted that "reflective thinking was the key to making experience educative" (p. 15). Regardless of the care and skill with which a faculty member designs the community service activities in a course, that design cannot fully achieve its ends unless similar care and skill are expended to design exercises that allow students to turn those activities into conscious learning.

However, because service learning goals are not limited to course- and discipline-specific expertise, reflection in a service learning context must facilitate a wider range of educational outcomes than it must elsewhere.

Besides providing the mechanism that links theory to practice in the technical sphere (i.e., Bringle and Hatcher's "course content"), reflection activities must also help students locate that technical sphere in a broader set of concerns. It is to this latter task that Barber (1997) refers when he notes that "[helping] create contributing, responsible citizens...is a task schools and colleges can be expected to undertake, for it reflects nothing more than a recognition of and recommitment to the traditional ideal of education as preparation of young people for civic life in a free society" (p. 228).

And yet, as traditional as such a task may be, it may also pose even more of a challenge than the task of designing course-specific community service assignments. For while some faculty may object to experiential assignments as unacceptably "vocational," even more will object to the task of developing engaged citizens as by and large "irrelevant"—that is, not irrelevant in general but irrelevant to the specific courses they teach. Like character education, many faculty see citizenship and democracy skills as matters of personal rather than academic development and, as such, the province of student, not faculty, affairs.

For this reason reflection, like community service activities, must be approached with considerable sensitivity to course-specific content. For if, as Schön (1995) and others have suggested, reflection is the natural process through which experience yields real discipline-specific understanding, so it also must be allowed to work as naturally as possible in making that experience yield other, broader kinds of understanding. In other words, while the concept of citizenship may be as appropriate in an accounting class as in a political science class, the way in which it is introduced, developed, and made a natural part of the course's concerns will necessarily differ. Indeed, even the vocabulary the disciplines use to articulate their sense of public obligation and public work (Boyte & Farr, 1997) will show considerable variation.

I clearly remember the time I approached the steering committee of the Massachusetts Support Center Accounting Assistance Project to discuss the possibility of project members becoming involved in my college's service learning program. Although I had prepared myself to "make the case" for such participation, I found myself instead on the receiving end of a mini-lecture on the importance of modeling professional responsibility for future accountants. During a visit to the American Chemical Society (ACS), I started the dis-

cussion by conceding the special difficulties chemistry instructors faced in engaging first-year students in socially relevant projects. The ACS staff members passed me a stack of publications explaining how to do precisely that!

There is, in short, within all disciplinary cultures ample opportunity to explore questions of civic participation, social responsibility, and personal priorities in ways that naturally complement rather than contradict more specific, technical concerns. Take, for example, the Accounting Education Change Commission's monograph *Intentional Learning: A Process for Learning to Learn in the Accounting Curriculum* (Francis, Mulder, & Stark, 1995). The publication nowhere explicitly mentions service learning. However, one finds, in a "Composite Profile of Capabilities Needed by Accounting Graduates," such nontechnical, citizenship-related items as "awareness of personal and social values"; "ability to interact with culturally and intellectually diverse people"; and "knowledge of the activities of business, government, and nonprofit organizations, and of the environments in which they operate" (pp. 94-95). To require, as service learning does, that higher education reestablish a vital connection between issues of disciplinary expertise and issues of broad, public concern need not mean de-contextualized "relevance." It will, however, require institutional leadership to help faculty recognize this fact.

**Quadrant C: Academic Culture**
It is at this point that most discussions of service learning end. If we were to return to the Bringle and Hatcher definition in its entirety, we would find that all of its concerns have now been addressed. Why, then, should the service learning matrix posit four rather than two quadrants? The answer lies in the fact that service learning is not simply a course-based undertaking with implications for the way in which faculty teach and the kinds of faculty development opportunities they need to succeed in their teaching. It is also, perforce, a larger departmental and institutional undertaking, and its implications for these two units are every bit as challenging as are its implications for individual faculty members.

For the most part, the kinds of departmental and institutional issues service learning raises can also be found in other academic contexts. In his influential paper "Making a Place for the New American Scholar" (1996), Eugene Rice identifies the assumptive world of the academic professional; that is, the "complex of basic assumptions" that has come to dominate and structure the work of faculty. These include a privileging of research above all other forms of scholarly activity, a privileging of pure research above applications, a privileging of specialization above connections and context, and a privileging of the internal values and priorities of the academy above the needs and concerns of non-members (p. 8 ff.). It is these assumptions that have shaped the professional socialization of "the large number of older, senior faculty who now head departments and influence tenure and promotion decisions." However, even as this assumptive world continues to shape the academy in its image, "institutional developments [have] pulled in another." Primary among these developments is the pressure to pay far more serious attention to undergraduate education and the larger community:

> As we moved into the 1990s...[the] priorities that had been central to the assumptive world of the academic professional began to be not necessarily challenged and rejected but added to. The junior faculty interviewed for the 'Heeding New Voices,' inquiry report that, in one sense, it is a new day on campus...Extensive peer review of one's publications continues to be what is valued most; but in addition to thorough student evaluation, one's teaching also has to be peer reviewed in multiple ways. While new faculty are, on the local level, being encouraged to engage in the very gratifying work of curricular development and reaching out to the broader community through newly initiated service learning programs, they are being told that their more cosmopolitan responsibilities to professional associations and their guild colleagues are to be their first priority.
>
> Some of the best new faculty are being attracted to a new set of priorities focused on the essential missions of our institutions. On the other hand, the old priorities—the assumptive world of the academic professional—remain intact (p. 10).

It is interesting that Rice should explicitly refer here to service learning, for few initiatives that characterize the emerging paradigm so vividly capture its implications for the departments and institutions in which future faculty will work. In this regard, service learning can be viewed as a kind of litmus test: departments and institutions that have fully recognized its significance and have provided for its operations have not only made a strong commitment to undergraduate education and civic outreach, they have also indicated a willingness to

explore the necessity of structural readjustments. Such readjustments will necessitate dealing with at least some of the following cutting-edge concerns.

**REINTEGRATION OF FACULTY ROLES.** One of the questions that most frequently surfaces at institutions where a significant number of faculty have embraced service learning is how one can best capture this work in annual reports and faculty profiles. A historian who has developed an upper-level seminar around community-based research is certainly not involved in faculty professional service in the traditional sense. Hence, despite the "service" profile of the project, it should perhaps more properly be placed in the category of "pedagogical innovations" unless, of course, it reflects the faculty member's own scholarly interests, enhances the work, and winds up being published in some form. In that case, it can also be entered under "research" or "scholarship" or "professional activity"— or whatever other suitable category happens to be used.

There are, in other words, few academic undertakings that so effectively point up both the incoherence and the inefficiency of the traditional tripartite division of faculty responsibilities. In an era of shifting expectations, such incoherence can have especially serious consequences. As James Votruba (1996), president of Northern Kentucky University, has noted:

> Traditionally, we have treated the academic trilogy of teaching, research, and service as if they were separate and conceptually distinct forms of professional activity. In times of limited resources, it is assumed that any attempt to strengthen one part of the trilogy must be done at the expense of the others. If outreach is to become a primary and fully integrated dimension of the overall academic mission, this "zero sum" mentality must be overcome (p. 30).

If colleges and universities are to reemerge as active citizens, they simply cannot afford to sustain this kind of inefficiency. By encouraging faculty to develop projects that make their work simultaneously productive in all three of the traditional categories, service learning helps both individual faculty and institutions do more with the resources available to them.

**REASSESSING ASSESSMENT AND RECOGNITION.** In discussing the implications of quadrant A (course-specific service activities), service learning challenges faculty to be much more deliberate in their course design and pedagogical strategies. One of the most important areas in which this heightened deliberateness must manifest itself is in matters of assessment—in developing measures of student performance more adequate to the complex, real-world dimensions of student work. The same can also be said for departments and institutions with regard to faculty work. Beyond the task of conceptualizing and capturing the multi-dimensionality of such work, there remains the task of judging its merits and rewarding it appropriately.

Here, of course, we go back directly to the issues raised by Boyer in Scholarship Reconsidered (1990). If the scholarships of integration, application, and teaching are to be regarded as genuinely equal to the scholarship of discovery (i.e., traditional research), there must be ways to assess and reward them with comparable confidence. As a pedagogy of process, closely allied to both the scholarship of teaching and the scholarship of application, service learning is concerned with "not only *transmitting* knowledge, but *transforming* and *extending* it as well" [original emphasis] (p. 24). By embracing activities in which "theory and practice vitally interact," it allows "[n]ew intellectual understandings [to] arise out of the very act of application" (p. 23).

Thus, service learning has a vested interest in undertakings such as the American Association for Higher Education's Peer Review of Teaching project and the New England Resource Center for Higher Education's Program on Faculty Professional Service and Academic Outreach. Departments and institutions that regard teaching as public work and/or that recognize the distinctive nature of community engagement activities "based on [a] faculty member's professional expertise" (NERCHE, n.d.) can in the long run more effectively support service learning than can those that profess progressive values but remain formally defined by traditional academic procedures and expectations.

VALIDATING NEW CURRICULAR COLLABORATIONS. Throughout this chapter, special attention has been paid to the important role played by course- and discipline-specific thinking in developing effective service learning initiatives. To some, such an emphasis on traditional, for the most part discipline-based courses may seem anachronistic, especially in the context of a progressive pedagogy such as service learning. Are we not constantly reminded, every time one steps outside the academy, that traditional discipline-based distinctions are indeed "academic"—in the narrowest sense of the word? Does not the future belong to interdisciplinary studies and problem-organized learning?

Such a charge should not be taken lightly. If academic specialization is largely responsible for the many "disconnects" that characterize our current system (Smith, 1990; Wilshire, 1990), should not service learning unambiguously align itself with programs that reject such specialization? In my opinion, such a move would be counterproductive. Whatever the liabilities of current discipline-based academic culture, that culture remains, in fact, the basis of most faculty members' professional identities. As such, it underlies both their sense of competence and the meaning of their work. For service learning to challenge these fundamentals— in addition to all the other givens it must challenge— would doom it to academic marginality for the foreseeable future.

However, service learning does indirectly challenge the trend toward ever greater specialization within the disciplines. By anchoring itself in real-world projects, it naturally serves to pull participating faculty members in the direction of functional and conceptual integration. Indeed, over and beyond such integration, it promotes new opportunities for dialogue among disciplinary participants. Enhanced collegiality and communication are almost always a side benefit of developed service learning programs.

Such collegiality and communication are not, of course, without practical consequences. Rarely have I facilitated a service learning workshop for faculty at the same institution without at least two participants from different disciplinary backgrounds discovering that they share issue-, problem-, or site-based interests. Such discoveries sometimes lead, right on the spot, to concrete plans for curricular collaboration—from the use of students in one course to serve as consultants to other students to the creation of learning communities organized around a single community service initiative.

## Quadrant D: Community Partnerships
The final quadrant of the service learning matrix directly addresses issues arising from the creation of academy-community partnerships. From a service learning perspective, the word partnership immediately demands definition. On the one hand, it may mean little more than those work sites or tasks identified by service agencies or community groups as appropriate for course-based student involvement. Such a concept of partnership differs little from the volunteer opportunity lists maintained by many student affairs offices. To be sure, utilization of such opportunities in a service

learning context demands that they be further defined (e.g., the service activity be carefully matched with academic needs, the community sponsor must be fully consulted as to priorities and goals). Nonetheless, these are adjustments that do not fundamentally challenge the notion of a casual, task-specific relationship.

On the other hand, partnership may also point to relationships that call for significant investments of time and effort on both sides, relationships designed to continue far beyond achieving specific tasks. Keith Morton (1995), associate director of the Feinstein Institute for Public Service at Providence College, has described that institute's "four or five...core partner[ships]" as involving "commitments [that] have taken the form of doing strategic planning together, intentionally developing interdependent agendas; supporting the work of the partner by actively developing other campus-based resources; and...down the road [possibly]...swapping or sharing (formally or informally) staff" (p. 30).

Such partnerships lie at the core of this fourth quadrant, for it is only here that the full potential of service learning as a strategy of academic citizenship can manifest itself. Service learning placements—like extension programs, faculty professional expertise, utilization of campus resources for community and civic purposes—clearly serve an important function and go a long way towards strengthening campus-community ties. However, it is only through full service learning partnerships that the academy and the community come together as equals for the purpose of better fulfilling their core missions. Only through the kinds of long-term interdependencies Morton describes is the community invited to become centrally involved in higher education's obligation to generate and communicate knowledge—even as higher education is invited to become centrally involved in the community's obligation to meet essential human needs.

Interdependency of this sort is necessarily transformative. It transforms academic engagement from a responsible action to a moral obligation. It transforms institutional citizenship from the concern of a designated office to the business of the campus as a whole. It is unsettling, subversive, shifting the very foundations of academic work from self-definition to joint purpose. It affects the way students learn, what they learn, and how they are assessed. It affects the way faculty teach, how they frame their research, and why they are recognized. It affects the agendas administrators set and the way in which they allocate resources, including money.

One allocation is of special importance, for on it largely depends the work not only of this fourth quadrant but also that of the other three. just as faculty cannot be expected to undertake the challenge of service learning course design and implementation without adequate recognition and academic support, so even the availability of such recognition and support may accomplish little unless faculty also have available to them structures that facilitate establishing and maintaining community partnerships. Currently there exists a variety of models that institutions can look to in developing structures of their own, but some functions and features cut across most arrangements (Troppe, 1996; Zlotkowski, 1998a). For example, most support structures assist faculty in identifying suitable partners and projects, facilitate student transportation to and from community sites, and monitor student participation as well as stakeholder satisfaction. Institutions like Brevard Community College have developed an elaborate, efficient, and inclusive protocol to help faculty, students, and community partners navigate all aspects of that institution's service learning activities.

As for the personnel needed to provide such support, successful programs almost always require the leadership of a professional staff person—someone familiar both with the local community and with an institution's faculty. Such a person must be able to work with off-campus groups in a knowledgeable, respectful way and yet also feel at home in the culture of higher education. "Bilingualism" of this sort is essential if the mutuality that must characterize service learning partnerships is to be cultivated and maintained.

Clearly, however, the presence of a single professional staff person—no matter how competent and energetic—is insufficient to meet all the logistical needs of a comprehensive service learning program. How, then, to meet those needs becomes one of the most important questions facing any institution seeking to develop such a program. Fortunately, this problem can turn into a blessing in disguise.

Colleges and universities seeking to develop service learning sometimes encounter opposition from an unlikely quarter: students already involved in cocurricular community service. This opposition often stems from a fear that if service learning is successfully developed, student efforts will be preempted by faculty-led activities. In point of fact, such a concern is groundless. In the first place, the kinds of needs—academic and social—that service learning seeks to meet are often quite different from the needs addressed by traditional volunteer programs. Just as service learning complements rather than replaces traditional internships, so it should also be seen as complementing rather than replacing other kinds of community engagement. Second, students have an important, and perhaps critical, role to play in the successful functioning of service learning programs.

That there can be a powerful relationship between community service and leadership development has been demonstrated in a variety of contexts. Robert Greenleaf's concept of servant leadership (1977) and the Astins' *A Social Change Model of Leadership Development* (Astin & Astin, 1996) represent only two especially relevant contributions to our understanding of this relationship.

What the work of people like Greenleaf and the Astins makes available to the service learning community is a solid theoretical and practical foundation for developing positions, functions, and arrangements that facilitate the service learning work of faculty even as they provide students with opportunities to develop special service-related skills of their own. Thus, for example, at the University of Utah's Bennion Center (Fisher, 1998),

> Many student leaders of...cocurricular projects serve as teaching assistants for new service learning courses. These undergraduate students essentially share with their faculty colleagues what they have learned through directing their own cocurricular projects (p. 225).

At Providence College's Feinstein Institute (Battistoni, 1998),

> Students have played a pivotal role in planning the new program and managing its activities. This has also been a conscious strategy, necessitated by both [a] commitment to democratic community and the fact that, as an academic program, the tendency for faculty to control the curriculum has had to be balanced by a strong student presence and voice (p. 183).

The Community Scholars program at Bentley College, the Student Ambassadors program at Miami-Dade Community College, and the Public and Community Service Scholars program at Augsburg College, despite many differences, all represent efforts to utilize and develop student leadership by making students structurally significant players.

## COLLATERAL BENEFITS

This discussion of the four quadrants of service learning practice has either explicitly or implicitly touched upon many of the ways in which this approach enhances both faculty effectiveness and student learning. If, moreover, Barr and Tagg (1995) are correct and higher education is in the midst of a major conceptual shift from education as a system for delivering instruction to education as a system for producing learning (p. 13), service learning's significance only increases. This is a function not only of the way in which it works but also of what it seeks to accomplish.

In a comprehensive article on Restructuring the Role of Faculty, Alan Guskin (1994), chancellor of the five-campus Antioch University System, makes an observation that is becoming increasingly important, namely, "that the primary learning environment for undergraduate students, the fairly passive lecture-discussion format where faculty talk and most students listen, is contrary to almost every principle of optimal settings for student learning." These principles, which Guskin draws from the work of Chickering and Gamson (1991), include student collaboration, active learning, time on task and respect for multiple learning styles.

Every one of these principles finds a natural home in service learning (as do also, if somewhat less distinctively, three other principles: student-faculty contact, prompt feedback, and high expectations). In contrast to the traditional lecture-discussion format, service learning encourages—in many instances, mandates—student-student collaboration on challenging real-world tasks, tasks that require an assortment of strengths and skills, including problem identification, process adjustments, and project ownership. By linking theory and practice, reflection and experimentation (Kolb, 1984), service learning opens up the learning process to accommodate a much wider variety of student learning styles than has traditionally been the case. The significance of such expanded access can hardly be underestimated.

Schroeder (1993), reported on the results of a series of studies on student learning styles across a fifteen-year period:

> In our initial studies, we focused most of our inquiry on two very broad learning patterns associated with sensing and intuition. The results indicate that approximately 60 percent of entering students pre-

fer the sensing mode of perceiving compared to 40 percent who prefer the intuitive mode...In general, students who prefer sensing learning patterns prefer the concrete, the practical, and the immediate...The path to educational excellence for sensing learners is usually a practice-to-theory route, not the more traditional theory-to-practice approach (pp. 23-24).

Schroeder goes on to point out that "on many campuses students who prefer the sensing learning pattern are now in the majority. This is particularly true for relatively non-selective institutions that do not place a premium on entrance examination scores." As for why so many students with a sensing preference are entering college, "[t]he reason is fairly obvious when we consider that approximately 75 percent of the general population has been estimated to prefer the sensing learning pattern" (p. 24).

I discovered the value of opening up the teaching-learning process quite by accident. For several years I had taught a values clarification course intended to help students better understand the way in which their mental models shaped their attitudes. In an attempt to introduce greater authenticity into our discussion of poverty and privilege, I arranged to have students spend some productive time working with the homeless. As a result, I found even typically taciturn students eager to share both their experiences and their new insights. Class discussions became dynamic, even passionate; journal entries swelled far beyond their required length.

Like many instructors, I do not have the luxury of taking student intellectual engagement for granted. In fact, most of my students approach their education from a decidedly utilitarian point of view. While I am, in fact, deeply sympathetic to their practical concerns, I am too committed to the value of liberal learning not to be troubled by what many of them sacrifice in their quest for marketable skills. By opening up the learning process through the introduction of community-based units, I had stumbled upon a way of reconciling diverse, even seemingly contradictory, educational values: students could follow their instinct to learn through concrete experience, remaining firmly in contact with the real world, while at the same time they grapple with situations that challenged their preconceptions and self-understanding.

Such bridge building lies at the heart of the service learning experience and provides the best metaphor for its value to colleges and universities as citizens. Service learning works to create new patterns of coherence in many areas of academic life: in the way it helps faculty naturally link their research, teaching, and service interests; in the way in which it fosters intra- and inter-department collaboration; and in the way it links faculty needs and student leadership opportunities.

Research conducted by UCLA's Higher Education Research Institute points to another kind of service-related bridge building. According to Astin, Sax, and Avalos (1996), service involvement (curricular and cocurricular) not only "encourages students to become more socially responsible, more committed to serving their communities, more empowered, and more committed to education," it also "encourages socialization across racial lines and increases commitment to promoting racial understanding in the years after college" (p. 16).

From the standpoint of America's changing demographic makeup, these results point in two equally significant directions. In the first place, the undergraduate community service experience may be one of our best hopes yet for resolving racial and ethnic tensions. But no less important is the social potential captured in the finding that community service encourages students to become "more empowered" and "more committed to education" (Astin, Sax, & Avalos, 1996, p. 16). Widespread anecdotal reports suggest that involvement in service learning has strong positive influences on minority retention. Given the way in which it opens up to students multiple paths to participation and achievement and draws leaders and role models from a variety of community-based organizations into the learning process, such an influence is not at all unlikely.

But perhaps the single most important bridge service learning helps build and sustain is the one between institutional rhetoric and institutional action, between professed values and actual practice. Whether an institution is a research university, an urban land grant, a liberal arts college, or a community college, the chances are excellent that its mission encompasses service or public purpose. Because service learning can—and in some cases does—affect virtually every aspect of a campus's operations, few other initiatives have the same potential to bring professed values and practice so thoroughly into alignment. Hence, institutions as diverse as St. John's University (New York), the University of Pennsylvania, Bates College, Middlesex Community College (Massachusetts), and Portland State University have deliberately turned to it as a primary means to live out more authentically their own self-identified missions and traditions—whether these are expressed in terms of religious commitment, public charter, research capability, or civic and personal values.

## CONCLUSION

This chapter began with a brief discussion of the present wave of interest in community service on America's campuses. Such interest, I conceded, may be cyclical, but there is good reason to believe that this time around it differs in several important respects from earlier manifestations. Community service as a voluntary, cocurricular undertaking is being complemented by course-based service learning and, through the latter, institutions of higher learning have become involved in academy-community partnerships in a new, potentially revolutionary way. As such, service learning's implications reach into almost every facet of the academic enterprise.

For this reason, service learning can be more challenging and, perhaps, more institutionally significant than outreach strategies that define community-related efforts in ways that leave an institution's core educational functions unaffected. And yet, as I have pointed out, Boyer's New American College, with its "cross-disciplinary institutes [organized] around pressing social issues"; its "[c]lassrooms and laboratories...extended to include health clinics, youth centers, schools, and government offices"; its "practitioners who...come to campus as lecturers and student-advisers," envisions nothing less.

In the October 31, 1997, edition of *The Chronicle of Higher Education*, the Carnegie Foundation for the Advancement of Teaching announced its four "Outstanding Professors of the Year." According to the descriptive statements that accompanied the announcement, the achievements of all four of these representatives of extraordinary undergraduate teaching involved an "[extension of] the learning process beyond the classroom." In the case of three of the four, this extension involved "encouraging...students to apply what they learn to real-life situations." In two of the four, such an extension "connect[ed] students directly with...public service institutions," thus "stressing the importance of the application of knowledge toward the improvement of the human condition" (p. A29). As in Boyer's characterization of the New Ameri-

can College, the term "service learning" nowhere explicitly appears in this announcement. Still, one can no more doubt its relationship to at least half of the work described here than one can its relationship to Boyer's own vision. That the organization he headed so ably for so long should single out for recognition precisely this kind of excellence cannot help but strike one as singularly appropriate.

## REFERENCES

American Association for Higher Education. (1996). AAHE's series on service learning in the disciplines. Washington, DC: Author.

Astin, H. S., & Astin, A. W. (1996). *A social change model of leadership development: Guidebook, version III.* Los Angeles: UCLA Higher Education Research Institute.

Astin, A. W., Sax, L. J., & Avalos, J. (1996). *Long-term effects of volunteerism during the undergraduate years.* Los Angeles: UCLA Higher Education Research Institute.

Barber, B. R. (1997). Afterword. In R. M. Battistoni & W. E. Hudson (Eds.), *Experiencing citizenship: Concepts and methods for service-learning in political science* (pp. 227-235). Washington, DC: American Association for Higher Education.

Barr, R. B., & Tagg, J. (1995). From teaching to learning: A new paradigm for undergraduate education. *Change, 27*(6), 12-25.

Battistoni, R. M. (1998). Making a major commitment: Public and community service at Providence College. In E. Zlotkowski (Ed.), *Successful service learning programs: New models of excellence in higher education* (pp. 169-188). Boston: Anker.

Boyer, E. L. (1990). *Scholarship reconsidered: Priorities of the professoriate.* Princeton, NJ: Carnegie Foundation for the Advancement of Teaching.

Boyer, E. L. (1994, March 9). Creating the new American college. *The Chronicle of Higher Education,* A48.

Bringle, R. G., & Hatcher, J. A. (1996). Implementing service learning in higher education. *Journal of Higher Education, 67,* 221-239.

Boyte, H. C., & Farr, H. (1997). The work of citizenship and the problem of service learning. In R. Battistoni & W. Hudson (Eds.), *Practicing democracy: Concepts and models of service learning in political science* (pp. 35-48). Washington, DC: American Association for Higher Education.

Chickering, A. W., & Gamson, Z. E (1991). Applying the seven principles for good practice in undergraduate education. In A. W. Chickering & Z. E Gamson (Eds.), *New directions for teaching and learning, No. 47: Seven princi-*

ples for good practice in undergraduate education (pp. 63-69). San Francisco: Jossey-Bass.

Coye, D. (1997). Ernest Boyer and the new American college: Connecting the "disconnects." *Change, 29*(3), 21-29.

Enos, S. L., & Troppe, M. L. (1996). Service learning in the curriculum. In B. Jacoby & Associates (Eds.), *Service learning in higher education: Concepts and practices* (pp. 156-181). San Francisco: Jossey-Bass.

Eyler, J., Giles, D. W. Jr., & Schmiede, A. (1996). *A practitioner's guide to reflection in service learning.* Nashville TN: Vanderbilt University.

Fisher, I. S. (1998). We make the road by walking: Building service learning in and out of the curriculum at the University of Utah. In E. Zlotkowski (Ed.), *Successful service learning programs: New models of excellence in higher education* (pp. 210-231). Bolton, MA: Anker.

Francis, M. C., Mulder, T. C., & Stark, J. S. (1995). *Intentional learning: A process for learning to learn in the accounting curriculum.* Sarasota, FL: Accounting Education Change Commission & American Accounting Association.

Greenleaf, R. K. (1977). *Servant leadership: A journey into the nature of legitimate power and greatness.* New York: Paulist Press.

Guskin, A. E. (1994). Restructuring the role of faculty. *Change, 26*(5), 16-25.

Jacoby, B., & Associates. (1996). *Service learning in higher education: Concepts and practices.* San Francisco: Jossey-Bass.

Kolb, D. (1984). *Experiential learning: Experience as a source of learning and development.* Englewood Cliffs, NJ: Prentice-Hall.

Levine, A. (1994). Service on campus. *Change, 26*(4), 4-5.

Miller, M. A. (1997). The advancement of teaching: An interview with the new head of the Carnegie Foundation for the Advancement of Teaching, Lee Shulman. *AAHE Bulletin, 50*(1), 3-7.

Morton, K. (1995). The irony of service: Charity, project, and social change in service-learning. *Michigan Journal of Community Service Learning, 2,* 19-32.

Porter, L. W., & McKibbin, L. E. (1988). *Management education and development: Drift or thrust into the 21st century.* New York: McGraw-Hill.

NERCHE report. (n.d.). Boston: New England Resource Center for Higher Education.

Rama, D. V., & Zlotkowski, E. (1996). Service learning and business education: Creating conceptual bridges. *NSEE Quarterly, 21,* 10-11, 26-27.

Rice, R. E. (1996). *Making a place for the new American scholar* (Working paper series: Inquiry #1). Washington, DC: American Association for Higher Education.

Schon, D. A. (1983). *The reflective practitioner.* New York: Basic Books.

Schon, D. A. (1987). *Educating the reflective practitioner.* San Francisco: Jossey-Bass.

Schon, D. A. (1995). The new scholarship requires a new epistemology. *Change, 27*(6), 27-34.

Schroeder, C. C. (1993). New students-new learning styles. *Change, 25*(5), 21-26.

Smith, P. (1990). *Killing the spirit: Higher education in America.* New York: Penguin.

Stanton, T. K. (1990). *Integrating public service with academic study: The faculty role.* Providence: Campus Compact.

Teaching Matters: The Carnegie Foundation for the Advancement of Teaching 1997 professors of the year (1997, October 31). *The Chronicle of Higher Education,* A29.

Troppe, M. (1996). *Two cases of institutionalizing service learning: How campus climate affects the change process.* Providence, RI: Campus Compact.

Votruba, J. C. (1996). Strengthening the university's alignment with society: Challenges and strategies. *Journal of Public Service and Outreach, 1,* 29-36.

Wilshire, B. (1990). *The moral collapse of the university: Professionalism, purity, and alienation.* Albany, NY: State University of New York Press.

Zlotkowski, E. (1995). Does service learning have a future? *Michigan Journal of Community Service Learning, 2,* 123-133.

Zlotkowski, E. (1996a). A new voice at the table? Linking service learning and the academy. *Change, 28*(1), 20-27.

Zlotkowski, E. (1996b). Opportunity for all: Linking service learning and business education. *Journal of Business Ethics, 15,* 5-19.

Zlotkowski, E. (1998a). *Successful service learning programs: New models of excellence in higher education.* Bolton, MA: Anker.

Zlotkowski, E. (1998b). A service learning approach to faculty development. In J. P. Howard & R. Rhodes (Eds.), *Service learning pedagogy and research.* San Francisco: Jossey-Bass.

# Pedagogy:
## Recommended Reading

### BOOKS & CHAPTERS

Ayers, W., Hunt, J.A., & Quinn, T. (Eds.). (1998). *Teaching for social justice.* New York, NY: Teachers College Press.

Burbules, N. (1993). *Dialogue in teaching: Theory and practice.* New York: Teachers College Press.

Campus Compact. (1998). *When community enters the equation: Enhancing science, mathematics and engineering education through service-learning.* Providence, RI: Campus Compact.

Cooper, D., & Julier, L. (eds.). (1995). *Writing in the public interest: Service-learning and the writing classroom.* East Lansing, MI: Michigan State University.

Creamer, E.G. (1999). Feminist pedagogy in action. In James-Deramo, M. (Ed.), *Best practices in cyber-serve: Integrating technology with service-learning instruction.* Blacksburg, VA: Virginia Polytechnic Institute Service-Learning Center.

Ender, M., Marsteller-Kowalewski, B., Cotter, D. Martin, L and DeFiore, J. (1996). *Service-learning and undergraduate sociology: Syllabi and instructional materials.* Washington, DC: American Sociological Association.

Furco, A., Bolotte, D., Chung, O., Keaton, T., Muller, P., & Nuttall, S. (1998). *Service-learning faculty development at community colleges.* Mesa, AZ: Campus Compact National Center for Community Colleges.

Furco, A. & Billig, S.H. (2002). *Service-learning: The essence of pedagogy.* (A volume in the Advances in Service-Learning Research series). Greenwich, CT: Information Age Publishing.

Hutchings, P. and Wutdorff, A. (Eds.). (1988). *Knowing and doing: Learning through experience.* San Francisco: Jossey-Bass.

Kendall, J., et al. (Eds.). (1990). *Combining service and learning: A resource book for community and public service, Volumes I and II.* Raleigh, NC: National Society for Internships and Experiential Education.

Klopp, C., Toole, P. & Toole, J. (2001). *Pondering learning: Connecting multiple intelligences and service-learning.* Clemson, SC: National Dropout Prevention Center.

Kraft, R.J. & Swadler, M. (Eds.). (1994). *Building community: Service-learning in the academic disciplines.* Denver: Colorado Campus Compact.

Oates, K.K. & Gaither, L. (2001). Integration and assessment of service-learning in learning communities. In B.L. Smith & J.M. McCann (Eds.), *Reinventing ourselves: Interdisciplinary education, collaborative learning, and experimentation in higher education.* Bolton, MA: Anker.

Rhoads, R. & Howard, J. (Eds.). (1998). *Academic service-learning: A pedagogy of action and reflection.* San Francisco: Jossey-Bass.

Walters, A., & Ford, M. (1995). *Writing for change: A community reader.* New York: McGraw Hill.

Walters, A., & Ford, M. (1995). *A guide for change: Resources for implementing community service writing.* New York: McGraw Hill.

Zlotkowski, E. (Ed.). (1996–2003). *Service learning in the disciplines, volumes 1–19.* Washington, DC: AAHE.

Zlotkowski, E. (1999). Pedagogy and engagement. In R. Bringle, et al. (Eds.), *Universities as citizens,* pp. 96–120. Needham Heights, MA: Allyn and Bacon.

### ARTICLES & REPORTS

Beckman, M. (1997). Learning in action: Courses that complement community service. *College Teaching, 45* (2), 72–76.

Carter, M., et al. (2002). Designing your community-based learning project: Five questions to ask yourself about your pedagogical and participatory goals. *Teaching Sociology, 30* (2), 158–173.

Checkoway, B. (1996). Combining service and learning on campus and in the community. *Phi Delta Kappan, 77* (1), 600–606.

Chickering, A., & Gamson, Z. (1987). Seven principles of good practice in undergraduate education. *AAHE Bulletin, 39* (7), 3–7.

Cohen, J., and Kinsey, D. (1994). Doing good and scholarship: A service-learning study. *Journalism Educator,* 48 (4), 4–14.

Coleman, J.S. (1977). Differences between experiential and classroom learning. In Keaton, M.T. (Ed.), *Experiential learning: Rationale, characteristics, and assessment.* San Francisco, CA: Jossey-Bass, 1977.

Coles, R. (1994, October 26). Putting head and heart on the line. *Chronicle of Higher Education,* p. A64.

Coles, R. (1988). Community service work. *Liberal Education,* 74 (4), 11–13.

Cooper, D. and Julier, L. (1995). Writing the ties that bind: Service-learning in the writing classroom. *Michigan Journal of Community Service-Learning,* 2, 72–85.

Corwin, P. (1996). Using the community as a classroom for large introductory sociology classes. *Teaching Sociology,* 24, 310–315.

Dublinsky, J.M. (2002). Service-learning as a path to virtue: The ideal orator in professional communication. *Michigan Journal of Community Service Learning,* 8 (2), 61–74.

Forsyth, A., Lu H. & McGirr, P. (2000). Service learning in an urban context: Implications for planning and design education. *Journal of Architectural and Planning Research,* 17 (3), 236–259.

Goldblatt, E. (1994). Van rides in the dark: Literacy as involvement in a college literacy practicum. *The Journal for Peace and Justice Studies,* 6 (1), 77–94.

Hayes, E., and Cuban, S. (1997). Border pedagogy: A critical framework for service-learning. *Michigan Journal of Community Service Learning,* 4, 72–80.

Hesser, G. (1995). Outcomes attributed to service-learning and evidence of change in faculty attitudes about experiential education. *Michigan Journal of Community Service Learning,* 2, 33–42.

Hondaagneu-Sotelo, P. and Raskoff, S. (1994). Community service-learning: Promises and problems. *Teaching Sociology,* 22, 248–254.

Herzberg, B. (1994). Community service and critical teaching. *College Composition and Communication,* 45 (3), 307–319.

Howard, J. (1998). A counternormative pedagogy. In R. Rhoads, & J. Howard (Eds.). *Academic service-learning: A pedagogy of action and reflection.* San Francisco: Jossey-Bass.

Kendrick, J.R. (1996). Outcomes of service-learning in an introduction to sociology course. *Michigan Journal of Community Service Learning,* 3, 72–81.

Kienzler, D. (2001). Ethics, critical thinking, and professional communication pedagogy. *Technical Communication Quarterly* 10 (3), 319–39

Langseth, M. & Troppe, M. (1997). So what? Does service-learning really foster social change? *Expanding Boundaries,* 2, 37–42.

Markus, G. Howard J., & King D. (1993). Integrating community service with classroom instruction enhances learning: Results from an experiment. *Educational Evaluation and Policy Analysis,* 15, 410–419.

Morton, Keith. (1993). Potential and practice for combining civic education and community service. In T. Kupiec (Ed.) *Rethinking tradition: Integrating service with academic study on college campuses.* Providence, RI: Campus Compact.

Parker-Gwin, R. & Mabry, J.B. (1998). Service-learning as pedagogy and civic education: Comparing outcomes for three models. *Teaching Sociology,* 26, 276–291.

Pompa, L. (2002). Service-learning as crucible: Reflections on immersion, context, power, and transformation. *Michigan Journal of Community Service Learning,* 9 (1), 67–76.

Rubin, M.S. (2001). A smart start to service-learning. *New Directions for Higher Education,* 114, 15–26.

Serow, R.C., Ciechalski, J., & Daye, C. (1990). Students as volunteers: Personal competencies, social diversity, and participation in community service. *Urban Education,* 25 (1), 157–168.

Stanton, T. (1994). The experience of faculty participants in an instructional development seminar on service-learning. *Michigan Journal of Community Service Learning,* 1, 7–20.

Strand, K.J. (2000). Community-based research as pedagogy. *Michigan Journal of Community Service Learning,* 7, 85–96.

Tai-Seale, T. (2001). Liberating service-learning and applying the new practice. *College Teaching,* 49 (1), 14–19.

*Teaching Sociology,* October 1998, 26(4). (Entire issue is devoted to experiential education.)

Varlotta, L. (2000). Service as text: Making the metaphor meaningful. *Michigan Journal of Community Service Learning,* 7, 76–84).

Zlotkowski, E. (1996). Linking service-learning and the academy: A new voice at the table? *Change,* 28 (1), 20–27.

Zlotkowski, E. (2001). Mapping new terrain. *Change,* 33 (1), 24–34).

# Reflection

## TITLES INCLUDED IN THIS SECTION

Reflection in Service-Learning: Making Meaning of Experience, BY ROBERT G. BRINGLE AND JULIE A. HATCHER

Reading, Writing, and Reflection, BY DAVID COOPER

Recommended Reading

## QUESTIONS FOR REFLECTION AND PLANNING

How would you define reflection within your discipline? Your course?

In what way can reflection serve as an assessment tool for your course(s)? How will you evaluate reflection?

Who should facilitate reflection, and how?

Is reflection an acceptable pedagogical tool at your institution? Where might its use be rooted in the institution's history or mission?

What role will the community play in the reflection process?

# Reflection in Service Learning:
## Making Meaning of Experience

by Robert G. Bringle and Julie A. Hatcher

TRADITIONAL METHODS OF INSTRUCTION based on lectures and textbook readings can be effective in some instances and for some types of learning, yet many educators seek methods to enhance traditional student learning and to expand educational objectives beyond knowledge acquisition. Two related issues illustrate the limitations of traditional methods. The first is context-specific learning. Students are taught a particular module of content, they are provided examples of how to solve particular types of problems, and then they practice solving these types of problems. However, when the nature of the problem is varied, or when similar problems are encountered in different contexts, students fail to generalize prior learning to these new circumstances or situations. The second issue that frustrates educators is the shallow nature of the content learned through traditional instruction and the degree to which it does not promote personal understanding. That is, although students may demonstrate rote learning of a particular educational module, that new information does not always enlighten understanding of their own lives and the world outside the classroom. When knowledge acquisition is viewed as the most important goal of education, the educational system fails to develop intellectual habits that foster the desire and capacity for life-long learning and the skills needed for active participation in a democracy.[1]

Recognizing these limits to traditional instructional methods, a Task Group on General Education, appointed by the American Association of Colleges in 1994, recommended that college instructors focus more attention on active learning strategies. Several types of active learning strategies identified in the report address these challenges (i.e., context-specific learning,

personally relevant learning) and successfully expand the educational agenda beyond the acquisition of knowledge. Recommended active learning strategies include using electronic and interactive media; promoting undergraduate research; structuring collaborative learning experiences; and developing problem-based learning.[2] The benefits of these active learning strategies include the promise that students are more engaged in the learning process. As a result, students are more satisfied with the learning experience, which in turn fosters academic persistence and success. In addition, educational outcomes are enriched, deepened, and expanded when student learning is more engaged, active, and relevant. Another type of active learning that holds similar promise is service learning.

## SERVICE LEARNING

Service learning is defined as a "course-based, credit-bearing educational experience in which students (a) participate in an organized service activity that meets identified community needs and (b) reflect on the service activity in such a way as to gain further understanding of course content, a broader appreciation of the discipline, and an enhanced sense of civic responsibility."[3] According to this definition, service learning is an academic enterprise. Although other forms of community service (e.g., volunteering) can have educational benefits, service learning deliberately integrates community service activities with educational objectives. This means that not every community service activity is appropriate for a service learning class. Community service activities need to be selected for and coordinated with the educational objectives of the course. Furthermore, the community service should be meaningful not only for the student's educational outcomes but also to the community. Thus, well-executed service learning represents a coordinated partnership between the campus and the community, with the instructor tailoring the service experience to the educational agenda and community representatives ensuring that the students' community service is consistent with their goals.[4] Thus, high-quality service learning classes demonstrate reciprocity between the campus and the community, with each giving and receiving.

The definition of service learning also highlights the importance of reflection. Reflection is the "intentional consideration of an experience in light of particular learning objectives."[5] The presumption is that community service does not necessarily, in and of itself, produce learning. Reflection activities provide the bridge between the community service activities and the educational content of the course. Reflection activities direct the student's attention to new interpretations of events and provide a means through which the community service can be studied and interpreted, much as a text is read and studied for deeper understanding.

## PHILOSOPHICAL BASIS FOR REFLECTION

The extensive work of John Dewey offers a philosophical foundation for the role that reflection assumes in the learning process as a bridge between experience and theory. Indeed, personal experiences, such as those gained through community service, allow theory to take on meaning when reflection supports an analysis and critical examination of the experience. Dewey contends that experience is as important as theory.

An ounce of experience is better than a ton of theory simply because it is only in experience that any theory has vital and verifiable significance. An experience, a very humble experience, is capable of generating and carrying any amount of theory (or intellectual content), but a theory apart from an experience cannot be definitely grasped even as theory. It tends to become a mere verbal formula, a set of catchwords used to render thinking.[6]

Too often, the presentation of a theory by an instructor or in a textbook is viewed by students as an empty, pedantic venture. It is through active learning and the interplay between abstract, remote content and personal, palatable experiences that student learning is deepened and strengthened.

According to Dewey, reflection is an "active, persistent, and careful consideration of any belief or supported form of knowledge in light of the grounds that support it."[7] Reflection consists of "turning a subject over in the mind and giving it serious and consecutive considerations."[8] Dewey acknowledges that experience by itself does not necessarily result in learning; experiences can be either "miseducative" or "educative." Experience becomes educative when critical reflective thought creates new meaning and leads to growth and the ability to take informed actions. In contrast, experiences are miseducative when they fail to stimulate critical thought and they more deeply entrench existing schemata. Dewey notes that communication, particularly face-to-face discourse, is a key to creating educative experiences. Communication with others leads not only to educational growth but also to social and moral development. Gouinlock is clear in identifying the moral dimensions of Dewey's educational philosophy. He notes, "The values, aims, and expected response of others play a critical role in stimulating revised interest in each participant. Accordingly, in a community where full and open communication exists, one finds an essential condition for the growth of new values and forms of behavior."[9]

Many forms of inquiry can produce reflection about the tensions between theory and application. Dewey specifies four conditions that maximize the potential for inquiry-based learning to be educative: (a) it must generate interest in the learner; (b) it must be intrinsically worthwhile to the learner; (c) it must present problems that awaken new curiosity and create a demand for information; and (d) it must cover a considerable time span and foster development over time.[10] Service learning classes structured to meet these four conditions can thereby create educative experiences for students. Because service learning extends the walls of the classroom into the community, students frequently encounter new circumstances and challenges. These experiences often create dissonance, doubt, and confusion. Dewey values such perplexity, for it is at that very point that reflection and thinking begin: "Thinking begins in what may fairly enough be called a forked-road situation, a situation that is ambiguous, that presents a dilemma, that proposes alternatives. . . . Demand for the solution of a perplexity is the steadying and guiding factor in the entire process of reflection."[11]

At the heart of Dewey's educational philosophy are three principles: (a) education must lead to personal growth; (b) education must contribute to humane conditions; and (c) education must engage citizens in association with one another.[12] When reflection activities engage the learner in dialogue and other forms of communication about the relationship between relevant, meaningful service and the interpretative template of a discipline, there is enormous potential for learning to broaden and deepen along academic, social, moral, and civic dimensions.[13] This occurs not only when reflection activities ask the learner to confront ambiguity and critically examine existing beliefs, but also when the retrospective analysis has prospective relevance that leads to informed future actions.[14]

## TYPES OF REFLECTION FOR SERVICE LEARNING

There are many examples of reflection activities (e.g., reading, writing, doing, telling) that can be used in service learning classes.[15] We have chosen to highlight a few that we feel are particularly worthwhile to use when working with college students. Many of them are based upon written work. Writing is a special form of reflection through which new meaning can be created, new understanding of problems can become circumscribed, and new ways of organizing experiences can be developed. Analysis through writing helps to make challenging experiences less overwhelming, fosters problem solving, and facilitates the exploration of the relationships between past learning, current experiences, and future action.[16]

JOURNALS. Student journals are common reflection activities in service learning courses because they are easy to assign and they provide a way for students to express their thoughts and feelings about the service experience throughout the semester. It is important that students know, at the beginning of the course, what is expected in a journal and how it is going to be used. Some journals, intended as personal documents, are never submitted for a grade. Journals may also be reviewed periodically by the instructor. Occasionally, journals are shared with other students or with community agency personnel. If journals are to be evaluated for a grade, then this policy should be made clear at the beginning of the semester and the criteria for grading the journal should be specified to the students.

Before assigning a journal, it is important to consider what learning objectives the journal is intended to

---

Table 1
**Types of Reflective Journals**

Key Phrase Journal: Students are asked to integrate an identified list of terms and key phrases into their journal entries as they describe and discuss their community service activities. Students may be asked to underline or highlight the key phrases in order to identify their use.

Double-entry Journal: For this journal, students use a spiral notebook. On the left side of the journal students describe their service experiences, personal thoughts, and reactions to their service activities. On the right side of the journal, they discuss how the first set of entries relates to key concepts, class presentations, and readings. Students may be asked to draw arrows indicating the relationships between their personal experiences and the formal course content.

Critical Incident Journal: Students focus on a specific event that occurred at the service site. Students are then asked to respond to prompts designed to explore their thoughts, reactions, future action, and information from the course that might be relevant to the incident. For example,

Describe an incident or situation that created a dilemma for you because you did not know how to act or what to say.
　　Why was it such a confusing event?
　　How did you, or others around the event, feel about it?
　　What did you do, or what was the first thing that you considered doing?
　　List three actions that you might have taken, and evaluate each one.

How does the course material relate to this issue, help you analyze the choices, and suggest a course of action that might be advisable?

Three Part Journal: Students are asked to respond to three separate issues in each of their journal entries: (a) Describe what happened in the service experience, including what you accomplished, some of the events that puzzled or confused you, interactions you had, decisions you made, and plans you developed. (b) Analyze how the course content relates to the service experience, including key concepts that can be used to understand events and guide future behavior. (c) Apply the course materials and the service experience to you and your personal life, including your goals, values, attitudes, beliefs, and philosophy.

Directed Writings: Students are asked to consider how a particular aspect of course content from the readings or class presentations, including theories, concepts, quotes, statistics, and research findings, relate to their service experiences. Students write a journal entry based on key issues encountered at the service site.

---

meet. Journals can be an effective way to develop self-understanding and connect the service experience to the course content. Journals can also be used during the semester to record information that is used in more formal reflective activities, such as a paper or class presentation. Our experience is, and other instructors concur, that unstructured journals too often become mere logs of events rather than reflective activities in which students consider their service activities in light of the educational objectives of the course. Table 1 identifies some ways that journals can be structured to transcend mere description and promote connections between the course content and the service activities.

EXPERIENTIAL RESEARCH PAPER. An experiential research paper is a formal paper based on the experiential learning theory.[17] Students are asked to identify a particular experience or set of events at a service site and to reflect upon and analyze the experience within a broader context in order to make recommendations for subsequent action. For example, in order to complete this assignment, students might be asked at mid-semester to identify and describe a perplexing, frustrating, or confusing experience at the service site. Students then identify an important social issue that may be underlying this circumstance (e.g., health care to homeless youth, eating disorders among adolescent girls, volunteer recruitment strategies). They identify the multiple perspectives from which the issue can be analyzed and how it might be the basis for making recommendations to influence community agency operations, policies, or procedures. Students then locate articles in professional journals and other relevant sources to provide a conceptual framework for the issue. During the second half of the semester, students use d-us research to write a formal paper that analyzes the social issue and includes recommendations.

**ETHICAL CASE STUDY.** At the service site students frequently encounter events that raise not only intellectual and practical, but also moral and ethical, issues. In this reflection activity, students are asked to write case studies of an ethical dilemma they confronted at the service site, including a description of the context, the individuals involved, and the controversy or dilemma they observed. Case studies can be written to include course content, as appropriate. Once the case studies are developed, they can provide the bases for formal papers, class presentations, or structured group discussions. These case studies are particularly well suited to an exploration and clarification of values because their diverse perspectives allow students to discuss the issue from alternative points of view. Lisman's seven-step method for discussing case studies can be adapted to service learning classes.[18]

**DIRECTED READINGS.** Some textbooks might not adequately challenge students to consider how knowledge within a discipline can be applied to the service site. This may particularly be the case for civic, moral, or systemic issues that students encounter. Additional readings that effectively probe these issues and prompt consideration of the relevance and limitations of course content can be assigned. The directed readings might come from the discipline. Alternatively, books that contain selected readings or chapters might be appropriate, including *Service-Learning Reader; Reflections and Perspectives on Service; Education for Democracy; The Call of Service and Common Fire.*[19] Students can be asked to write a two-page summary of the reading and its relevance to their service experience.

**CLASS PRESENTATION.** Students can share experiences, service accomplishments, or products created during their service in classroom presentations that use videos, PowerPoint, bulletin boards, panel discussions, or speeches. These presentations provide excellent opportunities for students to organize their experiences, develop creative displays, and publicly celebrate their accomplishments. Community agency personnel can be invited to these presentations.

**ELECTRONIC REFLECTION.** Reflective exercises and dialogue interactions can occur through various means. Service learning practitioners are currently exploring the manner in which electronic modalities can be used as replacements for or supplements to traditional reflection activities. The recent book edited by James-Deramo is an important resource for educators interested in using Web-based modes of communication (e.g., class home pages, chat rooms, on-fine survey forms), electronic mail, and class listservs to present material; structure discussions; submit reflective journal entries; and deal with issues at the service site. This resource also highlights ways to build learning communities among students and instructors by using technology.[20]

## ASSESSING REFLECTION

**SELECTION AND DESIGN OF REFLECTION ACTIVITIES.** Designing reflection activities for a service learning class requires careful thought about the nature, structure, and function of each component. These considerations must incorporate other class assignments, whether or not all students are involved in service learning. Optional service might limit the use of class discussion and the variety of forms and modalities of reflection. In addition, we have suggested that effective reflection should observe the following five guidelines: reflection activities should (a) clearly link the service experience to the course content and learning objectives; (b) be structured in terms of description, expectations, and the criteria for assessing the activity; (c) occur regularly during the semester so that students can practice reflection and develop the capacity to engage in deeper and broader reflection; (d) provide feedback from the instructor about at least some of the reflection activities so that students learn how to improve their critical analysts and develop from reflective practice; and (e) include the opportunity for students to explore, clarify, and alter their values.[21]

## Table 2
### Bradley's Criteria for Assessing Levels of Reflection

Level One
1. Gives examples of observed behaviors or characteristics of the client or setting, but provides no insight into reasons behind the observation; observations tend to become dimensional and conventional or unassimilated repetitions of what has been heard in class or from peers.
2. Tends to focus on just one aspect of the situation.
3. Uses unsupported personal beliefs as frequently as "hard" evidence.
4. May acknowledge differences of perspective but does not discriminate effectively among them.

Level Two
1. Observations are fairly thorough and nuanced although they tend not to be placed in a broader context.
2. Provides a cogent critique from one perspective, but fails to see the broader system in which the aspect is embedded and other factors that may make change difficult.
3. Uses both unsupported personal belief and evidence but is beginning to be able to differentiate between them.
4. Perceives legitimate differences of viewpoint.
5. Demonstrates a beginning ability to interpret evidence.

Level Three
1. Views things from multiple perspectives; able to observe multiple aspects of the situation and place them in context.
2. Perceives conflicting goals within and among the individuals involved in a situation and recognizes that the differences can be evaluated.
3. Recognizes that actions must be situationally dependent and understands many of the factors that affect their choice.
4. Makes appropriate judgments based on reasoning and evidence.
5. Has a reasonable assessment of the importance of the decisions facing clients and of his or her responsibility as a part of the clients' lives.

OUTCOME. Students differ in how easily they engage in reflection and how quickly they mature in ability to learn from reflection. Table 2 presents a set of criteria developed by Bradley to assess levels of reflection.[22] Presenting these criteria to students prior to reflection activities can be helpful in creating expectations about their own development as reflective learners. Students can also be asked to evaluate their reflection activities with the criteria prior to evaluation by the instructor This exercise provides opportunities for self-evaluation by the students as well as occasions to compare student and instructor assessments.

## CONSEQUENCES OF REFLECTION

Little research has been conducted on how the amount or type of reflection activity is related to student outcomes. Mabry conducted analyses across twenty-three different service learning classes. The results tabulated the responses of students who engaged in classroom reflection activities (e.g., discussion groups with other students, using experiences in class, being asked in class for examples from service experience) and participated in face-to-face discussions with site supervisors, course instructors, and other students attributed more learning to the service experience than did students who had not engaged in those reflection activities.[23] These effects were significant after controlling for demographic variables, pre-test variables, and other independent variables.

There may be other benefits for the learner who engages in reflection in addition to course-specific learning outcomes. Pennebaker, Kiecolt-Glaser, and Glaser's experimental study manipulated whether college students wrote on four consecutive days about either traumatic experiences or superficial topics. Those who wrote about the traumatic event, compared to the other group, had more favorable immune-system responses, less-frequent health-center visits, and higher subjective well-being.[24] Similar effects have been found in other studies conducted by Pennebaker and colleagues.

> Writing about emotional upheavals has been found to improve the physical and mental health of grade-school children and nursing home residents, arthritis sufferers, medical school students, maximum-security prisoners, new mothers, and rape victims. Not only are there benefits to health, but writing about emotional topics has been found to reduce anxiety and depression, improve grades in college, and...aid people in securing new jobs.[25]

Pennebaker also reports on analyses of the essay's content to determine if characteristics of the narratives were related to the writer's subsequent health and well-being. The most important factor that differentiated persons showing health improvements from those who did not was the improved ability to include causal thinking, insight, and self-reflection in their stories. Thus, reflection activities that promote personally meaningful as well as academically meaningful explorations of experiences encountered in service settings may yield health as well as intellectual benefits to students.

However, the instructors should keep in mind the risks associated with structured, ongoing reflection activities in a service learning course. Batson, Fultz, Schoenrade, and Paduano conducted studies that examined the effects that critical self-reflection can have on the perceived motives of someone who has helped others. Critical self-reflection is an honest attempt to answer the question, "Why really am I doing good?" Batson and his colleagues found that critical self-reflection caused a self-deprecating bias that eroded the attribution that helping was done for altruistic reasons.[26] The effect was particularly strong for individuals who valued honest self-knowledge and those who were cognizant of the personal gain they would receive by helping others. It is interesting that all three of these conditions (reflection on motives, promoting self-knowledge, and personal gains for helping—e.g., course credit) can exist in service learning courses.

## CONCLUSION

Higher education has experienced a tremendous growth in service learning courses during the 1990s. This growth has been supported by funds and technical assistance provided by the Corporation for National Service and Campus Compact to promote service learning. Through "Learn and Serve America: Higher Education" grants, the corporation has stimulated the creation of thousands of service-learning courses. Similarly, Campus Compact estimates that 11,800 service-learning courses are available to students on its member campuses. As service learning becomes a more integral part of the curriculum, the manner in which it can improve educational goals needs better understanding.

Altman describes three distinct types of knowledge: content knowledge (i.e., rote learning of content), process knowledge (e.g., skills), and socially relevant knowledge.[27] Traditional instructional methods may effectively produce content knowledge and possibly process knowledge. However, service learning can promote both content and process knowledge,[28] and it is particularly well-suited for developing socially relevant knowledge in students. How reflection activities are designed plays an important role in their capacity to yield learning, support personal growth, provide insight, develop skills, and promote civic responsibility.

Trosset found that students often view discussions with peers, particularly discussion about race, gender, and sexual preference, as primarily forums for advocacy and persuading others to accept new viewpoints on controversial issues.[29] Discussions were not viewed by students as ways to explore differences through dialogue. Droge and Heiss, however, found a contrasting picture:

students endorsed discussions with peers as opportunities to learn from others, to have their views challenged, and to use materials other than their personal experiences to inform and change their views.[30] These contrasting cases in higher education should alert educators to the different assumptions that students may bring to experiential and educational activities. Differences such as these will be present among service learning students. Creating a classroom climate of trust and respect is an essential element in fostering reflective practice among students; students who are more skeptical of the process can be supported in Liking personal risks in the learning process.

These differences also highlight how the structure of a reflection activity can influence the results of a service experience: whether they will be educative and lead to new ways of thinking and acting, or miseducative and reinforce existing schemata and stereotypes. For service learning to educate students toward a more active role in community, careful attention must be given to reflection. Reflection activities must allow students to discover the value of dialogue, embrace the importance of perplexity in the learning process, and develop the ability to make meaning of personal experience.

## REFERENCES

1. John Dewey, *Democracy and Education* (New York: Macmillan Inc., 1916).

2. Task Group on General Education, *Strong Foundations: Principles for Effective General Education Programs.* (Washington, D.C.: Association of American Colleges, 1994).

3. Robert G. Bringle and Julie A. Hatcher, "A Service-learning Curriculum for Faculty." *Michigan Journal of Community Service-Learning.* 2 (1995): 112.

4. Edward Zlotkowski, "Pedagogy and Engagement," in *Colleges and Universities as Citizens,* ed. Robert Bringle, Rich Games, and Edward Malloy (Boston: Allyn & Bacon, (1999): 9-120.

5. Julie A. Hatcher and Robert G. Bringle, "Reflections: Bridging the Gap between Service and Learning," *Journal of College Teaching.* 45 (1997): 153.

6. Dewey, *Democracy and Education,* 144.

7. John Dewey, *How We Think: A Restatement of the Relation of Reflective Thinking to the Educative Process* (Boston: D.C. Heath and Company, 1933),146.

8. Ibid., 3.

9. James Gouinlock, ed., *The Moral Writings of John Dewey* (New York: Prometheus Books, 1994), xxxvi.

10. Dwight E. Giles and Janet Eyler, "The Theoretical Roots of Service-learning in John Dewey: Towards a Theory of Service-learning," *Michigan Journal of Community Service Learning.* 1 (1994): 77-85.

11. Dewey, *How We Think*, 14.

12. Julie A. Hatcher, "The Moral Dimensions of John Dewey's Philosophy: Implications for Undergraduate Education," *Michigan Journal of Community Service Learning.* 4 (1997): 22-29.

13. Giles and Eyler, "The Theoretical Roots of Service-learning."

14. Dewey, *How We Think*.

15. Janet Eyler, Dwight E. Giles, and Angela Schmiede, *A Practitioner's Guide to Reflection in Service-learning: Student Voices and Reflections* (Nashville: Vanderbilt University, 1996).

16. James W. Pennebaker, *Opening Up: The Healing Power of Expressing Emotions*. New York: Guilford Press, 1990), 40.

17. David A. Kolb, Experiential Learning. *Experience as the Source of Learning and Development* (Englewood Cliffs, NJ.: Prentice-Hall, 1984).

18. C. David Lisman, *The Curricular Integration of Ethics: Theory and Practice* (Westport: Praeger Publishing, 1995).

19. Gail Albert, ed., *Service-learning Reader: Reflections and Perspectives on Service* (Raleigh: National Society for Experiential Education, 1994); Benjamin R. Barber and Richard M. Battistoni, eds., *Education for Democracy* (Dubuque: Kendall/Hunt, 1993); Robert Coles, *The Call of Service: A Witness to Idealism* (New York: Houghton Mifflin, 1993); Laurent A. Daloz, et al., *Common Fire: Lives of Commitment in a Complex World* (Boston: Beacon Press, 1996).

20. Michele James-Deramo, ed., *Best Practices in Cyber-Serve: Integrating Technology with Service- Learning Instruction* (Virginia Tech Service-Learning Center: Corporation for National Service, 1999).

21. Hatcher and Bringle, "Reflections."

22. James Bradley, "A Model for Evaluating Student Learning in Academically Based Service," *Connecting Cognition and Action: Evaluation of Student Performance in Service Learning Courses*, ed. Marie Troppe (Denver: Education Commission of the States/ Campus Compact, 1995).

23. J. Beth Mabry, "Pedagogical Variations in Service-Learning and Student Outcomes: How Time, Contact, and Reflection Matter," *Michigan Journal of Community Service Learning.* 5 (1998): 34.

24. James W. Pennebaker, Janice Kiecolt-Glaser, and Ronald Glaser, "Disclosure of Traumas and Immune Function: Health Implications for Psychotherapy," *Journal of Consulting and Clinical Psychology.* 56.2 (1988): 239-45.

25. Pennebaker, *Opening Up*, 40.

26. C. Daniel Batson, et al., "Critical Self-Reflection and Self-Perceived Altruism: When Self-Reward Fails," *Journal of Personality and Social Psychology.* 53 (1987): 594-602.

27. Irwin Altman, "Higher Education and Psychology in the Millennium," *American Psychologist.* 51 (1996): 371-98.

28. Randall E. Osborne, Sharon Hammerich, and Chanin Hensley, "Student Effects of Service-learning: Tracking Change across a Semester," *Michigan Journal of Community Service Learning.* 5 (1998): 5-13.

29. Carol Trosset, "Obstacles to Open Discussion and Critical Thinking: The Grinnell College Study," *Change.* 30.5 (1998): 44-49.

30. David Droge and Janet Heiss, "Discussion and Critical Thinking among College Students: Are Grinnell Undergraduates Weird?" (Northwest Communication Association, Coeur d'Alene, ID, April 1999)

# Reading, Writing, and Reflection

by David D. Cooper

"WHAT REALLY IRKED ME about Betty's decision," Rudy writes in his journal, "was that it should have been an editorial decision based on layout, design balance, etc. Instead, it was based on a phony rationale. The incident had an adverse effect on my outlook towards service at the Center." Rudy explains:

> When Betty and I discussed the final edits for the newsletter, she also explained to me that there was to be a change in the layout: [U.S.] Senator [Spencer] Abraham would not have his picture included in his story [about renaissance zones in Michigan]. Another individual, Flint Mayor Woodrow Stanley, had just sent a photo of himself to accompany his article. Mayor Stanley happens to be Black. Since Newt Gingrich's photo was already running with his story [on the Earning by Learning program Gingrich founded for inner-city youngsters], it would be "more balanced" if we ran a photo of the Black gentleman and withheld Abraham's, providing an element of diversity...I am simply tired of hearing we should/should not do something based on the color of a person's skin. This type of action does nothing to advance the fight against discrimination. It is a way for those in charge to give the appearance of a diversified newsletter...This one incident affected my outlook on the service I was doing.

As part of a required service learning component for his general education writing class, Rudy chose an assignment as newsletter assistant at his university's outreach office for economic development and urban affairs, where he works closely with Betty, editing articles that appear in the Center's monthly newsletter. The community placements chosen for students in Rudy's class were carefully selected as good sites for "real time" writing projects that address tangible and responsive audiences and link writing in a field of the student's choosing—in Rudy's case, public administration—with formal classroom based writing activities and instruction. In addition to writing for an agency, students are required to keep a written journal record that functions both as further writing practice and, more important, as opportunities for students to reflect critically and systematically on their service experiences.

In his next journal entry, Rudy relates an incident that has no ostensible bearing on diversity policy. At the prompting of his teacher, Rudy chooses instead to write about Betty herself, seeking some insight into her personality and the character of her commitment.

> As we were leaving the Center last Tuesday so that Betty could give me a ride home the family that lives next door to the Center arrived home. They were obviously an economically disadvantaged family, since they lived in a less affluent part of the city. As Betty was getting in the car, the little girl from next door called her name and came racing over. Immediately Betty gave the little girl a big hug, and asked about her day at school, etc. This scene may have had nothing to do with my work, and it may have been just a minor event in the grand scheme of things, but it touched me. Here was a woman that was so compassionate and caring, and here was a little girl who respected and appreciated this relationship so much. It really gave me a bit of insight into Betty's nature. It became clear why she was working at the Center. She was inherently a person with a great deal of love to give. That's simply a part of her make-up, and it was evidenced by this scene. One could tell that Betty truly believed that nothing, not even a poor economic

situation, could hinder this young girl's future. And I think I felt the same.

Even though Rudy takes pains to point out that the scene in the driveway "may have had nothing to do with my [actual] work," it still has powerful resonance for his attitude toward service and the legitimacy of his service-learning assignment at the Center. Indirectly, even covertly, Rudy's discovery of the depth and authenticity of Betty's commitment to economic Justice surely complicates, as his teacher may have hoped, that attitude of certainty he had earlier used to dismiss Betty's editorial decision as partisan and politically motivated.

## STRUCTURING CRITICAL REFLECTION: THE CRITICAL INCIDENT JOURNAL

The journals that Rudy and his classmates kept are modeled on the critical incident journal format devised by Stanton (1995). The "critical incident" technique differs from more traditional journal narratives in several ways. Primarily, as Stanton explains to students, "Rather than [providing] a descriptive record of daily life, a critical incident journal includes detailed analysis of only those incidents which change you or your perspective on your service experience...Rather than simply describing and interpreting an incident and the people involved," Stanton continues, "this reflective technique enables [you] to use the incident and its impact as a means for self-monitoring and personal exploration" (p. 59). In addition to identifying an event and describing its relevant details, the critical incident journal format requires students to pursue the three rhetorical steps of description, analysis, and reflection.

**STEP 1.** Describe your role in the incident. What did you do? How did you react? How did others react?

**STEP 2.** Analyze the incident. How well or how poorly did you understand the situation? Was your reaction—or the reaction of others—well informed or based on misinformation? How did you handle it? What would you do differently next time?

**STEP 3.** What impact did the incident have on you? Why do you view it as "critical"? How has the incident influenced your feelings about working at your placement site? What have you learned? How has your perspective on yourself or others been changed and/or reinforced? Where do you go from here?

When responding to his first journal entry, Rudy's teacher notes that he describes the incident surrounding Betty's photo layout decision with precision and good detail, but his reaction to it, she suggests, may be more emotive ("What really irked me . . .") than critically reflective. She encourages him either to revisit the incident in another entry or select a new incident to write about with special attention to fleshing out Step 3. Rudy's teacher also wisely defers direct comment on Rudy's conclusion that the episode over the picture layout evidences a phony diversity policy. Nor does she broach the issue of Rudy's boilerplate conservatism, a political alignment he had proudly and skillfully underscored in earlier journal entries as though itching to provoke her own liberalism. Instead, she focuses on the way Rudy "bookends" his journal entry with references to unarticulated changes in attitude. She encourages Rudy to spell out the exact changes in his outlook toward service brought about by the incident. In an effort to redirect his antagonism, she also urges him to write about another incident at the Center that either confirms or perhaps confounds his strong belief that Betty's editorial decision grew out of a bogus rationale for racial diversity.

With the help of the critical incident format, Rudy's teacher provides new conditions and ramifications that seek to redirect Rudy's natural powers of curiosity into investigations that are more intellectually responsible and more critically engaged. In doing so, she seizes on the rival interpretations that open Rudy's first passage to critical scrutiny—what John Dewey (1933) called "the strife of alternative interpretations" (p. 121). It may not be enough, she suggests, to be "simply tired of hearing" about racial diversity. She persists in posing questions that push Rudy to think in new ways, to reflect critically, and to question his own perceptions of what he considers a critical incident at the Center. Why, for example, should one choose pictures for a newsletter based on typographic considerations alone? Do race-based editorial decisions over layout send important and defensible messages to readers in support of diversity? Which of these competing interpretations has the rightful claim? What implications, she hints, might that "rightful claim" have for Betty's integrity?

## TRANSFORMING VALUES THROUGH REFLECTION

The narrative development between Rudy's two journal entries—from static indignation to dynamic reaffirmation, from annoyance to rectitude—captures, in fact, what Dewey considered as the primary function of reflective thought: "to transform a situation in which there is experienced conflict [or] disturbance of some sort, into a situation that is clear, coherent, settled, harmonious...Genuine thinking winds up, in short, with an appreciation of new values" (1933, pp. 100-101).

It is important to point out that Rudy continues to write favorably about articles and opinions advancing the conservative agenda. "The key to turning around the urban disadvantaged," he later writes, "lies in programs that promote rugged individualism, rather than encouraging people to expect a handout." His curiosity and powers of inquiry shift, however, to the moral integrity of those who act on behalf of policy and away from the validity or political viability of the policies themselves. Rudy's political conservatism begins to expand and take on a communitarian ring—once again illustrating Dewey's belief that "all reflective thinking is a process of detecting relations" (1933, p. 77). For example, Rudy writes that "one can show their [sic] compassion by forming ideas...such as [about how] people help themselves," and that urban renewal policies must "provide a greater good: helping the community as a whole." His new interests in moral consensus and the common good, moreover, reveal the kinds of social attitudes that naturally grow out of reflective thought and, as Dewey further believed, are indispensable to the nurture of democracy and responsible citizenship.

"The clear consciousness of a communal life, in all its implications," according to Dewey, "constitutes the idea of democracy" (Robertson, 1992, p. 341). That clarifying consciousness can be seen in Rudy's willingness to reevaluate his beliefs in light of Betty's different attitude about photo layout and diversity, Rudy's reconsideration of public policy in terms of the community as a whole, and ultimately (what he may have been most "touched by" when the child raced over to embrace Betty) his realization that one's own good cannot be easily separated from the good of others.

In many respects, Rudy's experience at the Center encapsulates a tension among service learning educators and practitioners that is best resolved through the use of structured critical reflection exercises and techniques like the critical incident journal. Should Rudy's teacher, to put it bluntly, set out to redirect, indeed redress, his political and social conservatism? Or is Rudy's social consciousness incidental to the academic

work going on at the intersection of his assignment at the Center and his enrollment in a writing class at his university? What is the proper character, in other words, of her intervention? Should the goal of a service-learning-infused curriculum be the preparation of students like Rudy for social action skills? Or should the goal be to develop intellectual competence and working knowledge in service of students' courses of academic study? To track Rudy's learning curve along separate social and cognitive spectra may beg, however, the wrong questions. Rudy's case may suggest that solving social problems vis-á-vis active community involvement and engaging intellectual processes may be more complementary than polarized. Rudy simultaneously learns to apply critical intelligence to his political beliefs while he engages in a practice of building democratic awareness and democratic community at the Center. He submits his political beliefs to the stimulus of critical reflection, not to a political litmus. He learns to formulate new questions about old habits of thought. He learns the important difference between an opinion passionately felt and powerfully held and a problem that needs to be solved and for which answers must be sought. He undergoes what Kolb (1984) describes as "learning [that] transforms...impulses, feelings, and desires...into higher-order purposeful action" (p. 22). If anything, ideology loses its exclusive and unchallenged grip on Rudy's political conservatism. His passion for rugged individualism now carries an ethical valence that transforms it into a more socially responsive conservatism: a conservatism, it could be said, with an articulate moral philosophy.

In the development of his narrative reflections, Rudy discovers that a valuation he previously held no longer works well for him. He could no longer satisfactorily dismiss Betty's editorial decision as politically motivated and, as such, rooted shallowly in ideological ground. He begins instead to experiment with alternative modes of valuation based on ethical and moral criteria and then to test those criteria experimentally to find out whether a life, as well as social policy, can be guided more satisfactorily according to them. Rudy is clearly more moved by the Betty who elicits the child's tender affections than he is by the Betty who makes an editorial decision based on racial balance. Given his teacher's encouragement to rethink his beliefs through the encounter with someone who believes differently, Rudy learns more about diversity—its complexity, its interpersonal ramifications, its socioethical consequences, its rootedness in the common good—than he

## EXPERIENTIAL ROOTS OF REFLECTIVE THINKING

In a word, Rudy undergoes what several generations of modern educational theorists, beginning with Dewey and cresting in the more recent work of Kolb, refer to formally as an experiential learning cycle that is driven, in large part, by the adaptive learning modality of reflective observation. Arguing for the reflexive nature of learning processes, Kolb (1984) acknowledges the dynamic spiral character of knowledge formation and its anchorage in a student's concrete, lived experience. Rudy's service learning assignment at the Center provides a good case for what Dewey and Kolb view as the "situatedness of reflective thinking" (Dewey, 1933, p. 99) that is both the indispensable agent and the object of knowledge formation. Follow the thread of an idea or "the stuff of knowledge far enough," Dewey writes, "and you will find some situation that is directly experienced, something undergone, done, enjoyed, or suffered, and not just thought of. Reflection is occasioned by the character of this primary situation. It does not merely grow out of it" (1933, p. 99).

Reflective thinking is not only an organic component in the learning cycle, it is simultaneously the very ground from which knowledge and belief spring. Reflective thinking, in short, is both process and product. As such, reflective thinking has become a key subject in the massive literature of experiential learning theory and, more recently, the operational linchpin of contemporary service learning pedagogy (Boud, Keogh, and Walker, 1984; King and Kitchener, 1994; Silcox, 1993).

## THEORETICAL FOUNDATIONS OF REFLECTIVE THINKING

Dewey (1933) presents one of the most durable cases, as Kolb (1984) acknowledges, for the critical primacy of structured reflective thinking in the educative process. Together with other significant works, Dewey (1916, 1938) left an intellectual legacy that best articulates that educative process through the guiding principles of experiential learning, including the cultivation and expression of a student's individuality, the transformation of the classroom into a venue for free and independent activity, inquiry, and thought, and the importance of learning through experience. Growing out of his abiding faith in the scientific method and experimentalism and his deep dedication to radical democracy as the model for progressive education, Dewey argues that reflective thinking is both the means and end that should be cultivated by education, properly considered.

Dewey defines reflective thinking succinctly as "active, persistent and careful consideration of any belief or supposed form of knowledge in the light of the grounds that support it and the further conclusions to which it tends" (1933, p. 9). Extending his definition into the sphere of pedagogical practice, Dewey argues that reflective thought results from "careful and extensive study,...purposeful widening of the area of observation [under study],...[and] reasoning out the conclusions of alternative conceptions, to see what would follow in case one or the other were adopted for belief" (1933, p. 8). For Dewey, reflective thinking is essential to the pragmatic application of the scientific attitude and outlook to human life and education. It therefore encompasses cognitive processes such as the logical management of an orderly chain of ideas to a controlling purpose and end, social or democratic functions called upon when public conflicts demand resolution through common problem solving and effective public discourse, and the ethical skills that Dewey adopts as the ground of reflective thinking: open-mindedness, whole-heartedness, and intellectual responsibility.

Reflective thinking is always inaugurated by what Dewey calls a "forked-road" situation in which a student faces an ambiguous dilemma that confronts him or her with the reliability and the worth of a previously held belief. "Difficulty or obstruction," Dewey continues, "in the way of reaching a belief brings us...to a pause. In the suspense of uncertainty[,]...demand for the solution of a perplexity is the steadying and guiding factor in the entire process of reflection" (1933, p. 14). Kolb synthesizes Dewey's point into one of the central premises of current experiential learning theory. "The process of learning," Kolb (1984) states, "requires the resolution of conflicts between dialectically opposed modes of adaptation to the world" (p. 29). Kolb is quick to add that "reflective observation abilities" are indispensable agents in that experience of adaptation.

Dewey takes pains to break down that process of engaging a dilemma into multiple aspects or "terminals" of reflective activity that span three progressive stages: problematization, hypothesis formation, and testing of the hypothesis. "Reflective thinking," Dewey summarizes, "involves (1) a state of doubt, hesitation, perplexity, mental difficulty, in which thinking originates, and (2) an act of searching, hunting, inquiring, to find material that will resolve the doubt, settle and dispose of the perplexity" (1933, p. 12). The movement from doubt to the disposition of a perplexity is engendered, first and foremost, by what Dewey insists are the critical conditions under which students must work and learn: "the provision of a real situation that arouses inquiry, suggestion, reasoning, testing, etc." (p. 283). This emphasis on the situatedness of reflective observation and its centrality to the learning process leads to a statement of Kolb's that has become a widely quoted catch phrase of the contemporary experiential learning movement: "Learning is the process whereby knowledge is created through the transformation of experience" (1984, p. 38).

## PRACTICING CRITICAL REFLECTION

Among the many successful efforts to render Dewey and Kolb's theories of reflective thinking into practical classroom application (Silcox, 1993; Goldsmith, 1995), Eyler, Giles, and Schmiede's 1996 *A Practitioner's Guide to Reflection in Service-Learning* stands out as particularly illuminating and incisive. They succeed in putting theory into practice, but, more important, their guide to reflection activities and techniques grows out of hundreds of structured interviews with students across the country enrolled in service learning courses. "The experiences of the students we encountered through this study," the authors write, emphasize "that reflection is the glue that holds service and learning together to provide [optimal] educative experiences" (p. 16).

The authors' research indicates that there are four principal criteria for successful application of reflective thinking to students' service learning experiences. They compress these criteria into "the 4 Cs of reflection." "Over the course of this study," they conclude, "certain themes have reappeared repeatedly as critical factors in effective reflective activity. The best reflection is Continuous in time frame, Connected to the 'big picture' information provided by academic pursuits, Challenging to assumptions and complacency, and Contextualized in terms of design and setting" (p. 21).

In using their interview data to structure reflection guidelines, Eyler, Giles, and Schmiede stress that reflection activities must flex according to various student learning styles. After all, students "learn to learn" in different ways. Therefore, faculty and coordinators involved with service learning should ideally offer a variety of reflection activities that accommodate differences across the range of student learning styles, which Eyler, Giles, and Schmiede identify as activists, reflectors, theorists, and pragmatists. In addition, the authors offer a "Reflection Activity Matrix" that reminds service-minded educators just how integral critical reflection is to other learning activities and modalities.

## FROM EXPECTATION TO EXPERIENCE

As service learning practitioners themselves, Eyler, Giles, and Schmiede realize that the most important element in effective reflection is also the most difficult and problematic for teachers to implement successfully: the challenge of pushing students to think critically and to engage issues in a more critically reflective way. Challenging reflection involves a hard balancing act. A teacher must be willing to intervene, pose tough questions, and propose often uncomfortable points of view for a student's consideration. A teacher must also be ready to back off and give support in order to nurture the independence and autonomy that are the lifeblood of experiential learning processes. Revisiting Rudy's service learning experience may suggest that achieving this balance is not strictly a matter of adopting frameworks and guidelines or following rules, but it is more a question of taking what service learning practitioners recognize as the path to critical learning: "Learning is best conceived as a process…grounded in experience, not in terms of outcomes," as Kolb puts it, and "a process…continuously modified by experience" (1984, pp. 26–27). In other words, a good teacher is prepared to set his or her students upon a journey to knowledge, and then be willing to go along for the ride.

Returning to Rudy's service learning assignment at the Center, much to his own credit he sets out to inquire into the meaning of what he learns and what difference it may have to his conservative beliefs. That search for meaning begins in Dewey's "forked-road" situation and it follows, as predicted by Kolb, a trajectory of transformation. On the one hand, Betty's editorial decision initially demonstrates to Rudy that diversity is only a matter of "appearances." Therefore, he is inclined to dismiss Betty's actions as arbitrary. But given the interpersonal realities Rudy faces in his actual working relationship at the Center (because his learning process is situated and grounded in lived experience), does it follow, as logically perhaps it must, that Betty is an arbitrary person? Should he not respect her?

Rudy's teacher occasions the ambiguity by inviting Rudy to probe into the implications that Betty's layout decision has for changes in his attitudes about working at the Center. He must squarely face the antagonism he writes about in his journal over this incident against the great enthusiasm he has when returning to work at the Center—for Rudy continues to speak about how "stimulating" his service has been and how he is "gaining a better understanding of the nuts and bolts of editing a newsletter...while also looking at Michigan's distressed communities and ways to revitalize them." Rudy's teacher also positions Rudy in such a way that he has to confront and work through some unstated assumptions he might be making. Is Betty an enforcer of orthodoxy? And what about the Mayor of Flint? Were it not for the color of his skin, would he deserve his picture on the newsletter cover? Paraphrasing Dewey, Rudy's teacher seizes on the real possibilities the incident harbors for Rudy to examine his assumptions more carefully and extensively, to widen the area of his inquiry into a cherished belief, and to follow his reasoning all the way to conclusions and alternatives he had not before considered due to the narrow depth of field compassed by his initial dismissal of Betty's decision as biased and unfair. Rudy's teacher problematizes his strongly held belief that diversity is a matter of "appearances" alone and "does nothing to advance the fight against discrimination." She provides impetus to Rudy's formation of a hypothesis concerning whether Betty's diversity policy is only skin-deep. Rudy tests the hypothesis. He probes into the reliability of a belief that once seemed so indisputable and obvious, and he finds it wanting in light of his discovery of Betty's real passion for community.

Rudy's learning occurs right at the place Kolb (1984) describes as "the interplay between expectation and experience," an interplay mediated by reflective thinking. Dewey (1933) reminds us that, like Rudy, we all have the tendency to believe that which is in harmony with desire. We take that to be true which we should like to have so, and contrary ideas have difficulty gaining lodgment. We draw weak conclusions as we fall to examine and test our ideas because of personal attitudes. When we generalize, we tend to make sweeping assertions based on only a few cases. Observation also reveals the powerful force wielded by social influences that have actually nothing to do with the truth or falsity of what is asserted and denied. As such, Kolb wisely concludes, "If the education process begins by bringing out the learner's beliefs and theories, examining them and testing them, and then integrating the new, more refined ideas into the person's belief systems, the learning process," as in Rudy's case, "will be facilitated" (1984, p. 27).

## REFERENCES

Boud, D., Keogh, R., and Walker, D. (eds.). *Reflection: Turning Experience into Learning.* New York: Routledge, 1984.

Dewey, J. *Democracy and Education.* New York: Free Press, 1916.

Dewey, J. *How We Think.* New York: Heath, 1933.

Dewey, J. *Experience and Education.* New York: Collier, 1938.

Eyler, J., Giles, D. E., and Schmiede, A. *A Practitioner's Guide to Reflection in Service Learning: Student Voices and Reflections.* Nashville, Tenn.: Vanderbilt University, 1996.

Goldsmith, S. *Journal Reflection: A Resource Guide for Community Service Leaders and Educators Engaged in Service Learning.* Washington, D.C.: The American Alliance for Rights and Responsibilities, 1995.

King, P. M., and Kitchener, K. S. *Developing Reflective Judgment: Understanding and Promoting Intellectual Growth and Critical Thinking in Adolescents and Adults.* San Francisco: Jossey-Bass, 1994.

Kolb, D. A. *Experiential Learning: Experience As the Source of Learning and Development.* Englewood Cliffs, NJ: Prentice Hall, 1984.

Robertson, E. "Is Dewey's Educational Vision Still Viable?" *Review of Research in Education,* 1992,18,335–381.

Silcox, H. C. *A How-to Guide to Reflection: Adding Cognitive Learning to Community Service Programs.* Philadelphia: Brighton Press, 1993.

Stanton, T. K. "Writing About Public Service: The Critical Incident Journal. In M. Ford and A. Watters (eds.), *Guide for Change: Resources for Implementing Community Service Writing.* New York: McGraw-Hill, 1995.

# Reflection:
## Recommended Reading

## BOOKS & CHAPTERS

Brookfield, S. (1995). *Becoming a critically reflective teacher.* San Francisco: Jossey-Bass.

Eyler, J., Giles, D., & Schmiede, A. (1996). *A practitioner's guide to reflection in service-learning: Student voices and reflections.* Nashville: Vanderbilt University Press.

Goldsmith, S. (1995). *Journal reflection: A resource guide for community service leaders and educators engaged in service-learning.* Washington, DC: The American Alliance for Rights and Responsibilities.

King, P.M. & Kitchner, K.S. (1994). *Developing reflective judgment: Understanding and promoting intellectual growth and critical thinking in adolescents and adults.* San Francisco: Jossey-Bass.

National Helpers Network. (1998). *Reflection: The key to service-learning.* New York: National Helpers Network Inc.

Reed, J. & Koliba, C. (1996). *Facilitating reflection: A manual for higher education.* Washington, DC: Volunteer and Public Service Center, Georgetown University.

Rhoads, R. & Howard, J. (Eds.). (1998). *Academic service-learning: A pedagogy of action and reflection.* New Directions for Teaching and Learning, No. 73. San Francisco: Jossey-Bass.

Schön, D. (1983). *The reflective practitioner: How professionals think in action.* New York: Basic Books.

Schön, D. (1987). *Educating the reflective practitioner.* San Francisco: Jossey-Bass.

Silcox, H. (1993). *A how-to guide to reflection: Adding cognitive learning to community service programs.* Philadelphia: Brighton Press.

Silcox, H. (1992). *An opportunity for experiential service-learning.* Philadelphia: Pennsylvania Institute for Environmental & Community Service Learning.

## ARTICLES & REPORTS

Campus Compact (n.d.). Using structured reflection to enhance learning from service. Available at www.compact.org/disciplines/reflection/index.html.

Conrad, D. & Hedin, D. (1990). Learning from service: Experience is the best teacher—Or is it?" In Kendall and Associates (Eds.), *Combining service and learning: A resource book for community and public service,* volume one (pp. 87–98). Raleigh, NC: National Society for Internships and Experiential Education.

Dunlap, M. (1997). The role of the personal fable in adolescent service-learning and critical reflection. *Michigan Journal of Community Service Learning, 4,* 56–63.

*Education and Urban Society,* February 1990. [Entire issue is a collection of articles on reflective practice.]

Eyler, J. (2001). Creating your reflection map. *New Directions for Higher Education, 114,* 35–43.

Kitchener, K.S. & Fisher, K.W. (1990). A skill approach to the development of reflective thinking. In D. Kuhn (Ed.), *Contributions to human development, 21: Developmental perspectives on teaching and learning thinking skills.* Basel, Switzerland: S Karger.

Kitchener, K.S., Lynch, C.L., Fisher, K.R., & Wood, P. (1993). Developmental range of reflective judgment: The effect of contextual support and practice on developmental stage. *Developmental Psychology, 29* (5), 893–906.

Kottkamp, R. (1990). Means for facilitating reflection. *Education and Urban Society, 22* (2), 182–203.

Litke, R.A. (2002). Do all students get it?: Comparing students' reflections to course performance. *Michigan Journal of Community Service Learning, 8* (2), 27–34.

Morton, K. (1993). Reflection in the classroom. In T. Kupiec (Ed.), *Rethinking tradition: Integrating service with academic study on college campuses.* Providence, RI: Campus Compact.

Scott, J. (1993). A journal workshop for coordinators. In J. Howard (Ed.), *Praxis II: Service-learning resources for university students, staff, and faculty.* Ann Arbor: Office of Community Service Learning, University of Michigan.

Trexler, C.J. (2001). Missing from our motto?: Learning to reflect. *The Agricultural Education Magazine, 74* (1), 4–5.

Wade, R.C. & Yarbrough, D.B. (1996). Portfolios: A tool for reflective thinking in teacher education? *Teaching and Teacher Education, 12* (1), 63–79.

Williams, D., & Driscoll A. (1997). Connecting curriculum content with community service: Guidelines for student reflection. *Journal of Public Service and Outreach, 2* (1), 33–42.

Williams, L.B. (1997). Slaughterhouse seven: Are there any epiphanies in killing chickens? *About Campus, 2* (4).

# Redesigning Curriculum

## TITLES INCLUDED IN THIS SECTION

Community Service Learning in the Curriculum,
BY JEFFREY HOWARD

Course Organization, BY KERRISSA HEFFERNAN AND
RICHARD CONE

Three Model Syllabi

Recommended Reading

## QUESTIONS FOR REFLECTION AND PLANNING

What could your students contribute to a community?
What could a community experience offer your
students?

Where would service be located in your course? What
are the logistical challenges with this model?

What significant changes will occur in your course as a
result of incorporating a service-learning component?
In your teaching methodology?

Which model of service-learning best describes your
service-learning course or courses?

Which model would be most appropriate to your
courses' goals and objectives?

How does or might your course incorporate the principles of engagement, reflection, reciprocity, and public
dissemination?

# Community Service Learning in the Curriculum

by Jeffrey Howard

MUCH OF THE ATTENTION AND SUPPORT for college student involvement in community service has focused on students' contributions to the community and on the development of students' lifelong civic responsibility. These are essential outcomes of a community service program. But there is more.

Community service learning, or service-learning as it is more commonly called, is a first cousin of community service. It, too, engages students in service to the community and contributes to the development of students' civic ethic. Where it differs is in its deliberateness about student learning. Though learning necessarily occurs in the act of serving in the community, with community service learning there is an intentional effort made to utilize the community service experience as a learning resource.

A number of possible avenues enable students to intentionally learn from their community service experiences. One option is for students to self-direct their learning, for example by keeping a reflective journal or by reading germane materials. A second option is for the campus community service program to provide a learning structure, such as a reflection guidebook or periodic seminars, for students placed in the community. Any of these intentional learning interventions would transform the community service to community service learning.

A third option is to have the community service integrated into an academic course. In this model, the community service experiences of the students are not just a sidebar but an integral component of the course. When used in this way, community service learning may be conceptualized as a pedagogical model that connects meaningful community service experiences with academic course learning.

## WHY INTEGRATE SERVICE INTO ACADEMIC COURSES?

There are some educationally sound reasons for integrating community service experiences into academic courses:

- faculty are well equipped to design effective assignments that enable students to capture the learning from their community service experiences

- students are more likely to intentionally learn because they are more accustomed to, and accountable for, learning in academic courses than in co-curricular activities

- community service experiences enhance academic learning

- community service experiences are important sources of knowledge and scholarship

- faculty can play a role in reducing the chances that students' stereotypes and preconceived notions about underserved populations are perpetuated

In addition, integrating service into the curriculum strengthens the prospect for the institutionalization of community service learning because:

- faculty are more likely to perceive community service as educationally valuable if the service occurs within, rather than outside of, the curriculum

- curricular efforts are a higher funding priority than co-curricular efforts

## PRINCIPLES OF GOOD PRACTICE IN COMMUNITY SERVICE LEARNING PEDAGOGY

The field of community service learning has a number of outstanding sets of principles of good practice, most notably the Johnson Foundation/Wingspread "Principles of Good Practice for Combining Service and Learning." However, these sets of principles have mostly focused on non-curricular community service learning programs. And though these prior principles have application to community service learning courses, they are insufficient for developing and implementing what is for many faculty a new kind of course. Therefore we offer the following set of principles of community service learning pedagogy, subscription to which will enable students' community learning to be fully integrated with, and utilized on behalf of, course learning.

The 10 principles below are derived from a host of sources, most notably the models depicted in this book, my 16 years of involvement with curriculum-based service-learning, and the candid responses of 10 University of Michigan academic leaders as part of the evaluation of our Kellogg Foundation grant.

None of these 10 principles are antithetical to, or inconsistent with, previously disseminated principles of good practice, and none of these will compromise the service that students provide in the community. On the contrary, these principles not only complement previously generated lists, but a number of them enhance the student's capacity to be of service in the community.

### Principle 1: Academic Credit Is for Learning, Not for Service

Credit in academic courses is assigned to students for the demonstration of academic learning. It should be no different in community service learning courses. Academic credit is for academic learning, and community service is not academic in nature. Therefore, the credit must not be for the performance of service. However, when community service is integrated into an academic course, the course credit is assigned for both the customary academic learning as well as for the utilization of the community learning in the service of the course learning. Similarly, the student's grade is for the quality of learning and not for the quality (or quantity) of service.

### Principle 2: Do Not Compromise Academic Rigor

Academic standards in a course are based on the challenge that readings, presentations, and assignments present to students. These standards ought to be sustained when adding a community service learning component. Though experience-based learning is frequently perceived to be less rigorous than academic learning, especially in scholarly circles, we advise against compromising the level of instructor expectation for student learning. The additional workload imposed by a community service assignment may be compensated by an additional credit, but not by lowering academic learning expectations. Adding a service component, in fact, may enhance the rigor of a course because, in addition to having to master the academic material, students must also learn how to learn from community experience and merge that learning with academic learning, and these are challenging intellectual activities that are commensurate with rigorous academic standards.

### Principle 3: Set Learning Goals for Students

Establishing learning goals for students is a standard to which all courses ought to be accountable. Not only should it be no different with community service learning courses, but in fact it is especially necessary and advantageous to do so with these kinds of courses. With the addition of the community as a learning context, there occurs a multiplication of learning paradigms (e.g., inductive learning, synthesis of theory and practice) and learning topics (e.g., the community, the population). To sort out those of greatest priority in the service of the course goals, as well as to best take advantage of the rich bounty of learning opportunity offered by the community, requires deliberate planning of the course learning goals.

### Principle 4: Establish Criteria for the Selection of Community Service Placements

To optimally utilize community service on behalf of course learning requires more than merely directing students to find a service placement. Faculty who are deliberate about establishing criteria for selecting community service placements will find that the learning that students extract from their respective service experiences will be of better use on behalf of course learning than if placement criteria are not established.

We offer three criteria as essential in all community service learning courses. First, the range of service placements ought to be circumscribed by the content of the course; homeless shelters and soup kitchens are learning appropriate placements for a course on homelessness, but placements in schools are not. Second, the duration of the service must be sufficient to enable the fulfillment of learning goals; a one-time two-hour shift at a hospital will do little for the learning in a course on institutional health care. And, third, the specific service activities and service contexts must have the potential to stimulate course-relevant learning; filing records in a warehouse may be of service to a school district, but it would offer little to stimulate learning in a course on elementary school education.

We also offer three guidelines regarding the setting of placement criteria. First, responsibility for ensuring that placement criteria are established that will enable the best student learning rests with the faculty. Second, the learning goals established for the course will be helpful in informing the placement criteria. And third, faculty who utilize the volunteer services office on campus or in the community to assist with identifying criteria-satisfying community agencies will reduce their start-up labor costs.

## Principle 5: Provide Educationally Sound Mechanisms to Harvest the Community Learning

Learning in any course is realized by the proper mix and level of learning formats and assignments. To maximize students' service experiences on behalf of course learning in a community service learning course requires more than sound service placements. Course assignments and learning formats must be carefully developed to facilitate the students' learning from their community service experiences as well as to enable its use on behalf of course learning. Assigning students to serve at a community agency, even a faculty approved one, without any mechanisms in place to harvest the learning therefrom is insufficient to contribute to course learning. Experience as a learning format, in and of itself, does not consummate learning, nor does mere written description of one's service activities.

Learning interventions that instigate critical reflection on and analysis of service experiences are necessary to enable community learning to be harvested and to serve as an academic learning enhancer. Therefore, discussions, presentations, and journal and paper assignments that provoke analysis of service experiences in the context of the course learning and that encourage the blending of the experiential and academic learnings are necessary to help ensure that the service does not underachieve in its role as an instrument of learning. Here, too, the learning goals set for the course will be helpful in informing the course learning formats and assignments.

## Principle 6: Provide Supports for Students to Learn How to Harvest the Community Learning

Harvesting the learning from the community and utilizing it on behalf of course learning are learning paradigms for which most students are under-prepared. Faculty can help students realize the potential of community learning by assisting students with the acquisition of skills necessary for gleaning the learning from the community and/or by providing examples of how to successfully do so. An example of the former would be to provide instruction on participant-observation skills; an example of the latter would be to make accessible a file containing past outstanding student papers and journals to current students in the course.

## Principle 7: Minimize the Distinction between Students' Community Learning Role and the Classroom Learning Role

Classrooms and communities are very different learning contexts, each requiring students to assume a different learner role. Generally, classrooms provide a high level of learning direction, with students expected to assume a largely learning-follower role. In contrast, communities provide a low level of learning direction, with students expected to assume a largely learning-leader role. Though there is compatibility between the level of learning direction and the expected student role within each of these learning contexts, there is incompatibility across them.

For students to have to alternate between the learning-follower role in the classroom and the learning-leader role in the community not only places yet another learning challenge on students but is inconsistent with good pedagogical principles. Just as we do not mix required lectures (high learning-follower role) with a student-determined reading list (high learning-leader role) in a traditional course, so, too, we must not impose conflicting learner role expectations on students in community service learning courses.

Therefore, if students are expected to assume a learning-follower role in the classroom, then a mechanism is needed that will provide learning direction for the students in the community (e.g., community agency staff serving in an adjunct instructor role); otherwise, students will enter the community wearing the inappropriate learning-follower hat. Correspondingly, if the students are expected to assume a learning-leader role in the community, then room must be made in the classroom for students to assume a learning-leader role; otherwise, students will enter the classroom wearing the inappropriate learning-leader hat. The more we can make consistent the student's learning role in the classroom with her/his learning role in the community, the better the chances that the learning potential within each context will be realized.

### Principle 8: Rethink the Faculty Instructional Role

Regardless of whether they assume learning-leader or learning-follower roles in the community, community service learning students are acquiring course-relevant information and knowledge from their service experiences. At the same time, as we previously acknowledged, students also are being challenged by the many new and unfamiliar ways of learning inherent in community service learning. Because students carry this new information and these learning challenges back to the classroom, it behooves service-learning faculty to reconsider their interpretation of the classroom instructional role. A shift in instructor role that would be most compatible with these new learning phenomena would move away from information dissemination and move toward learning facilitation and guidance. Exclusive or even primary use of the traditional instructional model interferes with the promise of learning fulfillment available in community service learning courses.

### Principle 9: Be Prepared for Uncertainty and Variation in Student Learning Outcomes

In college courses, the learning stimuli and class assignments largely determine student outcomes. This is true in community service learning courses too. However, in traditional courses, the learning stimuli (i.e., lectures and readings) are constant for all enrolled students; this leads to predictability and homogeneity in student learning outcomes. In community service learning courses, the variability in community service placements necessarily leads to less certainty and homogeneity in student learning outcomes. Even when community service learning students are exposed to the same presentations and the same readings, instructors can expect that the content of class discussions will be less predictable and the content of student papers will be

less homogeneous than in courses without a community assignment.

### Principle 10: Maximize the Community Responsibility Orientation of the Course

If one of the objectives of a community service learning course is to cultivate students' sense of community and social responsibility, then designing course learning formats and assignments that encourage a communal rather than an individual learning orientation will contribute to this objective. If learning in a course is privatized and tacitly understood as for the advancement of the individual, then we are implicitly encouraging a private responsibility mindset; an example would be to assign papers that students write individually and that are read only by the instructor. On the other hand, if the learning is shared amongst the learners for the benefit of corporate learning, then we are implicitly encouraging a group responsibility mentality; an example would be to share those same student papers with the other students in the class. This conveys to the students that they are resources for one another, and this message contributes to the building of commitment to community and civic duty.

By subscribing to this set of 10 pedagogical principles, faculty will find that students' learning from their service will be optimally utilized on behalf of academic learning, corporate learning, developing a commitment to civic responsibility, and providing learning-informed service in the community.

### FINAL NOTE

…community service learning is a comprehensive educational experience. In addition to contributing to the community, furthering students' social responsibility, and their general learning about the community, it is a teaching-learning model with myriad other learning benefits. It enhances academic learning. It offers students new learning paradigms as well as a chance to try on new learner and instructor roles. It renews investment in learning. It offers an opportunity to reconsider prior values, ethics, and attitudes. It offers an experience that counterbalances the curriculum's predisposition for theory. It provides experience with ambiguity and with variance in data significance, both of which in turn foster critical thinking. It encourages student self-direction and learning about self. It brings books to life and life to books. And, it provides opportunities for developing real world skills and real world knowledge.

# Course Organization

by Kerrissa Heffernan and Richard Cone

"How one understands service has direct implications for how one teaches. Whether one envisions service as a continuum, as a set of paradigms, or in another coherent, consistent way, coming to grips with one's understanding of service is an important step in selecting the type of service that will match the purpose of a given course, defining the impacts one expects service to have, and determining the criteria by which success or failure will be measured."

KEITH MORTON,
ISSUES RELATED TO INTEGRATING SERVICE-LEARNING INTO THE CURRICULUM
(IN JACOBY AND ASSOCIATES, 1996, P. 282)

There are four basic principles that should guide faculty in organizing and constructing a service-learning course:

1) **ENGAGEMENT**—Does the service component meet a public good? How do you know this? Has the community been consulted? How? How have campus-community boundaries been negotiated and how will they be crossed?

2) **REFLECTION**—Is there a mechanism that encourages students to link their service experience to course content and to reflect upon why the service is important?

3) **RECIPROCITY**—Is reciprocity evident in the service component? How? "Reciprocity suggests that every individual, organization, and entity involved in the service-learning functions as both a teacher and a learner. Participants are perceived as colleagues, not as servers and clients" (Jacoby, 1996 p. 36).

4) **PUBLIC DISSEMINATION**—Is service work presented to the public or made an opportunity for the community to enter into a public dialogue? For example: Do oral histories that students collect return to the community in some public form? Is the data students collect on the saturation of toxins in the local river made public? How? To whose advantage?

Once faculty have addressed these four principles, they should begin to plan the manner in which the service component will be presented in the syllabus. The presentation of service in the syllabus can be critical in shaping the educational outcomes for the course. Service cannot be presented as a mere sidebar to the course; rather, the syllabus should explain why this kind of service is a part of the course. This requires instructors to think about the explicit connections between their course and departmental objectives; between the university's mission and the community's expectations; and, perhaps most importantly, between their goals and their students' expectations (Woolcock, 1997, p. 10). These connections are further clarified for students in how faculty structure the service component in the syllabus. This is most often evident in how faculty conceptualize the course within a specific service-learning model.

## SIX MODELS FOR SERVICE-LEARNING

Whether creating a new course or reconstructing an existing course using service-learning, faculty should explore the appropriate model of service-learning. While one could argue that there are many models of service-learning, we feel that service-learning courses can basically be described in six categories:

### 1) "Pure" Service-Learning

These are courses that send students out into the community to serve. These courses have as their intellectual core the idea of service to communities by students, volunteers, or engaged citizens. They are not typically lodged in any one discipline.

---

**EXAMPLE:**

**CALIFORNIA STATE UNIVERSITY AT MONTEREY BAY**

Service Learning 200: Introduction to Service in Multicultural Communities: Course Focus: Youth and Elderly

*Purpose:* To prepare students for active and responsible community participation. To learn the skills, knowledge and competencies necessary for this type of participation, students will engage in an on-going process of service and reflection throughout the semester.

*Community-Based Assignment:* With faculty guidance, students will choose a service site that will allow them to learn about themselves and their community. For a minimum of three hours a week, for 10 weeks, students will be engaged in the work of a local community agency, school, or other organization. In addition to hands on work, time at the agency site will be spent observing, listening, and engaging in dialogue with community members.

One of the purposes of the community placement is to afford students direct experience in a community or sector of a community with which they do not have previous experience, and which they may have initially perceived as "other." The topics this section will focus on are infants, children, young people and people who are elderly. Some course readings, class discussions and activities and all placements for this section will focus on these topics. Several community agencies have agreed to serve as site placements for this section. Students will have the opportunity to learn more about them from class discussions and from the Service Learning Placement catalog distributed the third week of September. Students will be able to meet with agency staff at the Placement Fair held September 20.

Time spent in the classroom and in the community is of equal importance.

*Related Assignment:* Weekly journal, three service learning projects (one per month) with related essays. Final group service presentation (to be designed by students in conjunction with faculty).

CHALLENGES. Because service is the course content of pure service-learning, it is easier to build an intellectual connection between the course and the community experience. But pure service poses a danger in that the "content" of the course is service-learning, volunteerism, or civic engagement. It is not that these topics can't be taught in intellectually defensible ways. Many of these courses use a multi-disciplinary approach to examine the philosophical, social, and intellectual underpinnings that support a movement or a historical/philosophical approach to a phenomenon like volunteerism. But all too frequently, detractors criticize these courses as being lightweight excuses to give students credit for service with a reflective component that is more conversational than analytical (all in the guise of an intellectual frame). As a result, faculty often view these courses with a great deal of skepticism. There is also a danger that such courses may serve to marginalize service-learning because faculty may be reluctant to envision a more rigorous or content-specific model.

### 2) Discipline-Based Service-Learning

In this model, students are expected to have a presence in the community throughout the semester and reflect on their experiences on a regular basis throughout the semester using course content as a basis for their analysis and understanding.

---

**EXAMPLE:**
**SACRED HEART COLLEGE**
History 252: Medieval Europe

*Purpose:* This course aims to study the development of a distinctly European Western civilization that emerged from the Mediterranean and Classical world as well as other northern "barbarian" tribes. We will seek to understand the development of a distinctly "western civilization" in Europe by (1) focusing on political, economic and religious institutions, (2) by looking at the ideological and cultural system and the collective mentality, and (3) by looking at a variety of people who inhabited these worlds. In the medieval world each person had a fixed place in society, and entered their role through birth and "calling": they had a duty to live in society in a certain way.

*Community-Based Component:* (A course option in place of a paper.) You may do a student-teaching internship with sixth-graders at Winthrop School, Reed School or Moran School. Students will present units on the medieval world, work with reading skills, and design and run projects with the sixth graders.

*Related Assignments:* A written report of your experience (15 pages) is due at the end of the semester.

**CHALLENGES.** Discipline-based courses are generally easier to defend intellectually. But the link between course content and community experience must be made very explicit to students. And the more explicit the link, the more one limits the types of appropriate community experiences. This can make placement logistics and monitoring difficult and frustrating. Perhaps because of this constraint, discipline-based courses are more apt to use service in lieu of another assignment, as extra credit, or as a fourth credit. This can present additional challenges to the reflective component as not all students in the course are engaged in service.

### 3) Problem-Based Service-Learning (PBSL)

According to this model, students (or teams of students) relate to the community much as "consultants" working for a "client." Students work with community members to understand a particular community problem or need. This model presumes that the students will have some knowledge they can draw upon to make recommendations to the community or develop a solution to the problem; architecture students might design a park; business students might develop a web site; or botany students might identify non-native plants and suggest eradication methods.

---

**EXAMPLE:**

**UNIVERSITY OF UTAH**

Civil Engineering 571: Traffic Flow Theory

*Purpose:* Transportation studies encompass a wide range of disciplines. The Traffic Engineering Course has been designed to provide you with an insight into traffic control and management techniques.

*Community-Based Component:* Students in this class provide a needed service: The Millcreek Lion's Club and the county of Salt Lake have approached me requesting that I work with them to address traffic control problems in the Millcreek neighborhood. Traffic routed improperly has become a safety issue and has greatly contributed to the deterioration in the neighborhood, especially for seniors and children. Too much traffic on neighborhood streets has cut off access by foot and isolated parts of the neighborhood from what used to be a more cohesive unit. Students will work with the community residents to understand the problems, then to design traffic solutions. Students will present their findings and solutions to the community and the county in public meetings and will get feedback from both as to how to continuously improve the project.

*Related Assignments:* In addition to collecting research and designing solutions (presented in a series of reports), students will write about how their designs have been influenced by community concerns.

**CHALLENGES.** Problem-based service-learning attempts to circumvent many of the logistical problems faculty encounter by limiting the number of times that students go out into the community (students go into the community long enough to identify a problem and/gather data). The rationale is that students are responsible for surveying communities and identifying specific needs. Students are then responsible for coordinating their own schedules to develop a product in response to these identified needs. There are two difficulties associated with this approach:

1) The limited exposure of the students to the community minimizes the likelihood that their solution will address the full magnitude of the problem.

2) There is a danger in promoting the idea that students are "experts" and communities are "clients." This heightens the perception of many communities that universities are pejorative entities that promote insular ways of knowing and understanding the world.

## 4) Capstone Courses

These courses are generally designed for majors and minors in a given discipline and are offered almost exclusively to students in their final year. Capstone courses ask students to draw upon the knowledge they have obtained throughout their course work and combine it with relevant service work in the community. The goal of capstone courses is usually either exploring a new topic or synthesizing students understanding of their discipline. These courses offer an excellent way to help students transition from the world of theory to the world of practice by helping them make professional contacts and gather personal experience.

EXAMPLE:

PORTLAND STATE UNIVERSITY

In Other Words:

The Women's Community Education Project

*Purpose:* To design an outreach program to raise local teen girls' awareness of resources and activities at In Other Words and the Women's Community Education Project. To provide a space for teen girls to think, talk, and write about current issues in their lives.

*Community-Based Component:* Your primary task for this course is to make contacts with teen advocates in the Portland area and to conduct several rap sessions with teen girls, encourage them to participate in our project, solicit submissions, and design our 'zine. You will negotiate a secondary task applicable to our project. This task is an opportunity to use skills specific to your major and should reflect a personal interest in an issue related to teen girls or the bookstore.

*Related Assignment:* Portfolio, Capstone Plan, and proposal for group facilitation research reflective journal.

CHALLENGES. Capstone courses place much of the responsibility for placement on the student. It is assumed that the senior year is an appropriate time for students to bring their skills and knowledge to bear on a community problem, developing new knowledge in the process. Capstone courses generally offer communities students with specific skills who can invest a significant amount of time in research and practice. The danger is that when students graduate and leave the community, they take with them valuable knowledge and insights that cannot be easily replaced.

## 5) Service Internships

Like traditional internships, these experiences are more intense than typical service-learning courses, with students working as many as 10 to 20 hours a week in a community setting. As in traditional internships, students are generally charged with producing a body of work that is of value to the community or site. However, unlike traditional internships, service internship have regular and ongoing reflective opportunities that help students analyze their new experiences using discipline-based theories. These reflective opportunities can be done with small groups of peers, with one-on-one meetings with faculty advisors, or even electronically with a faculty member providing feedback. Service internships are further distinguished from traditional internships by their focus on reciprocity: the idea that the community and the student benefit equally from the experience.

EXAMPLE:

PROVIDENCE COLLEGE

PSP 401: Public Service Practicum

*Purpose:* The Practicum is designed to prepare you to work as a Community Assistant for the Feinstein Institute for Public Service. The Practicum is also designed to develop and improve the practical skills that will help you to work effectively as liaisons between service-learning courses and the community-based organizations that operate as service sites in these courses.

*Community-Based Component:* The Practicum is a year-long required course for the Public and Community Service Studies major. While the two semesters differ significantly in terms of course content and objectives, they complement each other. During the first semester your focus will be on developing a comprehensive knowledge of your site, the population it serves, and the neighborhood where it is located. You will be responsible for "managing" the service for the group of students assigned to your site. You will be asked to reflect upon your motivations, your intentions, and your impact in light of the relationships you develop over the course of the semester. During the second semester your focus will be on analyzing the relationship between the Feinstein Institute and your site and you will be asked to reflect upon and write about responsibility and impact at the institutional level. You will consider the history of the relationship between the Institute and the organization and be asked to make concrete recommendations regarding the advancement of the relationship in the future.

*Related Assignments:* Organizational action research, critical incident journal, grant application.

**CHALLENGES.** Service internships require students to produce a body of work that is of value to the community or to a specific community site. However, they generally require a level of oversight from the community partner that can be taxing. And, as with capstone courses, students graduate and leave the community site, taking with them valuable knowledge and insight that cannot be easily replaced.

### 6) Undergraduate Community-Based Action Research

A relatively new approach that is gaining popularity, community-based action research is similar to an independent study option for the rare student who is highly experienced in community work. Community-based action research can also be effective with small classes or groups of students. In this model, students work closely with faculty members to learn research methodology while serving as advocates for communities.

---

**EXAMPLE:**

**LEHIGH UNIVERSITY**

Economics 295 Regional
Economic Development Practicum

*Purpose:* This course will involve teams of students in community-oriented research projects. Students will participate in the design and execution of a specific research project identified by a Lehigh Valley development agency. The results of this research will be communicated both orally and in a written report to the agency.

*Community-Based Component:* Students may choose one of seven research projects identified by development agencies. For example:

- Transportation barriers to successful welfare to work transitions
- Community partner: Council of Hispanic Organizations

Students will assist the council by researching and documenting the extent to which women living in the inner city of Allentown are limited in their search for employment by the current configuration of bus routes. Student teams will meet with LANTA planners to identify ways in which routes could be changed or new services developed to enhance the possibility of successful transitions from welfare to work.

*Related assignments:* Large research paper and presentation.

**CHALLENGES.** Undergraduate community-based research shares many of the same pros and cons as traditional research-focused courses. This model assumes that students are competent in time management, are self-directed learners, and can negotiate diverse communities. These assumptions can become problematic and the ramifications of students' failures can impact the community.

These service models can assist faculty in conceptualizing service-learning within a specific disciplinary framework. For example, mathematicians and faculty in the hard sciences often react favorably to problem-based service-learning since it reflects their disciplinary training, which is primarily problem-based. Faculty in the humanities often respond favorably to disciplinary-based service-learning since it values the analysis and synthesis of information, which is reflective of disciplinary training in the liberal arts. But creating a service-learning course raises larger questions for faculty about the construction of knowledge.

## SOME REFLECTIONS ON THE CONSTRUCTION OF KNOWLEDGE

Introducing faculty to service-learning within the rubric of the six service-learning models may allow them to entertain larger questions about the construction of knowledge and the teaching-learning process.

Reflecting upon my own experiences creating and revising service-learning courses, I suspect that a significant challenge to my students' use of the syllabus was not just a lack of clarity but also the gulf between our (my students' and my) respective conceptions of knowledge. Many of the students I encountered in my courses seemed to conceive of thinking in an academic setting as linear and concrete. Lofty and abstract discussion of the emotional quality of working class women's lives during the progressive era were met with questions such as, "Will this be on the test?" or, my favorite question, "Do we need to know this?" While my students did enthusiastically engage in class discussions and grasp abstractions, these were not familiar classroom behaviors. Though I assumed that students were thinking about the possibilities information held, they generally preferred to remain in the now—to dwell on the immediate regurgitation of the information. Discussions with colleagues revealed that this gulf between my conception of knowledge (abstract) and my students' (concrete) was a common and taxing problem for faculty. Moreover, the various developmental levels (affective, emotional, and moral) of students further exacerbated this gulf.

As faculty, we are often drawn to teaching because it is about possibilities—about abstractions, ideas, and the possibilities inherent in our disciplinary interest. We construct our work environments so that they are highly autonomous and we assume that students prefer to think and work as we do. Our course syllabi often reflect our assumptions and our preferences about the acquisition and use of knowledge. But research suggests that many of our students are not of a like mind. When designing syllabi, instructors cannot dismiss the gap between how students have been taught to conceive of knowledge (concrete) and how faculty tend to perceive knowledge (abstract). Research confirms that many undergraduates perform best in learning situations characterized by "direct, concrete experience, moderate to high degrees of structure, and a linear approach to learning" (Schroeder, 1993 p. 22).

A well constructed service-learning course may assist students in several ways. As faculty, we might think of our syllabi as maps that guide students as they develop cognitively, affectively, emotionally, and morally over the course of the semester. But even when syllabi are linear and concrete, well-considered, and structured in a manner that is coherent and appealing to students, many students will simply ignore the information at hand. "The vast majority of difficulties in reasoning

demonstrated across a diverse population were not logical fallacies or other problems of a formal nature, but rather problems resulting from the subjects underutilization of available information" (Perkins, 1982 p. 32).

When we design a syllabus, we hope that it accurately reflects the intent of our courses. We hope our syllabi speak to students about the value of mastering the content or the discipline we love. We hope that the experience of being in our courses will challenge students intellectual and moral timidity; will serve as a measure to students of what they can aspire to be and understand. It is painful to realize that our discipline—our course—holds little more than a vague attraction for students; that the service placement we have so carefully cultivated is but one more responsibility a student must attend to each Thursday afternoon; that we have very little control over how our students prioritize and utilize information. I am not suggesting that the duty of faculty is one of leading the distracted, concrete learner through an "enjoyable" process. I am suggesting that we cannot diminish the importance of our (students' and faculty's) respective conceptions of the use of information and the construction of knowledge. As faculty, we should think of our syllabi as maps that guide students as they developmentally move over the course of the semester. Developing the map requires faculty to attend to a course sequence and an order, to create a syllabus that can bridge the gulf between faculty and students' conceptions of knowledge, and to assist students in learning how to utilize that information.

## REFERENCES

Jacoby, Barbara and Associates. *Service-Learning in Higher Education: Concepts and Practices.* San Francisco, CA: Jossey-Bass, 1996.

Schroeder, Charles. "New Students—New Learning Styles." *Change,* Sep-Oct., 1993, 25(4): 21–26.

Woolcock, Michael. *Constructing a Syllabus: A Handbook for Faculty, Teaching Assistants and Teaching Fellows, Second Edition.* Providence, RI: Brown University, 1997.

**DISCIPLINES: Biology, Engineering**

DR. MARYBETH LIMA
LOUISIANA STATE UNIVERSITY

## Course Designations
This is a service-learning course, and a communication intensive course

## Course Description
Effect of variability and constraints of biological systems on engineering problem solving and design; engineering units; engineering report writing; oral report presentation; laboratory demonstration of biological engineering analysis.

## Objectives
After completing this course, you should be able to:

1. Define and discuss engineering and biological engineering.

2. Have a better appreciation of yourself and your learning process, including why you picked this major.

3. Understand in some depth the area of biological engineering in which you want to study in which you are interested.

4. Communicate effectively with your community partner(s) and your peers, and apply rudimentary techniques for working together and resolving conflicts that result in the most success.

5. Conceptualize the process of engineering design, including the following: what is engineering design, how does one approach a problem using the engineering method, impact of social and technical factors on design, evaluation methods in design, and effective communication in the design process.

6. Understand the significance of service-learning, and how it affects your strength as a person and an engineering student.

7. Understand the significance of communicating, and how it affects your strength as an engineer.

## Course Approach
*This is a service-learning course.* Service-learning is defined as "a credit-bearing, educational experience in which students participate in an organized service activity that meets identified community needs and reflect on the service activity in such a way as to gain further understanding of course content, a broader appreciation of the discipline, and an enhanced sense of civic responsibility."

You will accomplish all of the learning objectives in this course by completing a service-learning project that concerns Biological Engineering and addresses a community need. This process is a mutual exchange of knowledge, information and service between the community (through community partners) and each of you.

This year, each section (Thursday and Friday lab sections) will be working in a groups of 3–4 students to *design a playground.* Each of these playgrounds will be designed by end of the semester, and will hopefully be constructed at some point in the future. Today we will discuss our approach, and will consult information on each community partner.

## Overall Approach

**WEEKS 1–4**

- Learn about engineering design and the engineering design method

- Learn about designing playgrounds

- Learn about your group members and create policies for decision making and management issues

- Information gathering on community partner and addressing community needs (meet with contact and community members, site visit)

**WEEKS 5–8**

- Continue information gathering with community partners (second site visit, further discussions with community partners) and professional playground designers

- Generate preliminary designs

- Initial check on designs by instructor

**WEEKS 9–13**

- Create and refine final design with input from instructor, community partners, and experts

**WEEKS 14–15**

- Presentation of final design to panel consisting of community partners and playground design experts

- Instructor and community partners take all designs and suggestions from panel, and streamline them into one consolidated design that best addresses community needs

**SUBSEQUENT TO SEMESTER:**

- Instructor (and interested students) presents streamlined design to community partners for further input, and a final design is agreed upon

- Fundraising for playground project is completed

- Construction will take place with community and student volunteers

## Community Partners

**SECTION 1.** Your community partners are the Old South Baton Rouge Community (centered at the Leo S. Butler Community Center) and Baton Rouge Green. You will be working with these groups to design a community park and playground using the SPARK model (www.sparkpark.com), in which school grounds are transformed into community parks. We will work with the community partners and the community to choose a location, and will then work with community members, including children, parents, and teachers at the school, to design the playground and park.

**SECTION 2.** Your community partner is the Louisiana School for the Deaf. The School for the Deaf has four playgrounds, an elementary school playground, a middle school playground, a high school playground, and a special needs playground. You will be involved with redesigning the special needs playground. Administrators at the School for the Deaf have chosen to tear down all existing equipment on the special needs playground and are in the process of "starting over." You will be working with the children, parents, teachers, therapists, and administrators at the School to design a playground for children with special needs.

## Student Portfolio

Each of you will be developing a portfolio this semester. *A portfolio is defined as "a purposeful collection of student work that tells the story of the student's efforts, progress or achievement in a given area."* Your purpose this semester is to learn about engineering, biological engineering, and yourself. Completing the assignments in this course will enable each of you to examine your motivations for choosing this major, and to learn more about biological engineering. This knowledge will help you to identify your personal and professional goals. Through portfolios, you will be documenting your path to a greater understanding of yourself and of this profession. You can use your portfolio for reference throughout your undergraduate career and beyond.

Investigators have established four levels of learning, which are as follows:

1. **INFORMATION:** student can define, repeat, list, name, label, memorize, recall and/or relate that information.

2. **KNOWLEDGE:** student shows an understanding and comprehension of the information gained in level 1,

and can describe, explain, compare/contrast, identify, discuss and/or summarize it.

3. **APPLICATION/ANALYSIS**: student can solve problems by applying knowledge in new situations, and can critically distinguish the logical components of other applications of that knowledge.

4. **WISDOM**: student can display professional judgment and the ability to synthesize, design, organize, plan, manage, teach and/or evaluate.

Investigators have also determined that approximately 85–90% of one's undergraduate education is spent in levels 1 and 2. My goal as an educator is to provide opportunities for students to participate in levels 3 and 4. Developing your portfolio is one way to accomplish this.

Your portfolio will consist of three parts:

1. **A PERSONAL WEB PAGE** that you will develop as part of this class;

2. **AN ENGINEERING JOURNAL**, which contains incidental or informal writing assignments that we will be doing throughout the semester; and

3. **HOMEWORK ASSIGNMENTS.**

Throughout the semester, you will have homework assignments, all of which will go into your portfolios. Obtain a notebook or binder immediately for your portfolio! In this way, you will be able to build the portfolio throughout the semester, instead of rushing to pull it together at the last minute. You will turn in your portfolios for comments from me at mid-semester.

Your final portfolio should contain the following:

1. **A TABLE OF CONTENTS**, including a description of the work done and the page on which it appears. An example is as follows:

2. **A SHORT INTRODUCTION** describing the purpose of your portfolio and what is contained in it; although this goes at the beginning of the portfolio, I suggest you write it at the end of the course.

3. **ALL THE WORK** you did in whatever order you'd like, as long as it makes sense and fits together.

4. **REFLECTION NARRATIVES**: After certain exercises, you will be asked to write a short statement describing what you thought and felt about that specific exercise. This is to help you to identify how and why you thought the exercise was useful (or not) to you, to help me identify if the exercise is one worth keeping and/or refining for next year's students.

Your portfolio requires a concluding **self-assessment narrative,** in which you write about your overall experience in the course, and evaluate the use of service-learning in your quest to achieve the objectives of this course.

Feel free to include anything that you find of help to your own learning process. This portfolio is for you, not for me. Engineering journals will be graded on completeness only, and not on what you said, how you said it, or grammar. The purpose of the engineering journal is for you to record all your thoughts, feelings and actions during the course of this class; please keep it with you at all times. These notes can be invaluable for many reasons; they may tell the story of how you develop into an engineer! Also, you may have great ideas that you forget about later; this is one excellent way to keep track of them.

## Homework Assignments

Homework assignments are intended to help you understand material. *I employ a resubmission process* for homework because of this reason: if you "mess it up" the first time, instead of just getting the grade and continuing, re-submissions allow you to concentrate on the mistakes you make and to fix them.

Re-submissions will not be accepted for any grade higher than 80%, except in special cases that I will designate. You may re-submit an assignment for any grade lower than this, and your final grade for that assignment will be the average of the original grade and the final grade. You are not required to re-submit any assignment, but if you choose to, you must re-submit within one week of the assignment being returned to you in class. If you happen to miss class the day the assignment is returned, you are still responsible for re-submitting it one week from the date in which it was returned in class. Your submission must include a written explanation of what (specifically) you didn't understand, and why you understand it now.

Homework must be turned in on time to receive full credit. Assignments must be turned in by 4:30 p.m. the day they are due in order to be considered on time. Late assignments will receive 20% off for each day that they are late. No re-submissions will be accepted for assignments turned in late.

## DISCIPLINES: Foreign Language, Ethnic Studies, Service Learning

GRESILDA A. TILLEY-LUBBS
VIRGINIA POLYTECHNIC INSTITUTE & STATE UNIVERSITY

Department of Foreign Languages & Literatures

Spanish 4984 CRN 15910

Spanish 5984 CRN 15953

### Justification for the Course
This is a service-learning course designed for Spanish majors and minors and other students who wish to have an immersion experience in the Latino community. The students will have the opportunity to interact in a personal way with members of the community, thereby enriching their understanding of the culture and the language. This is a grassroots program that will be driven by the needs of the Latino community. The course itself will be co-constructed by the students, the members of the Latino community who are involved in the project, and the instructor.

### Mission Statement
In facilitating a service-learning class, I plan to create an inviting and stimulating environment in which the students will form a learning community based on mutual respect and interests with the common goal of pursuing research and inquiry into the methodology and practice of working within a diverse community. They will construct their own knowledge so that it will be meaningful and applicable to their own projects and goals, thereby granting them ownership of the class and its outcome. They will design projects that will

immerse them in the Latino community. By means of reflection, they will constantly evaluate their progress, examining how the theory that they are reading is or is not present in their experiences in the community.

### Objectives
By the end of the semester, the students will be able to articulate what they have learned about service-learning within the Latino community. Through a variety of readings, in-services, guest speakers and reflections, they will be able to analyze how they can help people from Latin America to navigate within the community in which they are now living. They will have the opportunity to examine themselves by interactions with others.

### Principles of Service-Learning
This service-learning experience will be guided by the following principles which state that an effective program (Honnet & Poulen, 1989):

- engages people in responsible and challenging actions for the common good;

- provides structured opportunities for people to reflect critically on their service experience;.

- articulates clear service and learning goals for everyone involved;

- allows for those with needs to define those needs;

- clarifies the responsibilities of each person and organization involved;

- matches service providers and service needs through a process that recognizes changing circumstances;

- expects genuine, active, and sustained organizational commitment;

- includes training, supervision, monitoring, support, recognition, and evaluation to meet service and learning goals;

- ensures that the time commitment for service and learning is flexible, appropriate, and in the best interests of all involved; and

- is committed to program participation by and with diverse populations.

Honnet, E.P., and S.J. Poulen. (1989). *Principles of Good Practice for Combining Service and Learning, a Wingspread Special Report.* Racine, WI: The Johnson Foundation, Inc.

## Community Hours

During the first two class meetings, the students will have the opportunity to hear about the various services they will provide to families in the Roanoke Latino community. They will work in teams, going to their families' homes twice a week, often being called upon to:

- Provide transportation to medical, dental and social service appointments.

- Provide childcare at specified times.

- Provide transportation, babysitting, and a nurturing presence for women who want to attend group support sessions.

- Shop for groceries for families who are without sufficient food (I have a fund of about $500 in donations at this time that we can draw from).

- Shop for clothing for the children (depending on the situation, at Kmart, WalMart or Goodwill).

- Organize donations of clothing, toys, and furniture so that they are easily accessible.

- Deliver clothing, toys, furniture.

- Make phone calls to make appointments or to find out information about the available services.

- Translate brochures related to health care and social services.

- Interpret for people at medical and social service appointments where there no interpreter is provided.

- Act as an intermediary for communication with the children's school

- Work with individuals and families to help them with their English, either by tutoring or by teaching small classes.

- Teach basic survival skills, ranging from how to ride the bus to how to get a library card to be able to use the library facilities.

## Weekly Journal Reflections

The students will post a weekly reflection to the group email. The students should plan to read the reflections of the other students before class. This will greatly enrich the discussions that we have in class. With the exception of the first reflection, the reflections will focus on the assigned readings for the week and how the student sees it play out or not in the community. The first reflection will consist of personal narratives describing why the students chose to participate in service-learning and what they expect from the experience. The reflections should all be 2 pages, double spaced with one-inch margins on each side written on the computer in 12-point font. The reflections should be posted to the group e-mail by Saturday at midnight. The reflections may be written in Spanish or in English. Those students who are majoring or minoring in Spanish are highly encouraged to write in Spanish. There will not be a reflection on the weeks when the project proposals, the final transformation papers and the power point presentations are due.

## Final Transformation Paper

The final transformation paper will be due at the last class meeting on April 28. To write the final paper, the students should read back over the reflection papers that they have written over the course of the semester so that they can discuss how the service-learning experience compared to their expectations. This final paper should also cite the readings, discussing whether they helped the students to transform their thinking and perspectives in the course of the service-learning project. They should also discuss the effect the immersion experience had on their proficiency in Spanish. They should explore whether the course and its effects on them was what they expected. The paper should be between 8-10 pages double spaced with one-inch margins on each side written on the computer in 12-point font.

## DISCIPLINES: Writing, English

JOY MARSELLA
KAPI'OLANI COMMUNITY COLLEGE

This introduction to college writing will teach you to draft, revise, and edit your texts, keeping in mind your audience and purpose in writing. Working in the genre of the essay, you will write and revise six essays, two of them for publication in a class magazine. To provide you with help in the revision process, I'll organize collaborative writing groups so that you can get plenty of feedback on your writing; to provide guidelines for how to give good feedback in your writing groups, you will read Elbow and Belanoff's *Sharing and Responding*. Your reading in *The Best American Essays, College Edition* and in our own UH freshman English magazine *Fresh Review* will provide excellent models and suggest departure points for your own writing. The class will focus on three general kinds of essays—personal, analytic, and persuasive—thus providing a range of writing experience that will build a good base for future college writing at the same time it allows you to develop your own voice and style.

Much of the semester's writing and thinking will be directed toward the culminating assignment, which is the preparation of a writing portfolio, in lieu of a final examination, in which you present your writing, along with a cover letter reflecting on the writing. In this letter, you should select three essays which you wish to use as the basis of your grade for the semester, explaining how and why they reflect your best work.

To give you some perspective on your own writing skills, and to enable you to develop your own reading and writing abilities in the larger educational community, I am asking you to integrate your study in this expository writing class with a 25-hour service learning project. Service learning projects combine volunteerism in the community with the fieldwork typical of educational internships: the purpose is to serve recipients while providing learning experiences related to course content. The idea behind service learning is to help you gain a better understanding of the academic content of this course by applying your skills and knowledge to benefit society. Philosophically, service learning is grounded in experience as a basis for learning. If you wish your service-learning experience to be documented on your transcript, you can sign up for one credit of IS 291. If you elect this option, you will offer 30 hours across the semester in service.

Although you have the opportunity to tailor a service learning project to your own disciplinary interests and career goals in conference with me, I suggest two projects through which you can integrate your study of writing while serving the larger community:

- **MENTOR IN THE "TEENS READING THE PACIFIC" PROGRAM.** In this option you meet regularly with a small group of intermediate and/or high school students to discuss three or four books chosen from the Teens Reading list. Each reading circle will have four or five teenagers, and be led by you, a college student acting in the role of mentor and discussant. The circle members can meet either on school grounds or at branches of the public library to discuss the books. The purpose of this group, called a literature circle, is to provide an attractive, out-of-school, interactive setting so that young readers can discuss books in a non-threatening, non-graded way. You can help them develop a love for literature at the same time you reflect on reading and writing issues from our own class as they come up in the literature circles.

- **TUTOR IN A LOCAL PUBLIC SCHOOL CLASSROOM.** I'll put you in touch with teachers who will identify students and describe their language needs so that you can develop tutoring strategies.

I'll expect you throughout the semester to integrate the experiences in your service learning projects with our discussion of the assigned readings and with your own writing. Once you get your project set up, I'll ask you to write bi-weekly journals, reflecting on the experience and connecting it with class readings and discussions. Near the end of the semester, you'll draw on the journal reflections to write an essay that analyzes your service learning experiences and the language lessons you learned as a result of it.

# Redesigning Curriculum:
## Recommended Reading

## BOOKS & CHAPTERS

Billig, S. H., & Furco, A. (2002). *Service-learning through a multidisciplinary lens* (a volume in the Advances in Service-Learning Research series). Greenwich, CT: Information Age Publishing.

Campus Compact. (1998). *When community enters the equation: Enhancing science, mathematics, and engineering education through service-learning.* Providence, RI: Campus Compact.

Civian, J.T., Arnold, G., et al., (1996). Implementing change. In Gaff, J.G., & Ratcliff, J.L., *Handbook of the undergraduate curriculum: A comprehensive guide to purposes, structures, practices, and change.* San Francisco: Jossey-Bass.

Howard, J. (2001). Service-learning course design workbook. Companion volume to the Summer 2001 issue of *The Michigan Journal of Community Service Learning.* Ann Arbor: OCSL Press, The University of Michigan.

Heffernan, K. (2001). *Fundamentals of service-learning course construction.* Providence, RI: Campus Compact.

Murphy, C. & Jenks, L. (n.d.) *Integrating the community and the classroom: A sampler of postsecondary courses.* Springfield, VA: National Society for Experiential Education.

O'Grady, C.R. (Ed). (2000). *Integrating service-learning and multicultural education in colleges and universities.* Mahwah, NJ: Lawrence Erlbaum Associates.

Zlotkowski, E. (1996–2003). Service-learning in the disciplines, volumes 1–19. Washington, DC: American Association for Higher Education.

## ARTICLES & REPORTS

Barber, B., and Battistoni, R. (1993, June). A season of service: Introducing service learning into the liberal arts curriculum. *PS: Political Science and Politics, 26:* 235–262.

Cameron, M., et al. (2001). Learning through service. *College Teaching, 49* (3), 105–114.

Emanoil, P. (2000). Real-world learning. *Human Ecology, 28* (3), 20–25.

Freeman, S.A., Field, D.W. & Dyrenfurth, M.J. (2001). Using contextual learning to build cross-functional skills in industrial technology curricula. *Journal of Industrial Teacher Education, 38* (3), 62–75.

Fritz, J.M. (2002). A little bit of sugar: Integrated service-learning courses. *Sociological Practice, 4* (1), 67–77.

Gronski, R. & Pigg, K. (2000). University and community collaboration. *American Behavioral Scientist, 43* (5), 781–793.

Padmanabhan, G. & Katti, D. (2002). Using community-based projects in civil engineering capstone courses. *Journal of Professional Issues in Engineering Education and Practice, 128* (1), 12–19.

Patterson, A.S. (2000). It's a small world: Incorporating service-learning in an international relations course. *PS: Political Science and Politics, 33* (4), 817–822.

Ramaley, J.A. (2002). Creating a focus for the engaged institution: K–12 science and math reform. *The Journal of Public Affairs, 6,* 139–160.

Roakes, S.L. & Norris-Tirrell, D. (2000). Community service–learning in planning education: A framework for course development. *Journal of Planning Education and Research, 20* (1), 100–110.

Root, R. & Thorme, T. (2001). Community-based projects in applied statistics: Using service-learning to enhance student understanding. *American Statistician, 55* (4), 326–332.

Strage, A. (2000). Service-learning: Enhancing student learning outcomes in a college–level lecture course." *Michigan Journal of Community Service Learning, 7,* 5–13.

Swick, K.J. (2001). Service-learning in teacher education: Building learning communities. *The Clearing House, 74* (5), 261-265.

# Model Programs

## TITLES IN THIS SECTION

## QUESTIONS FOR REFLECTION AND PLANNING

What do you believe are/would be the elements of a successful service-learning course?

What structures exist at your institution that could facilitate the realization of those elements? (Allies)

What structures exist that would impede the realization of those elements? (Obstacles)

What aspects of the institution's mission, strategic plan, and/or curriculum reform efforts are conducive to expanding your service-learning program?

# From Accreditation to Strategic Planning:

## An Administrator's Interpretation of Service Learning

by Erin Swezey, *Loyola College*

FOUNDED IN 1852, Loyola College is a Catholic liberal arts college which enrolls 3,100 full-time students. Of these, 34% are Maryland residents and 66% are out-of-state residents. This urban Jesuit institution embraces an educational philosophy of developing "men and women for others" through service. Loyola employs 220 full-time faculty, two-thirds in arts and sciences and one third in the business school. The student/faculty ratio is 14:1. Tuition for the 1995-96 academic year is $14,260.

In 1989, as preparation for its regional ten-year accreditation, Loyola College in Baltimore, Maryland, developed an institutional strategic plan that revised its mission statement. This new mission, "challenging students to lead and serve in a diverse and changing world," rededicated the College to its recognized history of a strong liberal arts education and a religious tradition of service. The last of seven goals in this five-year plan states that a graduate of Loyola College "will be sensitive to racial and cultural diversity and dedicated to the service of others." As a direct response to this plan and in the same year, Loyola College hired a full-time administrator to establish an infrastructure to promote community service and eventually service learning. This position was funded from existing salary dollars and initially placed within campus ministry, a department which reported to the president.

In the fall of 1991, the president of Loyola College became interested in joining Campus Compact to promote campus-wide involvement in the college's community service effort. He held discussions with the academic provost and the director of community service. As a result of these discussions, the president formed a committee of faculty, administrators, students and service providers from the community to consider how Loyola could integrate service with academic study. The faculty membership represented a wide range of academic disciplines including the humanities, sciences and business. The committee, chaired by a faculty member, was first convened in January 1992 to develop and submit a service learning proposal to Campus Compact for their service learning institute.

Three institutional events influenced the development of this proposal to enhance service learning at Loyola College. First, the college experienced a groundswell of student involvement in service beginning in 1989. At the end of 1991, annual participant statistics compiled indicated that approximately 50% of the student body had participated in some form of service activity. Second, at the end of the spring semester 1990, the college council, Loyola College's governing body, unanimously approved a proposal to provide academic credit for community service linked to a course through a fourth credit option. (In conjunction with three credit courses, students may add an additional credit similar to an independent study by completing 56 hours of service and integrating their experiences with the course.) This option allows students to reflect upon and analyze their service experiences and to put into practice what they are learning in the classroom. The fourth credit option was first proposed at Loyola College by a Jesuit faculty member who knew of its value and benefit from Georgetown University. For over a year it had been tabled for discussion by the curriculum committee. But given the 1989 Strategic Plan of the College, there was renewed pressure to make a decision about this proposal. It was discussed for several meetings and finally, in a very narrow vote of 5-4, it was passed on to the college council for approval with a dissenting opinion. The third pivotal event occurred during the spring semester of 1991. A pilot program to integrate community service into the curriculum created service components within five elective, core and major courses. These pilot courses provided tangible examples for the potential of service learning at Loyola College as well as small group of credible faculty to lead future endeavors.

During the spring of 1992, the committee met regularly to produce a proposed action plan and developed the following problem statement: "Large numbers of Loyola students are participating in ongoing community service; yet the college lacks structured, ongoing academic contexts for rigorous reflection on those service experiences. While many faculty have expressed interest in providing such contexts, they lack the experience and methods necessary to integrate service into their academic courses." Working from this problem statement, a faculty team attended Campus Compact's 1992 Summer Institute on Integrating Service with Academic Study and drafted a two-year action plan for promoting the integration of community service into academic study on campus. This plan was a detailed statement of the college's understanding of the place of community service within its institutional mission as well as a two year, three part plan of practical activities and initiatives to move students and faculty toward a greater integration of service and reflections experiences into the academic and intellectual life of the campus.

The plan, "The Service Learning Initiative," had three objectives:

1. To recruit faculty and students who will explore ways to integrate service into existing courses and departmental efforts.

2. To provide faculty development opportunities to enhance and support this integration.

3. To assess the student learning outcomes and community benefits of service learning outcomes.

During the first year of implementation the committee focused on the first two objectives. Faculty who attended the Campus Compact Summer Institute and who had piloted some form of service integration with their courses presented the initiative and their initial course development efforts to 40 faculty at the annual fall faculty teaching workshop. Faculty from the com-

mittee invited these workshop participants for follow-up, small group lunch meetings to discuss their participation with the initiative and potential service learning course development. Many of the experienced faculty were aware of a related curriculum development, the Humanities Symposium, offering a series of lectures and discussions as well as the common text writing of Martin Luther King, Jr., Letter from the Birmingham Jail. This symposium would be held during the spring semester, allowing time for faculty to develop service components and to connect these experiences with the scheduled symposium enhancing reflection and academic integration. As a result of these efforts in the first year of implementation, faculty developed service components in seven courses. Nine courses offered the fourth credit option.

Critical to this new course development and the progress of the initiative was the administrative support provided by the newly established Center for Values and Service, the infrastructure first envisioned by Loyola College in 1989 and funded in 1992. The Center was established as a freestanding college department no longer directly connected to campus ministry, however, maintaining a collaborative spirit with the ministry effort. The Center reports to the academic provost. The leadership for the Center is shared in a collaborative model of co-directors, one a Jesuit faculty member who sits on the president's cabinet and the other, an administrator, who serves on the provost's dean's council. From the beginning, the Center has been funded primarily by the college's operational fund. Other funding includes private and federal grants as well as alumni donations and student fundraising efforts.

Simultaneous to this faculty recruitment effort, a faculty subcommittee of the service learning committee designed a faculty development series offered in the spring semester of 1993. This series included Friday afternoon reflection gatherings entitled "The Heart of our Community Service," examining the vision and identity of the initiative; a lecture entitled "Our Faith Doing Justice" given by a faculty member from a neighboring institution known for its service learning program; a faculty development workshop, "Writing in the Service Learning Classroom"; and at the end of the semester, an off-campus dinner for faculty who had integrated service into their course(s) that particular semester. This end-of-the-semester dinner provided time to evaluate these efforts and to generate pedagogical and logistical ideas and to air concerns for the next academic year. Given the accomplishments and faculty momentum during this first year of implementation, Loyola College submitted a mini-grant proposal to Campus Compact for implementation funds for the second year. The Service Learning Initiative received this funding to support faculty development programs, to establish student service assistant positions that would help faculty with service placements, logistical arrangements, as well as preparation and reflection, and to subsidize part of the expense with the service learning assessment project.

During the second year of implementation, Loyola encountered problems with faculty leadership and limited administrative support from the Center for Values and Service due to sabbaticals and administrative leave. The chair responsibilities for the service learning committee turned over twice, and with each new faculty chair, new visions and approaches emerged. The service learning committee spent many meetings discussing philosophy and pedagogical ideas. Many faculty engaged with the initiative for the past two years felt that Loyola had reached a plateau in the development of service learning. Energies seemed unfocused. Although there still remained individual effort, collective faculty leadership and collaboration seemed lacking.

Other obstacles in year two included faculty skepticism regarding the academic nature of service learning, as well as concern about the politicization of the classroom, an academic advising request for a listing of courses with service learning components to advise students wishing to avoid these courses, and faculty concern about how service learning endeavors were perceived by the Board on Rank and Tenure. The first obstacle was addressed in year one and two through the faculty teaching workshop and faculty development sessions as well as bringing skeptical faculty into the service learning effort and persuading them of the educational and community value through their own experience. The other two obstacles have only recently been addressed during the third year of implementation.

During implementation year two, three factors seemed to refocus and reshape the initiative. First, external speakers and consultants addressed Loyola's faculty to provide insight and inspiration. In September 1993, Robert Coles, Harvard professor and renowned author, spoke to the college community in a packed chapel seating 800 about his recently published book, *A Call to Service*. He also spoke to groups of students and faculty who were engaged in some way with service learning. In February 1993, a staff member from Campus Compact made a site visit. She met with many of the key players: students, faculty, service providers and administrators. Her report and recommendations spurred us on. With an implementation grant from Campus Compact, we were able to bring a faculty team from Bentley College to work with Loyola faculty, those already involved and those interested, to broaden and deepen our pedagogical thinking as well as ideas for community involvement.

Also during this year, Loyola began its service learning assessment project in earnest. One of the service learning committee members, a psychology professor, designed evaluation tools as well as a focus group process to be used initially with students. Faculty evaluations were also distributed and compiled. At the same time, an administrator from student affairs completed his doctoral research of a comparative study of students engaged in a service learning course and those enrolled in the same course without service. Finally, staff from the Center for Values and Service convened a group of service providers most involved in our service learning effort to discuss more effective ways of working together and developing relationships with the faculty. This gathering was followed by another lunch meeting inviting both providers and faculty to a dialogue. All of this information, feedback and valuative data helped the faculty, Center for Values and Service and the service learning committee to refocus direction and resources.

During year two, the faculty continued to gather for reflection on their progress and pedagogy. Two significant gatherings contributed to the third factor enabling the initiative to be reshaped and refocused. Early in spring semester 1994, the faculty from the service learning committee hosted a Friday night dinner at the home of a faculty member. This dinner was a pivotal event; it solidified a sense of community among the faculty engaged in service learning, enabled new faculty leadership to emerge and brought forth a serious commitment to service learning as innovative teaching. The dinner also served as an avenue to promote justice both within the curriculum and in the broader Baltimore community. From this meeting, the faculty agreed to design and attend a service learning retreat in May to share in more depth pedagogical strategies and curricular ideas.

These factors enabled the service learning committee to redirect its priorities and effort. This year's focus has been on developing faculty leadership, intra- and inter-disciplinary infrastructure, course development and deepening the pedagogy and integration in all service learning courses. To this end many faculty have agreed to coordinate various projects:

1. The design and implementation of an ongoing service learning colloquium.

2. The design and coordination of a divisional associates program. (Designating faculty to serve as divisional liaisons in the humanities, social sciences, natural sciences and business as well as discipline-specific consultants for service learning.)

3. The expansion of a college/community partnership with the Beans and Bread meal program to provide more college resources and expertise to respond to community needs in an adjacent facility and the surrounding neighborhood (e.g., youth programs, economic development, legal assistance, job training). This expansion will provide specific service learning opportunities for graduate courses in education, business, psychology, speech pathology and pastoral counseling.

4. The service learning assessment project determining student, faculty and community outcomes and impact.

These efforts have been funded and supported through Loyola's participation with the consortium of colleges and universities coordinated by the Shriver Center at University of Maryland, Baltimore County. Faculty have received course development grants, administrative support for service projects, student service/teaching assistants and funding for the design and development of service learning curricular and infrastructure projects. Over the past three years Loyola College has had 33 faculty participate in service learning either through teaching a course with a service learning component or the fourth credit option. The future is bright. As the 1995-96 academic year began, we implemented the service learning colloquium and the faculty associates program. We now offer 21 service learning courses. 14 of these are newly developed courses with service learning components. We have expanded service learning more intentionally in the business school and with graduate courses (of which we currently have three new courses). Learn and Serve monies and existing monies

from the business school fund two administrative staff, one to work specifically with arts and science faculty and one to work with the business faculty. One position is a full-time administrator and the other is a graduate assistant.

In a spring 1995 meeting, the service learning committee formed a subcommittee of faculty and students to meet with the academic advising department staff about course listings to address an ongoing concern to list courses with service components in registration publications. Academic advisors also had new concerns about requiring athletes to complete service learning components in courses when they coincide with their season play. This subcommittee met with the college officials involved to determine ways to resolve and address these areas of resistance that kept surfacing. In addition, the committee recommended that the Center for Values and Service, with the input and advice of the committee, design an attractive brochure about service learning and course offerings that would be used as a positive, educational marketing tool to encourage students to enroll in these courses.

The faculty have owned service learning as their initiative. The dean of arts and sciences has appointed a faculty liaison to the Center for Values and Service to provide faculty leadership. Also in May 1995, twenty-five faculty gathered for a day-long retreat to discuss pedagogical ideas and collaborative service learning efforts. Loyola College believes its contribution to the national scene comes from its strong foundation in the humanities. Many of the humanities faculty are involved. Therefore, Loyola plans to publish a handbook on service learning pedagogy from the perspective of the humanities disciplines. To gain this kind of faculty ownership demands perseverance and savvy strategy. Throughout this effort, we have sought diverse representation of faculty from various disciplines to ensure a broad base of support.

Loyola has intentionally invited faculty with skepticism and resistance into the initiative knowing that if they could be persuaded they would become strong champions. Finally, whenever possible, we have invited and encouraged faculty participation in local, regional and national service learning workshops and conferences. Faculty have become service learning spokespersons at board of trustees meetings, college strategic planning meetings and Shriver Center consortium meetings. Many of the faculty involved with service learning view this kind of involvement and leadership as one way to make a significant impact on the institution and for some, it has renewed their commitment to the institution even after receiving tenure and promotion.

As part of the ongoing faculty and institutional dialogue about service learning, the associate provost invited Eugene Rice, director, AAHE Forum on Faculty Roles and Rewards, to address Loyola's faculty at the August, 1995 Faculty Teaching Workshop. The faculty involved with service learning believed that this occasion would provide the opportunity to address tenure and promotion issues. All the faculty involved with service learning have received tenure, so it is the perception of the service learning committee that such involvement does not hinder tenure and in some cases may assist faculty members' service or teaching performance categories. As service learning faculty engage in scholarly and other professional activities, the issue of value and merit may arise. During the time of the initiative, one of the members of the service learning committee served on the board of rank and tenure. This faculty member helps in explaining what service learning is and what its merits are.

Loyola College is once again engaged in strategic planning for accreditation purposes. This time the discussion related to service is how to articulate service learning not only in the mission but also as part of the climate of learning at the college. It is a given that service learning is an important part of Loyola's educational endeavor. Today, much discussion occurs around innovative teaching and community partnerships that heretofore was not imagined. Implementation of these service learning initiatives requires time, vision, perseverance and faculty leadership.

# Rediscovering Our Heritage:

## Community Service and the Historically Black University

Beverly W. Jones, *North Carolina Central University*

## INTRODUCTION

FOUNDED IN 1910, North Carolina Central University (NCCU) is a four-year, historically black liberal arts institution with 19 departments, two programs, and five professional schools. It enrolls over 5,500 undergraduate and professional degree students. Of these, 89% are North Carolina residents.

Like most historically black institutions, North Carolina Central University was founded in order to " . . . seek the regeneration of the Negro," as outlined by W. E. B. DuBois in his seminal 1903 work *The Souls of Black Folks*. Seven years later, when James E. Shepard founded North Carolina Central University, he operationalized DuBois's vision in his mission statement for the university. For Shepard, the regeneration was possible only to the extent that the university was able to develop in young men and women the character and sound academic training requisite for real service to the nation. Service, in this context, could be considered a code word for community-based and commu-nity-focused regeneration.

The DuBois-Shepard service mission for higher education is even more relevant today, because many urban African-American institutions are surrounded by seamless poverty, epidemic crime, and physically deteriorating inner cities. Historically black institutions cannot be oblivious to these issues for, geographically, they are located in the heart of deteriorating African-American communities. Now, perhaps more than ever before, historically black institutions have come to realize that the plight of urban cities is inextricably tied to their future and must be addressed effectively and proactively.

## THE AFRICAN-AMERICAN TRADITION OF COMMUNITY THROUGH SERVICE

African-American notions of community service are rooted in a traditional African legacy of connectedness and intergenerational obligation. African metaphysics emphasized three basic aspects of humanity (Joseph, 1996). The first is the idea that individuals and communities have the capacity to celebrate life, even in despairing situations. The second idea is that individuals and communities are visionaries who have the creative power to manifest their visions. The third idea is that individual identity is communal. The individual operates in a network which provides economic, religious, and political functions. African mutual aid societies, for example, stressed moral instruction and provided financial aid for the burial expenses of their members.

Enslaved Africans brought this communal nature with them to the Americas as they were dispersed in the Diaspora. The tendency to form voluntary, benevolent organizations not only survived the slavery experience, but was significantly shaped by it. African-Americans in the slave community viewed themselves as a familial group with a common lifestyle and interests. Slave communities, in addition, protected and fed runaway slaves. Many slave narratives and interviews with former slaves exemplify this connection.

Beverly W. Jones. "Rediscovering Our Heritage: Community Service and the Historically Black University," in Edward Zlotkowski, ed. *Successful Service-Learning Programs: New Models of Excellence in Higher Education*, pp. 109–123. Bolton, MA: Anker Publishing. Copyright © 1998 by Anker Publishing. Reprinted with the permission of Anker Publishing.

During slavery, most African-Americans viewed family as a combination of extended family and friends in the community. This might include community leaders, conjurers, preachers, and peer group members. These individuals felt a responsibility to nurture, protect, and educate the younger members in the family. Younger slaves exhibited a respect for their elders and often cared for those members too old to care for themselves.

A cooperative slave community allowed African-Americans to survive the harsh conditions of slavery. Recognizing that their fates were connected, many slaves pooled their meager resources to benefit the entire community. Slaves built houses, sewed, weaved baskets, and washed for one another. In some instances slaves shared food from their garden patch if they were fortunate enough to have one. In addition, slave communities protected individual members from harsh conditions and abuse at the hands of the master.

Outside the slave community, black benevolence expressed itself in the creation of mutual aid societies, fraternal organizations, and churches. These institutions often operated like the extended family network in the slave quarters. Black benevolence groups provided financial resources among free blacks and helped to ease the transition from slavery to freedom. The earliest, formed in 1787, aided the development of the black church.

Throughout the African-American experience, the church has been instrumental in the struggle for black liberation and citizenship. Early black churches served as stations for the Underground Railroad. These institutions provided food, clothing, and shelter for many of the runaways escaping the bonds of slavery. Churches were also centers for education and recreation. The first historically black colleges and schools were associated with black churches that often provided financial and human resources.

The African-American communal mentality reached an apex during the civil rights movement. During the 1950s and 1960s, thousands of local grassroots organizations raised money, collected and distributed food, and recruited volunteers to participate in demonstrations and boycotts. In addition, black churches often served as centers for mobilization. During this mass movement for social justice, the black community looked within for resources, as it had during slavery and the first years of freedom.

African-Americans still exhibit communal tendencies in their institutions and associations. Black churches feed the hungry, provide shelter for the homeless, and offer educational activities. Some churches provide economic and social development programs in the black community. Black fraternal organizations and mutual aid societies also remain a major factor in the African-American quest for a better life. Organizations such as the Alpha Kappa Alpha sorority, the Kappa Alpha Psi fraternity, and others often provide college scholarships and operate senior citizens' organizations.

African-Americans have a long history of helping themselves and others in the community. This legacy of self-help and volunteerism has survived throughout the African Diaspora. Despite the harsh conditions African-Americans experienced during slavery, they pooled their resources and came through the terrible ordeal. This sense of community aided the transition from slavery to freedom and continues to support the black struggle for liberation. The current black perception of community service remains an extension of traditional African notions of family and community responsibility.

## THE SERVICE MISSION RE-EMERGES AS MORAL IMPERATIVE

Not surprisingly, many African-American universities were originally commissioned to serve local community needs and to solve community problems. However, in the wake of desegregation, many of these universities neglected their service focus in order to emulate and compete with white institutions. Thus, over time, instead of working to improve the nation's poor urban communities, HBCUs (Historically Black Colleges and Universities) abandoned them altogether, opting instead for purely academic/ theoretical goals. In doing this, HBCUs ceased to be active partners with the communities that had supported them when few others had dared. In the decades following the civil rights movement, these institutions seemed to forget the reciprocal benefits inherent in service-based relationships with their communities. Both parties have suffered from that amnesia. History has a way of repeating itself, however, and the current *zeitgeist* among institutions of higher learning in inner cities now favors university involvement in community regeneration. Reflecting this development, a number of HBCUs have begun to reassert themselves as community partners by tapping the rich source of helping hands and positive role models in their student bodies and faculties.

Among these universities, few have repositioned themselves more squarely in the service-learning camp than has North Carolina Central. This dramatic repositioning began as a top-down strategy in 1993. Under the leadership of Chancellor Julius Chambers, who based his strategy on both ethical and pedagogical considerations, the primary mission of the university became to promote the consciousness of social responsibility and dedication to the general welfare of the people of North Carolina, the United States, and the world. The university recognizes, however, the mutually reinforcing impact of scholarship and service on effective teaching and learning. North Carolina Central, therefore, encourages and expects faculty and students to engage in scholarly and creative as well as service activities that benefit the larger community. This lofty mission is akin to John Dewey's progressive idea that educational institutions should focus on developing the social intelligence of their students through service. Chambers, a former director of the Legal Defense Fund for the NAACP, transposed this Deweyan concept of pedagogical mission to the realm of moral responsibility. Thus, the ethical underpinnings of the mission have brought NCCU's educational focus full circle back to the DuBois-Shepard vision which served the university and its community so well in the early years of this century.

## FROM MISSION TO FRUITION

Once the service-based mission was adopted by the board of trustees in 1994, the chancellor turned his energies to two objectives which he believed were critical to making the mission a reality. These objectives were: 1) to revise general study requirements for freshmen and sophomores to include service components in core academic curricula, and 2) to require a minimum of 120 hours (15 clock hours per semester) of community service volunteer work as a condition for graduation.

In 1994, the university's General College Studies program was revised and renamed CFAS (Critical Foundations in the Arts and Sciences). Of the many course offerings involved, Personal and Social Development became the first to incorporate community service. To implement the above two objectives, Chambers established the Community Service Office (CSO)—which was later renamed the Community Service Program (CSP)—as an ombudsman between the university and

the Durham community. I, who was a tenured full professor of history, was asked to develop a five-year service plan for the university. The NCCU planning team included Rosa Anderson, Director of the Community Service Office and a Department of Human Sciences faculty member; Dr. Ted Parrish, Health Education Chair; Dr. Kenneth Chambers, Faculty Senate Chair; Dr. George Wilson, Criminal Justice Chair; Mr. Tyrone Cox, SGA member; and Mr. Derick Brown, SGA President. The plan included: 1) direct service to established community agencies by students, faculty, staff, and alumni; 2) a variety of means to incorporate service-learning into all academic courses; 3) development of university-community partnerships to improve the local urban community; and 4) creation of awards and university-wide activities to encourage an ethic of service on campus.

As a core discipline faculty member with experience in building service components into her course design even before the new mission was adopted, I brought credibility to the CSP and was named its director in 1994. To maintain my credibility among faculty, I retain a part-time teaching load (two courses per year) while serving administratively as head of the CSP. In addition, to ensure that community service would develop from concept to core and that the university would, in fact, become a community revitalization partner, a full-time staff of four was hired to implement the program year-round. With mission and department in place, NCCU joined the Campus Compact in 1995 in order to solidify its commitment and to link its campus-wide involvement in service to a nationwide arena. During that same year, I was invited to join the Invisible College, a national organization whose aim is to increase faculty involvement in service-learning.

## PROGRAM STRUCTURE

The CSP currently has a year-round staff of five: Beverly W. Jones, Director; Rosa Anderson, Assistant Director; Carla Alston, Student Placement Coordinator; David Williams, Service-Learning Coordinator; and Regina Barton, Administrative Assistant. I serve part-time and report to the provost and vice chancellor for academic affairs. Day-to-day operations are divided among the remaining four employees. In addition, a cadre of 20 student volunteers serves within and for the program in a variety of functions, from clerical work to program promotions.

The director's responsibilities include: 1) implementing service-learning policy; 2) securing funding; 3) serving as university spokesperson on matters related to service; 4) establishing collaborative institutional and interinstitutional activities; and 5) promoting opportunities for faculty and students to collaborate with noted service-learning practitioners such as Robert Coles, Edward Zlotkowski, and Ira Harkavy.

The assistant director reports directly to the director. Ms. Anderson coordinates departmental functions, maintains daily CSP operations, and supervises three full-time staff. She is responsible for program and staff development and evaluation, some fundraising initiatives and grantwriting, volunteer training, and program policy implementation. Other responsibilities include agency site monitoring, interinstitutional partnership development, coordinating nonprofit agency collaborations, and overseeing student reflection activities. Ms. Anderson is a member of the North Carolina Association of Volunteer Administrators and holds the Certification of Service-Learning Training from the North Carolina Department of Public Instruction.

The service-learning coordinator's responsibilities include the design and implementation of specific service-learning projects on and off campus. Mr. Williams identifies appropriate community service sites congruent with students' interests and career goals. He also assists community service sites in developing curricula and ensures continuity between the NCCU service-learning program and the community. The coordinator frequently visits departments on campus and assists in the development of workshops and conferences, but the position's primary purpose is to assist CFAS faculty in the incorporation of service into their courses. Mr. Williams taught social sciences at the secondary level, completed NTE certification, and maintains membership in Kappa Delta Pi.

The student placement coordinator has experience in customer service, salesmanship, and public relations—all of which help ensure smooth implementation of the Community Service-Learning Graduation Policy. Ms. Alston is responsible for student registration and placement, and maintains all records and statistics pertaining to student volunteerism. She conducts service site visits, monitors agency needs and concerns, and coordinates and analyzes all data gathered from the various service sites to gauge the impact of student efforts on each community site served. She is also responsible for officially documenting service hours, determining the impact of service on all stakeholders, and disseminating student and agency evaluations.

The administrative assistant is responsible for coordinating office operations, maintaining CSP budgets, and facilitating the grant writing process. She also takes care of all departmental written correspondence and CSP publications. Ms. Barton designs, composes, and serves as editor for the Community Service Program's monthly newsletter, *Truth and Service*. In addition, she plans and implements all conferences, town meetings, and workshops on community service and service-learning, and supervises the student volunteers who staff the CSP. Staying as current with inner-office technology as budgets allow and keeping a physical inventory are still other duties of the administrative assistant.

## STUDENT INVOLVEMENT

While the CSP provides guidance on community needs and requests, NCCU's policy is never to stifle student creativity. Freshman students are allowed to perform service both on and off campus. Many students like to perform service collectively rather then individually. This sense of communalism and group dynamics is integral to the African heritage of tribalism, which provides the context and the purpose of the African ethos.

Hence, many African-American students who perform community service are especially interested in activities and projects that relate to community development (e.g., assisting small businesses in marketing plans, designing community-based grassroots tutoring projects, conducting community needs assessments, and engaging in community capacity-building activities). Such linkages to service reinforce this sense of communalism and self-identity.

Since a key objective of the CSP is to promote an ethic of service, this heritage and the inclination of our students has led to a natural alliance among the Office of Student Affairs, the Student Government Association, and the CSP. The result has been projects such as the following:

- Project GRASP (Generating Resources to Address Social Problems) in which NCCU students work with targeted community agencies to attend to persons with health problems—physical, mental, and emotional—through the identification of coping strategies, resources, and referrals critical to ensuring quality of life.

- New Hope Project in which students from NCCU and Duke University organized a house course (a course taught by students and/or faculty in the dormitory) on homelessness and coordinated a city-wide effort to raise money and the awareness of citizens to the issues of homelessness.

- Project ASSIGN (After-School Session in Guided Nurture) in which NCCU students work with the child and family service unit of the social services department to provide at least minimal substance and social needs for families. Each student partners with a child to identify and address health, material, and educational needs as well as to provide mentorship.

- Project FACE (Friendly Association for Cultural Enrichment) in which students work with Holton Middle School students to address problems of youth literacy, negative behavior, and health and environmental concerns.

Cumulatively, these efforts have begun to address some of the most critical needs of our local community while also beginning to rebuild the community's trust in our resolve to be its long-term problem solving partner.

To cultivate student leadership, CSP has also established a Community Service Ambassadors Program. Ambassadors are upperclassmen who have been active in service from their freshman year on. The process of choosing an ambassador is highly selective. The candidates must have at least a 2.8 grade point average and must undergo an intensive screening process by the CSP staff. Ambassadors commit to activities such as placing and evaluating students, disseminating service information to NCCU departments and to the Durham community, assisting with student reflection activities, and conducting site visit evaluations. There are currently 24 ambassadors chosen per year.

## FACULTY INVOLVEMENT

Involving faculty has been more of a challenge. One promising start was to involve the English department in promoting the concept of service. Thus, in 1995, the CSP and the English department jointly developed and sponsored an annual community service essay competition, providing a forum for students to reflect upon and communicate the meaning of service to them per-

sonally. However, winners of the competition do not receive any monetary awards for their reflections. This would be antithetical to NCCU's philosophy of service-learning. Instead, they receive volunteer credit hours, have lunch with the chancellor and the board of trustees, and are celebrated in the campus media. The following excerpts from the first year's competition highlight the synergistic relationship between service and a student's intellectual and social development:

> Many of us have been taught the concept of being "our brother's keeper," but it takes more than thinking about it to make the idea work. It is one's own personal and committed action that really makes the difference. And the wonderful part of shouldering some of our neighbors' burdens by serving our community is that it all comes back to us. Giving service to others not only touches the lives of those being helped, but also helps to build our character, to provide much-needed interaction with others, and to improve the world in which we all dwell together.
>
> —Nacelle Johnson, first place essay, 1995

> There are a lot of blind people in the world. Until recently, I was one of them. Going on that midnight run changed my way of thinking, the way I treat homeless people, and the way I want to live my life. If you doubt this radical transformation, just try to think of yourself as the one who helps save her, the one who makes a difference. It's an insight that could change your life and the lives of those frightened children out there in all of our communities.
>
> —Kesha Moore, second place essay, 1995

> You would never believe how giving a few hours of your time each week can make a difference in someone's life ... I did not believe [this] until I became a volunteer for Communi-Care three years ago. A nonprofit, community-based organization originating in Statesville, North Carolina, Communi-Care focuses on positive intervention in the lives of children. And, while volunteers do their worthy work, they reap additional benefits—developing leadership and organizational skills, all while giving back to the community.
>
> —Cheryl Parker, third place essay, 1995

While the essay competition has proven to be a success, there is much more to be done to involve faculty. We acknowledge that service-learning at NCCU is still in an embryonic stage and has not yet been universally accepted by all faculty. However, a recent survey of faculty involvement indicated that there are at least 50 faculty members who are actively engaged in service-learning teaching or curriculum restructuring efforts. The survey also reported a heightened interest in service-learning among both old and new faculty. This increased faculty interest can be traced to three factors.

First, external speakers have provided insight and strategies. Edward Zlotkowski, from Bentley College in Massachusetts, conducted two workshops on restructuring courses for over 30 faculty members. Tom Ehrlich, former president of Indiana University and member of the Campus Compact Executive Board, validated the important role of higher education in the service movement in a keynote address to faculty and students. Robert Coles, Harvard professor and renowned author, spoke to the freshman class and faculty about his book *The Call of Service*. Ira Harkavy discussed with the faculty the salience of university-community partnerships in revitalizing inner cities. A symposium featuring Nancy Rhodes, then Director of Campus Compact; Dr. Gloria Scott, President of Bennett College; State Representative William Martin; and moderator Valeria Lee, Program Officer of the Z. Smith Reynolds Foundation, even convinced some reluctant administrators that community service is a bona fide pedagogical tool. The CSP has also made it a priority to introduce faculty from neighboring institutions involved in service-learning to NCCU faculty in order to discuss service-learning strategies. Another, related effort has been the distribution of a series of journal articles on service-learning to the faculty. Finally, the CSP has coordinated service-learning circles of faculty and students to reflect upon existing courses and the meaning of service.

A second factor responsible for increased faculty interest is of a rather different nature. In concert with the School of Education, the CSP has developed an evaluation tool for assessing the impact of community service-learning on faculty teaching, as well as student leadership and intellectual development. Twice a year, service sites are also evaluated by students, faculty, and CSP staff. And yet, despite these steps, there is still much room for strengthening the evaluative aspect of the program.

Still another strategy calculated to increase faculty interest concerns the reward system. We are currently recommending a rewriting of our tenure, promotion,

and merit increase policies to include curricular service activities. To that end, our provost and deans have reviewed copies of service policies from institutions such as Portland State University. It is our belief that, together, these activities have begun to create a critical mass of theory, insight, and practical information that is essential to convince faculty to adopt service-learning as an ongoing component of their courses.

## COMMUNITY REVITALIZATION: A PROJECT IN PROGRESS

Community revitalization is the goal of the Community Service Program's strategic plan. The reason we are working so hard on a variety of means to convince faculty of the efficacy of service-learning and the importance of university-community partnerships is that without committed faculty participation, the service mission and strategic plan of the university can only be empty promises. To nurture our fledgling program, therefore, we enthusiastically communicate and promote each genuine effort made by faculty members to contribute to the community revitalization effort. In this regard, one especially exemplary service-learning course is Health Education 4200, Aging and the Aged: Health Perspectives, in which students have produced taped interviews as part of prescribed home visits to elderly persons. In addition, they make a minimum of five visits to nursing homes where they do whatever they can to assist the staff and patients. Students in the class have also "adopted" two families and provided food items for their Thanksgiving and Christmas dinners. Many of the students have continued the relationships with the elderly beyond the end of the class.

With a $3,060 grant from the HBCU Campus Network, Environmental Biology 2600 was revised to incorporate a service-learning module designed to increase awareness of environmental hazards in the Durham community. Students focused on Legionnaires' Disease, a condition that stems from contaminated water in closed environments. During the spring semester 1995-96, students conducted a university-wide survey investigating student, staff, and faculty awareness of this disease and its reported incidence on campus; conducted a community-based survey to compare the university data with that of the Durham community; identified and formed liaisons with community organizations—health, environmental, and social—that deal with outbreaks of the disease; designed an information booklet on the disease, its history, prevention methods, and prescribed treatments; and selected the best techniques for demonstrating to the community the steps that should be taken to disinfect devices that may harbor Legionnaires' bacteria.

During the 1995 spring semester, public administration students met their service requirement by participating in an interdisciplinary health appraisal project with students in the geography department. The dual-discipline course was called Public Administration 2100. While public administration students administered a survey which tapped health perceptions and practices of students and faculty at NCCU, geography students input the data into a geographic information system (GIS) program. Public administration and geography students analyzed the data and assisted in summarizing the survey findings. The findings on health perceptions and practices at NCCU will become part of a larger collection of state survey information that will be forwarded to the Centers for Disease Control in Atlanta.

In addition to the service-based course offerings that have begun to remake our curriculum, a community project has been created which may prove to be the core of our long-term commitment to the community and its well-being. NCCU firmly believes that if the community is transformed, so will NCCU's students and the university itself. Thus, while many university-community partnerships use a bipolar approach to service delivery, the CSP favors a more holistic strategy. In 1993, in response to the city of Durhams Partnership Against Crime (PAC) efforts, North Carolina Central University joined city and county government, businesses, post-secondary institutions, and community residents for the purpose of revitalizing the most drug-infested, deteriorating local community—Northeast Central Durham.

A community-based committee of representatives from the local community, from NCCU, and from city and county government developed five task forces focused on: 1) family and child support, 2) economic development, 3) religion, 4) youth, and 5) health. Members of each task force included the same mix of university, community, and government representatives. An assets and needs survey was conducted by the Institute for the Study of Minority Issues at NCCU. The assets of the community indicated strong economic interest on the part of operating businesses, economic investment potential among black churches, and three public schools with quality education programs that could be leveraged for further development. A needs survey

indicated four concerns of the community: 1) reducing crime, 2) creating jobs, 3) developing health prevention programs, and 4) encouraging children to stay in school.

Though Northeast Central Durham is located eight miles from the university, North Carolina Central University responded to the expressed requests of the community through research projects, student tutors and mentors, technical grant writing, and curriculum restructuring support. Each activity and funding proposal was approved by the community-based committee. To date, the most promising result of this effort has come from the task force focused on family and child support. Though numerous meetings were necessary to solidify trust between partners, faculty from the School of Education and the Human Resources Department have now successfully fostered the concept of "community capacity-building" by assisting in the development of a Family Resource Center which serves as a one-stop delivery for children's needs. The center is operated by the community task force and volunteers. Smart Start and Family Preservation Grants totaling $350,000 now fund the necessary infrastructure to improve the quality of life for children and families in Northeast Central Durham. In addition, one elementary school in the community is receiving support from NCCU's School of Education and the human resources department to improve the curriculum and training techniques of teachers. Meanwhile, the health education department is providing lead testing and vision screening for the children.

The School of Business is also actively involved in this project, examining ways to work with the Economic Reinvestment Committee to spawn business incubators. Other discipline-based units, like the School of Nursing, have assessed their curricula and plan to incorporate quality of life issues and service support for this Durham community into their course activities. Since interinstitutional support is important in community revitalization efforts, Duke University has volunteered its medical staff and Durham Technical Community College has helped with adult and work-preparedness training. All along the way, the community has been directly involved in planning and implementation in partnership with CSP staff.

The Northeast Central Durham model has now become the collaborative structure for Durham's city revitalization efforts. As a result of the program's success to date, the city has created three other opportunity zones on which to focus service efforts: Southeast Central, Northwest, and Southwest Durham. Another community revitalization project that students have participated in is the Knolls Development bordering on Chapel Hill. This project began in 1991 when a health education class became aware of the toll that crack cocaine had taken on many of the people in the development. Crime was up; several drive-by shootings had occurred; young mothers were prostituting themselves for drugs; and a NCCU professor, who had committed to living in the community, had experienced the first break-in at his own home. An experienced organizer and field supervisor, the professor decided to place students in this troubled community for an eight-week period. Their assignment was to work directly with the community by 1) interviewing community leaders, 2) collecting and analyzing data, and 3) assisting neighborhood residents with planning and implementing programs designed to address community problems. In other words, while students learned to practice health education, they simultaneously served a low-income community.

In 1991–92, three students served the Knolls Development by helping neighbors plan and implement a summer enrichment program. Child safety had become a real concern to mothers in the area, following a drive-by shooting which accidentally injured a nine-year-old boy. The summer program had such a positive outcome on residents that one of the students, upon graduation, wrote a small grant proposal which the local school system funded. Other students were then assigned to help her, and a regular after-school program continued what the summer enrichment program had begun. This, too, was successful, and today the city of Chapel Hill funds this after-school program, which is operated by the local YMCA. Two students assigned to do their fieldwork in the Knolls Development formed the Knolls Development Association (KDA), through which students study the history of the community. Through the KDA, the community learned that the first black homeowner in the area was a former slave who had worked for Chancellor Caldwell of the University of North Carolina at Chapel Hill. It was also learned that the Knolls Development had had numerous strong leaders in the past, including an 80-year-old woman who still lives there today. It was she who had organized the community to petition both Carrboro and Chapel Hill for annexation many years ago. Both municipalities had refused to accept the development,

but when Chapel Hill elected its first African-American mayor, the community was finally annexed.

Lessons like these infused the fledgling organization with the belief that it, too, could succeed with its initiatives, particularly in addressing the crack problem and the housing crisis. By 1993, the NCCU professor who had moved to the community assigned more students to organize work crews from NCCU to assist in the remodeling of a few old houses that had been given to KDA by the Durham school board. With the success of this remodeling, more houses, loans, and grants followed. Every step of the way, several semesters' worth of students found opportunities to perform service for and learn about the Knolls Development, as well as to develop graphic displays showing what they had accomplished.

Since 1995, when the Community Service Program was formally adopted by NCCU as part of its curriculum, the mentor professor has used the display to tell the story of the Knolls Development to students anticipating their own community service work. He points out how many NCCU, Duke, and University of North Carolina students have participated in service-learning in the community. He notes the thousands of hours that these students have invested in building houses, developing brochures, and providing technical assistance to KDA. As the professor looks out his window, he can see two houses. One is a ranch-style house built by KDA and valued at over $110,000, but sold to a moderate income family for $54,000. A second is a two-story house, which was appraised at $75,000 when it was given to KDA. When it is completed, its value will be over $100,000, even though KDA will sell it for only $60,000. Since 1993, KDA has renovated or purchased for renovation 25 residential units for low to moderate income families. KDA has become a positive force in the Knolls Development and concomitantly in Chapel Hill, where affluent residents no longer wish that African-Americans would leave the Knolls Development for good. With only a community center and a dream in 1991, and with the ongoing support that now comes through The Community Service Program, KDA expects to complete projects that will exceed $3,000,000 in value by the year 2000.

## THE FUTURE OF SERVICE AT NCCU

Many faculty and administrators believe we have, by this point, correctly identified the elements necessary to create a reliable and long-lasting Community Service

Program. Our energy must now be focused on strengthening each existing component. Based on the results of projects such as those just outlined, the CSP will have to concentrate on increasing faculty support for service-learning, evaluating the efficacy of the Community Service Graduation Policy, strengthening community-university partnerships, and aggressively seeking external funding in the face of declining enrollment.

## LESSONS LEARNED: A SUMMARY FROM AN HBCU PERSPECTIVE

Overall, the success of the Community Service Program at North Carolina Central University can be attributed to the following:

- Visible top administrative support for the program, particularly during its start-up years

- Institutionalization of service as a driving force for university activities, through formal revision of the mission statement

- Formation of a core team of faculty, administrators, students, and community members to advocate for service-learning on campus and to serve on the Community Service Advisory Committee for the community at large

- Selection of a veteran faculty member to lead the program; also, providing a committee and professional staff to serve as a liaison among students, faculty, staff, and community agencies

- Application for faculty development funds to introduce faculty to the service-learning pedagogy from a variety of perspectives and through different voices

- Creation of numerous opportunities for faculty to discover how others in their discipline and across disciplines in similar types of institutions have implemented service-learning

- Existence of multiple approaches to build service into the university, including traditional direct service, service-learning, and university-community partnerships

- Service efforts that focus on a limited population, as in the case of Northeast Central Durham, so that real progress can be made and accurately assessed

The DuBois-Shepard service-based mission remains a challenge for NCCU, a reminder that regeneration is a broadly beneficial process and that regeneration through service requires continuous commitment. As our students, faculty, and staff have worked with our community in renewing itself-economically, socially, and environmentally-they have testified, almost as one, that the integrity of their learning and their self image is, and must be, grounded in the renewable soil of the community in which their university makes its home.

## REFERENCES

Coles, R. (1993). *The call of service*. Boston, MA: Houghton Mifflin.

Joseph, J. A. (1995). *Remaking America: How the benevolent traditions of many cultures are transforming our national life*. San Francisco, CA: Jossey-Bass.

# Model Programs:
## Recommended Reading

## BOOKS & CHAPTERS

American Association of Community Colleges. (1998). *Best practices in service learning: Building a national community college network*. Washington, DC: Community College Press.

American Association of Community Colleges. (1999). *Community colleges broadening horizons through service-learning, 1997–2000*. Washington, DC: Community College Press.

American Association of Community Colleges. (2000). *Creating sustainable service-learning programs: Lessons learned from the horizons project, 1997–2000*. Washington, DC: Community College Press.

Boone, E.J., Pettitt, J.M., & Weisman, I.M. (Eds.). (1998). *Community-based programming in action: The experiences of five community colleges*. Washington, DC: Community College Press.

Campus Compact. (1996). *Service matters: A sourcebook for community service in higher education*. Providence, RI: Campus Compact.

Duckenfield, M., & Swick, K.J. (Eds.). (2002). *A gallery of portraits in service-learning action research in teacher education*. Clemson, SC: National Dropout Prevention Center.

Iannozzi, M. (2001). *Examplars: Tusculum College*. Philadelphia: Knight Higher Education Collaborative.

Simon, L.A.K., Kenny, M., Brabeck, K., & Lerner, R.M. (Eds.). (2001). *Learning to serve: Promoting civil society through service-learning*. Norwell, MA: Kluwer Academic Publishers.

Vaughan, G.B. (2001). *Community colleges and democracy: Celebrating the American dream*. Washington, DC: Community College Press.

Zlotkowski, E. (Ed.). (1998). *Successful service-learning programs*. Bolton, MA: Anker Publishing.

## ARTICLES & REPORTS

Bringle, R.G., et al. (2000). Faculty fellows program. *American Behavioral Scientist*, 43 (5), 882–95.

Campus Compact (n.d.). Program models database. Available at www.compact.org/programmodels.

Cummings, C.K. (2000). John Dewey and the rebuilding of urban community: Engaging undergraduates as neighborhood organizers. *Michigan Journal of Community Service Learning*, 7, 97–108).

Degelman, C. (Ed.). (2001). Local government: The learning laboratory. *Service-Learning Network*, 8 (3).

Fogelman, E. (2002). Civic engagement at the University of Minnesota. *The Journal of Public Affairs*, 6, 103–118.

Hamner, J.B., et al. (2002). Community-based service-learning in the engaged university. *Nursing Outlook*, 50 (2), 67–71.

Hodge, G., et al. (2001). Collaboration for excellence: Engaged scholarship at Collin County Community College. *Community College Journal of Research and Practice*, 25 (9), 675–90.

Keefe, M., et al. (2000). The caring for the community initiative: Integrating research, practice, and education. *Nursing and Health Care Perspectives*, 21 (6), 287–92.

Meister, R.J. (1998). Engagement with society at DePaul University. *Liberal Education*, 84 (4), 56–61.

Moore, S.D. (2000). Winburn community academy: A university-assisted community school and professional development school. *Peabody Journal of Education*, 75 (3), 33–51.

O'Neill, H. (2000). Promising practices in programming: An annotated list of model programs. *New Directions for Student Services*, 90, 91–102.

Peterman, D. (2000). Service-learning in community colleges. *Community College Journal of Research and Practice*, 24 (4), 321–6.

Roschelle, A.R., Turpin, J., & Elias, R. (2000). Who learns from service-learning? *American Behavioral Scientist*, 43 (5), 839–48.

Schwinn, E. (2000, November 30). Maine college forges community ties through students' service work. *Chronicle of Philanthropy, 13* (4), 32–4.

Wallace, J. (2001). The problem of time: Enabling students to make long-term commitments to community-based learning. *Michigan Journal of Community Service Learning, 7,* 133–41.

# Student Development

## TITLES INCLUDED IN THIS SECTION

Long-Term Effects of Volunteerism During the Under-graduate Years, BY ALEXANDER W. ASTIN, LINDA J. SAX, AND JUAN AVALOS

Comparing the Effects of Community Service and Service-Learning, BY LORI J. VOGELGESANG AND ALEXANDER W. ASTIN

Recommended Reading

## QUESTIONS FOR REFLECTION AND PLANNING

How will you ascertain the appropriate service placement for the students in your course? How will you know students are prepared for the experience?

What is your institution's approach to student development? How is that evidenced?

Who on your campus understands and practices this institutional definition/philosophy of student development?

What student development outcomes can you integrate into your courses through service-learning?

# Long-Term Effects of Volunteerism During the Undergraduate Years

by Alexander W. Astin, Linda J. Sax, and Juan Avalos

AGROWING NUMBER OF colleges and universities in the United States have become actively engaged in encouraging their undergraduate students to participate in some form of volunteer service (Cohen & Kinsey, 1994; Levine, 1994; Markus, Howard, & King, 1993; O'Brien, 1993). Further, service is increasingly being incorporated into the curriculums of major and general education courses (Cohen & Kinsey, 1994; Levine, 1994). While relatively few colleges include service learning or volunteer service as a curricular requirement, the number is growing and such a requirement has become an increasingly frequent topic of debate (Markus, Howard, & King, 1993). That the top leadership in higher education has become increasingly supportive of service as part of the undergraduate experience is reflected in the phenomenal growth of Campus Compact, a consortium of colleges and universities dedicated to promoting service among students and faculty. Campus Compact now numbers well over 500 institutions.

One of the issues frequently raised by faculty and others who might be skeptical about the value of a service or volunteer experience is the one of efficacy: How is the student's educational and personal development affected by service participation? To date, empirical studies on the impact of service are quite scarce although evidence of the benefits of "involvement" in college is certainly abundant (Astin, 1993; Pascarella & Terenzini, 1991). While recent studies provide some evidence that service is associated with civic involvement and cognitive development, such research is generally limited because it relies on small samples of students from a single institution (Batchelder & Root, 1994; Giles & Eyler, 1994; Markus, Howard, & King, 1993). Although such studies have opened the door by providing a useful framework for the study of service, a consensus has indeed emerged about the urgency of collecting longitudinal, multi-institutional data on how students are affected by the service experience (Batchelder & Root, 1994; Cohen & Kinsey, 1994; Giles & Eyler, 1994; Giles, Honnet, & Migliore, 1991; Markus, Howard, & King, 1993; O'Brien, 1993).

Recently, the Higher Education Research Institute at UCLA completed a national study of the effects of President Clinton's Learn and Serve America Higher Education Program, an activity of the Corporation for National Service, which is designed to facilitate the development of volunteer service programs for college students. This longitudinal multi-institutional study allowed for the examination of the effects of service participation after controlling for students' precollege propensity to engage in service. Findings suggested that service participation is positively associated with a number of short-term cognitive and affective outcomes during the undergraduate years (Astin & Sax, 1998). Among other things, the study found that service participation positively affects students' commitment to their communities, to helping others in difficulty, to promoting racial understanding, and to influencing social values. In addition, service participation directly influences the development of important life skills, such as leadership ability, social self-confidence, critical thinking skills, and conflict resolution skills. Service participation also has unique positive effects on academic development, including knowledge gained, grades earned, degrees sought after, and time devoted to academic endeavors.

While the Astin and Sax (1998) study examined the short-term effects of service participation, the purpose of the study reported here is to determine whether service participation during the undergraduate years has any *lasting* effects on students once they leave college. Among the questions to be explored are: Does undergraduate service participation continue to affect the student's educational development after college? How are other postcollege behaviors influenced? Do the value changes that have been associated with service participation during college persist after the student leaves college?

## CONTEXT FOR THE STUDY

The long-term effects of college can be looked at from two different perspectives: First, how students in general develop once they leave college (the generic "impact of college"); and second, how postcollege development is affected by particular college *experiences*. The study reported here is of the latter type. While most studies of the long-term impact of college tend to focus on whether college attendance or degree attainment makes a difference (see Pascarella & Terenzini, 1991), few studies have been carried out to assess the long-term impact of particular college experiences such as community service.

To place this study in the larger context of the higher education research literature, we propose that our principal independent variable—participating in community service during the undergraduate years—be regarded as a form of student involvement (Astin, 1975, 1984, 1985). Briefly stated, the theory of *involvement* postulates that the benefits (i.e., "value-added") that students enjoy as a result of the college experience will be directly proportional to the time and effort that they invest in that experience. A large body of research shows that diverse forms of involvement are associated with a wide variety of positive student outcomes (Astin, 1977, 1993; Pascarella & Terenzini, 1991). The most potent forms of student involvement appear to be academic involvement (e.g., time spent studying and carrying out class assignments), interaction with peers, and interaction with faculty. While community service has so far received relatively little attention in student development research, it clearly qualifies as a substantial "investment of time and energy," and it ordinarily involves interaction with peers. In the case of course-based service, it would also be likely to increase both student-faculty interaction as well as the amount of time and energy that the students devote to the course.

## METHOD

An opportunity to explore this topic was afforded by the availability of a national sample of former college students that included longitudinal data collected at three time points: at the time of initial entry to college in the fall of 1985, four years later in 1989, and nine years after college entry during 1994–1995. These data were collected as part of the Cooperative Institutional Research Program (CIRP), which is sponsored by the American Council on Education and the Higher Education Research Institute (HERI) at the University of California, Los Angeles. The CIRP annually collects a broad array of student background information using the Student Information Form (SIF), and is designed to serve as a pretest for longitudinal assessments of the impact of college on students.

## THE SURVEY

### The Student Information Form

The SIF was mailed to campuses in the spring and summer of 1985 for distribution to first-year college students during orientation programs and in the first few weeks of fall classes. The 1985 SIF includes information on students' personal and demographic characteristics, high school experiences, and expectations about college, as well as values, life goals, self-concepts, and career aspirations. A total of 279,985 students at 546 participating colleges and universities completed the SIF.

### The 1989 Follow-up Survey

In 1989, HERI conducted a four-year longitudinal follow-up of students at four-year institutions who had completed the first-year survey in 1985. The 1989 follow-up survey includes information on students' college experience, their perceptions of college, and post-tests of many of the items that appeared on the 1985 freshman student survey. The follow-up sample of 93,463 of the original 279,985 first-year students was selected in three different ways. A initial sample of 16,658 students from 309 institutions was selected through stratified random sampling. This procedure was designed to best reflect the national distribution of students across different institutional types. A second follow-up sample of 34,323 students at 52 institutions was afforded through a grant from the Exxon Education Foundation for the purpose of studying general education outcomes. Finally, we surveyed an additional 42,482 students at 100 institutions through a grant from the National Science Foundation designed to study undergraduate science education. Ultimately, we had responses from 27,064 students from 388 colleges and universities, resulting in an overall response rate of 29.0 percent. (See Astin, 1993, for more details on this sample.)

### The Nine-Year Follow-up Survey

We conducted a second longitudinal follow-up survey in 1994–1995. This nine-year follow-up survey provides information on graduate school and early career experiences, as well as post-test data on many of the attitudinal and behavioral items appearing on the 1985 and 1989 surveys. This survey was sent to a sample of 24,057 students who had completed both the 1985 first-year and the 1989 follow-up surveys. A response rate of 51.4 percent was obtained, yielding a final sample of 12,376 from 209 institutions that had data at all three time points.[1]

## PRIMARY INDEPENDENT VARIABLE

The principal independent variable used in this study comes from the first (1989) longitudinal follow-up survey conducted four years after the student entered college. Students were asked, "During your last year in college, how much time did you spend during a typical week in volunteer work?" Students could respond along an eight-point continuum ranging from "none" to "over 20." After inspecting the distribution of responses to this question, we decided to collapse the top categories to create a five-category measure: (1) none, (2) less than 1 hour per week, (3) 1–2 hours per week, (4) 3–5 hours per week, and (5) 6 or more hours per week. The weighted percentage distribution of students' responses on this collapsed scale are as follows: 61.3, 13.3, 13.3, 7.0, 5.1. Thus, more than three students in five reported no involvement in volunteer service work during their last year of college, whereas only about one in twenty reported volunteering for six or more hours per week.

## DEPENDENT VARIABLES

The nine-year follow-up survey (1994–1995) provided a number of opportunities to assess the impact of volunteer service participation during college on postcollege outcomes. Our selection of dependent variables was guided by two considerations: First, the short-term outcomes (e.g., satisfaction, academic performance, interest in graduate school, and sense of personal empowerment) that recent research has shown to be affected by service participation (Sax, Astin, & Astin, 1996); and second, the theory underlying the concepts of volunteerism and service learning, which argues, among other things, that service participation deepens students' understanding of social problems such as environmental degradation, poverty, and racial tension, and strengthens their commitment to civic values. (See, for example, Barber, 1993; Newman, 1985). We were also interested in testing the argument, sometimes advanced by opponents of service-learning, that participation in community service "politicizes" students. Finally, although no previous research or theory suggests that service participation should enhance the student's earnings, preparation for graduate school, or sense of commitment or loyalty to the alma mater, we included such outcomes on a purely exploratory basis.

With these guidelines in mind, we selected 18 outcome measures comprising a diverse array of academic and nonacademic behaviors, attitudes, and goals. The majority of these items had been pretested when the students entered college and post-tested four years later in the first follow-up conducted in 1989. Dependent variables include: five behavioral outcomes (attended graduate school, highest degree earned, donated money to the undergraduate college, frequency of socializing with persons from other racial/ethnic groups, and hours per week spent in volunteer/community service work during the past year); five measures of values (the student's degree of commitment to participate in community action programs, help others in difficulty, participate in programs to clean up the environment, promote racial understanding, and develop a meaningful philosophy of life); two *ratings of the undergraduate college* (adequacy of preparation for graduate work and for job); and two *satisfaction measures* (with graduate school, with job). Additional dependent measures included: political leaning (five-point scale from far right to far left), degree aspirations, income, and agreement with the statement, "Realistically, an individual person can do little to bring about changes in our society." This last measure is included as a "negative" outcome measure; that is, one would expect that involvement in service work would tend to empower students with the conviction that they can indeed make a difference in the society.

## ADDITIONAL INDEPENDENT VARIABLES

Following the CAMBRA approach to causal modeling (Astin & Dey, 1996), we included a number of first-year student "input" variables as control variables. These included pretests on 12 of the 18 dependent variables. Such pretests were available on all outcomes except the two satisfaction measures, the two undergraduate college ratings, income, and donating money to the undergraduate college. Input variables also included a set of 13 variables that we found through exploratory analyses to predict students' precollege propensity to engage in service. These include: four *behavioral* measures (performed volunteer work, tutored another student, attended religious services, and smoked cigarettes); three measures of *values* (the student's degree of commitment to participate in community action programs, help others in difficulty, and be very well off financially); two *reasons for attending college* (to make more money and improve reading and study skills); self rating on leadership ability, and measures of racial background and religious preference. Student's gender, socio-economic status, and high school grades are additional inputs included in this study.

## ANALYSIS DESIGN

The principal purpose of the data analysis was to estimate the effects of volunteer participation during the undergraduate years on each of the eighteen postcollege outcomes. For this purpose, we employed the CAMBRA method of causal modeling, which utilizes blocked, stepwise linear multiple regression analysis to focus on changes in the partial regression coefficients for all variables at each step in the analysis (Astin & Dey, 1996). CAMBRA provides a powerful means of decomposing and comprehending multicollinearity in a complex multivariate data set.

The basic approach in CAMBRA is to view each step (or block) in stepwise regression as a new model, differentiated from the model defined by the previous step (or block) by the newly added variable (or block of variables). The power of CAMBRA resides in its ability to demonstrate how the addition of a new variable (or block of variables) affects the relationship between *every other* variable—both in *and* out of the model—and the dependent variable. Identifying changes in the "effect" of variables that are not part of the variables currently defining the model is possible because of a novel feature of SPSS regression that computes the "beta in" for each such variable. "Beta in" shows what the standard-ized regression coefficient for a nonentered variable would be if it were the one entered on the *next step*. By following step-by-step changes in betas (for variables in the model) and "beta ins" (for variables not yet in the model), the investigator can get a comprehensive picture of how multicollinearity is affecting the entire data set.

CAMBRA also allows the investigator to conduct a series of path analyses by observing how the coefficients for variables already entered are changed when later variables are entered. When an entering variable significantly diminishes the coefficient for an earlier variable, an "indirect" path has been identified. When an earlier variable's coefficient remains significant through the final step, a "direct" path has been identified. The unique situation that occurs when an entering variable *strengthens* the coefficient for an earlier variable (a condition not covered in most writings on path analysis) is called a "suppressor effect" (i.e., the entering variable has been "suppressing" the observed effect of the earlier variable on the dependent variable) (Astin, 1991; Astin & Dey, 1996).

Each CAMBRA analysis had four blocks: (a) entering first-year student (input) variables; (b) hours spent volunteering during the last year in college (the principal independent variable); (c) the first (1989) posttest; and (d) hours spent in volunteer/community service work during the past year (i.e., 1994–1995). We included all entering first-year student or input variables in the first block, not only to control for initial differences in the students' pretest performance on each outcome measure, but also to control for possible self-selection bias (i.e., the student's predisposition to engage in volunteer service work during college).

We included the third block—the initial (1989) posttest on the dependent variable—to determine the extent to which the long-term effects of undergraduate service participation could be explained by its short-term effect on the first posttest measure obtained four years after entering college. In other words, does undergraduate service participation have any effect on the student nine years after college entry (1994), above and beyond its short-term effect as assessed only four years after entering college (1989)?

We included hours per week spent in volunteer or community service work in 1994 as the fourth and final block to determine if the effects of volunteering during college could be explained by its effect on volunteering after college. In other words, do students develop a "habit" of volunteering which persists after college, and can this continuing involvement help to explain the effect of undergraduate service participation on other long-term outcomes?

In short, we included these final two blocks of variables to learn something about the factors that *mediate* the long-term effects of service participation during the undergraduate years. (Note that the fourth block obviously had to be excluded from the one regression in which hours per week spent in volunteer/community service work was the dependent variable.)

We conducted a separate CAMBRA analysis for each of the 18 dependent variables. We confined regressions involving income and job satisfaction to students who were employed full-time at the time of the follow-up. Similarly, we limited the two regressions involving graduate school to students who had either completed their graduate work or were enrolled in graduate work at the time of the follow-up. We also excluded subjects who were missing data on either the dependent variable or the principal independent variable (volunteer participation during the undergraduate years) from any analysis. The sample sizes thus ranged between 5,604 cases (the student's rating of how well the undergraduate college prepared him or her for graduate work) to 11,478 (the frequency with which students socialized with persons from other racial/ethnic groups). Because of these very large sample sizes, we used a very stringent confidence level ($p < .001$) to select input variables into each regression. However, to provide as comprehensive a picture of the findings as possible, we report all results that show effects of service participation (after controlling for inputs) at the $p < .05$ level.

## RESULTS

Before discussing the results of the multivariate analyses, it is useful to examine our principal independent variable in somewhat more detail. Table 1 shows a simple cross-tabulation between this variable and its counterpart, hours per week spent in volunteer/community service work at the time of the second follow-up in 1994–1995. Although the simple correlation between these two variables is quite modest ($r = .22$), how much a student volunteers during college can clearly have a substantial effect on how much that student volunteers after college. Thus, spending six or more hours per week in volunteer work during the last year of college, as compared to not participating in volunteer work,

nearly doubles the student's chances of being engaged in volunteer work in the years after college, and more than doubles his or her chances of spending either one, three, or six plus hours per week in postcollege volunteer/community service work. For example, 44 percent of those who spent six or more hours per week volunteering during their last year in college were spending at least one hour per week volunteering after college, contrasted to only 19 percent of those who did not volunteer during their last year of college.

To what extent does the student's engagement in service during high school relate to involvement during college and in the years after college? To explore this question we have performed a three-way cross-tabulation using the "pretest" measure of volunteer engagement, which comes from an item in the 1985 first-year student questionnaire that reads: "Performed volunteer work" (students were asked to indicate whether, during the past year, they had performed this activity "frequently," "occasionally," or "not at all"). Though this first-year student input variable showed very modest correlations with hours spent volunteering during college ($r = .18$) and five years after college ($r = .16$), it is associated with substantial differences on the other two measures. (See Table 2.) Of particular interest is the fact that, even after controlling for hours per week spent volunteering during college, the frequency of volunteer participation during high school *still* correlates with hours spent volunteering nine years later. This is especially true among students who engaged in volunteer work for less than one hour per week during college: Those who volunteered "frequently" in high school were more than twice as likely to devote at least some time to volunteer/community service work nine years later than those who did no volunteer work during high school (64% versus 30%). Table 2 thus shows that the "habit" of volunteering persists over a relatively long period of time. For example, among those who did no volunteer work during either high school or college, only 13 percent were spending one hour or more per week in volunteer work nine years after entering college. This figure more than triples, to 49 percent, among those who volunteered frequently during high school *and* averaged one or more hours of volunteer work during college.

Despite these consistencies, Table 2 also indicates that a good deal of volunteer engagement is situationally determined. Thus, among those students who were frequent volunteers in high school and who devoted one or more hours per week to volunteer work during college, fully one-third (33 percent) were not engaged in any volunteer or community service work nine years after entering college. At the same time, among those who did no volunteer work in either high school or college, nearly one-third (31 percent) devoted at least some time to volunteer or community service work nine years after entering college.

Thirteen of the 18 dependent variables showed significant effects from service participation during the undergraduate years. These findings are summarized in Table 3. The first column of coefficients indicates the effect of volunteering during college on each long-term outcome after all significant input variables have been controlled. All of the effects are in the expected direction, including the expected negative effect on the "disempowerment" measure, "Realistically, an individual person can do little to bring about changes in our society." Being a volunteer during college, in other words, is associated with a greater sense of empowerment in the years after college.

In the behavioral realm, participating in volunteer service during college is associated with attending graduate school, earning higher degrees, donating money to one's alma mater, socializing with persons from different racial/ethnic groups, and participating in volunteer/community service work in the years after college. In the value realm, volunteering during college is positively associated with five values measured in the postcollege years: helping others in difficulty, participating in community action programs, participating in environmental cleanup programs, promoting racial understanding, and developing a meaningful philosophy of life. Clearly, the positive short-term effects of volunteering during college on civic and social values observed in earlier studies (Markus, Howard, & King, 1993; Sax, Astin, & Astin, 1996) persist beyond college. Volunteering during college is also associated with higher degree aspirations as measured nine years after college entry and with the student's perception that his or her undergraduate college provided good preparation for work. This latter finding is consistent with the notion that participating in service work gives the student important practical experience in the "real world."

The second column of coefficients in Table 3 shows the effects of undergraduate service participation after controlling for the immediate postcollege measures obtained in 1989. What these coefficients tell us is whether undergraduate service participation continues to affect the nine-year outcome measures (the second

posttest) once its effects on the immediate postcollege outcomes (the first posttest) are controlled. The fact that every single partial beta coefficient shown in the second column is smaller than its corresponding coefficient shown in the first column suggests that most of the effects of undergraduate service participation are at least partially mediated by its short-term effects on the four-year outcomes. One of these effects appears to be entirely mediated in this fashion—the belief that individuals can do little to change society. Thus, in the regression, the highly significant (p < .0001) partial beta shown in column 1 is reduced to nonsignificance (p > .05) after controlling for the immediate postcollege outcomes. Not surprisingly, the largest reductions occur with value outcomes, all of which were posttested immediately after college as well as nine years after entering college.

The last column of coefficients in Table 3 shows the long-term effects of undergraduate service participation after controlling for involvement in volunteer work nine years after college. Controlling for the last variable has little effect, suggesting that few of the long-term effects of volunteerism during college can be explained by volunteerism after college. Only three additional outcomes—donating money to one's alma mater, participating in environmental cleanup, and developing a meaningful philosophy of life—are reduced to nonsignificance by controlling for postcollege volunteerism; and in all three instances, the changes in the coefficients are trivial. Indeed, these three outcome measures had beta coefficients that were only marginally significant (p < .05) after controlling for immediate postcollege outcomes. In short, these findings show that the long-term effects of undergraduate service participation cannot be explained simply in terms of its effects on postcollege volunteer engagement. This finding was perhaps to be expected, given that the simple correlation between undergraduate and postcollege volunteerism is only .22. Once again, these results suggest that the "habit" of volunteering is not the main determinant of who will get involved at any point in time but rather that much engagement in volunteerism is situationally determined.

## DISCUSSION

This study makes it clear that the short-term effects of volunteer service participation during the undergraduate years persist beyond college and are not simply short-term artifacts. While it is true that these longer-term effects are indeed mediated to some extent by the short-term effects measured at the time of college completion (especially in the area of values and attitudes), undergraduate service participation continues to have direct effects at least through the first five years following the completion of college. In the parlance of path analysis, we would say that undergraduate service participation has both "direct" and "indirect" effects on postcollege outcomes. Of equal importance is the finding that undergraduate volunteer participation affects students in both the affective and cognitive realms, including direct effects on educational outcomes, such as attendance at graduate school and the acquisition of higher degrees.

While service participation during the undergraduate years did not result in any significant effects on satisfaction with graduate school or on the student's perception of how well the undergraduate college prepared him or her for graduate work, it did show a significant positive effect on the student's perception of how well the undergraduate college prepared the student for work. And, while undergraduate service participation showed no measurable effect on either income or overall job satisfaction, it did show a significant positive effect on the student's aspiration for advanced degrees.

That undergraduate service participation should increase the likelihood that the student will actually donate money to the alma mater should be of particular interest to college officials and trustees. Most of the debate about including a "service requirement" in the undergraduate curriculum has focused on the *educational* efficacy of volunteer participation or service learning. While our earlier work shows clearly that service participation does indeed have beneficial effects in the academic area (Astin & Sax, 1998), this study suggests that there may be a considerable institutional self-interest in encouraging more students to participate in service work.

It is also important to point out that the long-term effects of undergraduate service participation are very consistent with the rationale underlying many service learning and volunteer programs in academia. Volunteering encourages students to become more socially responsible, more committed to serving their communities, more empowered, and more committed to education. That volunteering encourages socialization across racial lines and increases commitment to promoting racial understanding in the years after college is consistent with our recent short-term study (Astin &

Sax, 1998) showing that undergraduate service participation strengthens the student's interest in issues relating to multiculturalism and diversity.

Although service had favorable effects on 13 of 18 outcome measures, it is important to address those five outcomes which appear to be unaffected by service work during college. First, the fact that service participation does not appear to affect the student's political leanings seems to refute the argument that service participation "politicizes" students. Second, although we expected that participation in service during college might have a positive effect on satisfaction with graduate school and employment, even if only indirectly through its positive effects on satisfaction with college (Astin & Sax, 1998), service in fact had no effect on these two outcomes. It may be that job satisfaction and satisfaction with graduate school are both heavily dependent on situational factors such as pay and working conditions (in the case of employment), or financial aid and accessibility of faculty (in the case of graduate school). Finally, the two remaining outcomes with nonsignificant effects (income and preparation for graduate school) were included solely on an exploratory basis, with no previous research suggesting that they should be affected by service participation.

Several limitations of the current study should be noted. First, although the results are highly significant statistically, the coefficients shown in Table 3 are quite small. This is perhaps to be expected, given that our measures were relatively simple self-report questionnaire items and given that we were dealing with longitudinal changes over a relatively long span of time. Even so, it is important to recognize that even small coefficients such as these can be associated with important practical differences, especially when one looks at effects over the entire range of the variable. (See, for example, Tables 1 and 2, which are based on relatively weak correlations between the variables displayed.)

A potentially more important limitation is the nature of our independent variable, which is simply a generic assessment of the amount of time that students devoted to volunteer service work during the last year in college. We did not obtain specific information, for example, on service learning experiences (as opposed to simple volunteer work) or on the type of service performed or the location of the service. All of these issues are being addressed in studies of volunteer service we are currently conducting.

**NOTE**

1. We made successive reductions in the institutional sample to conserve costs and to have faculty survey data available. While the final sample of 12,376 includes students from all types of institutions at all selectivity levels, it overrepresents students who completed the bachelor's degree and students at the more selective institutions. An elaborate system of weights was used to partially correct for these biases using freshman data for students who did and did not return questionnaires. (For more on this weighting procedure, see Astin & Molm, 1972; Dey, 1997.) We conducted cross-tabular analyses using weighted data (Tables 1 and 2); however, since weighted regressions produced much the same results as the unweighted regressions (Dey, 1997), and because weighted regressions may be highly sensitive to outliers, regression results (Table 3) include only the unweighted results.

## REFERENCES

Astin, A. W. (1975). *Preventing students from dropping out.* San Francisco: Jossey-Bass.

Astin, A. W. (1977). *Four critical years.* San Francisco: Jossey-Bass.

Astin, A. W. (1984). Student involvement: A developmental theory for higher education. *Journal of College Student Personnel, 25,* 297–308.

Astin, A. W. (1985). *Achieving educational excellence.* San Francisco: Jossey-Bass.

Astin, A. W. (1991). *Assessment for excellence.* New York: Macmillan Publishing Company.

Astin, A. W. (1993). *What matters in college? Four critical years revisited.* San Francisco: Jossey-Bass.

Astin, A. W., & Dey, E. L. (1996). *Causal analytical modeling via blocked regression analysis (CAMBRA): An introduction with examples.* Los Angeles: Higher Education Research Institute, UCLA.

Astin, A. W., & Molm, L. D. (1972). Correcting for nonresponse bias in followup surveys. Unpublished manuscript, Office of Research, American Council on Education, Washington, DC.

Astin, A. W., & Sax, L. J. (1998). How undergraduates are affected by service participation. *Journal of College Student Development, 39*(3): 251–263.

Barber, B. R. (1993). *An aristocracy of everyone.* New York: Ballantine Books.

Batchelder, T. H., & Root, S. (1994). Effects of an undergraduate program to integrate academic learning and service: Cognitive, prosocial cognitive, and identity outcomes. *Journal of Adolescence, 17,* 341–355.

Cohen, J., & Kinsey, D. (1994). "Doing good" and scholarship: A service-learning study. *Journalism Educator, 48,* 4–14.

Dey, E. L. (1997). Working with low survey response rates: The efficacy of weighting adjustments. *Research in Higher Education, 38,* 215–227.

Giles, D. E., & Eyler, J. (1994). The impact of a college community service laboratory on students' personal, social, and cognitive outcomes. *Journal of Adolescence, 17,* 327–339.

Giles, D. E., Honnet, E., & Migliore, S. (Eds.). (1991). *Research agenda for combining service and learning in the 1990s.* Raleigh, NC: National Society for Internships and Experiential Education.

Levine, A. (1994, July/August). Service on campus. *Change, 26,* 4–5.

Markus, G. B., Howard, J. P. F., & King, D. C. (1993). Integrating community service and classroom instruction enhances learning: Results from an experiment. *Educational Evaluation and Policy Analysis, 15,* 410–419.

Newman, F. (1985). *Higher Education and the American Resurgence, 31.* Princeton, NJ: Carnegie Foundation for the Advancement of Teaching.

O'Brien, E. M. (1993). Outside the classroom: Students as employees, volunteers and interns. *Research Briefs, 4.* Washington, DC: American Council on Education.

Pascarella, E. T., & Terenzini, P. T. (1991). *How college affects students.* San Francisco: Jossey-Bass.

## AUTHORS

**ALEXANDER W. ASTIN** is Allan M. Cartter Professor of Higher Education and Director of the Higher Education Research Institute (HERI) at the University of California, Los Angeles.

**LINDA J. SAX** is Visiting Assistant Professor of Higher Education and Director of the Cooperative Institutional Research Program (CIRP), also at the University of California, Los Angeles.

**JUAN AVALOS** is Associate Director for Student Affairs Asssessment at California State University, Monterey Bay.

This study was made possible through grants from the Exxon Education Foundation and the Ford Foundation.

# Comparing the Effects of Community Service and Service-Learning

by Lori J. Vogelgesang and Alexander W. Astin
*University of California, Los Angeles*

*This paper presents results from a study that compares course-based service-learning and generic community service. The study was a quantitative, longitudinal look at over 22,000 students at diverse colleges and universities. Student outcome comparisons are made related to values and beliefs, academic skills, leadership, and future plans. Of particular interest is the finding that connecting service with academic course material does indeed enhance the development of cognitive skills. Limitations and directions for future research are identified.*

Service-learning represents a potentially powerful form of pedagogy because it provides a means of linking the academic with the practical. The more abstract and theoretical material of the traditional classroom takes on new meaning as the student "tries it out," so to speak, in the "real" world. At the same time, the student benefits from the opportunity to connect the service experience to the intellectual content of the classroom. By emphasizing cooperation, democratic citizenship and moral responsibility through service-learning, higher education connects to the wider community and enables students to contribute to the alleviation of society's urgent needs.

There is a mounting body of evidence documenting the efficacy of participating in service during the undergraduate years (Astin, Sax & Avalos, 1999; Batchelder & Root, 1994; Eyler, Giles & Braxton, 1997; Eyler & Giles, 1999; Hesser, 1995; Rhoads, 1997; Sax, Astin & Astin, 1996). Yet, though there is broad support for engaging students in community service, there has been some resistance to incorporating service into academic courses. The thinking has been that the place for service is outside the classroom—done on a student's "own time." Those who doubt that service-learning belongs in undergraduate curricula ask, What is the "value-added" for course-based service? For proponents of service-learning, it is important to be able to know whether engaging in service as *part of an academic*

course has benefits over and above those of co-curricular community service.

This study directly compares service-learning and co-curricular community service, in order to identify the unique contributions, if any, of course-based service beyond those of community service.[1] We address these issues through a quantitative longitudinal study of a national sample of students at diverse colleges and universities.

Research that contributes to understanding the educational value of course-based service is important for several reasons. First, it contributes to our understanding of how student learning takes place. Second, such understanding directly addresses faculty concerns about the value of participating in service as part of a course. As a recent study of federally funded service-learning programs points out, "at the institutional level, the most serious obstacle [to expanding and sustaining service programs] is faculty resistance to service-learning. Faculty are reluctant to invest the extra time that teaching service-learningcourses entails, and many are skeptical of the educational value of service-learning" (Gray et. al., 1999, p. 103). As a result of research on service-learning, faculty may not only gain a broader understanding of how learning takes place, but also be more likely to support service-learning if they see evidence documenting its educational value.

## METHOD

In this article, we report the results of quantitative analyses which directly compare service-learning and community service. For this purpose we do a longitudinal comparison of three student groups: service-learning participants, "generic" community service participants, and non-service participants.

### Participants

The data from this study were collected as part of the Cooperative Institutional Research Program (CIRP), with sponsorship from the American Council on Education. Conducted by the Higher Education Research Institute (HERI) at the University of California, Los Angeles, the CIRP annually collects data on entering first-year students using the Student Information Form (SIF), a questionnaire which is designed as a pre-test for longitudinal assessments of the impact of college on students. The College Student Survey (CSS), which provides longitudinal follow-up data, is typically administered four years after college entry.

This study uses 1998 CSS data, and draws on SIF data from 1991 through 1997. Most students who participated in the 1998 CSS completed their SIF in 1994 (69%). The remaining cases either entered college before 1994 (8%), or were at institutions that administer the CSS to students less than four years after college entry (22%). For instance, some schools administer the CSS to students at the end of their sophomore year. The total number of students in this study is 22,236. Detailed information on the data collection process for the 1998 CSS is available from HERI.

The sample represents most institutional types and selectivity levels, but two-year institutions are only marginally represented, and among four-year institutions, private four-year colleges are over-represented. Table 1 shows the number of institu-tions and students from each institutional type that participated in the study.

### Measures

PRINCIPAL INDEPENDENT VARIABLES. The main independent variables used in this study come from the 1998 CSS instrument: "generic" community service and "course-based" service (or service-learning). To measure the frequency of "generic" community service, students were asked: "Please indicate how often you per-formed volunteer work during the past year," and students could mark frequently, occasionally, or not at all.

To determine participation in service-learning, students were asked, "Since entering college, have you performed any community/volunteer service? If yes, how was the service performed?" Students were instructed to mark all that applied: as part of a course or class; as part of a collegiate-sponsored activity (sorority, campus org., etc.); or independently through a non-collegiate group (church, family, etc.). Students who indicated they had performed community/volunteer service as part of a course (regardless of whether they also marked another choice) were considered to have participated in service-learning.

These two service variables were coded into two partially overlapping variables:

- "Generic" service participation: participated in service (including service-learning) frequently (score 3), occasionally (score 2) or not at all (score 1).

- Service-learning: a dichotomous variable in which those who took one or more service-learning courses (score 2) were contrasted with non-service-learning participants (score 1) (i.e., non-service participants plus community service participants who were not in a service-learning course).

Note that these two variables differ only in the placement of the community service participants who did not take a service-learning course (see below for how these two variables were used in the analysis).

DEPENDENT VARIABLES. Existing research on community service influenced our choice of dependent variables. Since the study seeks to compare the effect of course-based service with the effect of "generic" community service, we chose outcomes that have been shown to be impacted by participation in any type of service.

Given the existing research, we chose eleven dependent measures, reflecting behavioral and cognitive outcomes as well as values and beliefs. Many of these items were pretested when students entered college. Dependent variables include:

Three measures of values and beliefs:

- degree of commitment to the goal of promoting racial understanding (4=essential, 3=very important, 2=somewhat important, 1=not important)

- degree of commitment to activism (see below)

- agreement with the statement "realistically, an individual can do little to bring about changes in our society" (4=agree strongly, 3=agree somewhat, 2=disagree somewhat, 1=disagree strongly);

Three measures of academic skills:

- GPA (grade-point average)

- growth in writing skills ("compared with when you entered college as a freshman, how would you now describe your writing skills?" 5=much stronger, 4=stronger, 3=no change, 2=weaker, 1=much weaker)

- critical thinking skills ("compared with when you entered college as a freshman, how would you now describe your ability to think critically?" 5=much stronger, 4=stronger, 3=no change, 2=weaker, 1=much weaker);

Three measures of leadership:

- growth in interpersonal skills ("compared with when you entered college as a freshman, how would you now describe your interpersonal skills?" 5=much stronger, 4=stronger, 3=no change, 2=weaker, 1= much weaker)

- leadership activities (see below)

- leadership ability ("compared with when you entered college as a freshman, how would you now describe your leadership abilities?" 5=much stronger, 4=stronger, 3=no change, 2=weaker, 1= much weaker);

And two measures of future plans:

- career choice (see below)

- plans to engage in community service during the forthcoming year (see below).

Several of the dependent variables reflect responses to more than one survey item. Commitment to activism is a composite measure of the eight items listed below. The first seven items are responses (4=essential, 3=very important, 2=somewhat important, 1=not important) to the item "indicate the importance to you personally of each of the following:" The last item (about politics) is a response to "for the activities listed below, please indicate how often you engaged in each during

the past year" (3=frequently, 2=occasionally, 1=not at all)

- influencing the political structure

- influencing social values

- helping others who are in difficulty

- becoming involved in programs to clean up the environment

- participating in a community action program

- keeping up to date with political affairs

- becoming a community leader

- frequency of discussing politics

The activism composite measure was factorially derived (alpha=.8021). The composite measure "leadership activities" was derived in an a priori manner, and includes the following dichotomous items:

- participating in student government,

- being elected to student office, and

- participating in leadership training.

The composite measure of "plans to engage in community service the following year," also derived in an a priori manner, includes:

- plans to do volunteer work, and

- plans to participate in a community service organization.

OTHER INDEPENDENT VARIABLES. In addition to the two principal independent variables—"generic" community service participation and taking a service-learning course—several freshman "input" or "control" variables were included in the analysis to minimize the potentially biasing effect of characteristics such as previously held beliefs and high school activities (Astin, 1993). These input variables from the SIF also include pretests for most of the dependent measures on the CSS. In examining writing, critical thinking and leadership ability, we chose to use self-perceived change during college as the dependent measure. Although there is no pretest that would allow us to assess actual change in writing, critical thinking, or leadership ability, we were able to control for self-rated writing ability and leadership ability at the time of college entry. Similarly, since "plan to engage in community service next year" does not have a pre-test on the SIF, we used the freshman response to "plan to engage in volunteer work" (in college) as a proxy.

Since we were interested in isolating the effect of service during college as distinct from antecedent factors that might predispose the student to engage in service, we also controlled for freshman self-selection factors that are known to predict subsequent participation in service (Astin & Sax, 1998; Sax, Astin & Astin, 1996). These eight variables include: sex (women are more likely than men to participate), doing volunteer work in high school, tutoring another student, attending religious services, being a guest in a teacher's home, commitment to participating in a community action program, endorsing "to make more money" as a reason for attending college (which is a negative predictor), and self-rated leadership ability. We also controlled for freshman student characteristics such as religious preference (4 dichotomous variables), parental education and income, and race (8 dichotomous variables), because some of the outcome measures may be affected by these characteristics (Astin, 1993).

In addition to entering student characteristics, activities and attitudes, we controlled for a set of college environmental variables, reflecting differences in college size, type and control. This was done in order to make sure that any observed effects of community service and service-learning are not confused with the environmental effect of attending a given kind of college. The nine institutional variables used in the regression are measures of institutional selectivity, size, and seven dichotomous variables reflecting type/control combinations (private university, public university, public college, non-sectarian college, Catholic college, Protestant college, and Historically Black College/University).

### Data Analyses
The purpose of the study was to see if participating in service as part of an academic course has any effects on each of the 11 outcome measures beyond those of "generic" community service. A secondary objective of the study is to replicate previously reported effects of service participation using a new sample of students and several new outcome measures.

For these purposes we utilized a method of causal modeling which uses blocked, stepwise linear regression analysis to study the changes in partial regression coefficients for all variables at each step in the analysis (Astin, 1991). The advantage of this form of analysis is that it allows us to observe and understand the effects of multicollinearity—especially involving the variables representing community service and service-learning—in a complex longitudinal data set.

The approach we used enables us to view each step or block in a stepwise regression as a new model, different from the previous steps or blocks because of the newly added variable in the model. We can see how the new variable or block of variables affects the relationship of the dependent variable to every other variable, both in and out of the model. All such changes in relationships can be seen because SPSS has a feature that computes the "Beta in" for each such variable. "Beta in" shows what the standardized regression coefficient for a nonentered variable would be if it were the variable entered on the next step. By tracking step-by-step changes in Betas (for variables already in the model) and in "Beta-ins" (for variables not yet in the model), we can understand how multicollinearity is affecting the entire data set. Because community service and service-learning are treated as independent measures in this study, we are able to examine closely how their relationship with the dependent variable is affected by the entry of every other variable (including each other).

For each of the eleven stepwise regressions in this study, there are thus three blocks of variables in the regression equation: (1) entering freshman (input) variables; (2) variables for college size and type; and (3) variables representing participation in generic community service and in service-learning. By placing all the entering freshman variables in the first block, we controlled for pre-test differences on each outcome measure as well as for each individual's predisposition to engage in service—the self-selection bias.

We entered our primary independent variables in the third block: "generic" community service and service-learning. As already noted, the service-learning variable is a dichotomous measure of whether the student participated in service as part of a course, and the "generic" community service reflects any kind of community service experience, including service-learning.

A separate analysis was conducted for each dependent measure. All subjects who were missing data on either the dependent measure, the pre-test of the dependent measure, or the primary independent variables (community service and service-learning) were excluded from the analysis. The final sample sizes thus ranged from 19,268 to 20,254. Analyses used a very stringent confidence level ($p < .001$) to select input variables in each regression, except for the career choice regressions, for which we used subsamples. The confidence levels for all regressions are noted in the results tables.

## RESULTS AND DISCUSSION

Of the 22,236 students in our study, 29.9% indicated that they had participated in course-based community service (service-learning), an additional 46.5% reported participation in some other form of community service (the sum of these two define "generic" community service participation), and 23.6% said they did not participate in any community service during college. Service-learning participants were more likely to say they performed volunteer work frequently (28.5%) compared to those who participated in non-course-based community service (22.7%).

Confirming earlier research (Astin & Sax, 1998), we found that there were certain characteristics that predispose students to participation in community service. Among the strongest predictors of participation in community service are volunteering in high school, being a woman, tutoring other students in high school, expressing a commitment to participate in community action programs, attending religious services, and not placing a high priority on making money.

In addition to confirming earlier research on the predictors of service, this study affirms some earlier findings about the *effects* of service participation. All eleven student outcomes are positively affected both by community service and by taking service-learning courses, even after "inputs" and "environments" (entering characteristics and institutional type) are controlled. We will briefly discuss these overall findings, and then address affective, academic, leadership and future plans outcomes in more detail.

In some cases—most notably with certain affective outcomes—community service appears to have a stronger effect than does service-learning.[2] Moreover, while both of these participation measures show significant partial correlations with the affective outcomes after inputs and college-type variables are controlled, for the self-efficacy and leadership outcomes the partial regression coefficient for service-learning shrinks to non-significance when generic service is entered into the equation. In other words, for these outcomes, the effect of service-learning is accounted for by the fact that students who engage in service-learning are also participating in generic community service.

In such comparisons between the effects of community service and service-learning, it is important to keep in mind a couple of considerations. First, service-learning is still an emerging form of pedagogy for faculty. Some faculty may not conduct service-learning well, or service placements might not work out for some students; we have not attempted to assess the quality of the service experience in these analyses. Given the range of such experiences that students might have, the possible effect of participating in a service-learning course may not be as strong as it might be if only "excellent" service-learning courses were analyzed.

Second, elements that make course-based service a potentially powerful pedagogy can also be found in some "generic" community service. For instance, co-curricular leadership development programs that require service might also have a strong reflection component (such as structured discussions with a student affairs professional). In such cases, one might expect the outcomes of such an experience to resemble outcomes that would be expected in service-learning courses, especially for the affective outcomes. These kinds of issues are important when comparing the effects of service-learning with those of community service.

Despite these considerations, there are a few outcomes for which service-learning is a stronger predictor than is community service. Further, for all academic outcomes as well as for some affective ones, participating in service as part of a course has a positive effect over and above the effect of generic community service. Service-learning participation is also a clearly superior predictor of choosing a service-related career, exhibiting a stronger effect than generic community service in almost all career choice analyses. We now discuss each group of outcomes in more detail.

### Values and Beliefs

We have intentionally chosen affective measures that reflect social concern and interest in civic engagement. In this way, our research directly addresses the extent to which community service and service-learning are tools that higher education can use to strengthen democracy by fostering a sense of civic responsibility and community participation in students.

Two of the three measures of values—"commitment to promoting racial understanding" and "commitment to activism"—are significantly affected by participation in course-based service over generic community service. A third outcome—the belief that an individual can effect change in our society—is impacted by service, but service-learning shows a significant effect only until generic service is controlled. In other words, service-learning does strengthen a student's sense of social self-efficacy, but only because it provides an opportunity to do community service. In this connection, it is important to realize that service-learning *would* have shown a significant direct effect on this belief if generic community service had not been included in the analysis.[3] Table 2 shows the Beta values at the end of each regression block for the outcome measures.

That service-learning has an independent effect both on a student's commitment to promoting racial understanding and activism is noteworthy. This suggests that service-learning provides a concrete means by which institutions of higher education can educate students to become concerned and involved citizens. (Recall that our measure of activism includes such things as helping others who are in difficulty, influencing the political structure, influencing social values and participating in community action programs.) In short, while participating in community service positively affects these values, participating in course-based service can strengthen them even more.

### Academic Outcomes

One of the most interesting findings of our study is the positive effect that participating in service has on all the academic outcomes: growth in critical thinking and in writing skills and college GPA (grade-point average). Table 3 shows the Beta values for community service and service-learning at the end of each of the three blocks of these regression analyses.

For all three academic outcomes, both community service and service-learning have a significant effect after controlling for "inputs" (including entering characteristics such as high school GPA) and institutional type. In other words, both kinds of service are associated with greater self-reported gains both in critical thinking and in writing skills, and higher college GPAs.

Of particular significance is the finding that service-learning has an effect on all these cognitive outcomes that is independent of the effect of community service. This is different from what we found with the affective outcomes just discussed, where the impact of service-learning is largely due to the fact that it provides an opportunity to engage in community service. In fact, for both writing skills and college GPA, the effect of service-learning is stronger than that of generic community service. Since these outcomes are academic in nature, one might expect that course-based service would provide benefits beyond those of generic community service. Though the differences are modest, it is important to keep in mind that we have not limited our analysis to what might be considered "ideal" service-learning courses (where academic learning and the service are both meaningful and connected in clear ways).

The reason that students who participate in service-learning courses exhibit higher GPAs is not entirely clear. Could it be that service-learning courses tend to be "easy" courses, that is, graded on a more lenient basis than other courses? While it may seem far-fetched to argue that a course or two will significantly improve a student's overall GPA, could it be that students who take service-learning courses tend to enroll in other courses that are "easy" as well?[4] Another explanation, of course, is that participating in service-learning helps to get students more engaged in the overall academic experience, thereby enhancing their overall academic performance. Clearly, these alternative interpretations need to be tested in further research.

Taken together, these findings present powerful evidence to suggest that connecting service with academic course material does indeed enhance the development of cognitive skills. In other words, even if the only goal of coursework is to strengthen students' cognitive development, this study suggests that service-learning has a place in the curriculum, and should not be relegated solely to co-curricular efforts.

### Leadership Outcomes

The leadership measures we examined—growth in leadership *ability*, involvement in leadership *activities* (being elected to student government office, participating in student office or participating in leadership training) and self-perceived growth in interpersonal skills—do not appear to benefit more from a service-learning experience than from involvement in generic community service. Service-learning does not retain its significance once generic service enters the regression, primarily because the effect of generic service is so strong. (The final coefficients for service-learning reach the .01 level of confidence for leadership ability and leadership activities, but not the .001 level.) See Table 4 for the Beta values of the leadership measures at key points in the regression analysis.

One possible explanation of these results is that academic courses incorporating service-learning focus more on cognitive skill development (critical thinking, writing, etc.) than on the development of leadership and interpersonal skills. Another possible explanation is that co-curricular leadership development programs (in contrast to service-learning courses) may in many cases be designed and operated by the students themselves, thereby affording them an opportunity to develop leadership skills not present in most service-learning courses. Or, co-curricular service programs designed to enhance leadership development may be designed more like service-learning courses, thereby producing the same effects in students.

### Career Outcomes and Plans for Future Service

Choosing a service-related career is more strongly affected by participating in community service and by service-learning than most other student outcomes. For the preliminary descriptive analyses, freshman career choices were grouped into two kinds of service-related careers:

- medical careers (clinical psychologist, dentist, nurse, optometrist, physician and therapist),

- non-medical service careers (elementary, secondary or college teacher, clergy, forester/conservationist, foreign service, law enforcement, school counselor, and principal).

Table 5 shows that students who participate in community service—regardless of freshman year career choice—are more likely than their nonparticipant classmates to say they plan to pursue a service-related career on the post-test. Moreover, those students who complete their service as part of a course exhibit the most dramatic shifts in career choice. For example, among those 3,942 students who indicated on the Freshman Survey that they were interested in pursuing a medical career, 71.3% of those who participated in service-learning confirmed their commitment to a service-related career on the follow-up survey; of those who were engaged in generic community service, 64.4% maintained their initial commitment, while among other students only 54.7% maintained their freshman commitment to a service-related career. The differences among the 2,635 freshman "undecided" students are particularly remarkable: 41.3% of those who engaged in service-learning during college planned to pursue a service-related career on the follow-up, compared to only 18.5% of undecided students who didn't participate in service.

The regression results for "plans to participate in community service" mirror those for the values and beliefs we examined, in that generic community service is the stronger predictor. However, in this case, service-learning maintains a unique (though slight) direct affect on the outcome measure. Not surprisingly, participation in (any kind of) service during college is a powerful predictor of plans to do so in the future.

Career choice regression analyses are limited to the sub-group of students for whom we had post-test career choice information. Since the dependent measure is necessarily dichotomous (chose a service career or a non-service career), we made a decision to eliminate the cases who marked "other" or "undecided" on the follow-up survey.

Because the various career-choice groups looked so different in our preliminary descriptive analyses, we chose to run four separate regressions, one each for:

1. the entering group that planned to pursue service-related careers (medical and non-medical were combined),

2. the group planning non-service-related careers as freshmen,

3. the group who chose "other" on the freshman survey, and

4. those who marked "undecided" on the freshman survey.

Table 6 shows the regression results for these four career-choice groups.

Service-learning appears to impact these career outcomes in two different ways. First, it affects students' career choices indirectly by providing an opportunity to participate in generic community service. This indirect effect is evidenced by the decrease in the Beta value for service-learning that occurs when community service enters the regression. For example, in the regression for undecided students, the coefficient for service-learning after controlling for inputs and institutional characteristics is .17, but drops to .13 when community service enters the regression. So service-learning has a unique ("direct") effect on initially undecided students, but also a weaker ("indirect") effect that is shared with community service. This same shared effect is evidenced in the case of generic community service, where the Betas show a decrease from .19 to .16 when service-learning enters the equation. However, the fact that the Betas for service-learning in all four groups retain most of their size even after community service is controlled suggests that service-learning's primary effect on career choice is a direct one.

Given that one's career choice often represents a lifelong commitment that consumes a large part of one's waking hours, there is perhaps no stronger expression of commitment to service than to choose a career that is service-based. Thus, the positive effects of service-learning on the student's career choice may well represent the most significant finding to emerge from this inquiry.

### Limitations and Future Research

Perhaps the greatest limitation of this study is that the quality of the community service and classroom experiences are not measured, and as Eyler and Giles' (1999) research suggests, "the quality of the service-learning makes a difference" (p. 187). Echoing other researchers and practitioners (Mabry, 1998; Zlotkowski, 1996), we suggest that future research focus on the specifics of the service experience.[5] For instance, how do factors such as training, type of experience, and length of experience affect student development?

Second, this study examines outcomes from the perspective of the student (self-reported measures). Research that provides different perspectives—faculty assessment of learning or standardized assessments—will also benefit our understanding of how learning takes place. The self-efficacy measures in this study are not intended to substitute for independently assessed skills, though one would expect the two to be related (e.g., one who believes he/she has good leadership skills is likely to become more effective than one who doesn't). Research examining the validity of self-reported

growth in cognitive learning in general suggests that self-reported growth is related to cognitive constructs (Anaya, 1999). A more detailed study of critical thinking in particular offers support for the use of self-reports to measure this construct (Tsui, 1999).

The analyses conducted on the academic outcomes in this study only begin to enhance our understanding of how students participating in service learning can benefit from the experience. There is still a need to understand how the learning of various disciplines might be enhanced by service-learning. This concern is being addressed directly by the American Association for Higher Education (AAHE) Series on Service-Learning in the Disciplines. There is also a need to better understand how different kinds of students might benefit (e.g. does race or gender matter?), and the benefits of placing a service-learning experience at different points in a student's college experience (e.g. first-year experience, in the major, or throughout the college years).

## CONCLUSION

The results of this study add weight to the belief that course-based service has benefits over and above those of "generic" community service. Because it is a longitudinal study, we have been able to control for many student and institutional characteristics which predispose students to participate in service, and which may shape the service-learning experience. Even when such student and institutional characteristics were controlled, service-learning has a significant effect on all eleven outcomes examined.

## NOTES

This research was funded in part by an anonymous donor.

The authors gratefully acknowledge the work of Elaine K. Ikeda and Jennifer A. Yee, who were part of a larger research project on the effects of service-learning, and who gave valuable feedback on earlier drafts of these findings.

1.  For this study, we define service-learning as service done as part of a course or class.

2.  In most cases this difference may be attributed simply to the greater variance in generic community service.

3.  Here we have a clear demonstration of the "multi-collinearity problem": Our conclusion about whether a particular variable (i.e., course-based service-learning) "affects" any given outcome may depend on what

other variables (i.e., generic service) are included in the analysis of that outcome.

4. Further analyses of these data suggest that college major does not play a significant mediating role between service-learning and college GPA (Astin, Vogelgesang, Ikeda, and Yee, 2000).

5. For a discussion of the effects of reflection on this particular set of students, see Astin, Vogelgesang, Ikeda & Yee (2000).

## REFERENCES

Anaya, G. (1999). College impact on student learning: Comparing the use of self-reported gains, standardized test scores, and college grades. *Research in Higher Education*, 40 (5), 499-524.

Astin, A. W. (1991). *Assessment for excellence: The philosophy and practice of assessment and evaluation in higher education.* New York: Macmillan/Onyx.

Astin, A. W. (1993). *What matters in college? Four critical years revisited.* San Francisco, CA: Jossey Bass.

Astin, A. W. & Sax, L. J. (1998). How undergraduates are affected by service participation. *Journal of College Student Development*, 39 (3), 251–263.

Astin, A.W., Sax, L.J., & Avalos, J. (1999). Long-term effects of volunteerism during the undergraduate years. *The Review of Higher Education*, 22 (2), 187–202.

Astin, A.W., Vogelgesang, L.J., Ikeda, E.K. & Yee, J.A. (2000). *How Service Learning Affects Students.* Los Angeles: University of California Los Angeles, Higher Education Research Institute.

Batchelder, T. H. & Root, S. (1994). Effects of an undergraduate program to integrate academic learning and service: Cognitive, prosocial cognitive, and identity outcomes. *Journal of Adolescence*, 17(4), 341–355.

Eyler, J. & Giles Jr., D. E. (1999). *Where's the learning in service-learning?* San Francisco: Jossey-Bass.

Eyler, J., Giles Jr., D. E., & Braxton, J. (1997). The impact of service-learning on college students. *Michigan Journal of Community Service Learning*, 4, 5–15.

Gray, M. J., Ondaatje, E., Fricker, R., Geschwind, S., Goldman, C. A., Kaganoff, T. Robyn, A., Sundt, M., Vogelgesang, L., & Klein, S. P. (1999). *Combining Service and Learning in Higher Education: Evaluation of the Learn and Serve America, Higher Education Program.* Santa Monica, CA: RAND.

Hesser, G. (1995). Faculty assessment of student learning: Outcomes attributed to service-learning and evidence of changes in faculty attitudes about experiential education. *Michigan Journal of Community Service Learning*, 2, 33–42.

Mabry, J. B. (1998). Pedagogical variations in service-learning and student outcomes: How time, contact and reflection matter. *Michigan Journal of Community Service Learning*, 5, 32–47.

Rhoads, R. A. (1997). *Community service and higher learning: Explorations of the caring self.* Albany: State University of New York Press.

Sax, L.J., Astin, A.W., & Astin, H.S. (1996). What were LSAHE impacts on student volunteers? In *Evaluation of Learn and Serve America, Higher Education: First Year Report.* Santa Monica, CA: RAND Corporation.

Tsui, L. (1999). Courses and instruction affecting critical thinking. *Research in Higher Education*, 40 (2), 185–200.

Zlotkowski, E. (1996). Linking service-learning and the academy: A new voice at the table? *Change*, 28 (1), 20–27.

## AUTHORS

**LORI J. VOGELGESANG** is director of the Center for Service Learning Research and Dissemination at the Higher Education Research Institute (HERI), University of California, Los Angeles. She has conducted research and evaluation of service learning programs for HERI and for RAND.

**ALEXANDER W. ASTIN** is Allan M. Cartter Professor of Higher Education and Director of the Higher Education Research Institute at the University of California, Los Angeles.

# Student Development:
## Recommended Reading

## BOOKS & CHAPTERS

American College Personnel Association. (1994). The student learning imperative: Implications for student affairs. In E.J. White (Ed.) *College student affairs administration*. Needham Heights, MA: Simon and Schuster.

Astin, A. W. (1991). *What matters in college? Four critical years revisited*. San Francisco: Jossey-Bass.

Baxter Magdola, M. (1992). *Knowing and reasoning in college*. San Francisco: Jossey-Bass.

Boyer, E. (1986). *College: The undergraduate experience in America*. Princeton, NJ: The Carnegie Foundation for the Advancement of Teaching.

Boyer, E. (Ed.). (1990). *Campus life: In search of community*. Princeton, NJ: The Carnegie Foundation for the Advancement of Teaching.

Delve, C. & Rice, K. (1990). The integration of service-learning into leadership and campus activities. In C.I. Delve, S.D. Mintz, & G.M. Steward (Eds.), *Community service as values education*. San Francisco: Jossey-Bass.

Dey, E., Astin, A.W., & Korn, W. (1991). *The American freshman: Twenty-five year trends, 1966–1990*. Los Angeles: Higher Education Research Institute, University of California-Los Angeles.

Fried, J., et al. (1995). *Shifting paradigms in student affairs*. Washington, DC American College Personnel Association.

Fried, J. (Ed.). (1997). *Ethics for today's campus: New perspectives on education, student development, and institutional management*. San Francisco: Jossey-Bass.

Kitchener, K. (1995). Ethical principles and ethical decisions in student affairs. In H. J. Canon & R. D. Brown (Eds.), *New directions for student services: Applied ethics in student services*. San Francisco: Jossey-Bass.

Kohlberg, L. (1969). Stage and sequence: The cognitive developmental approach to socialization. In D. A. Goslin (Ed.), *Handbook of socialization theory and research*. Skokie, IL: Rand McNally.

Levine, A., & Cureton, J.S. (1998). *When hope and fear collide: A portrait of today's college student*. San Francisco: Jossey-Bass.

Loeb, P. (1994). *Generation at the crossroads: Apathy and action on the American campus*. New Brunswick, NJ: Rutgers University Press.

McKay, V. (2001). Sociocultural context and service-learning inside and outside of the university classroom. In D.M. McInerney & S.Van Etten (Eds.), *Research on sociocultural influences on motivation and learning, volume one*. Greenwich, CT: Information Age Publishing.

Myers-Lipton, S. (1996). Service-learning: Theory, student development, and strategy. In M. Ender (Ed.), *Service-learning and undergraduate sociology*. Washington, DC: American Sociological Association.

Pascarella, E.T. & Terenzini, P.T. (1991). *How college affects students: Findings and insights from twenty years of research*. San Francisco: Jossey-Bass.

Radest, H.B. (1993). *Community service: Encounters with strangers*. Westport, CT: Praeger.

Sullivan C., Myers, A., Bradford, C., & Street, D. (1999). *Service-learning: Educating students for life*. Harrisonburg, VA: Institute for Research in Higher Education, James Madison University.

Sutherland, S.L. (1981). Patterns of belief and action: Measures of student political activism. Toronto: University of Toronto Press.

Zlotkowski, E. (2002). *Service-learning and the first-year experience: Preparing students for personal success and civic engagement*. Columbia, SC: National Resource Center for the First-Year Experience and Students in Transition.

## ARTICLES & REPORTS

Abernathy, T.V. & Obenchain, K.M. (2001). Student ownership of service-learning projects: Including ourselves in our communities. *Intervention in School and Clinic, 37* (2), 86–95.

Altbach, P.G. (1998). Perspectives on student political activism. *Comparative Education, 61* (1), 97–108.

Angelique, H.L. (2001). Linking the academy to the community through internships: A model of service-learning, student empowerment, and transformative education. *Sociological Practice, 3* (1), 37–53.

Astin, A.W. & Sax, L. (1998). How undergraduates are affected by service participation. *Journal of College Student Development*, 39 (3), 251–263.

Astin, A.W., Sax, L., & Avalos, J. (1997). Long-term effects of volunteerism during the undergraduate years. *Review of Higher Education*, 22 (2), 187–202.

Batchelder, T.H. & Root, S. (1994.) Effects of an undergraduate program to integrate academic learning and service: Cognitive, prosocial cognitive, and identity outcomes. *Journal of Adolescence*, 17 (4), 341–55.

Bennett, S. E.(1997, March).Why young Americans hate politics, and what we should do about it. *PS: Political Science and Politics*, 20(1).

Boss, J.A. (1994). The effects of community service work on the moral development of college ethics students. *Journal of Moral Education*, 23, 183–198.

Brotherton, P. (2002). Connecting the classroom and the community. *Black Issues in Higher Education*, 19 (4), 20–5.

Cone, R., Cooper, D.D., & Hollander, E. (2001, March/April). Voting and beyond. *About Campus*.

Dunlap, M. (1998, Fall). Voices of students in multicultural service-learning settings. *Michigan Journal of Community Service Learning*, 58–67.

Fitch, R.T. (1991). Differences among community service volunteers and nonvolunteers on the college campus. *Journal of College Student Development*, 32 (6), 534–540.

Frederickson, P.J. (2000). Does service-learning make a difference in student performance? *Journal of Experiential Education*, 23 (2), 64–74.

Gardner, J.N. (2001). Focusing on the first-year student. *Priorities*, 17.

Giles, D.E., Jr. & Eyler, J. (1994). The impact of a college community service laboratory on students' personal, social, and cognitive outcomes. *Journal of Adolescence*, 17 (4), 327–339.

Kaye, H. (1999, July 7). Life stirring on the campus. *Times Educational Supplement*, 1391, 13.

Koliba, C.J. (2000). Moral learning and networks of engagement. *American Behavioral Scientist*, 43 (5), 825–39.

Kuh, G.D. (1996). Guiding principles for creating seamless learning environments for undergraduates. *Journal of College Student Development*, 37 (2), 135–148.

Levine, A. (1999, February 26). The new generation of student protesters arises. *Chronicle of Higher Education*, 45 (25), A52.

Masci, D. (1998, August 28). Student activism. *CQ Researcher*, 32.

Moely, B.E., et al. (2002a). Psychometric properties and correlates of the Civic Attitudes and Skills Questionnaire (CASQ): A measure of students' attitudes related

to service-learning. *Michigan Journal of Community Service Learning*, 8 (2), 15–26.

Moely, B.E., et al. (2002b). Changes in college students' attitudes and intentions for civic involvement as a function of service-learning experiences. *Michigan Journal of Community Service Learning*, 9 (1), 18–26.

Myers-Lipton, S. (1996). Effect of service-learning on college students' attitudes toward international understanding. *Journal of College Student Development*, 37, 659–668.

Myers-Lipton, S. (1998). Effects of a comprehensive service-learning program in college students' civic responsibility. *Teaching Sociology*, 26, 243–258.

National Association of Secretaries of State (1999). *New millennium project—Part 1: American youth attitudes on politics, citizenship, government and voting*. Lexington, KY: NASS.

National Survey of Student Engagement. (2002). *From promise to progress: How colleges and universities are using student engagement results to improve collegiate quality*. Bloomington, IN: National Survey of Student Engagement.

Payne, C.A. (2000). Changes in involvement preferences as measured by the community service involvement preference inventory. *Michigan Journal of Community Service Learning*, 7, 41–45.

Sax, L., Astin, A., Korn, W., & Mahoney, K. (2000). *The American freshman: National norms for fall 2000*. Los Angeles: Higher Education Research Institute, University of California, Los Angeles.

Serow, R.C., & Dreyden, J.L. (1990). Community service among college and university students: Individual and institutional relationships. *Journal of Adolescence*, 25 (9), 553–566.

Shumer, R. (2001). Service-learning is for everybody. *New Directions for Higher Education*, 114, 27–34.

Skilton-Sylvester, E. & Erwin, E.K. (2000). Creating reciprocal learning relationships across socially-constructed borders. *Michigan Journal of Community Service Learning*, 7, 65–75.

Steinke, P., & Buresh, S. (2002). Cognitive outcomes of service-learning: Reviewing the past and glimpsing the future. *Michigan Journal of Community Service Learning*, 8 (2), 5–14.

Stephens, A. (1998, November 16). The new campus activists. *Community College Week*, 11 (8), 6.

Van Dyke, N. (1998). Hotbeds of activism: Locations of student protest. *Social Problems*, 45 (2), 205.

Waldstein, F.A. & Reiher, T.C. (2001). Service-learning and students' personal and civic development. *Journal of Experiential Education*, 24 (1), 7–14.

Wilcox, H.S. & Waagbo, J.W. (2001). Diversity learning: A different approach. *Community College Journal*, 71 (4), 24–27.

# Civic Engagement

## TITLES IN THIS SECTION

## QUESTIONS FOR REFLECTION AND PLANNING

Does your institution have civic education/civic engagement requirements for your students? Is service-learning currently being used as a strategy within your civic education curriculum? If not, how might it be?

Do your own courses have explicit or implicit civic engagement requirements? Do you make an explicit link between service-learning and those requirements?

To what degree do your students demonstrate the service/politics split? How might service-learning help them see a linkage between community engagement and political engagement?

# Civic Skill Building:

## The Missing Component in Service Programs?

by Mary Kirlin, *Indiana University-Purdue University Indianapolis*

What are the best ways to instill democratic values and create civically engaged citizens? Much political, public, and scholarly attention has recently been paid to these and similar questions. Service learning and community service for adolescents and young adults have received the most attention (Perry and Katula 2001). Civic education has also been studied but does not draw the same attention as service learning (Niemi and Junn 1999). The September 2000 issue of PS: *Political Science & Politics* addressed service learning in higher education, but service for high school students is also receiving increasing amounts of attention. Estimates are that 83% of high schools nationally offer community service opportunities (Westheimer and Kahne 2000), that half of all community colleges have service learning courses and that nearly two million college students at four-year institutions participate in service learning (Hepburn, Niemi, and Chapman 2000). While specific articulated outcomes vary widely, researchers suggest that students who participate in service programs will become more civically engaged (Yates and Youniss 1998), understand and become more tolerant of our diverse society, and improve classroom learning (Hepburn, Niemi, and Chapman 2000). Empirical research suggests some positive outcomes from service learning relative to student cognition and classroom learning but little evidence supports expectations that service learning encourages civic behaviors such as voting, contacting elected officials, and being active in community affairs (Perry and Katula 2001).

This paper suggests one reason for the weak empirical results relative to civic engagement is that many service and volunteer programs have failed to sufficiently address development of fundamental civic skills such as expressing opinions and working collectively to achieve common interests as part of their design. As a result, while some studies of service learning participants show enhanced compassion and interesting social problems generally, those attitudinal changes do not consistently translate into behavioral changes (Eyler, Giles, and Braxton 1997; Perry and Katula 2001). This paper reviews recent empirical studies of community service, service learning, and volunteering, and then frames the consistently strong evidence that participation in clubs and organizations during adolescence leads to higher levels of civic engagement during adulthood within the political participation model developed by Verba, Schlozman, and Brady (1995). I suggest that the reason such participation is linked to later civic engagement is less related to civic identity development as suggested by some (Yates and Youniss 1998; Youniss, McLellan, and Yates 1997), than it is to development of fundamental civic skills necessary for civic engagement.

I am interested in how adolescents learn to become active adult members of their communities—to become "engaged," not only in political activities such as voting and campaign work, but also in community improvement activities via civic and volunteer associations (similar to Campbell 2000). I focus on how adolescents learn the doing of democracy, that is, active participation, not simply cognitive knowledge of political systems. Building upon the premise that adolescence is a critical time for socialization and development (Erikson 1968), I ask, "What activities during adolescence lead to long-term civic engagement?"

## COMMUNITY SERVICE, SERVICE LEARNING AND VOLUNTEERING IMPACT CIVIC ENGAGEMENT WEAKLY

Service learning, community service, and volunteering have been put forwards mechanisms to increase civic engagement of individuals (Yates and Youniss 1998). Community service programs typically consist of requirements for students to volunteer a given amount of time in their community. Hepburn, Niemi, and Chapman (2000) remind us that service learning is similar to community service in its volunteer component but has explicit links to classroom curricula.

Perry and Katula (2001) produce interesting results with their comprehensive review of 219 empirical studies of the relationship between service (including service learning and community service) and citizenship. After cautioning that limited empirical studies, small sample sizes, and differing objectives and methodologies affect the ability to draw concrete conclusions, they conclude that a) service appears to favorably influence citizenship related cognitive understanding; b) service and volunteering appear to positively influence later volunteering and giving; and c) the type of service that produces the most consistent positive results is service learning. However, they find that existing research does not address the relationship between citizenship skills and behaviors sufficiently to draw conclusions. While attitudinal changes were somewhat common there was no evidence of behavior changes. Perry and Katula (2001, 15) observe that "given the centrality of active citizenship inmost theories and proposals for service, the paucity of research about citizenship outcomes, particularly behaviors, is noteworthy."

Hunter and Brisbin's (2000, 625) evaluation of college student's service-learning experiences in three locations is exemplary of the mixed findings common in empirical research in this area. Their study confirms that service-learning participants "learn about their community, further develop some academic skills and feel that they have helped members of their community." However, little to no change was indicated for self-reported attitudes towards political engagement.

Similarly, empirical evidence indicates volunteering has positive results for individuals on cognitive and attitudinal measures but weak results for increasing civic engagement of participants. A 1996 survey found approximately 60% of teens volunteered during the previous 12 months (Independent Sector 1997). Adolescent volunteers reported their experience helped them understand people who are different than themselves (48%) and to understand more about good citizenship (37%); but only 18% said they learned how to help solve community problems (Independent Sector 1997). A longitudinal study of the long-term effects of volunteering in college (Astin, Sax, and Avalos 1999) finds a positive—though tenuous—relationship between volunteering during college and later volunteering. Those who volunteered extensively in high school and college were twice as likely to be volunteering nine years later than those who did no volunteer work. However, among those that volunteered during high school and college, one-third were doing no volunteer work nine years later; of those who did no volunteer work in high school or college, 31% were volunteering nine years later.

Perry and Katula (2001, 27) ask why the relationship between attitudes and behavior in service programs doesn't appear to be strong. "Is the attenuation a result of service-learning pedagogy that does not translate into enough hands-on experience . . .? Or is it a function of institutions that do not reinforce service experiences?" Morgan and Streb (2001) suggest that students' voices in service learning projects are critical to achieving positive political engagement impacts. Other scholars suggest that service may not create an understanding of social interdependence or a sense of community responsibility (Raskoff and Sundeen 1998), or that motivations for service may be associated more with an individual's desire to help another rather than in a broader social or political understanding or commitment (Scrow 1991).

## CIVIC SKILL DEVELOPMENT DURING ADOLESCENCE IS CRITICAL

Basing their work on surveys of 15,000 adults, Verba, Schlozman, and Brady (1995) argue that adult participation in civic life requires three "participatory factors": desire to get involved (motivation); the ability to contribute something to the effort (capacity and skills); and some connection to the networks of individuals who ask others to become involved (networks). In a complex model, the authors trace "roots of participation" back to "initial characteristics" including gender, race and parent's education. They then identify three "pre-adult experiences" that affect later civic participation: education, discussion of politics at home, and participation in an extracurricular organization as an adolescent. The model continues with adult experiences that affect participation, but for purposes of this article, the "pre-adult" experiences are critical.

The pre-adult experiences affect the three participatory factors in the following manner. Education can lead to increased understanding of the importance of civic participation (motivation); provide money or time to contribute to civic endeavors (capacity); and introduce one to others concerned with civic life (networks). Discussion of politics at home can enhance the motivation to get involved. Finally, participation in organizations and clubs during adolescence can teach skills necessary for adult civic participation (capacity).

Verba, Schlozman, and Brady (1995) find that participation in high-school student government and other clubs was strongly associated with later civic engagement, and suggest that such membership teaches skills that are necessary for later involvement including "hands-on training in communication and organization skills." With the exception of sports, Verba, Schlozman, and Brady find this to be true regardless of the underlying nature and type of the club; participation in the chess or Spanish club is as effective for teaching civic skills as participation in student government.

Additional empirical research supports participation in organizations during adolescence as a predictor of future civic engagement. Like studies of service, the samples are sometimes small, but unlike service research, the five studies conducted between 1976 and 1995 came to similar conclusions, finding that individuals who were active in organizations during adolescence are two to four times more likely to be active in civic and political life than those who had not participated in organizations during adolescence (Beane, et al. 1981; Hanks and Eckland 1978; Ladewig and Thomas 1987; Otto 1976; and Verba, Schlozman and Brady 1995). Adolescent participants were also two to four times as likely as their nonparticipating colleagues to be officers in organizations as adults. Adults were studied 12 to 30 years after their adolescent participation. In most studies, they were asked to recall their participation; although in two of the studies, participants were drawn from a pool of those known to be alumni from particular organizations (4-H and a school-based community planning project). Organizations that predicted future activity included participation in 4-H, student government, and school-based clubs such as yearbook, debate team, and a course where students helped the community with long-term planning efforts.

A more recent empirical study confirms and expands these findings. I analyzed a statewide California YMCA high school model-legislature program to find that the 1,069 alumni (ages 18 to 72) were statistically significantly more likely than the general population to be involved in several civic engagement behaviors. Specifically, 96% are registered voters, 87% voted in the 2000 presidential election, 47% have contacted an elected official about an issue, 45% have attended a local board or council meeting, 43% have gotten together with others informally to work on community problems, 35% have contributed to a campaign, and 36% have served on aboard or been an officer in a group (Kirlin 2001). To control for income and education effects, I examined the civic engagement behaviors of three groups of alumni: those over 25 years of age who make less than $25,000 per year; those over 25 years of age who do not hold at least a bachelor's degree; and those whose parents held jobs that did not require a college degree (largely service or trades). All three groups of alumni were statistically significantly more involved than the general population on all measures of civic engagement except campaign contributions. At least in this case, participation in extracurricular activities positively affected adult civic engagement, regardless of the income and education of the participants or their parents.

Glanville (1999) investigated whether individuals who were active in organizations as adolescents had "self-selected" into organizations based on preexisting personality characteristics or political attitudes. She finds that sociability, leadership attitudes, and interest in and awareness of political issues only partially account for the association between participation in organizations and later political and civic engagement. The remainder is attributed to the participation itself. Self-selection based on predisposition to politics did not seem to affect my (2001) study either. I asked 263 alumni why they became involved in the YMCA model legislature program; only 32% indicated they liked politics and government, while 65% said their friends got them involved.

Conrad and Hedin's (1982a, 1982b, 1989) research demonstrates the role experiential and participatory education play in preparing students to be active civic-minded citizens. School-based experiential learning has a positive impact when, among other things, student decision making is encouraged by teachers. Similarly, a recent international study finds that high school students who reported "an open classroom environment where they were encouraged to discuss issues and take part in shaping school life" showed greater civic knowledge and were more likely to indicate they expected to vote as adults (Torney-Purta, et al. 2001, 8).

These findings begin to knit together the consistent conclusions about the importance of adolescent participation. Involving students in many levels of the learning process may facilitate the development of civic skills important for later civic engagement.

Some researchers argue that these studies suggest enhanced civic identity among adolescents increases adult civic engagement. Yates and Youniss (1998, 496) argue that adolescent participation in organizations creates "reference points that aid in the formation of political understandings and engagement," norms of participation that become imbedded in identity, leading to engagement in civic life. Hepburn (2000) suggests that research linking adolescent participation in clubs and organizations to later civic engagement creates a rationale for community service in high school, agreeing with the Yates and Youniss premise of civic identity development as a key component.

However, research indicates that the impact of adolescent experiences is more plausibly attributable to enhanced civic skills. Adolescents' participation in organizations matters for later civic engagement not because it creates a civic identity but because it teaches concrete skills critical for civic engagement. Returning to the Verba-Schlozman-Brady model (1995), recall the three factors necessary for political participation: motivation, networks and capacity/skills. Because the types of organizations yielding future civic engagement weren't always political or civic in nature, it does not appear that the primary benefit of adolescent participation in organizations is creating either the motivation for involvement (Verba's terminology) or civic identity development (Yates and Youniss's terminology). While network development is a plausible explanation for some of the relationship, and deserves research attention, the most logical explanation is that students are developing and practicing civic skills through their participation in organizations.

This argument is consistent with two additional findings from Verba, Schlozman, and Brady (1995). First, they find that participation in high school sports was negatively associated with later civic engagement. Conway and Damico (2001) have similar findings. While providing other benefits, organized sports provide little opportunity for civic skill development: the goal (winning) is predetermined, and adults undertake the planning for the season, organize the matches, and do most of the coaching. Opportunities for students to organize themselves, decide on objectives, and collectively make decisions are limited. The same may be increasingly true for service learning and community service; adults may have organized students too well, taking the fun (and civic skill learning) out of the effort.

The second important finding is that church participation, whether in adolescence or adulthood, is positively associated with civic engagement. Depending upon the particular institution, church can provide motivation and networks, and may also provide opportunities tolerant and practice civic skills. Members have the opportunity to set goals (a new childcare program or building), organize fellow members (a picnic or bazaar), and negotiate with others to determine the common good. Verba, Schlozman, and Brady (1995) find church participation to be an equalizer for economic and education factors that would otherwise predict low levels of civic engagement.

## PARTICIPANTS IN COMMUNITY SERVICE AND SERVICE LEARNING CAN GAIN CIVIC SKILLS

Democratic society inherently demands collective decision making. Thus, young adults must practice the skills necessary for civic engagement; cognitive understanding of democracy is not sufficient. Adolescent participation in organizations provides the opportunity for hands-on development of foundational civic skills such as working in groups, organizing others to accomplish tasks, communicating, and working out differences of substance or process on the way to accomplishing a goal. Patrick (2000, 5) suggests participatory skills of citizenship in democracy include "interacting with other citizens to promote personal and common interests, monitoring public events and issues, deliberating about public policy issues, influencing policy decisions on public issues and implementing policy decisions on public issues." The list is particularly useful because it is based on actions that infer skills, not simply knowledge. However, to be competent in Patrick's civic skills, several very basic underlying skills must be mastered. Table 1 makes some preliminary suggestions as to what those skills might be. Some of these are cognitive in nature but many must be practiced in order to develop mastery. The premise that

**Table 1: Underlying Skills Necessary for Civic Skills**

| Civic Skill | Underlying Skills |
| --- | --- |
| Monitoring public events and issues | • Understand distinctions between three sectors of society (public, nonprofit and private)<br><br>• Understand context for events and issues (what happened and why)<br><br>• Capacity to acquire and thoughtfully review news (read the local newspaper) |
| Deliberating about public policy issues | • Think critically about issues<br><br>• Understand multiple perspectives on issues |
| Interacting with other citizens to promote personal and common interests | • Understand democratic society (collective decision making as norm)<br><br>• Capacity to articulate individual perspective and interests<br><br>• Work with others to define common objective<br><br>• Create and follow a work plan to accomplish a goal |
| Influencing policy decisions on public issues | • Identify decision makers and institutions<br><br>• Understand appropriate vehicles for influencing decisions |

civic skill building can be important for later civic engagement has implications for program design and for research. Some relatively simple changes might greatly enhance the long-term civic-engagement effects of service and volunteer programs.

The most significant step is rethinking the front end of service and volunteer programs so that students have as much latitude as possible to learn and practice civic skills through the process of designing and organizing their activities themselves. This does not mean disengaging the service experience from the classroom content. Rather, it means facilitating students' discovery of what problems exist, whom they need to contact to address the issues, and what types of projects they will undertake. Giving students the opportunity to identify fellow students with similar concerns and then to decide what they will do about it is an important first step. Underlying this relatively simple step are several skills including voicing one's opinion, expressing interests, identifying like-minded individuals, and reaching consensus about action. Service and volunteer pro-

grams that provide preapproved lists of organizations ready to accept students for predetermined volunteer roles immediately remove several learning opportunities including understanding local events and identifying decision makers, stakeholders, and providers. Adults should facilitate learning by asking questions and providing support and encouragement—but not prepackaged experiences.

Similar adaptations of classroom efforts may benefit civic learning in the classroom. I have begun testing this approach in an introductory undergraduate public affairs course. At the beginning of the term, students identify a public issue they would like to influence (by reading the local newspaper) and work in small (self-selected) groups to identify background, stakeholders, decision makers, and important timelines for the issue they have chosen. They then actively work to influence the outcome by writing letters, meeting with officials, attending and speaking at public meetings, and generating interest from others through media and other means. Requiring the students to practice civic skills led one student to observe, "Everyone thinks they know how to be involved but I didn't really know until I did it." Students have anecdotally reported increased understanding of the newspaper and local events, a much clearer understanding of who makes decisions and how to access them, and most importantly, confidence that they could get involved in an issue that interests them.

Important research questions arise from this argument. The identification of specific civic skills is crucial to understanding their roles in future civic engagement and to increasing our ability to build civic skill development into programs. Patrick's (2000) list is a starting point, and I have begun to identify some of the underlying skills, but further refinement is needed. Researchers can then fill the gaps in research on civic skill and behavior development in service programs by testing and identifying successful service programs.

Confirming the hypothesis that civic skill building can crosscut many types of organizations and lead to later civic engagement is fundamental. It is important to understand both the activities of current adolescents and the structure of programs intended to increase civic engagement. Currently there is inadequate information on the variety of possibly relevant programs offered by schools and nonprofit organizations, as well as the experiences individual students have. My efforts to collect information about programs, attributes and numbers of participants from high schools in one Indiana county revealed very good data on numbers of students participating in sports but fragmented and incomplete information about students participating in nonsports activities. Some high schools had athletics directors with assistants while nonsports programs were assigned somewhat haphazardly to faculty and staff with no central coordination. Not surprisingly, schools reported approximately twice as many opportunities for sports participation as all clubs and organizations combined. Understanding what programs are available through schools and the broader community will help us to understand where civic engagement efforts may best be enhanced.

Additional research into the question of whether service and participation in organizations and clubs provide networks (as defined by Verba, Schlozman, and Brady 1995) will also be helpful. As people are increasingly mobile, networks developed during adolescence may be less important although practicing the skill of network development may still have importance for long-term civic engagement.

## REFERENCES

Astin, Alexander W., Linda J. Sax, and Juan Avalos. 1999. "The Long-Term Effects of Volunteerism During the Undergraduate Years." *The Review of Higher Education* 22:187–202.

Beane, J., J. Turner, D. Jones, and R. Lipka. 1981. "Long-Term Effects of Community Service Programs." *Curriculum Inquiry* 11:143–55.

Campbell, David. 2000. "Social Capital and Service Learning." *PS: Political Science & Politics* 33:641–45.

Conrad, Dan, and Diane Hedin, eds. 1982a. *Youth Participation and Experiential Education.* New York: Haworth Press.

Conrad, Dan, and Diane Hedin. 1982b. *Executive Summary of the Final Report of the Experiential Education Evaluation Project.* Minneapolis: University of Minnesota, Center for Youth Development and Research.

Conrad, Dan, and Diane Hedin. 1989. *High School Community Service: A Review of Research and Programs.* Madison, Wisconsin: National Center on Effective Secondary Schools.

Conway, Margaret, and Alfonso J. Damico. 2001. "Building Blocks: The Relationship Between High School and Adult Association Life." Presented at the Annual Meeting of the American Political Science Association, San Francisco.

Erikson, E.H. 1968. *Identity: Youth and Crisis.* New York: Norton.

Eyler, Janet, Dwight Giles, and John Braxton. 1997. "Report of a National Study Comparing the Impacts of Service-Learning Program Characteristics on Post Secondary Students." Presented at the Annual Meeting of the American Educational Research Association, Chicago.

Glanville, Jennifer L. 1999. "Political Socialization or Selection? Adolescent Extracurricular Participation and Political Activity in Early Adulthood." *Social Science Quarterly* 80:279–90.

Hanks, M., and Eckland, B.K. 1978. "Adult Voluntary Associations and Adolescent Socialization." *The Sociological Quarterly* 19:481–90.

Hepburn, Mary A. 2000. "Service Learning and Civic Education in the Schools: What Does Recent Research Tell Us?" In *Education for Civic Engagement in Democracy,* ed. Sheilah Mann and John J. Patrick. Bloomington: Indiana University, ERIC Clearinghouse for Social Studies/Social Science Education.

Hepburn, Mary A., Richard G. Niemi, and Chris Chapman. 2000. "Service Learning in College Political Science: Queries and Commentary." *PS:Political Science & Politics* 33:617–22.

Hunter, Susan, and Richard A. Brisbin. 2000."The Impact of Service Learning on Democratic and Civic Values." *PS: Political Science & Politics* 33:623–26.

Independent Sector. 1997. *Trends Emerging from the National Survey of Volunteering and Giving Among Teenagers*. Washington, DC.

Kirlin, Mary. 2001. "Adult Civic Engagement: Can Adolescent Extracurricular Activities Overcome Income and Education Barriers?" Indiana University Purdue University Indianapolis.

Ladewig, Howard, and John K. Thomas. 1987."Assessing the Impact of 4-H on Former Members." College Station: Texas A&M University, Cooperative Extension Service.

Morgan, William, and Matthew Streb. 2001."Building Citizenship: How Student Voice in Service-Learning Develops Civic Values." *Social Science Quarterly* 82:154–70.

Niemi, Richard, and Jane Junn. 1999. *Civic Education: What Makes Students Learn?* New Haven, CT: Yale University Press.

Otto, L.B. 1976. "Social Integration and the Status Attainment Process." *American Journal of Sociology* 81:1360–83.

Patrick, John J. 2000. "Introduction to Education for Civic Engagement in Democracy," In *Education for Civic Engagement in Democracy: Service Learning and Other Promising Practices*, ed. Sheilah Mann and John J. Patrick. Bloomington: Indiana University, ERIC Clearinghouse for Social Studies/Social Science Education.

Perry, James, and Michael C. Katula. 2001."Does Service Affect Citizenship?" *Administration and Society* 33:330–33.

Raskoff, Sally, and Richard A. Sundeen. 1998."Youth Socialization and Civic Participation: The Role of Sec-

ondary Schools in Promoting Community Service in Southern California." *Nonprofit and Voluntary Sector Quarterly* 27:66–87.

Torney-Purta, Judith, Rainer Lehmann, Hans Oswald and Wilfram Schulz. 2001. *Executive Summary of Citizenship and Education in Twenty-eight Countries: Civic Knowledge and Engagement at Age Fourteen*. Amsterdam: International Association for the Evaluation of Educational Achievement.

Verba, Sidney, Kay Lehman Schlozman, and Henry E. Brady. 1995. *Voice and Equality, Civic Voluntarism in American Politics*. Cambridge, MA: Harvard University Press.

Westheimer, Joel, and Joseph Kahne. 2000."Service Learning Required." *Education Week* 19 (20): 52.

Yates, Miranda, and James Youniss. 1998."Community Service and Political Identity Development in Adolescents." *Journal of Social Issues* 54:495–512.

Youniss, James, Jeffrey A. McLellan, and Miranda Yates. 1997. "What We Know about Engendering Civic Identity." *American Behavioral Scientist* 40:620–32.

## NOTE

This research was funded by a grant from the Indiana University Center on Philanthropy.

**MARY KIRLIN** is assistant professor of public affairs at IUPUI. She spent 15 years working in government and politics before coming to the academy. Her research focuses on adolescent civic socialization. The author wishes to thank Michael Leuthner and Jordan Olivetti for their research assistance.

# The Service/Politics Split:

## Rethinking Service to Teach Political Engagement

Tobi Walker,
*Eagleton Institute of Politics, Rutgers University*

OVER THE PAST FEW YEARS, I have experimented with a classroom exercise that encourages students to think about how they perceive service and politics. I ask the students to create lists of service activities and political activities in which they and their friends and families engage. The service list typically includes such activities as working in a soup kitchen, delivering meals to the homebound, tutoring in the school system, and cleaning up parks. The list of political activities usually includes things like voting, protesting, raising money, lobbying, letter writing, and running for office.

Turning students' attention to the list of community service activities, I ask them to give some adjectives that people might use to describe the listed projects. The students usually offer such descriptors as altruistic, caring, helping, selfless, and giving, as well as individualistic and one-on-one. Often, the students will also add the words selfish or insincere to describe those students who engage in community service to enhance their resume or earn academic credit.

Asked for adjectives that describe politics, the words come fast and furious—dirty, corrupt, ambitious, crooked, dishonest, compromising, slow. After the initial rush of negative descriptors and with little prompting on my part, students will also talk about politics as a means to affect social change and make a difference for groups of people.

I have used this exercise with audiences ranging from young women uninterested in politics, to young people planning careers in politics and policy making, to foundation officials. Invariably, the answers are the same, reflecting a dramatic split in thinking about service and politics as very different types of activities with very different value structures.

This exercise was developed after working with college students, primarily young women, for several years.[1] Most of these students were involved in community service, and most of them were filled with disgust, disillusionment, and even dread toward politics. They wanted to "make a difference" and they believed the best way to do that was by helping another person one-on-one. Working on policy, challenging decision-making structures, or engaging mainstream institutions rarely entered their thinking.

The interest in service as an alternative to politics seems to reflect a larger trend among 18 to 24 year olds. According to a recent study released by the National Association of Secretaries of State, there is a "large gap between political and non-political engagement. Less than 20% of young Americans voted in 1998 and just 16% report having volunteered in a political campaign. In contrast, 53% say they have volunteered in non-political organizations" (1999, 6). A recent study commissioned by the Panetta Institute (2000) found similar results. In a national survey of college students, 34% of the eligible voters voted in the 1998 election cycle, while 73% reported doing volunteer work in the past two years. Politics and government, the authors reported, were largely irrelevant to these students.

These findings, and my own work with young people, lead me to the conclusion that educators cannot simply assume that service contributes to political engagement. Rather, I fear, service has been positioned as a morally superior alternative, a belief reinforced through rhetoric and practice by parts of the commu-

Tobi Walker. "The Service/Politics Split: Rethinking Service to Teach Political Engagement." PS: *Political Science and Politics.* 33 (3), pp. 646–649. Copyright © 2000 by the American Political Science Association. Reprinted with the permission of Cambridge University Press.

nity service movement. The following quote from the newsletter of the Corporation for National Service (CNS), which as the major funder and supporter of national service and service learning sets the tone for the national movement, is telling. In describing why AmeriCorps participants were prohibited from attending the Stand for Children rally in Washington, DC, as members, the CNS general counsel wrote: "National service has to be nonpartisan. What's more, it should be about bringing communities together by getting things done. Strikes, demonstrations and political activities can have the opposite effect. They polarize and divide" (CNS 1996).

Corporation officials will argue, quite correctly, that they must prohibit political activities like lobbying, unionizing, working for candidates, and protesting to ensure congressional support. But rather than dismiss all political activities as divisive, they could use the political decision to narrowly define service activities as a lesson for AmeriCorps members about how politics works, about the kinds of compromises and choices that are necessary in a representative, pluralistic democracy.

It is argued that students involved in service are reconceptualizing engagement as localized activities where young people can "get things done" and immediately see results. However, if students only think of civic engagement as individual, results-driven activity, they are not necessarily challenging institutions in power. Feeding the hungry does nothing to disrupt or rethink poverty or injustice. Tutoring inner-city kids does nothing to secure more resources for schools or ensure that teachers are held accountable. As educators, our task is to take the students' experiences and help them understand the larger social and political context. Why are people hungry in a period of unprecedented U.S. prosperity? How does government address the problem? How does government create the problem? Should responsibility for addressing the issues lie primarily with government institutions or with religious groups or nonprofit agencies? How are the agendas of those social service organizations shaped by government regulation and funding? The pedagogical benefit of service is that it can provide students with experiences that can inform such potentially abstract debates. But to be able to understand and address these questions, students must understand and address systems of power. One way to approach this challenge is to help students think about service and politics not as two dis-

tinct activities—one moral, one corrupt—but rather as a continuum of activities.

Leading students to this view requires considering a different set of theoretical and practical roots for service pedagogy than those typically addressed. The roots of service as citizenship education have often been traced to the writings of William James. James argued that virtues instilled by military service are the "rock upon which states are built," building the values of the good citizen—obedience, a sense of the common good, responsibility to the larger society (1967, 668). As a pacifist, James sought an alternative means to inculcate those virtues and proposed mandatory service as a mechanism for creating citizens. His arguments were the basis for the establishment of the Civilian Conservation Corps, which is often cited as the model for state-supported national service. Other service theorists (e.g., Moskos 1988) have invoked James' ideas of "martial virtues" to argue that military service should be the model for community service as citizenship education, arguing that service teaches young people about their obligations to society.

This theoretical approach is problematic because it is based on and perpetuates a conception of citizenship that has historically been exclusively male. A better model for service as a citizenship education tool is the historical relationship between women and community service. Such an approach offers insights into how educators' can reconnect service to political participation.

For generations of women activists, service galvanized them to engage in, not flee from, politics. Excluded from politics by law and tradition, women contributed to public activity by engaging in community service. Through women's clubs, settlement houses, and social reform movements like temperance, women worked to exercise influence on issues and communities. To justify their entrance into the public sphere, women's activity was conceptualized as "moral housekeeping," the extension of women's caring work from the home to the public realm. Understood that way, women's work was not a challenge to institutions of power where men exercised decision-making authority and the association of women's public activity with service effectively deflated the perception of women's power.

Many women activists understood that service alone would not substantially increase women's power or bring about societal change. Some became involved in the campaign for suffrage, hoping their vote would increase their ability to affect decision making on social issues. For some women, work in reform and service movements galvanized their involvement in politics. Women's clubs developed legislative agendas on issues of concern such as food safety and child labor (Scott 1990).[2] Women involved in Hull House, one of the great exemplars of social service activity, moved into formal government positions and began organizing workers into unions.

In a political science class at Rutgers University, I used these examples from women's history as the model for how service can lead to political engagement.[3] In the class, students explored democratic theory, women's political history, and social change strategy. Outside the classroom, they engaged in a four-hour-per-week community service placement of their own choosing, organized and managed by the university's Citizenship and Service Education Program. At the end of the semester, students wrote a research paper on a policy issue related to their community service placement. For example, a student working at a local women's health clinic did research on federal health care reform initiatives. As part of their research, students were required to interview at least two people involved in the issue— one of whom was a community activist and one who held a formal policy-making position. Finally, we required students to develop a public advocacy campaign that would integrate their public policy research, their community service experience, and their understanding of how public policy is made and changed. The students were expected to approach the issue as citizens seeking to exercise their voice in institutions with decision-making power, not as service providers proposing new programs or policymakers devising legislation or regulation.

While the small class size precludes drawing strong conclusions, students did report gaining an increased understanding of the political process, a clearer sense of how citizens can affect that process, and increased skills for engagement. Without a doubt, the service experience enriched and complicated the students' academic learning. Students were exposed to people and to questions they never would have encountered in the classroom. Because they had the chance to work on an issue they cared deeply about, the students were more motivated to conduct research. For example, the difficulties that low-income women faced in obtaining health care appalled the student working in a local health clinic. Her outrage led her to conduct an in-depth study of the

various approaches to reform in which her analysis was both politically engaged and supported by information and research. Students also confronted the questions about the limitations of their service on the issues. In particular, the students working with children were deeply concerned about the practical and ethical implications of ending their service.

As personally rewarding as students found their service, and as much as it contributed to their learning, I was also very aware that the students needed better ways to think about how to create political and policy change. Serving in community agencies did not help students understand politics. For example, the students struggled with developing their advocacy plans. I had hoped that providing them the opportunity to be creative about an issue they cared about would excite and challenge students, but the vast majority had never thought about organizing others to take on an issue and engage decisionmakers. Very few had been part of such an organizing effort; they simply had no idea of how the process worked. These students understood how to serve; they did not know how to affect political change.

Service can and should be an integral part of the way that students learn about civic and political life, challenging them to think about engagement more broadly then voting or belonging to an interest group. Nevertheless, while educators expand the concept of civic engagement, they must never abdicate their responsibility to engage students in the mainstream institutions that have power over their lives.

## NOTES

My thanks to Susan J. Carroll and Katherine E. Kleeman for their comments on this article.

1. This exercise was developed with my colleague Debra Liebowitz as part of our work on NEW Leadership, a young women's political leadership education program at the Center for American Women and Politics, a unit of the Eagleton Institute of Politics at Rutgers, the State University of New Jersey.

2. Also see Baker (1984), McCarthy (1990), Pascoe (1990), Ryan (1979), and Welter (1966).

3. Ruth B. Mandel co-taught the course described in this article.

## REFERENCES

Baker, Paula. 1984. "The Domestication of Politics: Women and American Political Society, 1780-1920." *American Historical Review* 89:620-47.

Corporation for National Service. 1996. *National Service News* 4, June 17, 1.

James, William. 1967. "The Moral Equivalent of War." *The Writings of William James*, ed. John J. McDermott. New York: Random House.

McCarthy, Kathleen D. 1990. "Parallel Power Structures: Women and the Voluntary Sphere." In *Lady Bountiful Revisited: Women, Philanthropy, and Power*, ed. Kathleen D. McCarthy. New Brunswick: Rutgers University Press.

Moskos, Charles. 1988. *A Call to Civic Service.* New York: The Free Press.

National Association of Secretaries of State. 1999. *The New Millennium Project - Part I: American Youth Attitudes on Politics, Citizenship, Government and Voting* www.nass.org/nass99/youth.htm1. Washington, DC: NASS. Accessed: June 1999.

Pascoe, Peggy. 1990. *Relations of Rescue.* Oxford: Oxford University Press.

Panetta Institute. 2000. "Institute Poll Shows College Students Turned Off by Politics, Turned On by Other Public Service" www.panettainstitute.org/news1.htm1. Accessed: February 2000.

Ryan, Mary P. 1979. "The Power of Women's Networks: A Case Study of Female Moral Reform in Antebellum America." *Feminist Studies* 5(Spring): 66-85.

Scott, Anne Firor. 1990. "Women's Voluntary Associations: From Charity to Reform." In *Lady Bountiful Revisited: Women, Philanthropy, and Power*, ed. Kathleen D. McCarthy. New Brunswick: Rutgers University Press.

Welter, Barbara. 1966. "The Cult of True Womanhood, 1820-1860." *American Quarterly* 18:151-74.

**TOBI WALKER** is a senior education associate at the Eagleton Institute of Politics, Rutgers, the State University of New Jersey.

# What Should Be Learned through Service Learning?

by Michael X. Delli Carpini and Scott Keeter

S ERVICE LEARNING IS TYPICALLY distinguished from both community service and traditional civic education by the integration of study with hands-on activity outside the classroom, typically through a collaborative effort to address a community problem (Ehrlich 1999, 246). As such, service learning provides opportunities and challenges for increasing the efficacy of both the teaching and practice of democratic politics. To better understand these opportunities and challenges, it is necessary to make explicit the goals of service learning and to consider how these goals intersect those of more traditional approaches to teaching about government and politics. We believe that one place these sometimes competing models could find common ground is in the learning of factual knowledge about politics.

Underlying the pedagogy of service learning are the beliefs that a central mission of civic education is to produce active, engaged citizens and that this mission is more likely to be accomplished by allowing young Americans to directly experience "politics" as part of their education. As noted by Frantzich and Mann, this view is very compatible with the stated mission of the American Political Science Association:

> The founding of the APSA in 1903 marked the evolution of political science as a distinct academic discipline in colleges and universities. At the time, two educational objectives were claimed for the emerging discipline: citizenship and training for careers in public service.... For the student, direct experience was recommended to supplement formal instruction in government and politics (1997, 193).

Frantzich and Mann went on to show that while the definitions of public service and citizenship have evolved over time, training for both through a combination of classroom and "real world" experiences has remained a central responsibility for the discipline.

Despite this longstanding commitment to developing good citizens, there remains a tension between the educational and civic goals of the discipline. Not all members of our profession would agree that developing active citizens is or should be part of our mission. Perceiving political science as a discipline that observes, critiques, and seeks to understand public life can easily (and justifiably) lead individuals to embrace a teaching philosophy that dictates transmitting knowledge and cultivating a critical perspective rather than encouraging participation. Indeed, some political science theory and research suggests that, for some Americans at least, civic and political engagement is irrational, unnecessary, ineffective, and even harmful (see, e.g., Berelson 1952; Downs 1957; Edelman 1988; Ginsberg 1982; Neuman 1986; Olson 1971).

Being more dedicated to transmitting knowledge than creating engaged citizens would not automatically lead one to reject the value of experiential learning, but it would lead one to consider it valuable only to the extent that it enhances a student's understanding of government and politics. In short, a factual orientation would lead one to design service learning experiences that increased learning (of a certain kind) rather than service.

Of course, the choice between transmitting knowledge and creating engaged citizens is seldom so stark as this. It is fair to assume that most political science instructors believe there is a connection between understanding government and politics and being an effective citizen, even if they never ask students to experience public life as part of their coursework. Similarly, few advocates for service learning as a means for creating more engaged citizens would deny the importance of putting one's real-world experiences into the broader context provided by readings, lectures, discussions, and writing assignments. The challenge facing instructors, therefore, lies in clarifying the relationship between classroom and experiential learning. Put another way, the questions all instructors, whatever their teaching philosophy, must answer are, "What does the experience of participating in public life add to classroom learning?" and "What does classroom learning add to the participatory experience?" While there are numerous ways one might attempt to answer these questions, we suggest that one good answer to both is factual knowledge about politics.

At first blush, the learning of political facts would seem far removed from the goals and approaches most centrally identified with either the service learning movement or current thinking about effective classroom instruction. The central objective of service learning is the development of lifelong habits of engagement in democratic citizenship. Indeed, service learning is often held up as an alternative to the dry, objectified, often context-free memorization of facts associated with traditional classroom civics. At the same time, even those who believe classroom learning is valuable in and of itself often emphasize the teaching of skills such as critical thinking or effective argument over the learning of specific facts.

While we agree that rote memorization of facts does little to create either engaged citizens or educated students (Niemi and Junn 1999), we also believe that imparting factual knowledge about politics is necessary, if not sufficient, for creating both. Consider the current paradox: America's youth are highly engaged with volunteer activity and yet very disengaged from traditional political activity; they are more trusting of government than their elders and yet feel much less politically efficacious (National Election Studies 1998). Young people want to help solve society's problems, but most do not see how what the government does can worsen or ameliorate these problems. And those who do see this connection often lack the practical knowledge of the issues, players, and rules to be able to participate in politics effectively. Political knowledge is a key to seeing these connections and to understanding how to affect the system. Being informed increases the likelihood that a citizen will have opinions about the issues of the day and that those opinions will be stable over time and consistent with each other. It produces opinions that are arguably more closely connected to one's values, beliefs, and objective conditions. It facilitates participation in public life that effectively connects one's opinions with one's actions. And it promotes greater support for democratic values such as tolerance (Delli Carpini and Keeter 1996). Put simply, while one can debate the amount or content of information a person "needs" to know, it is difficult to imagine either an educated student or an engaged citizen who is unfamiliar with the substance, key actors, institutions, and processes of politics.

Granting that factual knowledge is a prerequisite for becoming an educated and engaged citizen, we can begin to answer the two-part question posed above. One anticipated outcome of service would be the learning of political facts. There are reasons to expect this. Research suggests that knowledge is both a spur to political interest and involvement and a consequence of such interest and involvement, often offsetting more structural correlates of knowledge such as class, gender, or ethnicity (Delli Carpini and Keeter 1996; Junn 1991; Leighley 1991; Tan 1980). Further, political learning is more likely to occur when the information is directly relevant to one's immediate circumstances and behaviors. It is likely that a service learning experience, properly constituted, could activate interest and demonstrate relevance in ways that would increase a student's receptivity to and retention of factual knowledge. In addition, how much an individual learns about politics is closely tied to the opportunity to learn. Well-designed service learning projects would expose students to a great deal of essential contextual information about substantive issues, key political actors, the law, policy making, political participation (and the barriers thereto), and other fundamentals of the operation of the political system, all of which would increase the likelihood of political learning.

All of the above suggests that including service as part of students' educational experience can increase their motivation and opportunity to learn about politics, which in turn could increase the likelihood of their continued engagement in public life. Indirect evidence for this can be found in the National Assessment of Educational Progress 1998 Report Card for the Nation

(U.S. Department of Education 1999), which found that students who engaged in some form of volunteerism in their community (either through schools or on their own) scored higher on a test of civic knowledge than did those who had not engaged in this kind of activity.

The key to success is likely to be found in the nature of the service experience and how well the experience is integrated into the classroom. Effective programs provide opportunities that are likely to lead students to both "bump into" and actively seek out information about politics that is relevant to their activities. At the same time, this specific information will be more easily learned, more likely to be retained, and more likely to be connected to broader kinds of political knowledge if the classroom curriculum is integrated with the service experience. It is in the classroom that specific, often disparate service experiences can be tied to larger issues of government and politics, helping to instill not only factual knowledge but also the motivations and skills likely to increase learning over time.

Research is needed on several fronts. What is the impact of service learning on both short- and long-term gains in knowledge? What specific kinds of service experiences and teaching techniques enhance this learning? At what age (or ages) is service learning likely to be most effective? But we already know enough to expect that the combination of experiential and classroom education—when properly designed—can be an effective way to produce citizens who are both educated observers of the political scene and more active participants in public life.

## REFERENCES

Berelson, Bernard. 1952. "Democratic Theory and Public Opinion." *Public Opinion Quarterly* 16:313–30.

Delli Carpini, Michael X., and Scott Keeter. 1996. *What Americans Know about Politics and Why It Matters*. New Haven: Yale University Press.

Downs, Anthony. 1957. *An Economic Theory of Democracy*. New York: Harper and Row.

Edelman, Murray. 1988. *Constructing the Political Spectacle*. Chicago: University of Chicago Press.

Ehrlich, Thomas. 1999. "Civic Education: Lessons Learned." *PS: Political Science and Politics* 32(June): 245–50.

Frantzich, Stephen, and Sheilah Mann. 1997. "Experiencing Government: Political Science Internships." In *Experiencing Citizenship: Concepts and Models for Service-Learning in Political Science*, ed. Richard Battistoni and William E. Hudson. Washington, DC: American Association for Higher Education.

Ginsberg, Benjamin. 1982. *The Consequences of Consent*. Reading, MA: Addison-Wesley.

Junn, Jane. 1991. "Participation and Political Knowledge." In *Political Participation and American Democracy*, ed. William Crotty. New York: Greenwood Press.

Leighley, Jan. 1991. "Participation as a Stimulus of Political Conceptualization." *Journal of Politics* 53:198–211.

National Election Studies. 1998. 1998 Post-Election Study <www.umich.edu/ñes/archives/studies.phtml>. Ann Arbor: Center for Political Studies, University of Michigan.

Neuman, Russell. 1986. *The Paradox of Mass Politics: Knowledge and Opinion in the American Electorate*. Cambridge, MA: Harvard University Press.

Niemi, Richard, and Jane Junn. 1999. *Civic Education:What Makes Students Learn*. New Haven: Yale University Press.

Olson, Mancur. 1971. *The Logic of Collective Action: Public Goods and the Theory of Groups*. Cambridge, MA: Harvard University Press.

Tan, Alexis. 1980. "Mass Media Use, Issue Knowledge and Political Involvement." *Public Opinion Quarterly* 44: 241–48.

U.S. Department of Education, National Center for Education Statistics. 1999. "Focus on Civics" <http://nces.ed.gov/nationsreportcard/civics/civics.asp>. National Assessment of Educational Progress 1998 Report Card for the Nation. Washington, DC: U.S. Department of Education.

## ABOUT THE AUTHORS

**MICHAEL X. DELLI CARPINI** is director of the public policy program of the Pew Charitable Trusts. Prior to coming to the Trusts, he was a professor of political science at Barnard College, Columbia University. He is author of *Stability and Change in American Politics: The Coming of Age of the Generation of the 1960s* (New York University Press, 1986) and, with Scott Keeter, of *What Americans Know about Politics and Why It Matters* (Yale University Press, 1996), as well as numerous articles and essays on public opinion, political socialization, and political communication.

**SCOTT KEETER** is professor of government and politics and chair of the department of public and international affairs at George Mason University. He is an election night analyst of exit polls for NBC News and a survey consultant for the Pew Research Center for the People and the Press. He is coauthor of three books, including *The Diminishing Divide: Religion's Changing Role in American Politics; What Americans Know about Politics and Why It Matters;* and *Uninformed Choice: The Failure of the New Presidential Nominating System.*

# What Is Good Citizenship?

## Conceptual Frameworks Across Disciplines

by Richard M. Battistoni

I F WE WANT TO ENGAGE all across campus in education for civic engagement, we need to go beyond the social sciences for conceptual frameworks that will inform the theory and practice of service-learning. While political and other social scientists have a rich tradition and language around concepts like democracy, citizenship, community, political participation, civil society, and public work, they obviously do not own these concepts, and given the evidence of declining political participation (especially among young people), they may not be communicating it very effectively or in a way that resonates with students. In fact, the more we engage in narrow or rhetorical definitions of service and citizenship, the more we may turn away both students and faculty—especially those outside the social science disciplines. This calls at once for all disciplines, which may have equally effective conceptual frameworks, to join into the discourse around a multidisciplinary civic education. To paraphrase a statement made by Vaclav Havel in one of his first New Year's Addresses as president of the Czech Republic, the public problems we face as a people are such that require the collaboration of "well-rounded people," those informed by a variety of perspectives and conceptual frameworks (Havel, 1997, p. 9).

In this spirit, more than a year ago I began a conversation with representatives from a number of different disciplinary associations about the language and conceptual frameworks that resonated with their own disciplines. Out of this initial conversation, I generated the following list of terms:

- social capital (or social trust)
- civic engagement
- civic responsibility

- citizenship
- democracy/democratic citizenship/ democratic participation
- democratic practice
- public or community problem solving
- the creation of a public
- "public intellectual"
- civic professionalism
- corporate/institutional citizenship
- social responsibility, social accountability (or public accountability)
- social issues
- social justice
- public agency, public capacity
- social ethics, civic ethics, public ethics
- public scholarship
- community identity
- community responsibility
- community building
- common ground
- altruism
- prosocial behavior
- reciprocity
- civic or public leadership
- the creation of "public intellectuals"
- civic obligation
- public life
- other-regardingness
- creation of a more democratic society

- civil society
- the not-for-profit sector
- preparation for multicultural/intercultural citizenship
- community partnerships

The list was whittled down, based on positive faculty responses, to the following seven conceptual frameworks for civic engagement that come from theory and practice found in disciplines outside the social sciences. While certainly not exhaustive of the possibilities, these frameworks may better lend themselves to integrating service-learning into the civic engagement curriculum for many faculty than those found in the social sciences. As with the preceding chapter, a matrix comparing the answers each framework brings to the question of citizenship, civic education, the associated civic skills needed for effective public life, along with each framework's disciplinary affinities, follows the narrative summary (see Figure 1).

## CIVIC PROFESSIONALISM

In discussing the concept of civic professionalism I draw primarily from the argument made by William Sullivan in his book *Work and Integrity* (Sullivan, 1995). Sullivan, a philosopher by discipline and one of the co-authors of *Habits of the Heart* and *The Good Society*, traces the ideal of professionalism and professional work to the social reformers writing at the turn of the twentieth century. Sullivan contends that under this ideal, professional work was characterized by three central features:

- specialized training in a field of codified knowledge usually acquired by formal education and apprenticeship,
- public recognition of a certain autonomy on the part of the community of practitioners to regulate their own standards of practice,
- and a commitment to provide service to the public which goes beyond the economic welfare of the practitioners (Sullivan, 1995, p. 2).

In fact, the three features were originally thought to be intimately related to each other. The professional drew her social status, and the concomitant financial rewards, from her technical knowledge and expertise. This expertise also bought the professional autonomy in the workplace, something deemed critical to job satisfaction. In exchange, the professional was conceived as owing something back to the society from whom she drew this status and autonomy. So as a kind of *quid pro quo*, professionals were expected to contribute their knowledge to the public: indirectly, through their deliberations over matters of civic concern; and directly, through *pro bono* work with disadvantaged citizens. Originally referring to those working in the "classic honorific occupations of medicine, the bar, and the clergy," the status of professional was extended broadly to include fields such as business, education, engineering, governmental bureaucracy, health care (beyond physicians), architecture, and planning. But Sullivan asserts that while professionalization has grown tremendously over the past century, its connection to the "culture of civic democracy" emblematic of the third feature of professional work has weakened severely. While professional work has risen in social status and desirability, the civic responsibility that was originally understood as the price a professional paid for social and economic recognition and personal autonomy has declined. What we are witnessing today, according to Sullivan, is a professional ethic where technical expertise has become decoupled from civic purpose.

Sullivan argues that we must revitalize the civic orientation that originally stood at the foundation of the professions. In the United States, where the professions "pioneered and continue to model a socially attuned way to organize work," (Sullivan,1995, p. 222), we need civically minded professionals more than ever. Clearly, the challenges that face our society today require even more professional expertise than those confronted by citizens during the Progressive era. "Few kinds of work would seem better fitted to these needs of the new era than professions with a civic orientation" (Sullivan, 237). In particular, Sullivan calls upon professional education to re-instill the civic dimension that seems lacking in contemporary discussions of professional ethics and integrity.

This concept of civic professionalism should have great resonance in a number of fields where service-learning has been used as a pedagogy. Professional school educators who already deploy community service as a method of teaching concepts and practices in disciplinary courses could expand service-learning to explore related civic themes. With this concept in mind, students engaged in curriculum-based community service in schools of business, education, engineering, the health professions, law, and planning could be encouraged to reflect on the civic dimensions of their anticipated work.

## Figure 1: Conceptual Frameworks in Non-Social Sciences Disciplines

| Conceptual Framework | View of Citizenship | Understanding of Civic Education | Associated Civic Skills | Disciplinary Affinities |
|---|---|---|---|---|
| Civic Professionalism | Professional work with a civic purpose | Learning about the civic traditions and values of the professions | Public Problem Solving<br><br>Civic Judgment | Professional Disciplines |
| Social Responsibility | Responsibility to larger society | Learning about the public problems most closely associated with chosen field of work | Political Knowledge (Issues)<br><br>Organizational Analysis | Health Professions<br><br>Business Disciplines<br><br>Computer Science |
| Social Justice | Bringing one's spiritual values to bear on social problems | Learning the principles of social justice and their application to public life | Civic Judgment<br><br>Collective Action | Religious Studies<br><br>Philosophy<br><br>Faith-Based Institutions |
| Connected Knowing; Ethic of Care | Caring for the future of our public world | Learning about others and their perspectives on the world | Critical Thinking<br><br>Coalition Building | Women's Studies<br><br>Psychology<br><br>Nursing |
| Public Leadership | Citizen as "servant-leader" | Learning the arts of collaborative leadership | Community Building<br><br>Communication | Management<br><br>Leadership Studies |
| Public Intellectual | Thinkers who contribute to the public discourse | Learning about the traditions of writers and artists who have served as public intellectuals | Civic Imagination & Creativity | Literature<br><br>Visual & Performing Arts |
| Engaged/Public Scholarship | Participatory action researcher | Learning about how scholarly research might contribute to the needs and values of the community | Organizational Analysis<br><br>Public Problem Solving | Journalism<br><br>Communications<br><br>Professional Disciplines<br><br>Land Grant Instit. |

## SOCIAL RESPONSIBILITY

Where civic responsibility may be a concept that needs reviving, social responsibility is a well-established idea in a number of professions. We now see organizations devoted to connecting professional work with social responsibility in such fields as medicine, business, computer technology, architecture, and planning.

One of the first and most well-known organizations pushing this approach is Physicians for Social Responsibility (PSR). Begun during the Cold War in 1961, PSR originated with an understanding that all doctors have an ethical as well as a professional responsibility to work toward the elimination of violence—with an original emphasis on curbing nuclear weapons—global environmental degradation, and social and economic inequities. Part of this ethic of the physicians' social responsibility involves civic engagement: one of the central values of PSR is that "citizens have a right to informed participation in such decision-making processes made by both government and industry which affect their health, welfare, and environment" (www.psr.org/aboutpsr.htm).

Other organizations have followed the lead of PSR. Business for Social Responsibility has the mission of "providing members with innovative products and services that help companies be commercially successful in ways that demonstrate respect for ethical values, people, communities, and the environment" (www.bsr.org). Computer Professionals for Social Responsibility declares itself to be "a public interest alliance of computer scientists and others concerned about the impact of computer technology on society" (www.cpsr.org).

Faculty members—particularly those in disciplines which prepare students for professions with corresponding "social responsibility" arms—might see this idea of social responsibility as a natural pathway to a form of civic engagement. For example, as part of a service-learning course that's a required component of pre-medical education, students could be directed to the PSR literature and website as one of the tools for reflection on their service. A local representative from PSR could be invited in to discuss with students the social responsibilities of people entering the medical profession. And these connections would be enhanced even further if the community service connected to the course were in the specific areas addressed by PSR, such as peace and nonviolence, the environment, or public health.

## SOCIAL JUSTICE

Notions of social justice may also provide powerful connections to civic engagement for faculty, particularly those teaching in faith-based institutions of higher education. While numerous definitions of social justice exist, David Hollenbach offers one of the better ones, connecting social justice—as developed in the context of the social teachings of the Catholic Church—and civic engagement:

> It refers to the obligations of all citizens to aid in the creation of patterns of social organization and activity that are essential both for the protection of minimal human rights and for the creation of mutuality and participation by all in social life (Hollenbach, 1988, p. 27).

A similar understanding can be found in the American Catholic bishops' pastoral letter on the economy:

> Social justice implies that persons have an obligation to be active and productive participants in the life of society and that society has a duty to enable them

to participate in this way (National Conference of Catholic Bishops, 1986, p. 36).

The logic of this framework is that social justice moves individuals to work in active solidarity with fellow human beings to seek the common good of all who live in their community. Under this conception, then, a just individual is necessarily a good citizen.

A social justice framework has much to recommend itself. Not only does it offer a powerful nonpolitical path to civic engagement (important given the current student turnoff from traditional politics as documented at the outset of this book). Additionally, for faculty teaching service-learning courses at faith-based colleges and universities, this perspective can provide a seamless link between student service, the specific subject matter of their courses, the institution's mission, and civic engagement.

There exists a growing body of literature connecting faith, justice, and citizenship, usually tied to specific faith traditions and texts. To give just one example, the Catholic social justice tradition contains within it a principle known as "subsidiarity." Subsidiarity requires, on the one hand, that problems be solved and decisions be made at the smallest level of association. The assumption is that smaller communities—local not-for-profit organizations, churches, civic groups—can more effectively and compassionately address the needs of their people, and that a distant, often unresponsive federal government or multinational business enterprise should therefore not usurp or replace the authority of the smaller body to act on behalf of its members. But the principle of subsidiarity also holds that when "the demands of justice exceed the capacities" of the smaller/local units, then government has an affirmative duty to act in solving social problems (National Conference of Catholic Bishops, 1986, p. 62). Teaching at Providence College, I have successfully introduced subsidiarity as a way of engaging my students who do community service from their faith backgrounds in conversations about politics and public problem solving. The principle of subsidiarity also fits nicely with discussions of mediating institutions and social capital formation, and with basic principles of grass roots community organizing, especially the efforts sponsored by the Industrial Areas Foundation, a network of community-based organizations that teach citizens in local neighborhoods how to work together effectively to achieve public ends (see Rogers, 1990; Fischer, 1997).

More generally, social justice is a conceptual framework that can help faculty in terms of guiding students' reflection on their service. A social justice perspective can help move service-learners from the "personal" that often characterizes service to the "political," because a "foundation in social justice requires that community service from a faith perspective move beyond charity and address the root causes that create the need for service within our society and world" (Swezey, 1990, p. 78). It also allows faculty to ask the question, "How do/will you incorporate social justice and service into your daily lives?"—an opening to increased civic engagement. Social justice frameworks can provide ties between course-based service-learning and co-curricular efforts of campus ministry offices. And finally, a social justice perspective complements reciprocal approaches to community partnerships:

> Paramount to the quest for justice is the building of authentic relationships between students and the individuals and communities with whom they serve. These relationships affirm the reciprocal learning inherent in service. Service in this context is not a doing to or for but a service with a person or group; enabling and empowering disenfranchised individuals and communities to be "agents of their own development and not just the beneficiaries of someone else's efforts." Together, the student and the individuals or communities being served plan and carry out the community service experience. The task of the service becomes secondary to the relationships that develop within the service experience. (Swezey, 1990, p. 87).

## CONNECTED KNOWING; "ETHIC OF CARE"

Faculty coming into service-learning from a feminist perspective may find pathways to civic engagement through the literature on "connected knowing" or "caring" as a social ethic. Building on the work of Carol Gilligan (1982), Belenky, Clinchy, Goldberger, & Tarule (1986) developed the concept of "connected knowing" as a way of describing a "proclivity toward thinking" they found in undergraduate women, to be contrasted from the dominant understanding of how we ought to think, what they call "separate knowing." The critical distinction between the two kinds of thinking, they argue, lies in whether we see ourselves as dispassionately detached or empathetically connected to the object known (and by extension to other "knowing beings"):

> The separate knower holds herself aloof from the object she is trying to analyze. She takes an imper-

sonal stance. She follows certain rules or procedures to ensure that her judgments are unbiased. ... Separate knowing often takes the form of an adversarial proceeding. The separate knower's primary mode of discourse is the argument.

> Connected knowers are not dispassionate, unbiased observers. They deliberately bias themselves in favor of what they are examining. They try to get inside it and form an intimate attachment to it. The heart of connected knowing is imaginative attachment: trying to get behind the other person's eyes and "look at it from that person's point of view" (Clinchy, 1989).

Based upon the research into women's ways of knowing, feminist thinkers have called upon institutions of higher education to value connected knowing, to be places where "people are encouraged to think about the things that they care about and to care about the things they think about" (Clinchy, 1989).

Speaking of "care," there also abounds in the feminist literature discussions of an "ethic of care," not only to describe the way women's engagement with others has been characterized, but also as a political ethic to be embraced (Noddings, 1984). Joan Tronto (1993, p. 103) defines "care" as human activity "that includes everything that we do to maintain, continue, and repair our 'world' so that we can live in it as well as possible. That world includes our bodies, our selves, and our environment, all of which we seek to interweave in a complex, life-sustaining web."

While the gendered origins or associations of connected knowing and/or caring can be contested, there should be no doubt that the feminist orientation toward knowledge and caring can be a powerful way of moving from personal to civic engagement. And this conceptual framework lends itself to the pedagogy of service-learning. Not only does much of community service work come out of the "caring professions," but a student's course-related service can be reflected through the conceptual lens of "caring." This even allows the community service connected to a course to be subjected to various critiques of "care" as a concept that may be oppressive to women particularly when service-learning programs or courses are disproportionately populated by women, as is the case on many campuses. (For an example of a service-learning course reflecting this conceptual framework, taught by a faculty member in philosophy, see Foos, 2000.)

## PUBLIC LEADERSHIP

At first blush, concepts associated with "leadership" would not seem to be compatible with notions of democratic citizenship. After all, "leaders" usually produce "followers," and the characteristics of followers appear on the surface to be inconsistent with those of the engaged citizen. In the U.S. context, Benjamin Barber has gone so far as to argue that "strong leaders have on the whole made Americans weak citizens…the conditions and consequences of leadership often seem to undermine civic vigor" (Barber, 1999, pp. 164–5).

There are, however, rich conceptions of public leadership that compliment understandings of engaged democratic citizenship. In fact, we can trace ideas about this kind of "transformational" democratic leadership at least as far back as Rousseau's *Social Contract,* with more contemporary versions found in the writings of John Dewey, James MacGregor Burns, and Saul Alinsky (see Dewey, 1916; Burns, 1979; Alinsky, 1969). Burns puts the reciprocal relationship between leaders and citizens in a democracy this way:

> Leadership is not a surrogate for participation in a democracy, it is its necessary condition. Without leaders, a citizenry is unlikely to remain active; without active citizens, responsive leaders are unlikely to emerge, and leaders who do emerge are unlikely to remain responsive. (Burns, 1979, p. 439)

Viewed this way, then, a leadership framework can be yet another pathway to engaged citizenship. And given the emergence of "leadership studies" as a growing area on college campuses—not only in business disciplines but as an interdisciplinary field on its own—connecting the study of public leadership to civic engagement may make sense. Moreover, recent philosophies of "steward" or "servant" leadership have strong connections with service-learning, and can serve as bridges between leadership studies, community-based learning, and civic education. (See Greenleaf, 1996; see also the Greenleaf Center for Servant-Leadership, at www.greenleaf.org. A good example of a university-based leadership program, one with strong service-learning connections, is the Jepson School of Leadership Studies at the University of Richmond; see: www.richmond.edu/academics/leadership.)

## THE PUBLIC INTELLECTUAL

So far, the different conceptual models of citizenship offered tend heavily toward the social sciences and pre-professional disciplines. To the extent that we might find connections to the humanities, it would be primarily philosophers or theologians who see concepts that resonate with their disciplines. There may be little conceptually for those in literature of the arts to latch on to, leading to the question, "What does citizenship have to do with us?" My conversations with faculty in the literary, visual, and performing arts suggest that the tradition of the "public intellectual" or the artist inspired to contribute to a political vision may be a powerful pathway to civic engagement in these fields.

What is meant by the term "public intellectual?" Simply put, public intellectuals are writers, artists, and thinkers "who address a general and educated audience…who contribute to open discussions" (Jacoby, 1987, p. 221). They are women and men of intellect or vision who are not content to share their work with a specialized, esoteric audience, but bring the power of their ideas to bear on the public problems or questions of the day. In a democracy particularly, where majorities and public opinion rule, it has been thought critical to society's growth and progress to have a class of people who can contribute their ideas and vision to general public discourse. Writing in the nineteenth century, Walt Whitman makes this case for such a contribution to democracy in the United States:

> Our fundamental want today in the United States, with closest, amplest reference to present conditions, and to the future, is of a class, and the clear idea of a class, of native authors, literatuses, far different, far higher in grade than any yet known, sacerdotal, modern, fit to cope with our occasions, lands, permeating the whole mass of American mentality, taste, belief, breathing into it a new breath of life, giving it decision, affecting politics far more than the popular superficial suffrage, with results inside and underneath the elections of Presidents or Congresses—radiating, begetting appropriate teachers, schools, manners, and, as its grandest result, accomplishing (what neither the schools nor the churches and their clergy have hitherto accomplish'd, and without which this nation will no more stand, permanently, soundly, than a house will stand without a substratum,) a religious and moral character beneath the political and productive and intellectual bases of the States (Whitman, 1999).

Following Shelley, who called poets "the unacknowledged legislators of the world," Whitman believed that American poets, writers, artists, and thinkers had a duty to contribute to the public discourse, to "become the justification and reliance of American democracy"

(Whitman, 1999, p. 49). This tradition of public intellectuals in the United States would carry from Whitman, Ralph Waldo Emerson, Herbert Melville, Margaret Fuller, and Mark Twain in the nineteenth century to such individuals as Herbert Croly, John Dewey, Langston Hughes, Walter Lippmann, and Frank Capra in the early decades of the twentieth century (for examples of modern artists who have served the function of public intellectual, see Barber & McGrath, 1982).

The concept of a public intellectual may seem antiquated to many today. Indeed, a number of scholars would argue that the public intellectual is a dying breed, owing to changes in the media and popular culture, university life and work, and the demands of modern science and technology (see Bender, 1993; Jacoby, 1987; Hollander, et al., 2001). Still, this is a conceptual framework that may resonate with faculty in the humanities (for an extension to economists, see Levine, 2001), offering a number of natural links to service-learning. Students engaged in literary or artistic service projects can be introduced to this tradition of civic engagement through written texts and other works of public or political art. This conceptual tradition can be tied to the skills of civic imagination and creativity, with course assignments designed to make explicit linkage between literature or art and public value.

## THE SCHOLARSHIP OF ENGAGEMENT, PUBLIC SCHOLARSHIP

As noted in the last section, the notion of the "public intellectual" may seem antiquated to many faculty, the product of a bygone era. In the past decade, many faculty, especially those involved in experiential or service-learning, resonate more deeply to notions of engaged or public scholarship. The idea of connecting academic scholarship to engagement owes much to Ernest Boyer. In a 1996 essay, Boyer claimed that higher education needed to "become a more vigorous partner in the search for answers to our most pressing social, civic, economic, and moral problems, and must reaffirm its historic commitment to what I call the scholarship of engagement." Building on his report for the Carnegie Foundation for the Advancement of Teaching, entitled *Scholarship Reconsidered*, Boyer argued that "the scholarship of engagement means connecting the rich resources of the university to our most pressing social, civic, and ethical problems" (Boyer, 1996, pp. 11–20). A number of scholars have built upon Boyer's foundations, making the case for the civic purposes of academic research and scholarship (see Benson and Harkavy, 1997; Checkoway, 2001). The American Association for Higher Education's Forum on Faculty Roles and Rewards has advanced these notions of "engaged scholarship," and AAHE has published a number of resources for faculty interested in connecting advanced scholarship with public purposes (see their website, at: www.aahe.org/ FFRR).

As a variation on the theme of engaged scholarship, Jeremy Cohen has recently offered what he thinks is a more civically minded conceptual framework for the research work done by faculty and students: public scholarship. According to Cohen, public scholarship gives both faculty and students the opportunity to "imagine their academic capacity as a way to contribute as citizen participants, in a community structure where their intellectual decisions do make a difference." As Cohen defines it,

> public scholarship as an approach assumes a duty to make university scholarship public and to use our discoveries in the interest of the community....The social act of public scholarship itself provides a laboratory in which students can view their work not as the isolated, self-indulged actions of a campus segregated from society, but as the contributions of citizens with membership in a larger community (Cohen, 2001, pp. 15–16).

This conceptual approach lends itself to a different kind of community service: "participatory action research" conducted by students and their faculty in collaboration with their community partners. Under this model, community-based organizations identify research projects that would contribute to their work, and universities—through service-learning curricula—provide their research resources as a form of service. Seen this way, service-learning as engaged or public scholarship can be a vehicle for faculty and students to reflect upon the public purposes of academic research, and the civic responsibilities of academic institutions. At Stanford, for example, the Haas Center for Public Service offers a "Senior Honors Research in Public Service Seminar," a full-year course that "provides an organizational structure to encourage and support participants committed to developing a thesis that meets criteria for academic excellence and also realizes the program's theme and goal, 'research as a form of public service'" (Cruz, 1998). Academic programs at the institutions such as the University of Pennsylvania and the University of Illinois are grounded in this approach (see Harkavy, 2000; Reardon, 1997).

# REFERENCES

Alinsky, Saul. 1969. "Native Leadership," in *Reveille for Radicals*. New York: Vintage, 64–75.

Barber, Benjamin R. 1999. "Neither Leaders nor Followers: Citizenship Under Strong Democracy," in *Education for Democracy*, Benjamin Barber & Richard Battistoni, eds. Dubuque, IA: Kendall/Hunt Publishing Company, pp. 164–172.

Barber, Benjamin R. and Michael McGrath, eds. 1982. *The Artist and Political Vision*. New Brunswick, NJ: Transaction Books.

Belenky, Mary Field, Blythe McVicker Clinchy, Nancy Rule Goldberger, and Jill Mattuck Tarule. 1986. *Women's Ways of Knowing: The Development of Self, Voice, and Mind*. New York: Basic Books.

Benson, Lee and Ira Harkavy. 1997. "School and Community in the Global Society," in *Universities and Community Schools*. University of Pennsylvania, Fall-Winter: 16–71

Boyer, Ernest. 1996. "The Scholarship of Engagement," in *The Journal of Public Service and Outreach*. Vol. 1, No. 1, pp. 11–20.Burns, James MacGregor. 1979. Leadership. New York: Harper & Row, Publishers.

Burns, James MacGregor. 1979. *Leadership*. New York: Harper & Row.

Checkoway, Barry. 2001. "Renewing the Civic Mission of the American Research University." *The Journal of Higher Education*. Volume 72, No. 2 (March/April): pp. 127–147.

Clinchy, Blythe McVicker. 1989. "On Critical Thinking and Connected Knowing." *Liberal Education*: 75: 14–19.

Cohen, Jeremy. 2001. "Shouting Fire in a Crowded Classroom: Public Scholarship from Holmes to Homeroom," *Campus Compact Reader*. Vol. 1, Issue 3 (Winter), pp. 11–17.

Cruz, Nadinne. 1998. "Introduction to the Reader: Program Vision and Purpose," *Public Service Research Program Course Reader*. Stanford: Haas Center for Public Service.

Dewey, John. 1916. *Democracy and Education*. New York: Macmillan Publishing Co.

Foos, Cathy Ludlum. 2000. "The Different Voice of Service," in *The Practice of Change: Concepts and Models for Service-Learning in Women's Studies*, Barbara Balliet and Kerrissa Heffernan, eds. Washington, D.C.: American Association for Higher Education.

Fischer, Robert. 1997. *Let the People Decide: Neighborhood Organizing in America*. Twayne Publishing.Gilligan, Carol. 1982. In a Different Voice: Psychological Theory and Women's Development. Cambridge, MA: Harvard University Press.

Gillian, Carol. 1982. *In a Different Voice: Psychological Theory and Women's Development*. Cambridge, MA: Harvard University Press.

Greenleaf, Robert K. 1996. *On Becoming a Servant Leader* (edited by Don M. Frick and Larry C. Spears). San Francisco: Jossey-Bass Publishers.

Havel, Vaclav. 1997. "New Year's Address to the Nation," in *The Art of the Impossible: Politics as Morality in Practice*. New York: Alfred A. Knopf.

Hollander, Elizabeth, John Saltmarsh, and Edward Zlotkowski. 2001. "Indicators of Engagement," in Simon, et al. (eds.), *Learning to Serve: Promoting Civil Society Through Service-Learning*. Norwell, MA: Kluwer Academic Publishers.

Hollenbach, David. 1988. *Justice, Peace, and Human Rights: American Catholic Social Ethics in a Pluralistic Context*. New York: Crossroad.

Jacoby, Russell. 1987. *The Last Intellectuals: American Culture in the Age of Academe*. New York: Basic Books.

Levine, Peter. 2001. "Public Intellectuals and the Influence of Economics," in *Higher Education Exchange*. Dayton, OH: The Kettering Foundation.

Levine, Peter. 2001. "Public Intellectuals and the Influence of Economics," in *Higher Education Exchange*. Dayton, Ohio: The Kettering Foundation.

National Conference of Catholic Bishops. 1986. *Economic Justice For All*. Washington, D.C.: National Conference of Catholic Bishops.

Noddings, Nel. 1984. *Caring: A Feminist Approach to Ethics and Moral Education*. Berkeley, CA: University of California Press.

Reardon, Kenneth. 1997. "Institutionalizing Community Service Learning at Major Research University: The Case of the East St. Louis Action Research Project," *Michigan Journal of Community Service Learning*. Volume 4.

Rogers, Mary Beth. 1990. *Cold Anger: A Story of Faith and Power Politics*. University of North Texas Press.

Sullivan, William M. 1995. *Work and Integrity: The Crisis and Promise of Professionalism in America*. New York: HarperCollins Publishers.

Swezey, Erin D. 1990. "Grounded in Justice: Service Learning from a Faith Perspective," in *Community Service as Values Education*, Delve, Mintz, & Stewart, eds. San Francisco: Jossey-Bass Publishers.

Tronto, Joan. 1993. *Moral Boundaries: A Political Argument for an Ethic of Care*. New York: Routledge.

Whitman, Walt. 1999. "Democratic Vistas," in *Education for Democracy*, Benjamin Barber & Richard Battistoni, eds. Dubuque, IA: Kendall/Hunt.

# Civic Engagement:
## Recommended Reading

### BOOKS & CHAPTERS

Astin, A.W. (1996). *Democracy at risk: What higher education can do.* Gettysburg, PA: Eisenhower Leadership Program, Gettysburg College.

Barber, B.R. (1998). *A place for us: How to make society civil and democracy strong.* New York: Hill and Wang.

Barber, B.R. (1990). Service, citizenship and democracy: Civic duty as an entailment of civil right. In W. Evers (Ed.), *National service pro and con* (pp. 27–43). Stanford, CA: Hoover Institution Press.

Barber, B.R., & Battistoni, R.M. (1999). *Education for democracy.* Revised edition. Dubuque, IA: Kendall/Hunt.

Battistoni, R.M. (2002). *Civic engagement across the curriculum: A resource book for service-learning faculty in all disciplines.* Providence, RI: Campus Compact.

Battistoni, R.M. (2002). Service learning and civic education. In Mann, S., & Patrick, J.J. (Eds.), *Education for civic engagement in democracy: Service learning and other promising practices.* Bloomington, IN: ERIC Clearinghouse for Social Studies/Social Science Education.

Battistoni, R.M., et al. (2003) *The engaged department toolkit.* Providence. RI: Campus Compact.

Bennett, J. Collegial Professionalism: The academy, individualism and the common good. Phoenix, AZ: ACE/Oryx Press.

Boyte, H. C. & Farr, J. (1997). The work of citizenship and the problem of service-learning. In *Experiencing citizenship: Concepts and models for service-learning in political science.* Washington, DC: AAHE.

Boyte, H. C. and Kari, N. (1996). *Building America: The democratic promise of public work.* Philadelphia, PA: Temple University Press.

Bringle, R. G., Games, R., & Malloy, E. A. (1999). *Colleges and universities as citizens.* Boston, MA: Allyn and Bacon.

Colby, A., Ehrlich, T., Beaumont, E., & Stephens, J. (2003). *Educating citizens: Preparing America's undergraduates for lives of moral and civic responsibility.* San Francisco: Jossey-Bass.

Ehrlich, T. (Ed.). (2000). *Civic responsibility and higher education.* Phoenix: Oryx Press.

Eyler, J. and Giles, D. E., Jr. (1999). *Where's the learning in service learning?* San Francisco, CA: Jossey-Bass.

Eyler, J., Root, S., and Giles, D.E., Jr. (1998). Service learning and the development of expert citizens: Service learning and cognitive science. In R. Bringle and D. Duffy (eds.) *With service in mind.* Washington, DC: American Association for Higher Education.

Guarasci, R. & Cornwall, G. H. (1997). Democracy and difference: emerging concepts of identity, diversity, and community. In R. Guarasci, G.H. Cromwell & Assoc., *Democratic education in America.* San Francisco: Jossy-Bass.

Harlacher, E. L. & Gollattscheck, J. (1997). *The community-building college: Leading the way to community revitalization.* Washington, DC: American Association of Community Colleges.

Holland, G. (1998). *A call for connection.* Novato, CA: New World Library.

Hollander, E., Salmarsh, J., & Zlotkowski, E. (2001). Indicators of engagement. In Simon, L.A.K., Kenny, M., Brabeck, K., & Lerner, R.M. (Eds.), *Learning to serve: promoting civil society through service-learning.* Norwell, MA: Kluwer Academic Publishers.

Jacoby, B., & Associates (Eds). (1996). *Service-learning in higher education: Concepts and practices.* San Francisco: Jossey-Bass.

Jacoby, B., & Associates (Eds). (2003). *Building partnerships for service-learning.* San Francisco: Jossey-Bass. Kellogg Commission on the Future of State and Land-Grant Universities. (1999, February). *Returning to our roots: The engaged institution.* Washington, DC: Author.

Knapp, M. et al. (1998). *Paths to partnership: University and community as learners and teachers in interprofessional education.* Lanham MD: Rowman and Littlefield.

Lappe, F. M. & DuBois, P. M. (1994). *The quickening of America: Rebuilding our nation, remaking our lives.* San Francisco: Jossey-Bass.

Lempert, D. (1996). *Escape from the ivory tower: Student adventures in democratic experiential education.* San Francisco: Jossey-Bass.

Lisman, C. D. (1998). *Toward a civil society: Civic literacy and service learning.* London: Bergin and Garvey.

Loeb, P. R. (1999). *The soul of a citizen: Living with conviction in cynical times.* New York: St. Martin's Press.

Mathews, D. (1999). *Civic intelligence in higher education and the practice of democratic politics.* Dayton, OH: Kettering Foundation.

Medel–Reyes, M. (1998). A pedagogy for citizenship: Service learning and democratic education. In Rhoades, R. A. & Howard, J. P (Eds.). *Academic service learning: A pedagogy of action and reflection.* San Francisco: Jossey-Bass.

Milner, H. (2002). *Civic literacy: How informed citizens make democracy work.* Hanover, NH: University Press of New England.

Mitchell, M. (1998). *A new kind of party animal.* New York: Simon and Schuster.

Morse, S.W. (Ed.) (1989). *Public leadership education: Preparing college students for their civic roles.* Dayton, OH: The Kettering Foundation.

Morse, S.W. (Ed.). (1990). *Public leadership education: Learning about civic life.* Dayton, OH: The Kettering Foundation.

Murchland, B. (Ed.). (1991) *Higher education and the practice of democratic politics: A political education reader.* Dayton, OH: Kettering Foundation.

Myers, S. (Ed.). (2002). *The democracy reader.* New York: International Debate Education Association.

Newman, F. (1985). *Higher education and the American resurgence.* Princeton, NJ: Carnegie Foundation for the Advancement of Teaching.

Nyden, P. et al. (1997). *Building community: Social science in action.* Thousand Oaks, CA: Pine Forge Press.

O'Connell, B. (1999). *Civil society: The underpinnings of American democracy.* Hanover NH: University Press of New England.

Orrill, R. (Ed.) (1997). *Education and democracy: Re-imagining liberal learning in America.* New York: The College Board.

Parsons, M. H., & Lisman, C. D. (1996, Spring). *Promoting community renewal through civic literacy and service learning.* San Francisco, CA: Jossey-Bass.

Putnam, R. D. (2000). *Bowling alone: The collapse and revival of America's community.* New York: Simon & Schuster.

Putnam, R. & Feldstein, L. (2003). *Better together: Restoring the American community.* New York: Simon & Schuster.

Rimmerman, C. (1998). *The new citizenship: Unconventional policies, activism and service.* Boulder, CO: Westview Press.

Rudisill, A. (1996). *Hope and power in partnership: A study of community-institution partnerships.* Berkeley, CA: University of California Press.

Schudson, M. (1998). *The good citizen: A history of American civil life.* New York: Free Press.

Sullivan, W. S. (1999). *Institutional identity and social responsibility.* Chevy Chase, MD: Council on Public Policy Education.

Westbrook, R. B. (1991). *John Dewey and American democracy.* Ithaca, NY: Cornell University Press.

## ARTICLES & REPORTS

American Association of State Colleges and Universities. (2002). *Stepping forward as stewards of place.* Washington, DC: AASCU.

American Council on Education. (1997). *Educational Record: The Magazine of Higher Education,* Summer/Fall, entire issue.

Ansley, F. & Gaventa, J. (1997). Researching for democracy and democratizing research. *Change,* 29, 46–53.

Astin, A.W. (1998, Winter). Higher education and civic responsibility. *NSEE Quarterly,* 24 (2) 18–26..

Astin, A.W., Sax, L.J. & Avalos, J. (1999). Long term effects of volunteerism during the undergraduate years. *The Review of Higher Education,* 22 (2), 187–202.

Bernstein, A. & Cock, J. (1997, November). Educating citizens for democracies young and old. *Chronicle of Higher Education.*

Boyer, E. L. (March, 1994). Creating the New American College. *The Chronicle of Higher Education.*

Boyte, H. C. (1991). Community service and civic education. *Phi Delta Kappan.*

Boyte, H. C. (1993, March). Practical politics. *The Atlantic Monthly.*

Campbell, D. E. (2000, Sept.) Social capital and service learning. *PS: Political Science and Politics,* v. 33 n3, 641–5.

Campus Compact. (2002). *Presidents' declaration on the civic responsibility of higher education.* Providence, RI: Campus Compact.

Carnegie Corporation of New York and the Center for Information & Research on Civic Learning & Engagement (CIRCLE). (2003). *The civic mission of schools.* New York: Carnegie Corporation of New York and CIRCLE.

*Change: The Magazine of Higher Learning.* January/February, 1997.

*Change: The Magazine of Higher Learning.* May/June, 1997.

Checkoway, B. (1997). Reinventing the research university for public service. *Journal of Planning Literature,* 11: 307–319.

Cordes, C. (1998, September). Community-based projects help scholars build public support. *The Chronicle of Higher Education.* 45,1.

Damon, W. (1998, October). The path to a civil society goes through a university. *The Chronicle of Higher Education*.

Delli Carpini, M. X. and Keeter, S. (2000, Sept.). What should be learned through service learning? *PS: Political Science and Politics*, v. 33 n3, 635–7.

Dobelle, E. S. (1998, Summer). Easy days are over. *Connections*, New England Board of Higher Education.

Edmondson, M. (1997, September). On the uses of a liberal education: As lite entertainment for bored college students. *Harper's Magazine*.

Ehrlich, T. (1997, Summer/Fall). Civic learning: Democracy and education revisited. *Educational Record*, 78(3,4).

Gabelnick, F. (1997). Educating a committed citizenry. *Change*, 29(1): 30–35.

Gamson, Z. (1997, January/February). Higher education and rebuilding civic life. *Change*.

Gamson, Z., Hollander, E. & Kiang, P. N. (1998, Spring). The university in engagement with society. *Liberal Education*, pp. 20–25.

Gaudiani, C. (1997, Summer/Fall). Catalyzing community: The college as a model of civil society. *Educational Record*, 78(3,4).

Greiner, W. R. The courage to lead: engaging universities and colleges in public problem solving. *Universities and Community Schools*, 5(1–2).

Hahn, C.L. (1999). Citizenship education: An empirical study of policy, practices, and outcomes. *Oxford Review of Education*, 25 (1), 231–250.

Harkavy, I. & Benson, L. (1998). De-platonizing and democratizing education as the bases of service-learning. *New Directions for Teaching and Learning*, 73, 11–20.

Hart, Peter D. (1998, August). *New Leadership for a New Century: Key Findings from a Study on Youth, Leadership, and Community Service*. Washington, DC: Hart Research Associates.

Heffernan, K. (2002). Civic lessons. *The Journal of Public Affairs*, 6, 69–82.

Holland, B. (1997, Fall). Analyzing institutional commitment to service: A model of key organizational factors. *Michigan Journal of Community Service Learning*, pp. 30–41.

Holland, B. A. & Gelmon, S. B. (1998, October). The state of the 'engaged campus.' *AAHE Bulletin*.

Hollander, E. L. (1998, October-November). Civic education: Is higher education losing? *Compact Current*, 12(4).

Hollander, E., & Saltmarsh, J. (2000, July/August). The engaged university. *Academe: Bulletin of the American Association of University Professors*, 86 (4), 29–31.

*The Journal of Public Affairs*. (2002). Supplemental Issue: Civic Engagement and Higher Education, Vol 6 (supp. 1).

Kahne, J. & Westheimer, J. (1996, May). In the service of what? The politics of service learning. *Phi Delta Kappan*.

Kettering Foundation. *Connections*, 9(1). *Kettering Review*. Spring, 1998.

Kielsmeier, J. C. (2000, May). A time to serve, a time to learn: Service learning and the promise of democracy. *Phi Delta Kappan*, v. 81 n9, 652–7.

Koliba, C. (1998, Fall). Lessons in citizen forums and democratic decision-making: A service learning case study. *Michigan Journal of Community Service Learning*, 5: 75–85.

Koliba, C. J. (2000, Feb.). Moral learning and networks of engagement. *American Behavioral Scientist*,43(5), 825–39.

Lee, L. (1999, January-February). Soul of the student citizen. *About Campus*, pp. 16–22.

Lichterman, P. (1995, November). Piecing together multicultural community: Cultural differences in community building among grass-roots environmentalists. *Social Problems*, 42(4).

Lisman, C. D. (1996, Spring). The engaged campus. *New Directions for Community Colleges*, 24(1).

Lisman, C. D. (1997, Spring). The community college service-learning movement: Successes and challenges. *Journal of Public Service and Outreach*, 2(1).

Mathews, D. (1997, Summer/Fall). Character for what? Higher education and public life. *Educational Record*, 78(3,4).

McGovern, E. (1998, November-December). Doing good work: When one person's cause is another person's dinner. *About Campus*.

McKenzie, R. (1996). Learning civic effectiveness. *NSEE Quarterly*, 22(2).

McTighe-Musil, C. (1999, Winter). Educating for global citizenship. *Liberal Education*, 85(1): 22–27.

Meister, R. (1999, Winter). Engagement with society at Depaul University. *Liberal Education*, 85(1): 56–61.

Morton, K., & Enos, S. (2002). Building deeper civic relationship s and new and improved citizens. *The Journal of Public Affairs*, 6, 83–102.

National Commission on Civic Renewal. (1998). *A nation of spectators: How civic disengagement weakens America and what we can do about it.* http://www.puaf.umd.edu/civicrenewal/finalreport/table_of_contentsfinal_report.htm.

Pascarella, E.T., Ethington, C.A., & Smart, J.C. (1988). The influence of college on humanitarian/civic involvement values. *Journal of Higher Education*, 59: 412–437.

Perry, J.S. & Katula, M.C. (2001, July). Does service affect citizenship? *Administration and Society*, v. 33 n3, 330–65.

Platt, C. (1998). Civic education and academic culture. *Liberal Education, 84* (1), 18–26.

Rhoads, R.A. (2000). Democratic citizenship and service-learning: Advancing the caring self. *New Directions for Teaching and Learning, 82,* 37–44.

Rifkin, J. (1996, January). Rethinking the mission of American education: Preparing the next generation for the civil society. *Education Week.*

Rubin, S. (1990). Service-learning: Educating for democracy. *Liberal Education,76:* 12–17.

Rudisill, A. (1996). *Hope and power in partnership: A study of community-institution partnerships.* Berkeley, CA: University of California Press.

Sax, L. & Astin, A. (1997, Summer/Fall). The benefits of service: evidence from undergraduates. *Educational Record, 78*(3,4).

Schon, D. A. (1995, November/December). The new scholarship requires a new epistemology. *Change, 27*(6): 26–39.

Siegel, S. & Rockwood, V. (1993). Democratic education, student empowerment, and community service: Theory and practice. *Equity and Excellence in Education, 26:* 654–670.

Smith, M. W. (1994, Fall). Community service learning: striking the chord of citizenship. *Michigan Journal of Community Service Learning, 1:* 37–43.

Stevens, C.S. (2003). Unrecognized roots of service-learning in African American social thought and action, 1890–1930. *Michigan Journal of Community Service Learning,* Winter, 25–34.

Walker, T. (2000, Sept.). The service/politics split: Rethinking service to teach political engagement. *PS: Political Science and Politics,* v. 33 n3, 646–9.

Westhoff, L. (1995, Spring). The popularization of knowledge: John Dewey on experts and American democracy. *History of Education Quarterly,* 2747.

Williams, D., et al. (2002). Toward an understanding of civic capacity: An anatomy of community issues that matter to students. *The Journal of Public Affairs, 6,* 241–264.

Zehr, M. A. (1996, May/June). Getting involved in civic life. *Foundations News & Commentary.*

Zlotkowski, E. (1996, January/February). A new voice at the table: Linking service-learning and the academy. *Change,* pp.21–27.

# Civic Engagement Resources on the Web

## AAC&U's Civic Engagement Page

*www.aacu-edu.org/issues/civicengagement*

This site contains links to AAC&U initiatives, publications, and resources that support the organizations "vision of liberal learning [which] includes a strong focus on developing students' civic capacities, their sense of social responsibility, and their commitment to public action." Included is a link to the Center for Liberal Education and Civic Engagement, a collaborative initiative between AAC&U and Campus Compact.

## American Political Science Association Civic Education Network

*www.apsanet.org/CENnet*

This site provides links to teaching materials, funding sources, and other organizations that support civic education.

## Campus Compact

*www.compact.org and www.actionforchange.org*

In addition to its many service-learning resources, the Campus Compact website contains resources in support of civic education, including a link to Campus Compact's Raise Your Voice campaign, which is aimed at increasing civic participation among college students.

## Center for Civic Education

*www.civiced.org*

Although much of the material is on this site is for K-12 educators, higher education faculty will find valuable resources as well.

## Center for Democracy and Citizenship, University of Minnesota

*www.publicwork.org*

Based on Harry Boyte's concept of citizenship as public work, the Center works to support initiatives that strengthen students' civic capcities.

## Center for Information and Research on Civic Learning and Engagement (CIRCLE)

*www.civicyouth.org*

CIRCLE provides funding to support research in civic education. The site contains links to publications and resources of interest to civic educators.

## Civic Practices Network (CPN)

*www.cpn.org/index.html*

This site contains links to internal and external resources that support the Network's mission of "revitalizing our democracy to tackle the complex problems of the 21st century [through] broad exchange and continually refining the civic wisdom of what works and what empowers citizens to work together."

## Civics Online

*www.civics-lnline.org*

From the homepage: "Civics Online is a collaborative, online project providing a rich array of primary sources, professional development tools, and interactive activities to help in the teaching of civics."

## CIVNET

*www.civnet.org*

CIVNET provides online resources and services for teachers, scholars, and policymakers in order to promote civic education at all levels.

## Close Up Foundation

*www.closeup.org*

The Close Up Foundation provides state, local, and national experiential learning opportunities in civics and government. The website contains links to a variety of civic education resources.

### The Democracy Collaborative

*www.democracycollaborative.org*

From the homepage: "The Democracy Collaborative undertakes integrated activities aimed at leveraging the resources of higher education institutions in support of democratic renewal, civic participation, and community building."

### The Kettering Foundation

*www.kettering.org*

The Kettering Foundation promotes programs that strengthen participatory democracy. The website contains links to publications and resources that facilitate and inspire public problem solving.

### The National Alliance for Civic Education

*www.cived.net*

This website provides updates on news and events related to civic education and contains links to civic education resources and publications.

### The National Endowment for Democracy

*www.ned.org*

The National Endowment for Democracy publishes the *Journal of Democracy*, and provides grants to support civic education and democratic capacity building. The website is a good source for scholarly materials related to civil society and participatory democracy.

### Sustainable Communities Network— Civic Engagement

*www.sustainable.org/creating/civic.html*

As the header on this webpage notes, this site "provides resources for encouraging civil discourse and involvement."

# Community Partnerships

## TITLES IN THIS SECTION

The State of the "Engaged Campus": What Have We Learned About Building and Sustaining University and Community Partnerships? BY BARBARA A. HOLLAND AND SHERRIL B. GELMON

Higher Education/Community Partnerships: Assessing Progress in the Field, BY DAVID J. MAURRASSE

Recommended Reading

## QUESTIONS FOR REFLECTION AND PLANNING

What is the nature of campus-community partnerships at your institution? How does the surrounding community perceive your institution?

What have been your own experiences with community work? Collaborative work?

What would be the nature of a community partnership that could address the pedagogical goals of your course(s)?

What community sites do you feel would best be suited to meet those goals? How might your course goals intersect with the goals of the community/agency?

Do you work with one or two community partners consistently, or do you place your students in multiple sites? What are the relative advantages and disadvantages of each approach?

# The State of the "Engaged Campus":

## What Have We Learned About Building and Sustaining University-Community Partnerships?

by Barbara A. Holland and Sherril B. Gelmon

DOZENS OF INSTITUTIONS have discussed, pondered, argued, and waffled over the importance of university community relationships and their relevance to the academic core and mission. What forms should these partnerships take? Is this scholarly work? How do we avoid being overwhelmed by community needs? Why and how should we apply our intellectual energies to community issues?

Fortunately, there is a growing understanding of how intrinsic and extrinsic community-university partnerships might enhance the academy. While university-community interactions may not be relevant to the mission of all institutions, for many they have become a way to build relationships with the immediate community, improve image and support, and increase funding or recruitment and retention of students.

University-community interactions usually take basic and now familiar forms, such as service-learning, internships, practica, and capstones—all involving students in community-based learning. Faculty are also key to these learning strategies, and the partnership with community representatives often leads to additional opportunities for faculty to engage in a wide variety of scholarly activities, such as applied research, technical assistance, evaluation, and participatory action research.

But what do we know about the form and nature of the partnership relationships themselves? The many essays and articles written in the last few years have been dominated by "calls to action" that describe the importance and value of directing higher education's attention and intellectual assets toward our various communities and cities. These essays often focus on imponderable questions about how such partnerships should be developed and maintained.

Once the notion of the engaged campus took hold, many institutions looked for partnerships that would serve their own interests by allowing them to use the community and its problems as study subjects. This one-sided approach to linking the academy and the community is a deep-seated tradition that has, in fact, led to much of the estrangement of universities and colleges from their communities. Those very communities—necessary to fulfill the state of engagement—resent being treated as an experimental laboratory for higher education and resist the unidirectional nature of the campus efforts. As academics, we are trained as experts and tend to imagine community partnerships in which the institution identifies a need and offers an expert solution to the otherwise apparently hapless (or helpless) community.

Some faculty are skeptical about the appropriateness of applying knowledge to community issues and express concern about losing their scholarly agendas to nonacademic interests. Questions are raised about the relationship of this new kind of scholarly work to more traditional scholarly priorities. However, faculty and administrators alike see the potential for enhancing community relations, student learning, and overall scholarly performance of the institution through applied scholarship and various forms of community-based learning.

Many institutions—public and private, large and small, urban and rural—have taken up the idea of more active community engagement and have been pioneers in exploring mutually beneficial relationships. They have had to do so without the guidance of prior research or experience; they have acted largely on faith that community interactions would prove to be valuable and rewarding for faculty and students. As a result, much has been learned on a trial-and-error basis.

## LEARNING FROM MULTIPLE INITIATIVES

During the last two years, we have been involved in several national projects and local studies that permitted an in-depth exploration of many examples of university-community relationships. These include:

- The Health Professions Schools in Service to the Nation (HPSISN), funded by the Corporation for National Service and the Pew Charitable Trusts.

- The Interdisciplinary Professional Education Collaborative (IPEC), funded by the Institute for Healthcare Improvement and the federal Bureau of Health Professions.

- The assessment of the impact of service-learning across the curriculum at Portland State University, funded by the Corporation for National Service and internal sources.

- The Healthy Communities initiative of the metropolitan Portland region, one of 25 sites in the national Community Care Network (CCN) program, funded by the W.K. Kellogg Foundation and administered by the Hospital Research and Educational Trust.

- Independent research on organizational change and the nature of university-community relationships at a variety of public and private institutions.

In that exploration, we have used a systematic approach that considered the impact of various community-based learning initiatives on the community, the faculty, the students, and the institution. By analyzing each of these constituencies separately and collectively, we have learned a great deal about how campuses can be more successful in building and sustaining community partnerships that are effective for all who are involved.

## WHEN YOU'VE SEEN ONE PARTNERSHIP, YOU'VE SEEN ONE PARTNERSHIP

We found wide variety in the forms and types of community partnerships, reflecting differences in the his-

tory, capacity, culture, mission, and challenges faced by institutions and communities. Institutions must examine their missions and consider the relevance of service to core academic purposes. In addition, the level and types of service activities that a campus can engage in will be shaped by the role of the institution in the community and the nature of the community's capacity to address their own issues. For example, when West Virginia Wesleyan College, a HPSISN site, set out to design service-learning courses, they discovered that their small rural community had little social service infrastructure to serve as a natural organizing framework for partnerships. Thinking creatively, they began with a door-to-door assessment of community needs and developed a focus for their service-learning activities.

## A MATCH MADE IN HEAVEN, OR THE RESULT OF A DATING SERVICE?

Partnerships should reflect academic program strengths, and academic programs and scholarly agendas should reflect, at least in part, regional characteristics and challenges. Campuses should develop selected arrays of partnerships and cultivate them well, rather than engage in random activities. Portland State University has devoted considerable effort in the identification of partnerships that meet community-identified needs while also developing academic strengths and meeting curricular objectives. Many partnerships that may begin with a specific service-learning course requirement evolve over time and become the basis for more complex joint planning, evaluation, or other mutually beneficial activity. The Allegheny University of the Health Sciences, an IPEC site, has initiated a major community development project in an underserved area known as the Eleventh Street Corridor in Philadelphia, but only after careful reflection and determination that there was clear potential for mutual benefit.

## THE COMMUNITY KNOWS WHO IT IS; DO YOU?

A common failing of universities working with communities is the assumption that they can develop a single, uniform definition of who and what the "community" is, or that such a definition is necessary. The definition of community is itself a difficult challenge; who is the community? is best answered in the context of each institution and community and each chosen area of shared effort. Again, the community that the university works with is defined in part by the degree of fit with institutional academic strengths. Our findings indicate that the natural development of university-community partnerships begins with work between the university and well-organized local agencies and organizations that have the capacity and sophistication to interface with the more bureaucratic university. Over time, these relationships demonstrate the lasting commitment of the university and contribute to the development of trust. These developmental steps are key to gaining access to the deeper, more complex, informal fabric of the community and key populations.

The community must take a leadership role in defining what the university or college will do in the community setting. Community sites participating in a partnership of the George Washington University and George Mason University (participants in both the HPSISN and IPEC programs) have been carefully selected so that specific populations and contexts complement program goals. However, each community site participates in planning the curricular experiences and in defining needs and designing service activities that match those needs well.

## LEADERSHIP MATTERS

The interpretation of the role of community engagement in an institution's mission must involve a discussion among all levels of campus leadership, including faculty. While it is critically important that executive administrators consistently articulate the level of institutional commitment, they cannot unilaterally create and sustain partnerships or mandate faculty and student involvement. Community engagement as a core academic and scholarly activity involves the identification and support of faculty leaders and mentors who will sustain partnership activities over time and integrate engagement into their overall scholarly agenda. It is important to keep in mind that institutional involvement in community service does not devalue traditional scholarship, nor does every faculty member have to adopt service as part of their agenda. Community engagement requires a broader view of scholarship so that those faculty for whom service makes scholarly sense can be evaluated and rewarded for their efforts.

Each institution must decide the level and type of engagement that best reflects its mission and then test that decision by listening to the community. Then campus leaders must work to ensure that a critical mass of

faculty have the skills and support to fulfill that commitment. Leaders also contribute by ensuring adequate infrastructure to support the partnerships. The community-based teaching activities at many institutions, such as the University of Kentucky, the University of Scranton, Portland State University, and the University of Utah, are strengthened by a campus-wide center for service or volunteerism that provides faculty development programs and other assistance to faculty and students.

## IT'S THE CURRICULUM, STUPID!

We found partnerships that incorporate aspects of student learning to be the most mutually sustainable and comfortable paths to creating and testing relationships between the campus and the community. The community feels a sense of reciprocity in helping students develop civic responsibility and respectful understanding of critical human issues while learning new skills and exploring careers. For faculty, engagement in community-based learning through course instruction is less threatening than partnerships that may seem to impinge on their research agendas or may not be recognized by reward systems. Experimentation with community relationships through teaching allows faculty to explore linkages to the rest of their scholarly work. Students report that they learn much more about the community and find links to their academic goals when service is done as part of a course and not as an extracurricular volunteer activity. Students who participate in required course-based service-learning show greater personal transformation than those in optional programs. However, the issue of required service-learning remains controversial.

## WE ALL HAVE SOMETHING TO GIVE AND SOMETHING TO GAIN

Most people understand that successful partnerships focus on mutual benefits. We describe effective partnerships as knowledge-based collaborations in which all partners have things to teach each other, things to learn from each other, and things they will learn together. We have seen that an effective partnership builds the capacity of each partner to accomplish its own mission while also working together.

Sustainability is directly associated with an ongoing sense of reciprocity related to the exchange of knowledge and expertise. The University of Utah (a HPSISN site) places pharmacy and nursing students as companions in a seniors housing facility. Not only did students remark on what they gained from their service-learning experiences but the housing manager also played a role in the classroom as a facilitator of structured reflection, a key element of service-learning.

In many campus settings, community partners began with the view that they would not be accepted as coteachers because of their different experiences and credentials. Both they and faculty were often surprised at how professional expertise, extensive social and communication networks, and entrepreneurial skills allowed community partners to assume key roles in the student learning experience.

## THE LEARNING NEVER STOPS

As knowledge-based organizations focus on learning, collaborations inevitably evolve and change. Effective partnerships require a shared commitment to ongoing, comprehensive evaluation from the earliest stages of the relationship. A commitment to evaluation helps build trust and confidence between partners, especially when the community sees that the campus is open to criticism and that there is an authentic commitment to improvement.

Advisory groups were organized at most institutions as a way of gaining input. When advisory groups also played a strong role in evaluation, the partnership tended to expand into new community networks and collaborations. As a community-based organization, the Portland Healthy Communities initiative (a CCN site) has relied heavily on student and faculty participation since its inception. The nature of university involvement has varied over time, depending on the initiative's view of community needs. Projects have included strategic planning, staffing of action groups, membership on an oversight council, administrative and policy support, evaluation, use of geographic mapping and information systems technologies, website development, and facilitation of community meetings. The range of activities in the partnership is not limited but is designed to reflect both assets and needs. Evaluation has been critical to tracking those evolutionary changes and supporting improvement in the relationship.

## CONCLUSION

While partnerships take many purposes and forms, there are common features associated with "success," which most define as sustainability.

Sustainable partnerships have the following characteristics: (1) there are mutually agreed-upon goals; (2) success is defined and outcomes are measured in both institutional and community terms; (3) control of the agenda is vested primarily in community hands; (4) effective use and enhancement of community capacity are based on clear identification of community resources and strengths; (5) the educational component has clear consequences for the community and the institution; and (6) there is an ongoing commitment to evaluation that involves all partners.

The challenge facing higher education is twofold: first, making the changes in curricula and institutional culture that encourage partnerships with communities based on mutual learning as well as mutual benefit; and second, learning how to do this well.

The notion of the engaged campus will, no doubt, be sustained as a critical aspect of the mission of many institutions. We hope others involved in partnership evaluations will share their findings and learning widely so that higher education may grow in its effectiveness in working beside and within communities to develop rewarding and sustainable relationships.

BARBARA A. HOLLAND, formerly at Portland State University, is associate provost for strategic planning and outreach at Northern Kentucky University and executive editor of *Metropolitan Universities*.

SHERRIL B. GELMON teaches health management and policy as an associate professor of public health at Portland State University and is a senior fellow at the Center for the Health Professions of the University of California-San Francisco.

# Higher Education/ Community Partnerships:

## Assessing Progress in the Field

by David J. Maurrasse, *Columbia University*

Urban institutions of higher education around the country have increasingly been investing in partnerships with their local communities. The burgeoning movement, with deep historical roots, is beginning to emerge from its infant stages, raising numerous important questions about the role of assessments of these efforts and the availability of external and internal resources. I rely on my own participant observation as a funder of such partnerships, and now an evaluator of themm to address: What are effective measurements of the progress of higher education/community partnerships? What is the significance of this movement's stage in development as it relates to the availability of resources and the appropriateness of evaluation? I also rely on my observations of the field of corporate social responsibility to address: Does the current stage of development of the corporate social responsibility movement shed any light on how we should think about resources and evaluation in the higher education/community partnership movement? While it is essential that higher education/community partnerships ultimately stress concrete outcomes that improve lives, evaluations of these efforts should primarily stress processes. Process is no minor factor in a movement that heavily depends on relationships. For example, if trust and communication does not exist between partners, it will be difficult to achieve effective outcomes. Corporate social responsibility may not mirror higher education/community partnerships, but it addresses some similar issues regarding the accountability of major institutions to society. As a more developed movement, it does provide some lessons for how we think about measuring the progress of higher education/community partnerships.

I N MY RECENTLY COMPLETED BOOK, *Beyond the Campus*, I compared four diverse institutions of higher education and their community partnerships (Maurrasse, 2001). The University of Pennsylvania, San Francisco State, Xavier of New Orleans, and Hostos Community College of the South Bronx are all situated within a burgeoning movement to enhance the public engagement of higher education. While at the Rockefeller Foundation, I conducted a field assessment of these types of partnerships, traversing about the country looking for the strengths, weaknesses, and future possibilities of higher education/community partnerships. Other foundations, such as Surdna and Casey, were in a similar position, scanning the field and testing the waters. Still other ther foundations, such as Kellogg and Fannie Mae, actually developed more explicit funding initiatives. The most complete funding initiative for these efforts is most likely housed in the federal government at the Department of Housing and

Urban Development's (HUD's) Office of University Partnerships.

Eventually, my Rockefeller field assessment led to some grants, which touched all of the institutions profiled in *Beyond the Campus*, as well as some other universities, a couple of national initiatives, and a few intermediary organizations. As my travels produced some indicators of successful partnerships, I am now in the position of determining how to measure those indicators against actual grants. In other words, how do you measure the progress of higher education/community partnerships? While the field has a sense of the indicators of success, no one has quite figured out how to fairly and accurately assess the progress of these highly complicated efforts. The Urban Institute is conducting the assessment of HUD's funding initiative. The Fannie Mae Foundation has also recently completed an assessment. The necessary thinking is happening around the country, but does the higher education/community partnership movement have the necessary time, space, and resources to blossom into a full-fledged national effort?

While universities and corporations are different types of institutions, are there lessons to be learned from the corporate social responsibility movement, which has been addressing institutional/community partnerships over a longer period of time?[1] Furthermore, corporations tend to have more resources than institutions of higher education, enabling greater ongoing financial support for the development of the movement. Comparisons between the corporate social responsibility movement and the higher education/community partnerships movement could take on myriad angles. This paper deals specifically with evaluation, and the interaction between evaluation and funding sources.

With the funding community's increasing emphasis on outcomes, evaluation becomes critical to any burgeoning social movement that depends upon external support. The higher education/community partnerships movement is in its early stages despite the deep historical roots of the teaching, research, and service triumvirate. This current movement is highly urban in character and far more centralized than the multiple independently driven efforts on any campus. If higher education/community partnerships are to demonstrate progress, they likely require another ten-year window to allow for relationships to emerge, and outcomes to follow. Therefore, perspective is essential. One can evaluate, seeking, above all, quantitative achievements or one can evaluate the effectiveness of processes. One can also do both. Nevertheless, if the foundation community prioritizes results, then the higher education/ community partnerships movement is going to increasingly face pressure to deliver impressive outcomes. If the movement is not sufficiently developed to produce those outcomes, then it will likely fold.

The corporate social responsibility movement has created an evaluation industry. Social auditing, for example, is designed to assess the relative social accountability of corporations (Waddock & Smith, 2000). It can be both encouraging and punitive. In the higher education/community partnerships movement, similar aims are involved. Many institutions of higher education verbally promote service. In fact, it is often the case that some sense of social responsibility is written in the mission statements of colleges and universities. Corporations are different in this regard, since they are not driven by social missions. However, corporations are still accountable to society. Social pressures can break a

corporation (Burke, 1999). Since many corporations are publicly owned, shareholders have a direct influence over their direction. While shareholders have historically scrutinized the management of corporations in relation to the "bottom line," shareholder activism has ushered in scrutiny over social aspects. Socially responsible investment funds have introduced formal financial consequences for the relative social accountability of corporations. Again, this can be both encouraging and punitive. The higher education/community partnerships movement would likely benefit from more formal efforts both to encourage effective community partnerships and to introduce consequences for failure.

While many institutions of higher education promote their sense of social responsibility, some don't make the grade. The current stage of the higher education/community partnerships movement is a necessary phase to introduce indicators of success and develop the models that can improve partnerships. However, at some point, the movement should increase its expectations. The funding community is right to expect outcomes, especially those that enhance the well-being of communities. However, the movement is in a particular cycle at this juncture, and probably requires support in building the necessary formal vehicles.

In corporate social responsibility, companies are evaluated from numerous directions. They are accountable to their communities (neighborhoods, advocacy organizations), their sources of income (consumers and shareholders), and to themselves. Therefore, evaluation methods are required from each of these groups. Some are formal, while others are not. With higher education/community partnerships, colleges and universities are accountable to their communities (neighborhoods, community based organizations, etc.), their sources of income (foundations, donors/alumni), and themselves. The corporate social responsibility movement has begun to effectively leverage these key points of influence to enhance the social conscience and accountability of corporations. The higher education/community partnerships movement needs to develop mechanisms to leverage the points of influence on colleges and universities. In other words, foundations, communities, and the colleges and universities themselves require effective evaluation methods in order to enhance the success and longevity of the movement.

## INDICATORS OF SUCCESSFUL HIGHER EDUCATION/COMMUNITY PARTNERSHIPS

What are higher education/community partnerships seeking to achieve? A tension between the interests of institutions of higher education and those of communities naturally surfaces in partnerships. As discussed extensively in *Beyond the Campus*, mutual gain is the optimum goal because it produces incentives on both sides. But many are beginning to realize that institutions of higher education are beginning to gain more mileage out of community partnerships than are communities. The institutions of higher education tend to have more power than other neighborhood-based entities, allowing them to drive the agenda. Moreover, community change, especially when poor and disenfranchised populations are concerned, tends to take far more time to demonstrate significant results (Aspen, 1997). Enhancing entire communities, as opposed to enhancing particular individuals, is far more challenging. Institutions of higher education can gain quicker benefits from partnerships, whether it is public relations or experiential learning opportunities for students. One indicator of success would be that institutions of higher education expect to ensure that communities gain from partnerships. Another would be that institutions of higher education recognize how they benefit to the point where they attempt to centrally incorporate community partnerships into their missions and operations. One last indicator, given these realities, would be that institutions of higher education stand committed to long-term change in communities.[2]

On the topic of mutual gain, higher education is gradually becoming more conscious of the cost of not having healthy relations with the local community. The corporate social responsibility movement is still developing in this area, but more are working to develop mathematical models that demonstrate the cost of not being socially responsible (Waddock & Smith, 2001). Whether it is the money saved in lawsuits or the divestment of shareholders over human rights violations, if the corporation understands the financial consequences, it is more likely to think responsibly. Not to suggest that corporations are allocating enough resources toward social responsibility, but higher education is certainly not devoting sufficient resources to community partnerships. On the one hand, foundation support is necessary to improve the movement. On the other, colleges and universities must provide greater support to these efforts. They will be more likely to do so if they under-

stand the cost of unhealthy community relations. Foundation and higher education financial support are not mutually exclusive. They are, in fact, dependent on each other. Foundations will be more likely to support partnerships when they see demonstrated, long-term financial commitment to community partnerships in higher education. Institutions of higher education could opt to wait for foundations to provide more support before they allocate greater internal resources. However, this scenario would likely limit the movement's access to foundation resources. The movement has gotten the attention of foundations; it needs the internal resources to leverage external funds.

The notion of corporate social responsibility takes many forms, including not just community relations, but environmental accountability, diversity in hiring and contracting, labor rights, and human rights. The full universe in which major institutions and industries exist requires some degree of social conscience at every level. The corporate social responsibility movement has effectively fleshed out the corporate universe and injected a comprehensive sense of accountability— think before you dump, hire, fire, inspect, set prices, leave town, enter town, procure, speak, and on. The higher education/community partnerships movement has only scratched the surface; it has not pushed higher education to see the interrelationship between its labor practices and its community relations, for example. The movement needs time to develop a comprehensive sense of social responsibility in higher education.

As it stands, higher education/community partnerships are heavily dependent upon relationships. Subsequently, they require significant time. If an institution of higher education has a negative history with the community, the relationship could take several years to develop any genuine mutual trust. It is for this reason that evaluation of these partnerships should pay significant attention to process, especially in the early stages of this movement. Even when the field is far more developed, process will continue to be essential, as trust and communication are constants. Nevertheless, financial supporters of these efforts should have the patience to allow these efforts to develop genuine relationships. Once relationships are developed, outcomes can take many forms.

## MY EXAMPLE OF A MEASUREMENT TOOL

In my own evaluation of the grantees of the Rockefeller Foundation, I have had to manage my own expectations of one-year grants. My measurement tool essentially targeted indicators—signs that the partnerships were moving in the right direction. Of course, some of them are far more developed than others. Institutions and geographical areas are different. Also, all of the grants to institutions of higher education focused on specific projects; thus, they tell us only so much about an institution's overall community partnership. When funding these efforts, it was also important to me to support a national initiative designed to enhance the effectiveness of higher education/community partnerships.[3]

My measurement criteria are as follows:

- Residents were integral in shaping the direction of the proposed work.

- Administrators supported the proposed work; they saw community partnerships as consistent with the institution's mission.

- Prospects for residents' self-sufficiency were enhanced by the grants; resident capacity was improved.

- Principle investigators were sensitive to community needs and well trained/equipped to carry out the tasks.

- Higher education and community representatives, by the end of the grant, felt a sense of mutual gain.

- The lessons from the grant, for better or worse, were positioned to influence the broader field. Conversely, the grantee borrowed lessons from the field in the implementation of the project.

- The institution of higher education was not only philosophically, but structurally, prepared to support the project's implementation.

- The grantee was able to leverage additional support of varying types (internal and external), especially financial.

- Residents were knowledgeable about how best to take advantage of the institution's resources.

- Both higher education and community representation transcended a small handful of especially committed people.

- Structural holes were effectively filled by brokering /intermediary entities when necessary.

- Resident participation was able to reach the most disadvantaged, transcending larger nonprofits and local "leaders."

- The project was connected to a broader collaborative rather than an isolated effort.

This model is designed to identify progress in the processes that may lead to future success. My "theory of change" (Connel & Kubisch, 1998) centers on potential. It suggests that particular indicators insinuate a path that will lead to certain outcomes. The model also implies particular types of outcomes. Significant gain for residents, for example, is critical to the model, as are the college or university's willingness to institutionalize these efforts and the connection of the grant to broader efforts in the particular institution and around the country. This entire model is based on my conversations with local and national participants in the field, which were designed to identify the strengths, weaknesses, and future possibilities in the field. The lack of institutionalization, the dominance of the institutions over the community even in partnership, the disjointed nature of these efforts, the significance of trust, and many similar ideas surfaced repeatedly over the course of my research.[4]

## DISCUSSION

In conclusion, the higher education/community partnership movement (at least this historical incarnation of it) is beginning to mature. However, it needs to develop more nationally consistent expectations and models before we can expect significant outcomes. The movement appears to be putting the key pieces in place, outside of a few exceptional examples. Those examples should be promoted to demonstrate to institutions of higher education, communities, and supporters (financial or political) the potential of these efforts. The external funding community should support the movement in this phase of development. Researchers of partnerships should continue to assess particular examples, and write about both the successes and failures. The research should be closely aligned with the national efforts in the movement, so that the key participants in taking partnerships to national (and international) scale are armed with useful data.

Researchers should also compare and contrast the experience of the higher education/community partnerships movement with other similar efforts in order to add insight into common practices and pitfalls that may assist in shaping the expectations of all parties involved. The corporate social responsibility movement does this in some regard. Evidently, corporate social responsibility, at the very least, tells us about where higher education/community partnerships can go. This is not to say that corporate social responsibility, or the closest cousin, corporate community relations, has led to significant change in poor and disenfranchised communities. However, it has effectively spun a web of interrelated corporate practices around the notion of social responsibility. Because of the social mission of higher education, and the natural historical interplay between teaching, research, and service, higher education may have more potential than corporations to improve the lives of poor and disenfranchised communities. The higher education/community partnerships movement should be able to borrow lessons from the social responsibility efforts of other types of institutions while recognizing the uniqueness of academia.

As many scholars and practitioners have noted, evaluation depends upon a "theory of change"—what are you trying to achieve? Service learning at colleges and universities is often evaluated based on the numbers of campus representatives involved. Indeed, this is based on a theory of change, one, which prioritizes involvement at the institution. One could evaluate the same efforts with a completely different focus—did the service learning benefit community residents? The movement should agree on its priorities, and educate the funding community of its reasoning. I prefer to stress evaluating mutual gain between the institution and the community, which would allow for both of the aforementioned assessment approaches to service learning to suffice. The mutual gain approach also provides incentive for the institutions to be involved, yet it incorporates checks and balances to ensure that community interests do not get overlooked. On the topic of community interests, residents and community-based organizations are more likely to achieve their interests if they know for what to ask. Efforts to increase the capacity of communities to work with institutions of higher education (and all types of major institutions) would

likely enhance the prospects of achieving outcomes that benefit neighborhoods.

Finally, the funding community should continue to pay attention to the higher education/community partnerships movement. Foundations have, too often, vacated an area of focus prematurely (Letts, Ryan, & Grossman, 1997). As it stands, foundations really have not significantly submerged themselves into partnerships; they have remained cautious. After all, why do major institutions like colleges and universities need external support to make sure that they are good neighbors? Resources in institutions of higher education tend to be highly restricted, first of all. Secondly, foundations already significantly fund traditional research. Traditional research can be enhanced by applied research that also happens to benefit communities. But institutions of higher education themselves should make more significant investments in community partnerships because they gain significant mileage. As previously mentioned, researchers should develop models for calculating the cost of not being a good neighbor. As Trinity College in Hartford experienced, enrollment and alumni giving increased, partly due to the institution's significant engagement in the local community. Overall, a great deal of work is to be done to enhance the effectiveness of partnerships. There is a role for researchers, any stakeholder in higher education, communities, policymakers, and financial supporters.

## NOTES

1. This is not another attempt to hail the efficiencies of the private over the public and nonprofit sectors. In fact, much of the corporate social responsibility movement was catalyzed by nonprofits. The corporate social responsibility movement happens to focus on the accountability of major institutions. Moreover, institutions of higher education are increasingly resembling corporations in theory and practice. What I find interesting is that the corporate social responsibility and higher education/community partnership movements are not drawing lessons from each other.

2. These are just a few examples; over the course of my research, several other indicators were revealed.

3. The recently formed Association for Higher Education/Community Partnerships (ACHEP) is a national trade association of representatives of institutions of higher education and community organizations and residents, which is designed to enhance, promote, and sustain partnerships. The founders of the organization are some of the grantees of the Department of Housing

and Urban Development's Community Outreach Partnership Centers funding initiative.

4. *Beyond the Campus* provides a more in-depth discussion of the strengths, weaknesses, and future possibilities in the higher education/community partnerships movement. It also describes and analyzes particular case studies to provide evidence of some of the critical issues facing partnerships.

## REFERENCES

Alperson, M. (1996). *Measuring Corporate Community Involvement*. The Conference Board, New York.

Aspen Institute. (1997). *Voices from the Field: Learning from the Early Work of Comprehensive Community Initiatives*. The Aspen Institute, Washington, DC.

Bollier, David (for the Business Enterprise Trust). (1996). *Aiming Higher: 25 Stories of How Companies Prosper by Combining Sound Management and Social Vision*. The American Management Association, New York.

Brummer, J. J. (1991). *Corporate Responsibility and Legitimacy: An Interdisciplinary Analysis*. Greenwood Press, Westport, CT.

Burke, E. M. (1999). *Corporate Community Relations: The Principle of the Neighbor of Choice*. Quorum Books, Westport, CT.

Connel, J. P. & Kubisch, A. (1998). *Applying a Theory of Change Approach to the Evaluation of Comprehensive Community Initiatives: Progress, Prospects, and Problems*. The Aspen Institute, Washington, DC.

Denzin, N. K. & Lincoln, Y. (2000). *The Handbook of Qualitative Research*. Sage Publications, Thousand Oaks, CA.

Karake-Shalhoub, Z. A. (1999). *Organizational Downsizing, Discrimination, and Corporate Social Responsibility*. Quorum Books, Westport, CT.

Letts, C., Ryan, W. & Grossman, A. (1997, March-April). Virtuous capital: What foundations can learn from venture capitalists. *Harvard Business Review*, Harvard Business School Publishing, Boston, MA.

Light, P. (2000). *Making Nonprofits Work: A Report on the Tides of Nonprofit Management Reform*. The Aspen Institute and Brookings Institution Press, Washington, DC.

Maurrasse, D. (2001). *Beyond the Campus: How Colleges and Universities Partner with their Communities*. Routledge Press, New York.

Nelson, C. & Watt, S. (1999). *Academic Keywords: A Devil's Dictionary for Higher Education*. Routledge Press, New York.

Plein, L. Christopher, D., Williams, G. & Hardwick, D. M. (2000, October). Making engagement work: University outreach and welfare reform in West Virginia. *Journal of Public Affairs Education* Vol. 6, No. 4, National Association of Schools of Public Affairs and Administration, Washington, DC.

Waddock, S. & Smith, N. (2000, Winter). Corporate responsibility audits: Doing well by doing good. *Sloan Management Review*, Massachusetts Institute of Technology Sloan School of Management, Cambridge, MA.

# Community Partnerships:
## Recommended Reading

## BOOKS & CHAPTERS

Bonnen, J.T. (1998). The land-grant idea and the evolving outreach university. In R.M. Lerner & Simon, L.A.K. (Eds.), *University-community collaborations for the twenty-first Century: Outreach scholarship for youth and families.* New York: Garland.

Center for Community Partnerships. (n.d.). *Universities and community schools.* Philadelphia: Center for Community Partnerships, University of Pennsylvania.

Cotton, D. & Stanton, T. (1990). Joining campus and community through service-learning. In C. Delve, S. Mintz, & G. Stewart (Eds.), *Community service as values education* (pp. 101–110). San Francisco, CA: Jossey-Bass.

Hill, J. (Ed.) (1991). *You haven't to deserve: A gift to the homeless.* Atlanta, GA: Task Force for the Homeless.

Jacoby, B. (Ed.). (2003). *Building partnerships for service-learning.* San Francisco: Jossey-Bass.

Kemmis, D. (1945). *Community and the politics of place.* Norman, OK: University of Oklahoma Press.

Kretzman, J.P. & McKnight, J.L. (1993). *Building communities from the inside out: A path toward finding and mobilizing a community's assets.* Chicago: Urban Affairs and Policy Research Neighborhood Innovations Network, Northwestern University.

Lawson, H.A., & Hooper-Briar, K. (1994). *Expanding partnerships: Involving colleges and universities in interprofessional collaboration and service integration.* Oxford, OH: The Danforth Foundation and the Institute for Educational Renewal, Miami University.

Lerner, R. M., & Simon, L.A.K. (Eds.). (1998). *University-community collaborations for the twenty-first century: Outreach scholarship for youth and families.* New York: Garland Publishing.

Maurrasse, D. (2001). *Beyond the campus: How colleges and universities form partnerships with their communities.* New York: Routledge.

McKnight, J. (1995). *The careless society: Community and its counterfeits.* New York: Basic Books.

Minnesota Campus Compact. (1999a). *From charity to change: Model campus-community collaborations from Minnesota and the nation.* St. Paul, MN: Minnesota Campus Compact.

Minnesota Campus Compact. (1999b). *From charity to change: A notebook of resources from model campus-community collaborations from Minnesota.* St. Paul, MN: Minnesota Campus Compact.

Rhoads, R. (1997). *Community service and higher learning: Explorations of the caring self.* Albany: State University of New York Press.

Shorr, L.B. (1989). *Within our reach: Breaking the cycle of disadvantage.* New York: Doubleday.

Shorr, L. (1997). *Common purpose: Strengthening families and neighborhoods to rebuild America.* New York: Anchor Books.

Sigmon, R. (1998). *Building sustainable partnerships: Linking communities and educational institutions.* Springfield, VA: National Society for Experiential Education.

Stack, C. (1974). *All our kin: Strategies for survival in a black community.* New York: Harper and Row.

Torres, J. (Ed.). (2000). *Benchmarks for campus/community partnerships.* Providence, RI: Campus Compact.

Vidal, A., et al. (2002). *Lessons from the community outreach partnership center program.* Washington, DC: U.S. Department of Housing and Urban Development Office of Policy Development and Research. Available at www.oup.org/researchandpubs/copc/lessonslearned.html.

Walker, S. (Ed.) (1993). *Changing community.* St. Paul, MN: Greywolf Press.

Winer, M., and Karen, R. (1994). *Collaboration handbook: Creating, sustaining, and enjoying the journey.* St. Paul, MN: Amherst H. Wilder Foundation.

Zimpher, N.L., Percy, S.L., & Brukardt, M.J. (2002). *A time for boldness: A story of institutional change.* Bolton, MA: Anker Publishing.

## ARTICLES & REPORTS

Adams, H. (1995). A grassroots think tank: Linking writing and community building. *Democracy and Education*, Winter.

Arches, J., Darlington-Hope, M., Gerson, J., Gibson, J., Habana-Hafner, S., & Kiang, P. (1997). New voices in university–community transformation. *Change*, 29 (1), 36–44.

Boyle-Baise, M., Epler, B. & McCoy, W. (2001). Shared control: community voices in multicultural service-learning. *The Education Forum*, 65 (4), 344–53.

Cone, D., & Payne, P. (2002). When campus and community collide: Campus-community partnerships from a community perspective. *The Journal of Public Affairs*, 6, 203–218.

Ducharme, E., Sargent, B. & Chaucer, H. (n.d.) The necessary elements. In N. Carriulo (Ed.), *Beginning and sustaining school college partnerships*. Winchester, MA: New England Association of Schools and Colleges.

Edwards, B., Mooney, L. & Heald, C. (2001). Whom is being served? The impact of student volunteering on local community organizations. *Nonprofit and Voluntary Sector Quarterly*, 30 (3), 444–61.

Ferrari, J.R. & Worrall, L. (2000). Assessments by community agencies: How the "other side" sees service-learning. *Michigan Journal of Community Service Learning*, 7, 35–40.

Forrant, R. (2001). Pulling together in Lowell: the university and the regional development process. *European Planning Studies*, 9 (5), 613–628.

Gamson, Z., Holland, E. & Kiang, P. (1998). The university in engagement with society. *Liberal Education*, Spring.

Gelmon, S., Holland, B., Seifer, S., Shinnamon, A & Connors, K. (1998). Community-university partnerships for mutual learning. *Michigan Journal for Community Service Learning*, 5, 97–107.

Goodrow, B. & Meyers, P.L. (2001). The Del Rio project: A case for community-campus partnership. *Education for Health: Change in Learning and Practice*, 13 (2), 213–20.

Harkavy, I. & Puckett, J. (1991). Toward effective university-public school partnerships: An analysis of a contemporary model. *Teachers College Record*, 92, 556–581.

Holland, B. (2001). A comprehensive model for assessing service-learning and community-university partnerships. *New Directions for Higher Education*, 114, 51–60.

Kretzman, J. (1993). School participation in local community economic development: Ideas for getting started. Evanston, IL: Institute for Policy Research, Asset-Based Community Development, Northwestern University. Available at www.northwestern.edu/ipr/abcd.html.

Kreutziger, S.S., et al. (1999). The campus affiliates program. *American Behavioral Scientist*, 42 (5), 827–39.

McHugh-Engstrom, C. and Tinto, V. (1997). Working together for service-learning. *About Campus*, July-August.

Mayfield, L., Hellwig, M. & Banks, B. (1999). The Chicago response to urban problems: Building university-community collaborations. *American Behavioral Scientist*, 42 (5), 863–875.

Morton, K. (1997). Campus and community at Providence College. *Expanding Boundaries: Cooperative Education Association*, Spring, 8–11.

Peacock, J.R., Bradley, D.B., & Shenk, D. (2001). Incorporating field sites into service-learning as collaborative partners. *Educational Gerontology*, 27 (1), 23–36.

Pearson, N. (2002). Moving from placement to community partner. *The Journal of Public Affairs*, 6, 183–202.

Reardon, K.M. & Shields, T.P. (1997). Promoting sustainable community/university partnerships through participatory action research. *NSEE Quarterly*, 23 (1), 22–25.

Saltmarsh, J. (1998). Exploring the meaning of community/university partnerships. *NSEE Quarterly*, 23(4).

Sandmann, L.R. & Baker-Clark, C.A. (n.d.) Characteristics and principles of university-community partnerships: A delphi study. Available at www.anrecs.msu.edu/research/sandmann.htm.

Seifer, S. (1998). Service-learning: Community-campus partnerships for health professions education. *Academic Medicine*, 73 (3), 273–277.

Speer, P.W. & Hughey, J. (1996). Mechanisms of empowerment: Psychological processes for members of power-based community organizations. *Journal of Community and Applied Social Psychology*, 6, 177–187.

Walsh, M.E., et al. (2000). The Boston College-Allston/Brighton partnership: Description and challenges. *PJE:The Peabody Journal of Education*, 75 (3), 6–32.

Ward, K. & Wolf–Wendel, L. (2000). Community-centered service-learning: Moving from doing for to doing with. *American Behavioral Scientist*, 43 (5), 767–80.

Weinberg, A.S. (1999). The university and the hamlets: Revitalizing low-income communities through university outreach and community visioning exercises. *American Behavioral Scientist*, 42 (5), 800–13.

W. W. Kellog Foundation. (n.d.) Community partnerships toolkit. Available at www.wkkf.org/Pubs/CustomPubs/CPtoolkit/CPToolkit/default.htm.

Zimmerman, M.A., & Rappaport, J. (1988). Citizen participation, perceived control, and psychological empowerment. *American Journal of Community Psychology*, 16, 725–750.

SECTION 10

# Community-Based Research

## TITLES IN THIS SECTION

Principles of Best Practice for Community-Based Research, BY KERRY STRAND, SAM MARULLO, NICK CUTFORTH, RANDY STOEKER, AND PATRICK DONOHUE

Recommended Reading

## QUESTIONS FOR REFLECTION AND PLANNING

What does community-based research look like on your campus? To what degree does it reflect the practices described in these readings?

How might community-based research link your undergraduate research and service-learning goals?

Where does community-based research fit within your own research and teaching goals? Could you adapt those goals to incorporate community-based research?

How would you respond to colleagues that argue that community-based research is not "real" research?

# Principles of Best Practice for Community-Based Research[1]

Kerry Strand, *Hood College*
Sam Marullo, *Georgetown University*
Nick Cutforth, *University of Denver*
Randy Stoecker, *University of Toledo*
Patrick Donohue, *Middlesex County College*

Community-based research (CBR) offers higher education a distinctive form of engaged scholarship and a transformative approach to teaching and learning. In this article, we propose a CBR model that is genuinely collaborative and driven by community rather than campus interests; that democratizes the creation and dissemination of knowledge; and that seeks to achieve positive social change. We demonstrate how this model translates into principles that underlie the practice of CBR in four critical areas: campus-community partnerships, research design and process, teaching and learning, and the institutionalization of centers to support CBR.

COMMUNITY OUTREACH HAS BECOME PART and parcel of the missions of an increasing number of American colleges and universities. Several forces are driving this trend toward campus-community engagement. One is growing criticism of higher education's apparent insensitivity to the challenges faced by their adjacent neighborhoods: urban decay, environmental threats, growing economic inequality, and unmet needs of vulnerable children, families, and whole communities in areas such as education, health care, housing, criminal and juvenile justice, and employment (Marullo & Edwards, 1999). A second force for change comes from the widespread perception that the intellectual work of the professorate is unnecessarily narrow and largely irrelevant to societal concerns. This criticism is best developed in Ernest Boyer's (1990) widely-cited *Scholarship Reconsidered*, in which he argues that the "scholarship of discovery"—in the pursuit of new knowledge—should not be the only valued and rewarded form of scholarship. He suggests that the scholarships of integration, pedagogy, and especially application are other forms of scholarship that are undervalued and largely neglected, although they offer the potential for encouraging intellectual work that is truly useful and relevant in modern society. A third force driving the trend toward community engagement has to do with students, particularly

the growing concern that despite our best intentions, graduates leave our institutions largely disengaged from political issues, disenchanted with the ability of government to effect positive change, and disinclined and ill-equipped to assume an active role in civic life. Here the implication is that we need to re-think what and how we teach in order to ensure that we truly engage students, not only with their communities but also with the learning process in general.

As a result of all this, a growing number of colleges and universities have forged partnerships with a wide variety of community groups and agencies—schools, social service agencies, neighborhood organizations, businesses, and health care providers—to share institutional resources and expertise as well as provide students experiential learning opportunities beyond what is possible in traditional college classes. One particularly promising activity that has grown out of these campus-community partnerships is what has come to be called community-based research (CBR). CBR is collaborative, change-oriented research that engages faculty members, students, and community members in projects that address a community-identified need. It differs in important ways not only from traditional academic research, but also from the sort of charity-oriented service-learning that has come to be practiced and promoted at many colleges and universities. Indeed, the distinctive combination of collaborative inquiry, critical analysis, and social action that CBR entails makes it a particularly engaging and transformative approach to teaching and engaged scholarship. Moreover, its potential to unite the three traditional academic missions of teaching, research, and service in innovative ways makes it a potentially revolutionary strategy for achieving long-lasting and fundamental institutional change.

All this suggests that CBR is a next important stage of service-learning and engaged scholarship, and explains the growing interest in CBR among professors, students, and community members—especially those who are committed to service-learning. However, in contrast to the significant body of literature about service-learning that has emerged over the last decade, very little has been written about CBR. In this paper, we draw on our own extensive and varied experiences with CBR as teachers, researchers, administrators, scholars, and community activists to propose a CBR model based on what we see as its three central features: collaboration, democratization of knowledge, and social change. We then discuss how this CBR model translates into principles that govern its practice in four critical areas: campus-community partnerships; research design and process; teaching and learning; and institutionalizing CBR on our campuses.

## HISTORY AND PRINCIPLES OF CBR

CBR has a long history and diverse intellectual roots that are reflected in the terms variously used to describe it: action research, participatory research, popular education, empowerment research, participatory action research, and others. Practitioners of research that is participatory and community-based come from many different fields in and outside of academia and work in many different parts of the world—all of which make a precise history and commonly-accepted definition of CBR a bit problematic. Nonetheless, most community-based researchers draw from several common historical and modern strands. The first is the popular education model, which is widely associated with the work of Paolo Freire (1970). Freire advocated for education as a political tool to effect social change at local and global levels, arguing that learning that raises people's consciousness and enhances their understanding of oppressive social conditions can lead to social transformation. This model similarly shaped the work of the

Highlander Folk School (now the Highlander Research and Education Center) founded by Myles Horton in Tennessee in1933 (Horton, 1989). The second important influence on current CBR comes from what might be called the *participatory research model*. This approach grew mainly out of liberation struggles in the Third World over the past few decades and has been adapted, as well, to research with traditionally disadvantaged groups in North America. The PR (participatory research) and PAR (participatory action research) approaches are rooted in a critique of traditional Western social science research, whose rigidity, presumed objectivity, and authority of researchers and research expertise undermine community development efforts (Hall, 1992; Park, 1992). Finally, CBR also traces some of its roots to the "action research" approach introduced by Kirstein (1948), who used it as a tool to increase worker productivity and satisfaction through promoting democratic relationships in the workplace. Lewin's work is considered a more conservative influence on CBR because it de-emphasized community participation and failed to challenge existing power arrangements.

Our CBR model draws on these diverse historical influences, but also embodies core tenets that make CBR relevant to higher education, especially as a response to the challenges that colleges and universities currently face in exploring partnerships with communities in addressing pressing problems. These features clearly differentiate CBR from "business as usual" in American higher education—that is, both from conventional academic research and from conventional approaches to teaching and learning that have long dominated at both the graduate and undergraduate levels. The three central features are:

1. CBR is a collaborative enterprise between academic researchers (professors and students) and community members.

2. CBR seeks to democratize knowledge by validating multiple sources of knowledge and promoting the use of multiple methods of discovery and dissemination.

3. CBR has as its goal social action for the purpose of achieving social change and social justice.

### Collaboration

CBR's purpose is to create or discover knowledge that meets a community-identified need, but the role of community members goes beyond simply identifying the research topics or question. Indeed, the ideal CBR project is one that is fully collaborative—that is, where community people work with professors and/or students at every stage of the research process: identifying the problem, constructing the research question(s), developing research instruments, collecting and analyzing data, interpreting results, producing the final report, issuing recommendations, and implementing initiatives. This sort of collaboration—in which everyone at the research table is a teacher, learner, and contributor to the final product—means that research roles and relationships are very different from those characterizing conventional academic research. Such research, of course, often does not involve communities at all. But even when it does, there is typically a clear distinction between researcher and researched, such that the researcher is an "outside expert" with a limited and task-oriented relationship with the community, in contrast to the more multifaceted, informal, and long-term relationship that characterizes CBR.

The collaborative nature of CBR makes it a highly effective mode of teaching, learning, and empowerment for everyone involved. Students benefit from the best combination of experiential and intellectual learning strategies. As equal members of CBR research "teams" they learn how to listen to others, deliberate about problems and issues, arrive at solutions mutually, and work together to implement them—all skills that are important in the increasingly team-oriented work-world. This sort of collaboration is capacity-building for community organizations and individuals as well. Training and resources brought to the table by the college or university are transferred to the community partner such that the organization may become self-sufficient and research-capable. And collaboration also enhances the quality of the research in myriad ways, as community members bring to the research table ideas, perspectives, language, and knowledge that inform every stage of the group's work.

## Democratization of Knowledge
The second central tenet of CBR refers to the distinctive ways that this sort of research defines and discovers knowledge. In the same way that CBR requires the equal participation of academics and community partners in the research process, it also values equally the knowledge that each brings to that process—both the experiential, or "local," community knowledge and the more specialized knowledge of faculty and students

(who, we should note, often bring "local" knowledge as well). CBR insists on the democratization and demystification of knowledge as it challenges some basic assumptions about knowledge itself: what constitutes valid knowledge, how it is best produced (and by whom), and who should control it.

CBR also recognizes and, where possible, incorporates multiple and unconventional methods of knowledge discovery. Methods of data collection are developed or chosen not only based on their scientific rigor and appropriateness to the research question, but also because they have the potential for drawing out knowledge that is most relevant and useful; and because they invite the involvement of all the research "stakeholders" in identifying, defining, and struggling to solve the problem that has been identified. This focus on relevancy and usefulness also means that researchers must be flexible and willing to rely on a variety and multiplicity of data collection methods and instruments, to work to develop unconventional ones, and even to change methodological direction mid-study if it means that the results will be more empowering, more useful, and/or more clearly aligned with community needs.

Last, CBR also requires innovative thinking about the *dissemination* of knowledge. Here, again, the value of the research resides in its potential to produce results that can be used by the community. This means that academics used to thinking in terms of formal jargon-laden research reports and rigid scholarly standards of proof must think first of the need to present results in a form that is comprehensible to neighborhood organizations, politicians, agency personnel, and others who might make use of the research findings. Although this does not preclude formal research reports, it does require that researchers demystify the language of research reporting, present results with clarity and brevity, and consider multiple and even unconventional methods to communicate research findings.

## Social Change and Social Justice
This third tenet of CBR distinguishes it, once again, from conventional academic research, whose primary aim is to advance knowledge in a discipline. CBR is undertaken in the interest of community needs and priorities, and the information it produces might address any of community-based organizations' numerous purposes: improving their programs, promoting their interests, identifying or attracting new resources, understanding or assessing needs of their

target populations, explicating issues and challenges, creating awareness of the need for action, or designing strategies for change. In other words, CBR contributes to an information base from which community organizations and agencies can plan and act. At the same time, the research process itself sometimes contributes to social change by empowering and helping to build capacity among community members. Moreover, simply the fact of their coming together to identify collective needs and talk about potential solutions may help revitalize democracy in the community and set into motion structures and processes for social change that extend beyond any particular research project—an outcome that is suggested by Freire's popular education model.

Our approach allows for a broad definition of "community" that includes many different kinds of organizations and agencies that work with, by, or on behalf of community members. At the same time, the commitment to social justice that is central to our model means that the communities with whom we collaborate in CBR consist of—or represent—people who occupy positions of social, economic, and/or cultural disadvantage: they have fewer opportunities and limited access to resources due to the way that the larger society's institutions, social structures, or policies operate. To say that our ultimate goal is to achieve some measure of social justice, then, is simply to say that while the social change that we are able to effect with anyone CBR project may be quite limited, our hope is to make some contribution to changing the social arrangements that create and sustain inequality and injustice.

The CBR model we propose requires campus-community collaboration around meeting a community-identified need; new approaches to defining, discovering, and disseminating knowledge; and a commitment to social action for social change. Now we turn to the task of explicating just how these general features translate into somewhat more specific principles that operate in each critical area of CBR: creating and sustaining campus-community partnerships; designing and conducting the research itself; ensuring its value as a teaching and learning experience; and institutionalizing CBR on our campuses.

## DEVELOPING AND SUSTAINING CAMPUS-COMMUNITY PARTNERSHIPS

Mutually beneficial campus-community partnerships are the bedrock of successful CBR. However, creating and sustaining partnerships that are truly equal, collaborative, productive, and long-lasting presents many challenges. What are some principles that govern successful campus-community partnerships that are at the core of CBR? We have identified ten.

The first three principles of successful community-campus partnerships help us to understand what motivates partners to undertake CBR projects together. They delineate some of the important orientations toward one another that successful partners either bring with them or develop jointly in working together. Specifically, successful partners:

- Share a worldview,

- Agree about goals and strategies, and

- Have mutual trust and mutual respect.

Academics and community members can only work well together when they share those elements of a worldview relevant to their work. These include philosophical assumptions about people, communities, and society (Are people capable of governing themselves? What should be the role of government in meeting human needs in a society?) as well as an understanding of what their "community" is. While community partners may have a fairly clear sense of the community they represent, it may be more problematic on the campus side as there may be ideological and political ramifications associated with committing resources to one group as opposed to another, and the faculty member may even be at odds with the administration about whose interests ought to be paramount.

Agreement about goals and strategies is also important at the beginning stages of a partnership. Here the partners need to have a clear and shared understanding about what they hope to achieve in their work together and how they hope to achieve it—that is, what the different team members' roles and contributions will be, how much input from other community members will be sought, who will make key decisions at different research stages, and so on. Third, partners must come together sharing, or at least preparing to share, mutual trust and respect. Each partner must trust that the other can be counted on to "do the right thing:" exercise good judgment, keep the other's interests in mind, and work for the ongoing success of the partnership. It is also important that each partner share, or work to develop, a faith in the collaborative process itself. This means they have confidence in the partnership: that it is worth developing and sustaining, even as it faces hurdles—and perhaps even failures—along the way. Finally, another important dimension of mutual respect and trust is predicated on the assumption that in CBR, multiple sources and kinds of knowledge are both valid and essential to address community needs. When each person at the research table—professor, student, agency staff, community member—is seen as an indispensable source of ideas and information growing from their own experiences, then mutual trust and respect find a fertile setting in which to flourish and grow.

Successful partnerships also depend on certain interaction patterns and norms. These typically emerge over time and tend to be self-perpetuating, such that effective interactions among CBR team members fuel further effective interaction and collaboration. Specifically, partners in successful CBR relationships:

- Share power,

- Communicate clearly and listen carefully,

- Understand and empathize with each other's circumstances, and

- Remain flexible.

In the context of CBR, with its commitment to collaboration, shared power means that wherever possible, campus and community partners participate more or less equally in shaping decisions about their work together—ideally, with the balance of power tipped toward the community when it comes to basic project decisions. These include what the research question or focus will be, and shaping and implementing change strategies implied by the research. In reality, however, sharing power presents significant challenges to campus-community collaborations facing embedded hierarchies based on differences in class, race, institutional power, and expertise (Shefner & Cobb, 2002). However, when community members are afforded less authority than their academic counterparts, the research is likely to be less valuable to the community, and the partnership reproduces the very sort of inequities that CBR seeks to challenge and change. This makes the goal to share power especially compelling.

Clear and careful communication is another essential principle of effective partnerships. CBR brings together a mix of people from very different worlds and requires that they engage in conversations to accomplish a challenging and complex task: designing and executing a research project. To do this, partners from both sides must work to avoid the dangers of what Freire calls "alienating rhetoric" (1970, p. 77). All participants must strive to understand and be understood, and this means avoiding the inaccessible language of their discipline or community, clarifying meanings and assumptions that might be obscure to outsiders, and otherwise working to develop a common discourse that make subsequent partner interactions inclusive and fruitful. And it almost goes without saying that everyone at the research table not only must be an effective communicator, but also a patient and careful listener.

Just as successful partners learn how to communicate across sociocultural divides, they must also learn to recognize and deal with the various institutional constraints that may obstruct their working together. Community organizations and higher education institutions are very different in size, financial stability and cash flow, organizational structure and accountabilities, levels of bureaucracy, interorganizational relations, and reward structures. They also operate on very different schedules and have different priorities that shape deadlines, due dates, and "time off." Although these differences can frustrate the growth of strong CBR partnerships, they can be overcome by partners who are committed to good communication, trust, and empathy with one another's circumstances and constraints. Perhaps more than anything else, flexibility (along with some good humor) can go along way toward helping partners work through logistical and other challenges.

The last three principles governing effective partnerships have to do with desired outcomes or results of partnering. A CBR partnership's most obvious objective is to produce useful research. However, successful partnerships are also ones in which:

- Partners' primary interests or needs are met,

- Partners' organizational capacities are enhanced, and

- Partners adopt shared, long-range social change perspectives.

Academic and community partners' needs and interests are bound to diverge in some significant ways beyond their common goal to produce useful and quality research findings. On the academic side, some priority is likely to be given to providing students valuable learning experience, and perhaps enhancing the faculty member's teaching credentials or producing publishable research that otherwise furthers their career. The institution might have some goals as well, such as improving its community image, and recruiting and retaining students. On the community side, partners seek concrete benefits for the agency and individuals involved in the research. They need research reports of sufficient quality and usefulness, but also may have some subtle interests: satisfying funders, smoothing interagency political tensions, or bringing together a disorganized community. Recognizing and helping each other meet these different needs is important to strong CBR partnerships.

The most successful CBR partnerships are also those that work to increase participants' skills and knowledge on both campus and community sides of the partnership, so that at the project end, everyone is better prepared to make subsequent partnerships even more productive. This is true for faculty and students who—if they acquire technical skills, information, and familiarity with the community—are able to do more and better work on their next project. Similarly, community members and agency staff who develop a solid understanding of the research process, along with strategies for working effectively with students, can use that knowledge to make the next project more successful.

Last, an important principle of successful CBR partnerships is that partners need to develop and share a long-term perspective, meaning they keep a collective eye on long-term goals and recognize that each short-term CBR project can make an incremental contribution toward the larger goal of fundamental social change. These longer-term goals are likely to fall into three general areas. The first is change in higher education: helping to make the institution more relevant to the community anymore effective in preparing students to be active, engaged, knowledgeable citizens. The second has to do with the balance of power in the community—to help marginalized groups gain more influence by becoming better organized, more proficient advocates for themselves and their constituents, and better able to mobilize resources on their own behalf. The third area of change is in society-at-large. When it is done well, CBR models participatory democracy at its best and helps participants acquire knowledge, skills, and commitments that they carry to other projects, organizations, classes, jobs, and communities throughout their lives. Given the modest impact of most single CBR projects, a long-term perspective is also important to avoid burnout and retain commitment to the ongoing work of the partnership.

## RESEARCH DESIGN AND PROCESS

A second critical part of CBR is the design and conduct of the research itself. Here, again, our concern is how the central features of the CBR model that we propose—collaboration, democratization of knowledge, and social change—bear on the myriad decisions about the research itself. CBR is both different from, and similar to, conventional academic research. CBR draws on conventional methodological protocols and procedures defined within each discipline and insist on systematic and rigorous inquiry that characterizes research at its best. At the same time, CBR demands new ways of thinking about every aspect of the research process.

First, collaboration means that, ideally, everyone involved participates in discussions and decisions at every stage of the research. This helps to ensure that the research is both useful and valid—a result of incorporating the perspectives and ideas of community members into decisions about measures, samples, and modes of data collection. And when community members also participate in carrying out the research, their commitment and capacity are enhanced. However, in reality, this sort of uniformly equal participation throughout the research process is often hard to achieve for various reasons related to the nature of the project, type of community represented, characteristics of the organization with which one is working, and the interests and inclinations of participants from both the campus and community sides of the partnership. Nonetheless, we would argue that involving the community is absolutely critical in two research stages in particular: identifying the research question and making decisions about how the results will be used. Here we suggest that that community involvement is non-negotiable and despite the many challenges, every effort should be made to give priority to the community's voices and interests.

Second, CBR's *unconventional approach to defining and discovering knowledge* has many different implications for the design and execution of research projects. The important validation of many types of knowledge that comes with true collaboration is one such implication. CBR recognizes multiple sources of expertise: abstract, generalized knowledge of the professor, detailed hands-on experiential knowledge of community members, and the fresh perspective brought by students unencumbered by community traditions and academic canons. This does not mean that academics have nothing special to contribute to the research. On the contrary, they bring both their research expertise and an outsider's perspective that may reveal trends, patterns, and questions not apparent to those immersed in the community's social world. At the same time, as we have pointed out, nonacademics contribute to the research in many important ways: providing language, perspective, history, insight, and much practical information that strengthen the study and enhance the validity and power of results.

Another way that this new approach to knowledge bears on the research itself is that researchers must be prepared to employ any number and variety of data collection methods to achieve the goal of producing information that meets CBR's most important criterion: usefulness to the community. CBR requires that we eschew a rigid "cookbook" approach to social research in favor of flexibility and creativity—which might mean using not only qualitative as well as quantitative approaches, but also even creative media such as video, art, community theatre, or song to present results. CBR must be "user-friendly," hardly a requirement that academics usually consider in research design and execution.

CBR also frequently requires that researchers step outside their discipline and explore topics that may be quite outside their own disciplinary boundaries. Here again, community needs drive the research, and real-world problems are seldom just sociological, or biological, or economic, or physical. Because answers to questions raised in CBR transcend disciplines, here again everyone becomes both a teacher and a learner, willing to acknowledge the limits of their own knowledge and go outside their intellectual "comfort zones" to pursue new information and understandings.

Finally, CBR's *social action* orientation has important implications for the way we think about and conduct research, starting with the important realization that although social change is CBR's ultimate purposes, academics in particular should not take on a project thinking that the research itself will somehow "save the day" for the partnering group or organization. When the partner is an agency, even the most compelling research results will likely bring about, at most, a minor change in policy, programming, or service delivery—or perhaps a small change in the organization itself. Successful social change at the grassroots level is even more problematic, as academic researchers (and even more, students) are typically unwilling or ill-equipped to engage in the sort of organizing work that is requisite to bringing about any sort of "popular education" or political mobilization of the community (Stoecker, 1999). Rather, a more realistic and useful stance is one that recognizes CBR's limits—particularly, one that sees it as just one part of the larger social change agenda of an agency or organization. By seeking to understand that larger agenda, the researchers can more effectively tailor their research to its aims, while at the same time accepting the very real limits of their own social change objectives.

## TEACHING AND LEARNING

Next we consider how the principles governing CBR are brought to bear on teaching and learning. Although much evidence documents that service-learning generally produces a range of positive attitudinal, interpersonal, and academic learning outcomes, researchers and practitioners have recently acknowledged that some service-learning experiences are more valuable than others. They have also begun to identify some different benefits and limitations associated with different kinds of community-based learning experiences. Eyler and Giles (1999) find that positive student learning outcomes are in part dependent on the quality of the service-learning placement and that a "high quality" placement is one in which students can do meaningful work, exercise initiative, have important responsibilities, engage in varied tasks, and work directly with practitioners or other community members, and where their work is clearly connected to the course content. Along the same lines, Mooney and Edwards (2001) suggest that what they call "advocacy service-learning"—emphasizing social justice, social change, real community collaboration, and critical analysis of the structural roots of problems—produces benefits for students that may be absent or de-emphasized in more conventional or "charity-oriented" service-learning experiences. That is, students whose community-based experience requires that they collaborate with community members, critically analyze the sources of problems, consider alternative responses, confront political and ideological barriers to change, weigh the merits of legislative or other political strategies, and experience their own potential for social action are more likely to develop the leadership skills, political awareness, and civic literacy that represent developmentally richer forms of service-learning. The CBR model we propose here would seem to provide students with just these sorts of experiences.

Another and related appeal of CBR is that its core features—collaboration, democratization of knowledge, and a social change/social justice agenda—dovetail well with the goals of what is often called "critical pedagogy." Varieties of critical pedagogy, including feminist pedagogy, have made their way into classes at every educational level and inspire the work of teachers committed to teaching and learning in ways that fundamentally challenge and transform—rather than reproduce and legitimate—existing social arrangements, including what are considered some of conventional education's most oppressive features. Although definitions of critical pedagogy vary, they tend to center on three major goals (adapted from Hartley, 1999), each of which is also embodied in CBR's principles and practices.

**1) A FOCUS ON COLLECTIVE/COLLABORATIVE LEARNING THAT DE-EMPHASIZES HIERARCHY, INCLUDING AUTHORITY DIFFERENCES BETWEEN TEACHER AND STUDENT.** Perhaps the most obvious consequence of collaboration that is part of our CBR model is that it undermines conventional status differences between campus and community partners. However, with students participating as equal members of a CBR team, other status and authority differences—between professor and student as well as those based on age and experience—are blurred as well. When students work alongside community members and the professor as teachers, learners, and researchers, they are also empowered as they acquire a sense of efficacy about their own abilities and potential contributions.

**2) A DEMYSTIFICATION OF CONVENTIONAL KNOWLEDGE, INCLUDING THE NOTION THAT OBJECTIVITY IS IMPOSSIBLE, THAT KNOWLEDGE IS NOT NEUTRAL, AND THAT PEOPLE'S "LIVED EXPERIENCES" ARE VALID SOURCES OF KNOWLEDGE.** CBR contrasts with conventional academic research, as it also resembles critical pedagogy, with its insistence that scientific research can never be value free, that knowledge is a form of power that should be collectively produced and controlled, and that "local knowledge" of the community is as valid and important to the research as researcher expertise (Small, 1995). In critical pedagogy, these principles are most often applied to the classroom setting, where the students' experience and knowledge, rather than the teacher's authority, is the starting point for learning. This becomes a way of validating "positionality"—the distinctive perspectives and worldviews of students with diverse social characteristics that render them marginal in conventional classrooms and within conventional knowledge frameworks. In CBR, the affirmation of "lived experience" extends to and empowers both community members and students, two groups whose authority does not hold sway in conventional educational or research contexts. Moreover, CBR models for students alternative ways of thinking about the production and control of knowledge: why we do research and who should control knowledge that is produced (Strand, 2000).

**3) A FOCUS ON TEACHING FOR SOCIAL CHANGE.** Critical pedagogy asserts that education ought to be liberatory rather than oppressive, transformative rather than oriented toward maintaining the status quo. It should contribute to social betterment by challenging existing social relations and structures of privilege, and by empowering students with knowledge, skills, and inclinations that prepare them to be active agents of social change in their lives. CBR does all this. In the course of their involvement in CBR, students develop: the capacity to think critically and analytically about existing structures of oppression and injustice, skills that prepare them to operate as effective change agents in the public sphere, a commitment to values of social justice and human dignity, and a belief in their own and others' ability to apply their knowledge and skills to bring about improvement in people's lives.

A final and related way that CBR translates into effective teaching and learning has to do with what is commonly referred to as "civic education." Most colleges and universities share a commitment to graduating students who are prepared for democratic citizenship, and yet there is widespread concern about the apparent failure of institutions to achieve this, as evidenced by the political apathy, cynicism, disengagement, individualism, and pessimism that characterize even many of our most accomplished graduates. While service-learning (and, indeed, any sort of volunteer work) does seem to raise students' social and civic consciousness (Eyler & Giles, 1999), a number of critics suggest that preparation for active citizenship requires more than just moral commitments and predispositions. More important are the knowledge and skills necessary to take thoughtful and concerted political action to bring about social change (see Astin, 1999; Barber, 1992; Boyte & Kari, 2000; Kahne & Westheimer, 1996). These include what CBR is most likely to impart: the capacity to think critically about social policiesand conditions, the ability to access and evaluate information, the skill to work with others on projects that recognize and require multiple contributions, and a sense of political efficacy that will drive one to take on the challenges of active citizenship in a participatory democracy.

## INSTITUTIONALIZING CBR AND TRANSFORMING THE ACADEMY

Last, we turn our attention to the principles underlying CBR's effective institutionalization on our campuses and in our communities. When we talk about social change in relation to CBR, we typically think first about its contribution to change in the community. However, in important respects the most significant kind of transformation CBR promises is in colleges and universities themselves, to define, support, and reward their historical missions of teaching, research, and service. In a more immediate sense, CBR practitioners are calling on these institutions to provide organizational and administrative structures necessary to support and sustain CBR work and community partnerships. It is possible (and not uncommon) for individual faculty members to develop partnerships and involve students in CBR projects quite on their own, without any formal institutional supports. However, the different tasks or functions connected with CBR are accomplished far more effectively when institutions organize formally to support this work, in the form of a program-based CBR office, a campus-based center, or even a local/regional consortium.

CBR is complex work that is most effectively carried out with the help of an administrative structure, campus or community-based, organized to address seven functions or tasks. Institutional organization for CBR must do more than carry out these seven functions, however. It must also embody the core features of the CBR model that we propose. In other words, true collaboration, new approaches to defining and acquiring knowledge, and a commitment to social change must become manifest in the structures constructed to undertake this work. The seven tasks or functions are:

- mobilize resources,

- build multiplex (deep) relationships among collaborators,

- create appropriate divisions of labor,

- manage information and authority relations,

- devise rules and control mechanisms for undertaking research projects,

- manage external relationships, and

- construct sustainability mechanisms.

The research process is complex and requires multiple skills and concurrent tasks, and individual researchers are limited by how many activities they can undertake at once, and their own skills and resources. Any given CBR project might require administering an office, coordinating logistics, ordering supplies, designing a Web page or flyer, translating a questionnaire, attending community meetings, identifying funding sources, managing a staff, producing a mailing, and many other tasks—all of which require resources such as time, money, transportation, technical support, equipment, and familiarity with certain aspects of the community. An administrative structure that engages in ongoing and development activities makes it far easier to identify and *mobilize the many different kinds of resources*, including people, that are necessary to support and sustain CBR.

An organization's *division of labor* is how it uses the resources it has mobilized—in this instance, the range of specialized knowledge and experience that different people bring to a CBR project and partnership. An administrative structure makes it far easier to coordinate and ultimately integrate people with complementary expertise and interest, and create working teams that are more effective and efficient in completing a project. This structure also makes it possible to manage the *multiplexity of relationships* that may emerge from the many different roles and role interrelations of CBR partners and participants. Community organizations in a CBR partnership are also involved in delivering services or organizing their community, managing grants, fundraising, doing community outreach, and advocating in various ways for constituents. Students involved in a CBR project are also taking (other) classes, holding jobs, volunteering in the community, and participating in campus clubs and organizations. Faculty members engaged in CBR may be working on more than one research project, teaching courses, involved in service projects on and off campus, writing grant proposals, and working on articles or books. In short, CBR participants are all likely to be juggling multiple roles and relationships—which may even include interacting with one another in different capacities and along different dimensions. Managing these multiplex role relations is easier when there is an administrative structure in place to help coordinate and support them.

Every CBR project, but especially larger ones, also requires some organized means for *managing information and establishing ordered interactions among the components of the process*. Decision-making authority in modern organizations, and particularly in CBR enterprises, is typically delegated throughout a structure, with participants at various levels being empowered to make particular decisions. Likewise, information flow usually works best when it proceeds in all directions so that those at the top are sharing knowledge and information with others at all levels, thereby enhancing the capacity for sound decision-making throughout the organization. The development and widespread use of electronic information sharing via email, the Internet, and the Web make greater information flow possible, but they also pose extra challenges in the form of information overload. This makes the development of clear, effective, and relevant communication channels among all the research participants—students, faculty members, and community members—all the more important.

An administrative organization is also useful as a source of *rules and control mechanisms for the research process*. Because CBR must be a multi-person partnership among stakeholders with different roles, expertise, and vested interests, organization mechanisms are needed to govern the process—in contrast to traditional academic research, where the "expert" researcher makes unilateral decisions about the research design and process, guided by the principles and norms of the institution and discipline. CBR centers or offices develop both informal and formal mechanisms to govern the CBR process. Formal mechanisms might include memoranda, research protocols, and agreements about control and ownership of data. These more formal agreements must be supplemented by informal everyday practices: face-to-face interactions, email communication, informal memos, and regular staff meetings of people from every constituency involved in the research.

Because any CBR project is part of a larger social change initiative, a CBR organization also works to influence the larger society through lobbying, organizing, advocacy, and effectively using media. In the most sophisticated CBR structure, the work of *managing external relations* may be handled by professional experts, such as information specialists and lobbyists. More commonly, these tasks are shared by many different people from the campus and community sides of the project. Finally, the ultimate goals of CBR—to empower those in need, to expand opportunities and resources to the disadvantaged, to mitigate structured inequalities—are obviously long-term and thus require sustained efforts. Even a CBR center or office that successfully carries out the tasks necessary to complete one or more successful research projects will have difficulty continuing its work over time without seeing that some *sustainability mechanisms* are in place. These include a clear, collaboratively-articulated vision; diverse and ongoing sources of support; strong leadership; an organizational administrative structure well-suited to its work; a plan for continuing mobilization and building human resources (internal and external); and an ongoing evaluation process to ensure quality research and effective partnership practices (adapted from Torres, Sinton, & White, p. 23).

## CONCLUSION

We have proposed a CBR model that is collaborative and community-driven, that democratizes the creation and dissemination of knowledge, and is committed to social change for social justice. CBR offers higher education a powerful and innovative means for combining the traditional academic missions of teaching, service, and scholarship. It also has the potential to help colleges and universities become relevant to their adjacent communities in ways that can ultimately transform both. As CBR gains momentum on campuses and in communities across the country, the challenge is to ensure that these ideals are translated into principles and practices that do not simply reproduce old arrangements, but bring real benefits to communities and fundamental changes to higher education.

## NOTES

We gratefully acknowledge the support of the Corporation for National and Community Service and the Bonner Foundation, with special thanks to Robert Hackett for being a keen critic, a tireless supporter, and a much-valued friend.

1. This essay is based on *Community-Based Research and Higher Education: Principles and Practices* by Kerry Strand, Sam Marullo, Nick Cutforth, Randy Stoeker, and Patrick Donohue (Jossey-Bass, 2003).

## REFERENCES

Astin, A. (1999). Promoting leadership, service, and democracy: What higher education can do. In R. Bringle, R. Games, & E. Malloy (Eds.), *Colleges and universities as citizens* (pp. 31–47). Boston, MA: Allyn & Bacon.

Barber, B. (1992). *An aristocracy for everyone: The politics of education and the future of America*. New York: Oxford University Press.

Boyer, E.L. (1990). *Scholarship reconsidered: Priorities of the professorate*. Princeton, NJ: Carnegie Foundation for the Advancement of Teaching.

Boyte, H. & Kari, N. (2000). Renewing the democratic spirit in American colleges and universities. In T. Ehrlich (Ed.), *Civic responsibility and higher education* (pp. 37–61). American Council on Education and Oryx Press.

Brown, L. D., & Tandon, R. (1983). Ideology and political economy in inquiry: Action research and participatory research. *Journal of Applied Behavioral Science,19*, 277–294.

Edwards, B., & Marullo, S. (1999). Editors' introduction: Universities in troubled times—institutional responses. *American Behavioral Scientist, 42*(5), 754–765.

Eyler, J., & Giles, D.E. (1999). *Where's the learning in service-learning?* San Francisco: Jossey Bass.

Freire, P. (1970). *Pedagogy of the oppressed*. New York: Continuum.

Hall, B.L. (1992). From margins to center? The development land purpose of participatory research. *American Sociologist, 23*, 15–28.

Hartley, H. (1999). What's my orientation? Using the teacher-as-text strategy as feminist pedagogical practice. *Teaching Sociology, 27*, 398–406.

Horton, A.I. (1989). *The Highlander Folk School: A history of its major programs, 1932–1961*. Brooklyn, NY: Carlson Publishing.

Kahne, J., & Westheimer, J. (1996). In the service of what? *Phi Delta Kappan, 77*, 592–600.

Lewin, K. (1948). *Resolving social conflicts*. New York: Harper & Brothers.

Marullo, S. (1996). The service-learning movement in higher education: An academic response to troubled times. *Sociological Imagination, 33*(2), 117–137.

Mooney, L. A. & Edwards, B. (2001). Experiential learning in sociology: Service-learning and other community-based learning. *Teaching Sociology, 29*(2), 182–94.

Park, P. (1992). The discovery of participatory research as a new scientific paradigm: Personal and intellectual accounts. *American Sociologist, 23*(4), 29–43.

Shefner, J., & Cobb, D. (2002). Hierarchy and partnership in New Orleans. *Qualitative Sociology, 25*(2), 273–297.

Small, S. (1995). Action-oriented research: Models and methods. *Journal of Marriage and the Family, 57*, 941–56.

Stoecker, R. (1999). Are academics irrelevant?: Roles for scholars in participatory research. *American Behavioral Scientist, 42*(5), 840–854.

Strand, K. (2000). Community-based research as pedagogy. *Michigan Journal of Community Service Learning, 7*, 85–96.

Torres, J., Sinton, R., & White, A. (2000). *Establishing and sustaining an office of community service*. Providence, RI: Campus Compact.

## AUTHORS

**KERRY STRAND** is a professor of Sociology at Hood College (MD), where she has worked with students and community partners on almost two dozen CBR projects over the past five years. She has published papers and presented numerous talks and workshops on service-learning, CBR, and other topics related to undergraduate teaching and learning. She is co-author (with Sam Marullo, Nick Cutforth, Randy Stoecker, and Patrick Donohue) of *Community-Based Research and Higher Education: Principles and Practices* and is currently working on an anthology for students in undergraduate social science research methods courses.

**SAM MARULLO** is associate professor and chair of the Department of Sociology and Anthropology at Georgetown University. He is director of the Community Research and Learning (CoRAL) Network of Washington, DC. He regularly teaches a year-long CBR seminar for undergraduates, Project D.C., which is the capstone course for students with a concentration in Social Justice Analysis.

**NICK CUTFORTH** is associate professor of Educational Leadership in the College of Education at the University of Denver. He directs DU's Community Based Research Project and coordinates the Colorado Community Based Research Network. He is coeditor (with Don Hellison) of *Youth Development and Physical Activity: Linking Universities and Communities* (Human Kinetics, 2000). He is co-author (with Kerry Strand, Sam Marullo, Randy Stoecker, and Patrick Donohue) of *Community-Based Research and Higher*

*Education: Principles and Practices* (Jossey-Bass, 2003).

**RANDY STOECKER** is professor of Sociology at the University of Toledo. He has been the evaluation coordinator for the Bonner Foundation's Community Research Project, which supports most of the networks in this article. He has experience with a wide range of CBR projects over the past 15 years, and moderates the COMM-ORG online conference on community organizing and development at http://comm-org.utoledo.edu.

**PATRICK DONOHUE** is an assistant professor of Political Science at Middlesex County College (MCC) in Edison, New Jersey, where he also directs the MCC Community Scholars Corps and MCC Community-Based Research Center. He is the co-author of *Community Based Research: Principles and Practices for Higher Education* and the former acting director of the Trenton Center for Campus-Community Partnerships.

# Community-Based Research:

## Recommended Reading

## BOOKS & CHAPTERS

Boyer, E.L. (1990). *Scholarship reconsidered: Priorities of the professoriate.* Princeton, NJ: Carnegie Foundation for the Advancement of Teaching.

Boyte, H.C., & Kari, K.N. (1996). *Building America: The democratic promise of public work.* Philadelphia: Temple University Press.

Fetterman, D.M. (2000). *Foundations of empowerment evaluation.* Thousand Oaks, CA: Sage.

Greenwood, D., & Levin, M. (1998). *Introduction to action research.* Thousand Oaks, CA: Sage.

Kretzman, J.P., & McKnight, J.L. (1997). *Building communities from the inside out: A path toward finding and mobilizing community assets.* Chicago: ACTA Publications.

Mikler, M., Wallerstein, N., & Hall, B. (2002). *Community-based participatory research for health.* San Francisco: Jossey-Bass.

Murphy, D., Scammell, M., & Sclove, R. (1997). *Doing community-based research: A reader.* Amherst: Loka Institute.

Nyden, P., et al. (Eds.). (1997). *Building community: Social science in action.* Thousand Oaks, CA: Pine Forge.

O'Fallon, L.R., Tyson, F.L. & Dearry, A. (Eds.). (2000). *Successful models of community-based participatory research, final report.* Washington, DC: National Institute of Environmental Health Science. Available at www.niehs.nih.gov/external/outreach.htm.

Park, P., et al. (Eds.). (1993). *Voices of change: Participatory research in the United States and Canada.* Westport, CT: Bergin and Garvey.

Sclove, R.E., Scammell, M.L., & Holland, B. (1998). *Community-based research in the United States: An introductory reconnaissance, including twelve organizational case studies and comparison with Dutch science shops and the mainstream American research system.* Amherst, MA: The Loka Institute.

Strand, K.J., et al. (2003). *Community-based research and higher education: Principles and practices.* San Francisco: Jossey-Bass.

Stringer, E. (1999). *Action research: A handbook for practitioners.* Thousand Oaks, CA: Sage.

Whyte, W.F. (Ed.). (1991). *Participatory action research.* Thousand Oaks, CA: Sage.

Williams, L. (1997). *Grassroots participatory research.* Knoxville, TN: Community Partnership Center, University of Tennessee.

Witkin, B.R., & Altschuld, J.W. (1995) *Planning and conducting needs assessment: A practical guide.* Thousand Oaks, CA: Sage.

## ARTICLES & REPORTS

Ansley, F., & Gaventa, J. (1997). Researching for democracy and democratizing research. *Change, 29,* 46–53.

Benson, L., & Harkavy, I. (1996). Communal participatory action research as a strategy for improving universities and social sciences: Penn's work with the West Philadelphia Improvement Corps as a case study. *Educational Policy, 10,* 202–223.

Brown, L.D., & Tandon, R. (1983). Ideology and political economy in inquiry: Action research and participatory research. *Journal of Applied Behavioral Science, 19,* 277–294.

Cancian, F.M. (1993). Conflicts between activist research and academic success: Participation research and alternative strategies. *American Sociologist, 24,* 92–106.

Edward Ginsberg Center for Community Service and Learning. (2003). *Michigan Journal of Community Service Learning, 9* (3), entire issue.

Harkavy, I., & Puckett, J.L. (1994). Lessons from Hull House for the contemporary urban university. *Social Services Review, 68,* 299–321.

Lynch, J. (1993). Community participation in community needs assessment. *Journal of Applied Sociology, 10,* 125–136.

Nyden, P., & Wiewel, W. (1992). Collaborative research: Harnessing the tensions between researcher and practitioner. *The American Sociologist, 23* (4), 43–55.

Reardon, K.M., & Shields, T.P. (1997). Promoting sustainable community/university partnerships through participatory action research. *NSEE Quarterly, 23* (1), 1, 22–25.

Sandmann, L.R., et al. (2000). Managing critical tensions. *Change, 32* (1), 44–52.

Sclove, R. (1997). Research by the people, for the people. *Futures, 29* (6), 541–549.

Small, S.A. (1995). Action-oriented research: Models and methods. *Journal of Marriage and Family, 57*, 941–955.

Stoeker, R. (1999). Making connections: Community organizing, empowerment planning, and participatory research in participatory evaluation. *Sociological Practice,* 1, 209–232.

# SECTION 11

# Assessment

## TITLES INCLUDED IN THIS SECTION

## QUESTIONS FOR REFLECTION AND PLANNING

What assessment method(s) do you currently utilize in your courses?

How will you assess/evaluate student outcomes in service-learning? What outcomes will you evaluate?

How will you know if the desired outcome that drove the design and implementation of the service-learning component was achieved? (What outcomes do you want to measure? What is the purpose for generating this information? What would constitute success?)

What role will the community play in assessing the student? The course?

# An Assessment Model for Service-Learning:

## Comprehensive Case Studies of Impact on Faculty, Students, Community, and Institution

by Amy Driscoll, Barbara Holland, Sherril Gelmon, and Seanna Kerrigan

*A comprehensive case study model of assessment developed at Portland State University responds to the need to measure the impact of service-learning on four constituencies (student, faculty, community, and institution). The case studies blend quantitative and qualitative measures in order to determine the most effective and practical tools to measure service-learning impact and to provide feedback for continuous improvement of practice. Insights from the design process and preliminary results have potential value for institutions with similar agendas for service-learning and community partnerships.*

I N THIS TIME OF DRAMATIC TRANSFORMATIONS IN higher education, one very visible change on many campuses is the expansion of partnerships between colleges and universities and community agencies, organizations, and other constituencies. Those partnerships take many forms from campus to campus, but a typical connection is service-learning— the integration of community service with the academic content of course work. Service-learning responds to the call for higher education to improve the quality and productivity of instruction and to "become more engaged in addressing the nation's many problems" (Edgerton, 1995). As more and more educational institutions heed the call, the need to evaluate and interpret both the outcomes and the impacts of service-learning has grown.

At Portland State University (PSU) service-learning has long been present in the curriculum, but in fragmented forms with scattered visibility. When we revised our general education curriculum in 1993, our commitment to broad integration of service-learning became focused and supported, and clearly connected to our university mission. The first year (1994) of deliberate campus-wide focused service-learning was marked with high levels of enthusiasm and faculty claims of exciting impact. Aware that our enthusiasm and claims must give way to hard data and demonstrated outcomes, faculty and administrators held a series of meetings to develop an assessment plan uniquely targeted to service-learning courses. We began by searching for other models of assessment for service-learning and found that program evaluations dominated the literature (Shumer, 1991). We soon became aware that we were part of a larger national community seeking to ameliorate the "scarcity of replicable qualitative and quantitative research on the effects of service-learning on student learning and development, the communities in which they serve, or on the educational institutions" (Giles, Honnet, & Migliore, 1991, p.2). This paper describes our efforts to study and document the impact of service-learning and to develop an assessment model that contributes to service-learning practice. We were also committed to establishing a "culture of evidence" at Portland State University (Ramaley, 1996) to document our reform efforts.

## LITERATURE REVIEW

We began our conceptualization process by reviewing the theoretical and development literature on service-learning. Like PSU faculty, the proponents of service-learning in journals and other publications have been enthusiastic about its potential. Claims for its success include enhanced relevance of course content, changes in student attitudes, support for community projects and needs, and increased volunteerism (Ehrlich, 1995; Giles & Eyler, 1994; Harkavy, 1992). Those same supporters also acknowledged the gaps in our knowledge about the effects of service-learning and the difficulty in measuring those effects. As Eyler and Giles (1994) point out, the outcomes of service-learning have not been clearly conceptualized, nor is there agreement about the intent of service-learning. Such dissension and lack of clarity have contributed to the lack of significant progress in the development of assessment measures. We decided to address the lack of clarity of outcomes as we began our assessment plan.

Another challenge to the assessment of service-learning is that the benefits are spread among different constituencies: students, faculty, the community, and the institution. Colleges and universities have typically struggled with the assessment of student learning and institutional impact. Currently there are and have been multiple projects focused on student outcomes (Bringle & Kremer, 1994; Cohen & Kinsey, 1994; Giles & Eyler, 1994; Hesser, 1995; Markus, Howard, & King, 1993; Wechsler & Fogel, 1995), but the profession has concentrated little effort toward assessing faculty impact, and has only begun thinking about the process of assessing community impact. The issue of multiple constituencies is a major challenge to the task of assessing service-learning if institutions are to effectively evaluate the full ramifications of a commitment to integration of service-learning in the curriculum. This is especially important to the partnership concept that PSU embraces as the essence of its urban mission. Thus, the commitment to assessing the experiences and impact for multiple constituencies was a guiding principle of this study.

## CONTEXT FOR DEVELOPMENT

Before describing the conceptual development of our assessment plan, it is important to acknowledge the context in which we worked. Portland State University, an urban institution, had recently reformed the undergraduate curriculum in an effort to fulfill our mission, to better accommodate our non-traditional student population, and to attend to research on effective teaching and learning. Service-learning was integrated throughout the new curriculum in freshmen experiences, service-learning courses, and in graduation requirements. This comprehensive approach to the integration of community service influenced the design of an assessment model. The newness of our service-

learning integration and its comprehensive impact across campus called for an exploratory and formative assessment approach. This meant that our model would have to ensure the collection of assessment data that could provide feedback for continuous improvement and sufficient breadth to serve the diverse forms of service-learning in our curriculum. The design would also have to honor PSU's commitment to mutually beneficial partnerships with the community, and therefore, provide data of value to our community partners.

## CONCEPTUAL DEVELOPMENT OF AN ASSESSMENT MODEL

In response to the paucity of assessment approaches in the literature and with attention to our campus-wide service-learning approach, we decided to test the use of comprehensive case studies as a structural approach to the assessment and description of our service-learning courses. An additional objective was to develop assessment strategies that would be adaptable to other community service activities throughout our general education curriculum.

The comprehensive case studies were designed not only to assess and describe our service-learning courses, but to pilot multiple forms of assessment instruments. We needed to explore many mechanisms for measuring the impact of our courses in order to determine which approaches and tools would provide the best and most informative data. We were reminded by Giles and others (1991) that there was a "myriad of potential effects to be derived from combining service and learning in the educational enterprise" and by Hesser (1995) that the "variables to be controlled are almost infinite," so our intent was to be as comprehensive as possible for the draft of our case study model.

The first step in designing the case study model, that of defining purposes, attended to our commitment to a comprehensive approach directed by well-defined goals. Our purposes were:

1. To describe and assess the impact of service-learning courses on multiple constituencies.

2. To develop and pilot an exploratory case study model that integrates continuous improvement with educational assessment theory and practice, that measures a maximum number of impact variables

for multiple constituencies, and that tests a broad range of potential measurement tools.

3. To monitor both data collection and data analysis to determine the most effective assessment approaches and tools to measure service-learning in order to develop a practical and valid assessment model for future use.

4. To consider the lessons learned from the comprehensive case studies in order to develop assessment models for other community service activities on campus.

As we proceeded from these purposes to the articulation of hypotheses for our study, we encountered the need to define outcomes of our community-based learning courses. Just as the literature described, our courses did not have clear or specific outcomes regarding effects of service-learning participants. Much of our development work became the task of defining desired impact. If we claimed that service-learning courses had an impact on students or community or other constituencies, what did the impact look like? How could we establish that there was an impact? Before designing measures, a comprehensive definition of impact was needed for each of the constituencies. A set of potential impact variables for each constituency was developed in a participatory fashion that considered each group's perspective. We conducted a series of reviews of the impact variables with members of the four constituencies (students, faculty, community, institution) and made recommended revisions until there was agreement on their inclusiveness. An example of an impact variable for students is "awareness of community." To measure the impact variables, we developed indicators and drafted appropriate tools to capture the existence of an indicator or measure changes in an indicator. Building on the previous example for "awareness of community," indicators were determined as "knowledge of community history, strengths, problems, and issues," as well as "definition of community." Our design suggested that those indicators could be measured by means of interviews, journal analysis, focus groups, and surveys. Figures 1, 2, 3, and 4 display the variables, indicators, and appropriate measurements for each of the four constituencies.

Once the range of impact variables for all four constituencies was determined, the case studies were designed to make a broad assessment of a maximum number of impact variables for all constituencies. Indicators and appropriate measurement of each impact variable directed the case study design to blend quantitative and qualitative approaches. Further, it was anticipated that the case studies could demonstrate the potential for linking teaching, research, and service. With the impact variables providing measurement direction, the resulting hypotheses of our comprehensive case study research were:

1. Participation in service-learning courses will have an impact on students.

2. Participation in service-learning courses will have an impact on faculty.

3. Participation in service-learning courses will have an impact on community.

4. Participation in service-learning courses will have an impact on the institution.

5. Service-learning courses will transform the teaching and learning paradigm the university from a traditional instructional model to an interactive learning model.

Our hypotheses were intentionally broad to support our comprehensive approach and the wide range of impact variables. The last hypothesis resulted from earlier exploratory observations in classrooms in which service-learning was integrated with course work.

## STUDY METHODOLOGY

As indicated earlier, the broad range of variables, indicators and appropriate measurement tools and approaches demanded a blend of quantitative and qualitative approaches. Some of the approaches were to be used in a pre-post format, others were to be used for ongoing assessment throughout a course, and others were to be used for a one-time measurement. An overview of the indicators and appropriate measurement revealed three major categories of mechanisms or data collection procedures. The categories are illustrated in Figure 5. They include in-person assessment, independent reflection measures, and review of existing documentation. The in-person assessment is composed of interviews of students, faculty, and community representatives; focus groups to be conducted with students and community groups; and bi-weekly classroom observations of service-learning courses. The independent reflection measures are meant to capture journalized reflections of faculty and students, and pre-post

## Figure 1: Student Variables, Indicators, and Measurements

| Variables | Indicators | Measurements |
|---|---|---|
| Awareness of community | Knowledge of community history, strengths, problems, definition | Interview, journal analysis, focus groups, survey |
| Involvement with community | Quantity/quality of interactions, attitude toward involvement | Interview, surveys, journal analysis, focus groups |
| Commitment to service | Plans for future service | Surveys, focus groups |
| Career choices | Influence of community placement job opportunities | Surveys, interview, focus groups |
| Self awareness | Changes in awareness of strengths, limits, direction, role, goals | Surveys, interview |
| Personal development | Participation in additional courses, extracurricular activities | Interview, journal analysis, focus groups, survey |
| Academic achievement | Role of community, experience in understanding and applying content | Interview, survey, grades, focus groups |
| Sensitivity to diversity | Attitude, understanding of diversity, comfort and confidence | Journal analysis, reflections, survey, interviews |
| Autonomy/ independence | Learner role | Interview, class observation |
| Sense of ownership | Learner role | Class observation, interview |
| Communication | Class interactions, community interactions | Class observation, community observation |

## Figure 2: Faculty Variables, Indicators, and Measurements

| Variables | Indicators | Measurements |
|---|---|---|
| Involvement with community | Quantity/quality of interactions/contacts | Logs, surveys, interview, journals |
| Awareness of community | Definition of community, knowledge of history, strengths, problems | Interview, written comments, journals |
| Level of volunteerism | Valuing personal volunteerism, actual volunteerism | Vita, interview, survey |
| Professional development | Influence of community-based learning in conference/seminar attendance | Vita, interview, journals |
| Scholarship | Influence of community-based learning in articles., presentations, etc. | Vita, artifacts |
| Teaching methods | Influence of community-based learning in class format, organization, interactions | Class observation, journals, surveys, teaching and learning continuum |
| Faculty/student interaction | Content, variety, frequency, direction | Class observation, teaching and learning continuum |
| Philosophy of teaching/learning | Faculty/student roles, outcomes, pedagogy, curriculum | Interview, class observation, syllabus analysis, journals, teaching and learning continuum |
| Role in community-based teaching | Self perceptions of role | Log, interview, survey, journals |

## Figure 3: Community Variables, Indicators, and Measurements

| Variables | Indicators | Measurements |
|---|---|---|
| Nature of partnership | Present and future activities | Interview, syllabus |
| Involvement with community | Contribution to community, achievement of goals of the agency and course | Interview, survey, focus groups |
| Perceived capacity to serve clients | Number of clients, services, value added | Interview, focus groups, survey |
| Economic benefits | Cost of services provided by faculty/students, funding opportunities | Interview, survey |
| Social benefits | New connections, networks | Interview |
| New insights about operations/activities | Changes in goals, activities, operations | Interview |
| Awareness of PSU | Changes in image, confidence, knowledge of programs | Interview, focus groups, CAE log |
| Establishment of ongoing relationships | Changes in levels, nature, breadth of contacts, future partnerships | Interview, focus groups |
| Identification of prospective employees | Actual hirings | Interview, survey |
| Satisfaction with PSU interactions | Level of communication/interaction with students/faculty | Interview, Survey |

## Figure 4: Institutional Variables, Indicators, and Measurements

| Variables | Indicators | Measurements |
|---|---|---|
| Role in community | Numbers of types of requests for assistance from community, changes in enrollment and transfer patterns | CAE log, IRP reports, IASC interview |
| Orientation to teaching and learning | Number of faculty involved in community-based learning, focus/content of professional development activities, focus/content of dissertations, enrollment and transfer patterns | CAE log, survey (NG), content analysis of grants, dissertation, class observations |
| Resource acquisition | Contribution levels, site visits by other campuses, grant proposals and awards related to service, changes in enrollment/transfer patterns | CAE log, Currently, IRP reports |
| Image in community (local, state, national, int'l) | Number of media reports, number of site visits by other campuses, number of publications, conference presentations, contributions | CAE log, Currently, PR reports |

**Figure 5: Mechanisms to Measure Impact**

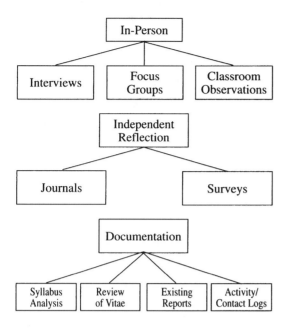

surveys of students, faculty, and community representatives. The review of existing documentation will include analysis of syllabi, review of faculty vitae, analysis of institutional reports (admissions data, alumnae surveys, etc.), and activity/contact logs.

## PILOT STUDY

During Winter quarter 1996 the comprehensive case study model was piloted in four service-learning courses at Portland State University. These courses were selected to ensure diversity of disciplines, faculty with previous experience in service-learning, and variation in the kind of service. The courses being studied include a graphics design course in the School of Fine and Performing Arts, a public health course on programs for children and families in the School of Urban and Public Affairs, a technical writing course in the College of Liberal Arts and Sciences, and an introductory education course in the School of Education. Graduate research assistants assisted the project team with classroom and community observations, interviews of faculty, students, and community members, and focus groups with students and community members. Students, faculty, and the research assistants maintained reflective journals during the entire quarter.

In the process of data collection, it was apparent that most of the assessment strategies were documenting

impact for the four constituencies as well as providing formative assessment information, that is, feedback for continuous improvement of service-learning courses. Our classroom observations began to reveal a non-traditional paradigm of teaching in some of the classes. Faculty and student reflections in interviews and focus groups indicated affirmation of the value of service-learning experiences. Those general trends were immediately obvious in the process of collecting data, but there is an enormity of data to be analyzed before drawing final conclusions.

At the time of this writing, data analysis is only partially completed. Preliminary findings from student interview data show support for all of the predicted student impact variables, especially awareness of and involvement with community, self awareness, personal development, academic achievement, sensitivity to diversity, and independence as a learner. Community interviews also support the predicted variables, especially perceived capacity to serve clients, economic benefits, social benefits, new insights about operations, and awareness of PSU. There is strong support for the variable, satisfaction with PSU interactions, and additional related community impact variables emerged from the data. Analysis of faculty vita indicate that community service teaching experiences have begun to influence scholarship in the form of research, conference presentations, and publications. It would be premature to draw any conclusions at this time, but we are encouraged by results from the partial analysis.

We predict that some of our assessment strategies will provide useful and significant information, and that some of our strategies will not. Our immediate intent is to use the results of our data analysis to refine the case study model for use with more courses during the 1996-97 academic year. Our long-term goal is to produce a practical and valid package of assessment strategies that can be embedded in all of our service-learning courses and adapted for other community service activities.

## SUMMARY

A comprehensive case study model of assessment developed at Portland State University responds to the concerns and questions about the impact of service-learning, accommodates the range of constituencies influenced by service-learning, and seeks to address the paucity of approaches for measuring service-learning outcomes. In addition, for the PSU community, the case study approach has the potential to support and inform institutional efforts to monitor the role of service-learning in the fulfillment of the urban mission. The model was developed by a team of faculty and administrators, with input from students and community representatives. The case study design is a blend of quantitative and qualitative measures to assess the impact of a service-learning course on faculty, students, community, and institution. Although analysis of the case studies is in progress, insights from the design process and from preliminary results have potential. value for institutions with similar agendas for service-learning and community partnerships.

## NOTE

Funding for this project was provided by the Corporation for National Service and the Center for Academic Excellence at Portland State University. The authors wish to acknowledge the assistance of MJ Longley, Carolyn Martin, and Amy Spring.

## REFERENCES

Bringle, R. G., & Kremer, J. F. (1993). An evaluation of an intergenerational service-learning project for undergraduates. *Educational Gerontologist, 19,* 407–416.

Cohen, J., & Kinsey, D. (1994). "Doing good" and scholarship: A service-learning study. *Journalism Educator,* 4–14.

Edgerton, R. (1995). Crossing boundaries: Pathways to productive learning and community renewal. *AAHE Bulletin,* 48 (1), 7–10.

Ehrlich, T. (1995). Taking service seriously. *AAHE Bulletin,* 47 (7), 8–10.

Eyler, J., & Giles, D. E. (1994). Research and evaluation in community service: The higher education agenda. Racine: Proceedings from the Wingspread Service Learning Conference.

Giles, D. E., & Eyler, J. (1994). The impact of a college community service laboratory on students' personal, social, and cognitive outcomes. *Journal of Adolescence, 17,* 327–339.

Giles, D.E., & Eyler, J. (1994). The theoretical roots of service-learning in John Dewey: Toward a theory of service-learning. *Michigan Journal of Community Service Learning,* 1 (1), 77–85.

Giles, D. E., Honnet, E., & Migliore, S. (1991). *Setting the agenda for effective research in combining service and learning in the 1990's.* Raleigh, NC: National Society of Experiential Education.

Harkavy, I. (1992). The mission of the Center for Community Partnerships. *Almanac,* 4–5.

Hesser, G. (1995). Faculty assessment of student learning: Outcomes attributed to service-learning and evidence of changes in faculty attitudes about experiential education. *Michigan Journal of Community Service Learning, 2,* 33-42.

Markus, G. B., Howard, J. P. F., & King, D. C. (1993). Integrating community service and classroom instruction enhances learning: Results from an experiment. *Educational Evaluation and Policy Analysis, 15,* 410–419.

Ramaley, J. (1996). Personal communication.

Shumer, R. (1991). Setting a research agenda for service learning. Unpublished article.

Weschler, A., & Fogel, J. The outcomes of a service-learning program. *National Quarterly Society for Experiential Education, 20* (4), 6–7, 25–26.

# How Do We Know That Our Work Makes A Difference?

## Assessment Strategies for Service-Learning and Civic Engagement

by Sherril B. Gelmon, Dr.P.H., *Portland State University*

## ABSTRACT

*Institutions committed to civic engagement and service learning must be able to demonstrate the impact of these initiatives. Understanding and articulating "impact" requires knowledge and expertise in the use of various assessment methods, in order to design the measurement of impact, analyze the findings and report the results. This paper provides an overview of practical methods and tools for assessment planning and implementation, and offers suggestions for readers to begin assessment design for their own programs.*

## CONTEXT FOR ASSESSMENT

INCREASINGLY A SHIFT is being observed in higher education from an "old way" emphasizing teaching to a "new way" emphasizing learning. Barr and Tagg (1995) described this as moving from a conceptualization of a college as a place that exists to provide instruction to thinking of a college as an institution that exists to produce learning. If one thinks of the core issues of teaching and learning—such as knowledge, focus, curriculum definition, instruction, design, student role, and organizational change—a framework can be created to illustrate the transition from old to new way, as shown in Table 1 (Holland et al., 1996). Most of the issues show movement from the "old" to the "new" ways—not to deny any of the good characteristics of the old way, or to suggest that they all must be eliminated, but rather to emphasize the "new" ways of thinking about higher education that represent this shift from teaching to learning. Service-learning and other forms of community-based education all demonstrate characteristics of the new way, emphasizing application of knowledge, team and community focus for learning, collective instruction and curriculum definition, integrated sequencing of courses, and active learning by students. All of these characteristics are important to take into consideration as one contemplates assessing the impact of such programs.

## SERVICE LEARNING AND THE ENGAGED CAMPUS

As institutions speak about the concept of the "engaged campus," others want to be able to know what engagement is and whether this is a true descriptor of their own institution. What does an engaged campus look like? What is different about faculty? What are the characteristics of the students? What can be observed about community-campus partnerships? All of these are questions that can begin to frame a campus-based assessment of engagement.

One method that is suggested for increasing civic engagement is the use of service learning as an instructional strategy. The published literature on assessing the impact of service learning across a broad range of constituencies is not very extensive; much of the literature has focused on the impact on students as individuals and on student learning. Therefore many campuses find it difficult to articulate how a service learning program can be assessed, let alone how the results of such an assessment contribute to a local understanding of civic engagement.

The 1999 report of the Kellogg Commission on the Future of State and Land Grant Universities, *The Engaged Institution*, offers a set of characteristics that form a seven-part "test" of engagement (Kellogg Commission,

Sherril B. Gelmon. (2002). "How do we Know our Work Makes a Difference? Assessment Strategies for Service-Learning and Civic Engagement." *Metropolitan Universities: An International Forum.* 11 (2), pp. 28–39. Copyright © 2000 Metropolitan Universities: An International Forum. Reprinted with permission of Metropolitan Universities: An International Forum.

**Table 1: Moving from Teaching to Learning**

| "Old Way" | Issue | "New Way" |
|---|---|---|
| Acquisition | Knowledge | Application |
| Individual | Focus | Team/Community |
| By faculty | Curriculum definition | By faculty, community, students |
| Banking | Instruction | Collective |
| Prescribed courses | Design | Integrated sequence |
| Passive | Student learning | Active |
| Sporadic reform | Change | Continuous improvement |

1999). Similarly, the 1999 "Presidents' Fourth of July Declaration on the Civic Responsibility of Higher Education" (Campus Compact, 1999) includes a draft of a "Campus Assessment of Civic Responsibility" that provides the basis for institutions to conduct a baseline assessment of civic engagement by involving administrators, trustees, faculty, staff, students, alumni and community partners in a deliberative self-assessment process.

## WHY DO ASSESSMENTS?

Why do we do assessments? The primary reason is often to provide immediate feedback to enable program leaders to make incremental changes during the program, responding to needs and concerns. Over the longer term, assessment data can provide the basis for program planning and for redesign and improvement. Assessments increasingly are called for by funding agencies, as evidence of the value received for the money invested in a program through a grant. Almost all accrediting agencies (both institutionalized and specialized/professional) have instituted specific requirements for documentation of explicit assessment processes and evidence of routine use of assessment data in program improvement. With ever-increasing calls for accountability, and particularly for resource accountability, there are regular demands for clear assessment data.

## BEGINNING THE ASSESSMENT PROCESS

Assessment serves a useful purpose as a mechanism to tell the story of what you have learned from your work—articulating the learning for yourself, and articulating the learning for others. In beginning any assessment, one should ask a series of key questions. The answers to these questions will frame the design of your assessment:

- What is the aim of your assessment?

- Who wants or needs the assessment information?

- What resources are available to support the assessment?

- Who will conduct the assessment?

- How can you ensure the results are used?

These questions are important for a number of reasons. The assessment should have an aim and a stated purpose. Without a purpose there may be little reason to carry forward the work of the assessment. The person or agency who wants or needs the assessment may dictate the nature of the work carried out—is this mandated by a funder, is it part of an accreditation or other regulatory review, is it part of an individual's personal performance review? It is necessary to know what resources will support the assessment and who will do the work; often assessments are designed without a clear understanding of the resource implications, and the result is frustration because the plans do not match with the realities of available resources and expertise. Finally it is important to be able to ensure that the results will be attended to and used; few things are as frustrating as designing and conducting a comprehensive assessment of a program and then having the results ignored. "Results" are facts and do not in themselves suggest anything.

Organizations and individuals are continuously changing and adapting. A structured assessment initiative helps those organizations and the individuals who participate in them to monitor activities, identify changes, and develop plans for continually improving their work. In the academic setting, much of this work will be done by faculty who are by nature inquisitive and spend much of their professional time asking questions, answering these questions, and developing ideas for the next set of questions. This is the essential nature of assessment. Gray (1997) has noted that such activity requires understanding innovation, identifying leadership, and facilitating change strategies to accomplish the goals of assessment.

Assessment may vary in the scope of its focus and may consider different constituencies, depending on its purpose. In the context of institutional review for regional accreditation, the assessment program might be university-wide. A department or program might undertake assessment—for internal review purposes, for professional review (by a state governmental entity or a specialized/professional accreditor), or as part of departmental/program planning. Campus-wide general education programs are often the focus of assessment in order to gain greater understanding of these cross-departmental programs that have an impact on multiple student populations within the university. Much of the assessment literature focuses on assessment of students—their learning, their performance, their preparation for various careers. It can be argued, however, that this provides a narrow perspective, as to gain a true comprehensive assessment picture one must also consider faculty, institutional mandates, community agencies, and other key stakeholders. Unfortunately, such broad assessment may consume significant resources and therefore many institutions focus only on student assessment.

## WHO SHOULD BE INVOLVED IN ASSESSMENT?

Successful assessment requires bringing together key players in the activity being assessed, and helping these individuals to step outside of their normal roles and create a new culture—one that facilitates these players pooling their collective interests to focus on the program, service, department, or other entity/activity being assessed. As a result, assessment can have a significant transformational impact on the organization (Magruder et al., 1997).

There is considerable debate about the merits of centralized vs. decentralized responsibility for assessment. In some institutions, a central office has been developed, providing a focus within the institution's administrative structure for assessment and serving as a campus-wide resource (see, for example, Palomba, 1997). Establishment of a central office is viewed as evidence of the institution's commitment to assessment and its validation of the importance of assessment activities. A downfall of a central office is that many faculty and departments may come to view assessment as the singular responsibility of that office, and not something that they need to be involved in. This may be overcome by using the central office as a resource that supports, encourages, and facilitates departmental or programmatic assessment while clearly remaining "hands-off" from routine assessment activities—encouraging buy-in to institution-wide assessment activities and disseminating assessment results. Those with the most knowledge of the activity to be assessed (e.g. departmental faculty) should be the ones designing, implementing, and analyzing the assessment activities and results.

## COMMON THEMES AND CONCERNS IN BEGINNING ASSESSMENT

A number of concerns are often raised at the beginning of assessment efforts. One has to do with identifying appropriate and affordable expertise. In academic institutions, despite the presence of a number of disciplines where one might expect to find assessment or evaluation expertise, there are often few if any individuals who have particular expertise to design, lead and manage curricular assessments. In some institutions such expertise may be found, but the few individuals with expertise are requested by everyone and are unable to meet the many needs of all university interests (and these individuals' scholarly interests may lie in other areas).

A second concern relates to conceptualizing assessment—What is to be assessed? When? For whom and for what purposes? The core questions previously identified can help to answer these questions and frame the assessment project, but it may take considerable discussion to reach agreement on framing the assessment plan. Once the assessment is conceptualized, the next concern often encountered has to do with implementation—who is responsible, what resources do they have, what leverage do they have for people to participate in assessment activities and cooperate in responding to data needs in a timely manner.

Yet another concern relates to selection of assessment methods. If plans and needs are clearly set out and agreed upon, there may be greater agreement upon methods—but many experiences in the academic setting suggest that each participant may feel that he or she is the expert who should dictate the method (and therefore resist other methods). One of the results of this methods debate is often the ongoing qualitative vs. quantitative discussion—leading to questions of appropriateness, validity of results, generalizability, and other challenges. These questions then lead to discussions of rigor, specification of methodological needs, and ultimately to design issues which may go beyond the resources available to support the assessment work.

The final concern encountered frequently rests with the uses of assessment findings. Once again, these concerns may be avoided if there is discussion and agreement from early in the process on what will be done with the data. Perceptions of a "closed" process or one that may be intended to result in program closure or termination of faculty/staff positions will compromise the assessment process. These may be exacerbated by uncertainty about the uses of the data; thus an open process with clear intentions of use will assist greatly in facilitating the assessment activities.

## RESISTANCE TO ASSESSMENT

The best designed plan with the most open process may still be met with resistance. The threat of findings—and in particular what may be done with those findings—may be real or perceived. If outside experts are brought in (either to augment or to supplement internal experts), these outsiders may be intimidating—just as in any other external review or site visit where individuals fear airing their "dirty laundry" in public. Skeptics may question the rigor of the assessment plan and its methods, and may not be willing to accept that com-

promises in the "pure" scientific method are sometimes necessary to meet deadlines imposed by the academic calendar (such as courses defined by an 11-week quarter system). There are issues of training to develop internal capacity to conduct and manage the various components of the assessment, as well as around issues of supervision, data collection, confidentiality, and data management. Finally, resistance arises when the environment is politically charged and there is skepticism about the political motivation for a new interest in assessment. Of particular concern may be a perception that there is competition for resources and the assessment initiative will provide the data to resolve who gets access to certain resources or privileges in future.

While each situation is unique, there are some generally agreed upon responses that may help to overcome this resistance. Agreement upon the purposes of the assessment, public sharing of these purposes, and adherence to the purposes and scope of the assessment will help to establish the authenticity and sincerity of the assessment effort. Energy should be invested by the leaders of the assessment initiative to build buy-in for the value of assessment. Roles and tasks should be clearly defined early in the process, and leaders should implement mechanisms for regular reporting, sharing of findings, updates, and airing of concerns.

## ASSESSMENT AS AN IMPROVEMENT STRATEGY

Assessment can be viewed as a strategy for improvement—an integrated set of activities designed to identify strengths and areas for improvement, and to provide the evidence that will serve as the basis for future program planning and enhancements. Assessment becomes most valuable only when viewed as a value-added routine activity and not just a burdensome add-on or "busywork".

This approach to assessment builds upon the "Model for Improvement" (Langley, Nolan, et al., 1998) which has been used widely throughout various industries, including higher education and health care. The model consists of three basic elements that form the basis for initiating assessment:

- "What are we trying to accomplish?" The statement of aims clarifies the purpose of the assessment.

- "How will we know that a change is an improvement?" This clarifies current knowledge and identifies the new knowledge gained when the assessment is completed.

- "What changes can we try that will result in improvement?" This helps to define what activities might be tried as initial improvement activities using the new knowledge.

In applications of this model in education, the following questions are useful to frame the assessment process:

- How is learning conducted (for example, service learning or learning grounded in community-university partnerships)?

- How does this pedagogical method become part of the curriculum—how is it introduced, how is it developed, how is it integrated?

- How can this educational method be improved?

- How do individuals using this method know that a change is an improvement (i.e., what comparisons can be made using pre- and post- data)?

In thinking of assessment as an improvement effort, one can delineate issues that otherwise might not be obvious, describe strategies that could be replicated in future, highlight areas where further work is needed, celebrate successes (which might otherwise go unrecognized), and focus thinking which otherwise might not be focused. The results also provide the basis for shared learning with others—sharing lessons learned, and transmitting knowledge to facilitate others' learning. This sharing might be done through internal communications within the organization, or through broader external dissemination via presentations at professional meetings, publications in professional literature, and postings on websites. In short, people experienced in assessment can help others—as we all would like to be helped (or would like to have been helped) by experts so as to avoid making the same mistakes and to accelerate the process through others' key learning.

## WHAT IS THE IMPACT OF ASSESSMENT EFFORTS?

Assessment efforts result in many benefits; for example, strengths in curriculum may be identified, validating existing knowledge and providing data to support continuation of these curricular activities. Similarly, deficiencies may be identified, providing evidence and jus-

tification for making changes—in individual courses, by adding/deleting courses, or by reconfiguring curriculum requirements or sequencing. Assessment may also be helpful in identifying areas where faculty resources might be reallocated, and where faculty may be recognized for excellence or assisted to remedy deficiencies. Institutional assessment is vital in order to consider broader issues of resources allocation (human, fiscal, physical, information, technological and other resources), to inform public relations and marketing strategies, and to consider possible changes or realignments in organizational relationships and strategies. Some useful descriptions of experience with assessment at institutions are provided by Palomba (1997) and Williford (1997).

One of the key factors in assessment, as in any other evaluation or improvement effort, is the obvious use of the results. Assessment is often resisted because of a lack of understanding of the motivation for assessment, the intended purposes and outcomes, and the perception that the results will not be shared or used. High visibility of assessment initiatives must be accompanied by high visibility of serious consideration of the results and evidence of use by decision-makers. Assessment results may inform decision-makers not only about curricular issues, but also about research and scholarly activity, public service, community image, and other key issues.

## WHAT ARE SOME PRACTICAL APPROACHES TO ASSESSMENT?

Over the past five years a multi-constituency approach to assessment has been developed, initially for use in the assessment of service-learning and now being used in broader applications of a range of community-based learning. This approach initially was developed at Portland State University as part of an assessment of the general education program (Driscoll, Holland, et al., 1996), and was designed to explicitly assess the impact of service learning on students, faculty, the institution, and the community. The model was further developed for assessment of the impact of service learning in health professions education for the Health Professions Schools in Service to the Nation (HPSISN) program (Gelmon, Holland, and Shinnamon, 1998; Gelmon, Holland, Shinnamon, and Morris, 1998; Gelmon, Holland, Seifer, et al., 1998.). This evaluation added a fifth component of community partnerships as a focus for assessment. In both of these cases the goal of the assessment was to learn about the implementation of service learning and its differential impact on various constituencies.

Subsequently the model has been applied in other assessments of the impact of learning in the community. Two examples are: 1) the assessment of the Community-Based Quality Improvement in Education for the Health Professions (CBQIE-HP) program (Gelmon and Barnett, 1998; Gelmon, White, Carlson, and Norman, 2000), where interdisciplinary teams of health professions students worked on specific community health improvement projects; and 2) the evaluation of the Portland Tri-County Healthy Communities Initiative (Gelmon, McBride, Hill, et al., 1999), a community development approach to build community collaborations that address specific community health problems. Each of these projects involved students, faculty and community partners working on community health improvement problems as part of academic course-based work. These various projects will be illustrated throughout this discussion as examples of assessment applications.

The methodology for all of these assessments was based on the development of a conceptual matrix which was derived from project goals, and which framed the assessment plan, guided the development of assessment instruments, and structured the data analysis and reporting. This approach, sometimes referred to as the "Concept-Indicator Method" approach (Gelmon, Holland, and Shinnamon, 1998), involves four primary questions:

- What do we want to know? This helps the evaluator to articulate the aim of the assessment, based upon the project goals.

- What will we look for? This leads the evaluator to identify core concepts that are derived from the project goals and the aim of the assessment.

- What will we measure? For each core concept, relevant measurable indicators are specified which will enable the evaluator to measure change or status.

- How will we gather the evidence to demonstrate what we want to know? At this stage, the evaluator identifies or develops appropriate methods and tools by which to collect the information for each indicator, and identifies sources of the data.

An example of the matrix from the HPSISN service-learning program (Gelmon, Holland, and Shinnamon, 1998) is shown in Table 2 for the research question "How has the HPSISN program affected university-community partnerships with respect to service learning in health professions education?" While there is a direct linear relationship between each concept and the related indicators, there is no such linear relationship to the methods and sources. In reality some methods

**Table 2: Sample Matrix for University-Community Partnerships**

| What will we look for? (concepts) | What will we measure? (indicators) | How will it be measured? (methods) | Who will provide the information? (sources) |
|---|---|---|---|
| Communication between partners and the university | • Nature of relationship<br>• Form and patterns of community involvement in university activities<br>• Kinds of communication | • Surveys<br>• Interviews<br>• Focus groups<br>• Direct observation | • Community partners<br>• Faculty<br>• Students<br>• Institutional administrators |
| Nature of partnership | • Kind of activities conducted<br>• Frequency<br>• Method of initiation | • Interviews<br>• Activity logs<br>• Syllabus review<br>• Faculty journals | • Community partners<br>• Faculty<br>• Institutional administrators |

## Table 3: Sample Matrix for Community Development Initiatives

| What will we look for? (concepts) | What will we measure? (indicators) | How will it be measured? (methods) | Who will provide the information? (sources) |
|---|---|---|---|
| Building community health improvement capacity | • Community development training<br>• Problem-solving skill development<br>• Management within fixed resources<br>• Adaptability | • Community survey<br>• Task force survey<br>• Document review<br>• Interviews<br>• Focus groups<br>• Direct observation | • Community database<br>• Governing Council<br>• Task force members<br>• Healthy Communities staff<br>• Health systems leadership group |
| Collaboration | • Community representation on Governing Council<br>• Community representation on task forces<br>• Satisfaction with partnerships<br>• Relationship to health systems<br>• Participation in related initiatives | • Observations<br>• Focus groups<br>• Task force survey<br>• Document review<br>• Interviews | • Governing Council<br>• Health systems leadership group<br>• Task force members<br>• Community database |

would be used for each indicator, and some sources would provide data for each method, but not all sources would be involved in each method and not all methods would address each indicator.

This illustration highlights two of the key concepts related to impact on university-community partnerships. Identification of these concepts provided specific direction to the evaluation team and to the participating sites in focusing on the elements of the partnerships that were most relevant to the assessment.

The evaluation of the Portland Tri-County Healthy Communities Initiative was part of a national evaluation of the W.K. Kellogg-funded "Community Care Network" demonstration project (Gelmon, McBride, Hill, et al., 1999). Two of the project strategies related to facilitating health sector participation in collaborative community development activities, and serving as a regional resource and clearinghouse for information. As a result, different kinds of key concepts were identified for this evaluation, as compared to those presented for the HPSISN project. Table 3 illustrates some of this project's methodology.

In this case, the emphasis of the project was not on service learning but rather on the role of the Healthy Communities initiative in achieving various community development goals. The service-learning component involved students participating in various parts of the initiative as part of course-based learning; thus this matrix does not emphasize the role of students and faculty, but rather places more emphasis on the community partners in the various activities (of which the students' home university was one).

Another example is offered from the CBQIE-HP program where interdisciplinary teams of health professions students worked on specific community health improvement projects (Gelmon and Barnett, 1998; Gelmon, White, Carlson, and Norman, 2000). In this project one area of interest was assessing whether the integration of an improvement philosophy into community-based learning projects accelerated health improvement and accentuated benefits. The question of benefits was considered from the perspective of benefits to students, faculty, the academic institution, and the community, as well as the benefits of the partnership. Table 4 illustrates some of the methodology related to benefits to students.

This illustration provides information that may be more readily applicable to assessment of service-learning programs in other institutions, since it places con-

**Table 4: Sample Matrix for Benefits to Students**

| What will we look for? (concepts) | What will we measure? (indicators) | How will it be measured? (methods) | Who will provide the information? (sources) |
|---|---|---|---|
| Commitment to community service | • Attitude toward involvement<br>• Level of participation over time<br>• Plans for future service | • Survey<br>• Focus group<br>• Interviews<br>• Reflective journal | • Students<br>• Community partners<br>• Faculty<br>• Community-based learning coordinator |
| Personal and professional development | • Changes in awareness of personal skills and capacities<br>• Communication skills<br>• Self-confidence<br>• Leadership activities | • Interviews<br>• Observations<br>• Focus groups<br>• Reflective journal | • Students<br>• Faculty<br>• Community-based learning coordinator |

siderable emphasis on benefits to students. Similarly, the Portland State University application considered impact on students, but also assessed impact on faculty (among other constituencies). A portion of the Portland State matrix is shown in Table 5 (Driscoll, Gelmon, et al., 1998).

There are many other descriptions in the literature of programmatic, departmental, and institutional approaches to assessment. The reader is encouraged to look further for other illustrations that may have most relevance to her/his own assessment needs, and to draw upon the experiences in the literature to shape an assessment plan most relevant to individual needs.

## COMPLETING THE ASSESSMENT CYCLE

This article has focused on the methods used to conceptualize an assessment plan, and offered illustrations of a variety of projects addressing service-learning and civic engagement. Once data is collected, assessment leaders must be prepared to engage in extensive data analysis, synthesis, discussion, and report-writing. Methods should be selected based on the kind of data that will be gathered, as well as issues such as ease of data collection, ease of data analysis, and time and costs involved in both collection and analysis. However, consideration must also be given to the richness of the data that can be derived from various methods. Methods such as interviews, focus groups, observations, and reflective journals will provide extensive and detailed information, which will necessitate a major time commitment to transcribe and analyze. In contrast, surveys will provide less detail and individual stories, but are relatively easy, inexpensive, and time-efficient to administer and to analyze. Assessment leaders who do not have familiarity and expertise with various assessment methods should ensure they engage an expert to advise during instrument development as well as data analysis.

A final step in the process is to report the results. A fairly typical method is to write an assessment report that describes project goals, what was done, what was measured, and the results. The reporting of results should be guided explicitly by the matrix (using the concepts as major headings and the indicators as subheadings); this will facilitate synthesis of findings and presentation in a report. It is also common for assessment results to form the basis for scholarly presentations and publications. Care should be given to ensuring that no confidential information is disclosed, and that the institution has given permission for its assessment findings to be released in a public forum.

Consideration should also be given to alternative forms of reporting to ensure wider and more rapid dissemination. For example, summaries of key findings could be presented in poster format and displayed by a campus cafeteria or in the library. Selected results and rich

**Table 5: Sample Matrix for Impact on Faculty**

| What will we look for? (concepts) | What will we measure? (indicators) | How will it be measured? (methods) | Who will provide the information? (sources) |
|---|---|---|---|
| Awareness of community | • Definition of community<br>• Specific definition of community site<br>• Ability to describe conditions, needs, assets of community partner<br>• Knowledge of strengths and resources of community partner | • Interviews<br>• Reflective journal<br>• Classroom observation | • Faculty<br>• Students<br>• Community partners<br>• Community-based learning coordinator (or community-university partnerships coordinator) |
| Scholarship emphasis | • Connection of community-based learning to scholarly agenda<br>• Evidence of community-based scholarship to publications, presentations, grants | • Interviews<br>• Surveys<br>• Portfolio review<br>• Curriculum vitae review<br>• Reflective journal<br>• Artifacts (papers, grant proposals, presentations) | • Faculty<br>• Community-based learning coordinator<br>• Institutional research office<br>• University administrators |

stories from participants could be integrated into a university website. Alternative forms of reporting can also be used. For example, in the Healthy Communities initiative a detailed evaluation report was prepared for the local board and for the national demonstration program; this was then edited considerably and reformatted into a brief "Report to the Community" in a community-friendly format with photographs. This report has been used widely by the community agency for promotional purposes and as documentation in grant proposals.

Assessment provides a valuable mechanism for communicating the value of our work. In particular, when seeking to document the effect of a pedagogy such as service-learning it is vital to be able to provide the evidence that the program is making a difference. Good assessment requires collaboration and a commitment to invest time and energy in the work. The very nature of assessment necessitates a long-term perspective, as the assessment effort is never complete. Nonetheless, continuous investment in assessment will provide the necessary information to continue to respond to the needs and assets of those involved in higher education

and to seek continued improvement of the programs and services we provide.

## REFERENCES

Barr, R. B. and J. Tagg. (1995). From teaching to learning: A new paradigm for undergraduate education. *Change* 27 (November/December): 13–25.

Campus Compact. (1999). *Presidents' Fourth of July Declaration on the Civic Responsibility of Higher Education*. Providence, RI: Campus Compact.

Driscoll, A., B. Holland, S. Gelmon, and S. Kerrigan. (1996). An assessment model for service learning: Comprehensive case studies of impact on faculty, students, community and institution. *Michigan Journal of Community Service Learning* 3 (Fall): 66–71.

Driscoll, A., S. B. Gelmon, B. A. Holland, S. Kerrigan, M.J. Longley, and A. Spring. (1998). *Assessing the impact of service learning: A workbook of strategies and methods*. Portland: Center for Academic Excellence, Portland State University.

Gelmon, S. B. and L. Barnett, with the CBQIE-HP Technical Assistant Team. (1998). *Community-based quality* improvement in education for the health professions: Evaluation report, 1997–1998. Portland: Portland State University.

Gelmon, S. B., B. A. Holland and A. F. Shinnamon. (1998). Health professions schools in service to the nation: 1996–1998 final evaluation report. San Francisco: Community-Campus Partnerships for Health, UCSF Center for the Health Professions. [available from http://futurehealth.ucsf.edu/ccph.htm]

Gelmon, S. B., B. A. Holland, A. F. Shinnamon and B. A. Morris. (1998). Community-based education and service: The HPSISN experience. Journal of Interprofessional Care 12 (#3): 257–272.

Gelmon, S.B., B. A. Holland, S. D. Seifer, A. F. Shnnamon, and K. Connors. (1998). Community-university partnerships for mutual learning. Michigan Journal of Community Service Learning 5 (Fall): 97–107.

Gelmon, S. B., L. G. McBride, S. Hill, L. Chester, and J. Guernsey. (1998). Evaluation of the Portland Health Communities Initiative 1996–1998. Portland: Healthy Communities and Portland State University.

Gelmon, S. B., A. W. White, L. Carlson, and L. Norman. (2000). Making organizational change to achieve improvement and interprofessional learning: Perspectives from health professions educators. Journal of Interprofessional Care 14 (No. 2): 131–146.

Gray, P. J. (1997). Viewing assessment as an innovation: Leadership and the change process. In P. J. Gray and T. W. Banta, eds. The campus-level impact of assessment: progress, problems, and possibilities. New Directions for Higher Education 100 (Winter): 5–15. San Francisco: Jossey-Bass Inc.

Holland, B.A., A. Driscoll, S.B. Gelmon, and S. Kerrigan. (1996). An assessment model for service learning: Comprehensive case studies of impact on faculty, students, community and institution. Paper presented at the American Association of Higher Education Annual Conference, Chicago, IL.

Holland, B. A. and S.B. Gelmon. (1998). The state of the "engaged campus": What have we learned about building and sustaining university-community partnerships? AAHE Bulletin 51 (October): 3–6.

Kellogg Commission on the Future of State and Land-Grant Institutions. (1999). Returning to our roots: The engaged institution. Washington, D.C.: National Association of State Universities and Land-Grant Colleges.

Langley, G. J., K. M. Nolan, T. W. Nolan, C. L. Norman, and L. P. Provost. (1996). The improvement guide. San Francisco: Jossey-Bass Inc.

Magruder, J., M. A. McManis, and C. C. Young. (1997). The right idea at the right time: Development of a transformational assessment culture. In P. J. Gray and T. W. Banta, eds. The campus-level impact of assessment: progress, problems, and possibilities. New Directions for Higher Education 100 (Winter): 17–29. San Francisco: Jossey-Bass Inc.

Palomba, C. A. (1997). Assessment at Ball State University. In P. J. Gray and T. W. Banta, eds. The campus-level impact of assessment: progress, problems, and possibilities. New Directions for Higher Education 100 (Winter): 31–45. San Francisco: Jossey-Bass Inc.

Shinnamon, A. F., S. B. Gelmon, and B. A. Holland. (1999). Methods and strategies for assessing service learning in the health professions. San Francisco: Community-Campus Partnerships for Health, UCSF Center for the Health Professions. [available from http://futurehealth.ucsf.edu/ccph.htm]

Williford, A. M.. (1997). Ohio University's multidimensional institutional impact and assessment Plan. In P. J. Gray and T. W. Banta, eds. The campus-level impact of assessment: progress, problems, and possibilities. New Directions for Higher Education 100 (Winter): 47–57. San Francisco: Jossey-Bass Inc.

# Assessment:
## Recommended Reading

## BOOKS & CHAPTERS

Eyler, J., & Giles, D. (1999). *Where's the learning in service-learning?* San Francisco: Jossey-Bass.

Gelmon, S., Holland, B., & Shinnamon, A. (1998). *Health professions schools in service to the nation: Final evaluation report.* San Francisco: Community-Campus Partnerships for Health.

Gelmon, S., et al. (2001). *Assessing service-learning and civic engagement: Principles and techniques.* Providence, RI: Campus Compact.

Oates, K. & Leavitt, L.H. (2003). *Service-learning and learning communities: Tools for integration and assessment.* Washington, DC: Association of American Colleges and Universities.

Waterman, A.S. (Ed.). (1997). *Service-learning: Applications from the research.* Mahwah, NJ: Lawrence Erlbaum Associates, 1997.

## ARTICLES & REPORTS

Alliance for Service Learning. (1993). Standards of quality for school-based service-learning. *Equity & Excellence, 26* (2), 71–73.

Batchelder, T.H. & Root, S. (1994). Effects of an undergraduate program to integrate academic learning and service: Cognitive, prosocial cognitive and identity outcomes. *Journal of Adolescence, 17,* 341–356.

Blumenthal, D.S., Jones, A., & McNeal, M. (2001). Evaluating a community-based multiprofessional course in community health. *Education for Health: Change in Learning and Practice, 14* (2), 251–6.

Bringle, R. & Hatcher, J.A. (2000). Institutionalization of service-learning in higher education. *The Journal of Higher Education, 71* (3), 273–90.

Driscoll, A., Holland, B., Gelmon, S., Kerrigan, S. (1996). An assessment model for service-learning: Comprehensive case studies of impact on faculty, students, community, and institutions. *Michigan Journal of Community Service Learning, 5,* 66–71.

Gelmon, S.B. (2000). Challenges in assessing service-learning. *Michigan Journal of Community Service Learning, 7,* 84–90.

Gelmon, S.B. (2000). How do we know our work makes a difference? Assessment strategies for service-learning and civic engagement. *Metropolitan Universities: An International Forum, 11* (2), 28–39.

Gray, M., et al. (2000). Assessing service-learning. *Change, 32* (2), 30–40.

Greene, D. & Diehm, G. (1995). Educational and service outcomes of a service integration effort. *Michigan Journal of Community Service Learning, 2,* 54–62.

Grzelkowski, K. (1986). Merging the theoretical and the practical: Community action research as a process and as a goal. *Teaching Sociology, 14,* 110–118.

Knapp, M. (1995). How shall we study comprehensive, collaborative services for children and families? *Educational Researcher, 24,* 5–16.

Long, A.B., et al. (2001). Organizing, managing, and evaluating service-learning projects. *Educational Gerontology, 27* (1), 19–22.

Markus, G.B., Howard, J. & King, D. (1993). Integrating community service and classroom instruction enhances learning: Results from an experiment. *Educational Evaluation and Policy Analysis, 15* (4), 410–419.

Olney C. & Grande S. (1995). Validation of a scale to measure development of social responsibility. *Michigan Journal of Community Service Learning, 2,* 43–53.

Payne, C.A. (2000). Changes in involvement preferences as measured by the community service involvement preference inventory. *Michigan Journal of Community Service Learning, 7,* 41–45.

Shiarella, A.H. & McCarthy, A.M. (2000). Development and construct validity of scores on the community service attitudes scale. *Educational and Psychological Measurement, 60* (2), 286–300.

Subramony, M. (2000). "The Relationship Between Performance Feedback and Service Learning." *Michigan Journal of Community Service Learning,* 7, 65–75.

## SECTION 12

# Academic Culture

### QUESTIONS FOR REFLECTION AND PLANNING

How is service defined within the context of your institution's academic culture?

To what degree does your institution acknowledge service as a legitimate form of scholarship?

How might your service-learning courses reflect service as scholarship?

Where is service located at your institution? Co-curricular? Curricular? Both?

To whom on your campus would you turn for assistance in developing a community partnership?

# The Scholarship of Engagement

by Ernest L. Boyer

AMERICAN HIGHER EDUCATION IS, as Derek Bok once poetically described it, "a many-splendored creation." We have built in this country a truly remarkable network of research universities, regional campuses, liberal arts and community colleges, which have become, during the last half-century, the envy of the world.

But it's also true that after years of explosive growth, America's colleges and universities are now suffering from a decline in public confidence and a nagging feeling that they are no longer at the vital center of the nation's work. Today, the campuses in this country are not being called upon to win a global war, or to build Quonset huts for returning GIs. They're not trying to beat the Soviets to the moon or to help implement the Great Society programs. It seems to me that for the first time in nearly half a century, institutions of higher learning are not collectively caught up in some urgent national endeavor.

Still, our outstanding universities and colleges remain, in my opinion, one of the greatest hopes for intellectual and civic progress in this country. I am convinced that for this hope to be fulfilled, the academy must become a more vigorous partner in the search for answers to our most pressing social, civic, economic, and moral problems, and must reaffirm its historic commitment to what I call the scholarship of engagement.

The truth is that for more than 350 years, higher learning and the larger purposes of American society have been inextricably interlocked. The goal of the colonial college was to prepare civic and religious leaders, a vision succinctly captured by John Eliot, who wrote in 1636: "If we nourish not learning, both church and commonwealth will sink." Following the revolution, the great patriot Dr. Benjamin Rush declared in 1798 that the nation's colleges would be "nurseries of wise and good men, to adapt our modes of teaching to the peculiar form of our government." In 1824, Rensselaer Polytechnic Institute was founded in Troy, New York, and RPI was, according to historian Frederick Rudolph, a constant reminder that America needed railroad builders, bridge builders, builders of all kinds. During the dark days of the Civil War, President Abraham Lincoln signed the historic Land Grant Act, which linked higher learning to the nation's agricultural, technological, and industrial revolutions. And when social critic Lincoln Steffens visited Madison in 1909, he observed, "In Wisconsin, the university is as close to the intelligent farmer as his pig-pen or his tool-house."

At the beginning of this century, David Starr Jordan, president of that brash new institution on the West Coast, Stanford, declared that the entire university movement in this country "is toward reality and practicality." Harvard's president, Charles Eliot, who was completing nearly forty years of tenure, said America's universities are filled with the democratic spirit of "serviceableness." And in 1896, Woodrow Wilson, then a 40-year-old Princeton University professor, insisted that the spirit of service will give a college a place in the public annals of the nation. "We dare not," he said, "keep aloof and closet ourselves while a nation comes to its maturity."

Frankly, I find it quite remarkable that just one hundred years ago, the words "practicality" and "reality" and "serviceability" were used by the nation's most distinguished academic leaders to describe the mission of higher learning which was, to put it simply, the scholarship of engagement. During my own lifetime, Vannevar Bush of MIT formally declared, while in Washington serving two presidents, that universities which helped win the war could also win the peace, a statement which led to the greatest federally funded research effort the world has ever known. I find it fascinating to recall that Bush cited radar and penicillin to illustrate how science could be of practical service to the nation. The goals in the creation of the National Science Foundation which led to the Department of Defense and the National Institutes of Health were not abstract. The goals were rooted in practical reality and aimed toward useful ends.

In the 1940s, the GI Bill brought eight million veterans back to campus, which sparked in this country a revolution of rising expectations. May I whisper that professors were not at the forefront urging the GI Bill. This initiative came from Congress. Many academics, in fact, questioned the wisdom of inviting GIs to campus. After all, these men hadn't passed the SAT, they'd simply gone off to war, and what did they know, except survival? The story gets even grimmer. I read some years ago that the dean of admissions at one of the well-known institutions in the country opposed the GIs because, he argued, they would be married, many of them; they would bring baby carriages to campus, and even contaminate the young undergraduates with bad ideas at that pristine institution. I think he knew little about GIs, and even less about the undergraduates at his own college.

But, putting that resistance aside, the point is largely made that the universities joined in an absolutely spectacular experiment, in a cultural commitment to rising expectations, and what was for the GIs a privilege became, for their children and grandchildren, an absolute right. And there's no turning back.

Almost coincidentally, Secretary of State George C. Marshall, at a commencement exercise at Harvard in 1947, announced a plan for European recovery, and the Marshall Plan sent scholars all around the world to promote social and economic progress. Ten years later, when the Soviets sent Sputnik rocketing into orbit, the nation's colleges and universities were called upon once again, this time to design better curricula for the nation's schools and to offer summer institutes for teachers.

And one still stumbles onto the inspiration of that time. I remember as commissioner, having lunch in Washington. We thought we were talking privately about the federal program to help teachers under the

Eisenhower administration, only to find we were being overheard at the next table, which you should always assume in Washington. And the man stopped by and said, "I just wanted to tell you that I was one of the NDA fellows at that time, and I've never had a better experience in my life." And the inspiration of the teachers who came back from the summer institutes touched teachers all across the country. The federal government and higher education had joined with schools toward the renewal of public education.

Then in the 1960s, almost every college and university in this country launched affirmative-action programs to recruit historically bypassed students and to promote, belatedly, human justice.

I've just dashed through three and half centuries, more or less. What I failed to mention were the times when universities challenged the established order, when they acted appropriately both as conscience and social critic, and that, too, was in service to the nation. And there were other times when campuses were on the fringes of larger national endeavors, standing on the sidelines, failing to take advantage of opportunities that emerged.

Still, I am left with two inescapable conclusions. First, it seems absolutely clear that this nation has throughout the years gained enormously from its vital network of higher learning institutions. And, at the same time, it's also quite apparent that the confidence of the nation's campuses themselves has grown during those times when academics were called upon to serve a larger purpose: to participate in the building of a more just society and to make the nation more civil and secure.

This leads me, then, to say a word about the partnership today. To what extent has higher learning in the nation continued this collaboration, this commitment to the common good?

I would suggest that in recent years, the work of individual scholars, as researchers, has continued to be highly prized, and that also, in recent years, teaching has increasingly become more highly regarded, which of course is great cause for celebration. But I believe it's also true that at far too many institutions of higher learning, the historic commitment to the "scholarship of engagement" has dramatically declined.

Almost every college catalog in this country still lists teaching, research, and service as the priorities of the professoriate; yet, at tenure and promotion time, the harsh truth is that service is hardly mentioned. And even more disturbing, faculty who do spend time with so-called applied projects frequently jeopardize their careers.

Russell Jacoby, in a fascinating book titled *The Last Intellectuals*, observes that the influence of American academics has declined precisely because being an intellectual has come to mean being in the university and holding a faculty appointment, preferably a tenured one, of writing in a certain style understood only by one's peers, of conforming to an academic rewards system that encourages disengagement and even penalizes professors whose work becomes useful to nonacademics or popularized, as we like to say. Intellectual life, Jacoby said, has moved from the coffee shop to the cafeteria, with academics participating less vigorously in the broader public discourse.

But, what I find most disturbing—as almost the mirror image of that description—is a growing feeling in this country that higher education is, in fact, part of the problem rather than the solution. Going still further, that it's become a private benefit, not a public good. Increasingly, the campus is being viewed as a place where students get credentialed and faculty get tenured, while the overall work of the academy does not seem particularly relevant to the nation's most pressing civic, social, economic, and moral problems. Indeed, it follows that if the students are the beneficiaries and get credentialed, then let students pay the bill. And I've been almost startled to see that, when the gap increases in the budget, it's the student, and the student fees, that are turned to automatically after all—it's a private benefit, and let the consumer, as we like to say, pay the bill.

Not that long ago, it was generally assumed that higher education was an investment in the future of the nation—that the intellect of the nation was something too valuable to lose, and that we needed to invest in the future through the knowledge industry.

I often think about the time when I moved, almost overnight, from an academic post in Albany, New York, to a government post in Washington, D.C. These were two completely separate worlds. At the university, looking back, I recall rarely having serious dialogues with "outsiders"—artists, or "popular" authors, or other intellectuals beyond the campus. And yet, I was fascinated by Derek Bok's observation, on leaving his tenured post at Harvard, that the most consequential shifts in public policy in recent years have come not from academics, but from such works as Rachel Carson's *Silent Spring*, Ralph Nader's *Unsafe at Any Speed*, Michael Harrington's *The Other America*, and Betty Friedan's *The Feminine Mystique*—books which truly place the environmental, industrial, economic, and gender issues squarely in a social context.

I teach occasionally at the Woodrow Wilson School, in the public policy center, and I open the first class by asking, "How is public policy shaped in America? Where does it originate? How does the debate get going?" And almost always the undergraduates will start with the president, then Congress, or they might think of the state legislature. Then I ask them, has anyone ever heard of Rachel Carson, or Michael Harrington, and a kind of bewildered look appears. And yet the truth is that out of the seminal insights of such intellectuals public discourse begins, and very often Congress is the last, not the first, to act, trying to catch up with the shifting culture. So it is with the academy. One wonders why discourse between faculty and intellectuals working without campus affiliation can't take place within the academy itself.

But, on the other hand, I left Albany and went to Washington, and I must say that I found government to be equally—or I'll go one step further—even more startlingly detached. In Washington, we did consult with lawyers and political pressure groups, driven usually by legislative mandates, and certainly by White House urges. But rarely were academics invited in to help put our policy decisions in historical, or social, or ethical perspective. And looking back, I recall literally hundreds of hours when we talked about the procedural aspects of our work and the legal implications, but I do not recall one occasion when someone asked, "Should we be doing this in the first place?," a question which I suspect could have been asked only by a detached participant with both courage and perspective.

Recently, I've become impressed by just how much this problem, which I would describe as impoverished cultural discourse, extends beyond government to mass communication where, with the exceptions of "MacNeil/Lehrer News Hour" and "Bill Moyer's Journal," the nation's most pressing social, economic, and civic issues are endlessly discussed primarily by politicians and self-proclaimed pundits, while university scholars rarely are invited to join the conversation.

Abundant evidence shows that both the civic and academic health of any culture is vitally enriched as scholars and practitioners speak and listen carefully to each other. In a brilliant study of creative communities throughout history, Princeton University sociologist Carl Schorske, a man I greatly admire, describes the Basel, Switzerland, of the nineteenth century as a truly vibrant place where civic and university life were inseparably intertwined. Schorske states that the primary function of the university in Basel was to foster what he called "civic culture," while the city of Basel assumed that one of its basic obligations was the advancement of learning. The university was engaged in civic advancement, and the city was engaged in intellectual advancement, and the two were joined. And I read recently that one of the most influential commentators didn't achieve his fame from published articles, but from lectures he gave in the Basel open forum.

I recognize, of course, that "town" is not "gown." The university must vigorously protect its political and intellectual independence. Still, one does wonder what would happen if the university would extend itself more productively into the marketplace of ideas. I find it fascinating, for example, that the provocative PBS program "Washington Week in Review" invites us to consider current events from the perspective of four or five distinguished journalists, who, during the rest of the week, tend to talk only to themselves. And I've wondered occasionally what "The Week in Review" would sound like if a historian, an astronomer, an economist, an artist, a theologian, and perhaps a physician, for example, were asked to comment. Would we be listening and thinking about the same week, or would there be a different profile and perspective? How many different weeks were there that week? And who is interpreting them for America?

What are we to do about all of this? As a first step, coming back to the academy itself, I'm convinced that the university has an obligation to broaden the scope of scholarship. In a recent Carnegie Foundation report titled *Scholarship Reconsidered,* we propose a new paradigm of scholarship, one that assigns to the professoriate four essential, interlocking functions. We propose, first, the scholarship of discovery, insisting that universities, through research, simply must continue to push back the frontiers of human knowledge. No one, it seems to me, can even consider that issue contestable. And we argue, in our report, against shifting research inordinately to government institutes, or even to the laboratories of corporations that could directly or indirectly diminish the free flow of ideas.

But, while research is essential, we argue that it is not sufficient, and to avoid pedantry, we propose a second priority called the scholarship of integration. There is, we say, an urgent need to place discoveries in a larger context and create more interdisciplinary conversations in what Michael Polanyi of the University of Chicago has called the "overlapping [academic] neighborhoods," or in the new hyphenated disciplines, in which the energies of several different disciplines tend enthusiastically to converge. In fact, as Clifford Geertz of the Institute for Advanced Study has argued, we need a new formulation, a new paradigm of knowledge, since the new questions don't fit the old categories.

Speaking of bringing the disciplines together, several years ago, when physicist Victor Weisskopf was asked what gives him hope in troubled times, he replied, "Mozart and quantum mechanics." But where in our fragmented intellectual world do academics make connections such as these? We assume they live in separate worlds, yet they may be searching for the same interesting patterns and relationships, and finding solutions both intellectually compelling and aesthetic. I remember during the days of the lift-offs at Cape Kennedy, I was always fascinated when the rockets lifted successfully into orbit. The engineers wouldn't say: "Well, our formulas worked again." They would say, almost in unison, the word "beautiful." And I always found it fascinating that they chose an aesthetic term to describe a technological achievement. But where do the two begin and end?

Beyond the scholarship of discovering knowledge and integrating knowledge, we propose in our report a third priority, the scholarship of sharing knowledge. Scholarship, we say, is a communal act. You never get tenured for research alone. You get tenured for research and publication, which means you have to teach somebody what you've learned. And academics must continue to communicate not only with their peers but also with future scholars in the classroom in order to keep the flame of scholarship alive. And yet, the truth is that on many campuses it's much better to prepare a paper and present it to colleagues at the Hyatt in Chicago than to present it to the students on campus, who perhaps have more future prospects than one's peers.

Finally, in *Scholarship Reconsidered,* we call not only for the scholarship of discovering knowledge, the scholarship of integrating knowledge to avoid pedantry, and the sharing of knowledge to avoid discontinuity, but also for the application of knowledge, to avoid irrelevance.

And we hurriedly add that when we speak of applying knowledge we do not mean "doing good," although that's important. Academics have their civic functions, which should be honored, but by scholarship of application we mean having professors become what Donald Schön of MIT has called "reflective practitioners," moving from theory to practice, and from practice back to theory, which in fact makes theory, then, more authentic—something we're learning in education and medicine, in law and architecture, and all the rest. And incidentally, by making knowledge useful, we mean everything from building better bridges to building better lives, which involves not only the professional schools but the arts and sciences as well.

Philosophy and religion also are engaged in the usefulness of knowledge, as insights become the interior of one's life. Recently I reread Jacob Bronowski's moving essay on science and human values, which was written after his visit in 1945 to the devastation of Hiroshima. In this provocative document, he suggests that there are no sharp boundaries that can be drawn between knowledge and its uses. And he insists that the convenient labels of pure and applied research simply do not describe the way that most scientists really work. To illustrate his point, Bronowski said that Sir Isaac Newton studied astronomy precisely because navigating the sea was the preoccupation of the society in which he was born. Newton was, to put it simply, an engaged scholar. And Michael Faraday, Bronowski said, sought to link electricity to magnetism because finding a new source of power was the preoccupation of his day. Faraday's scholarship was considered useful. The issue, then, Bronowski concludes, is not whether scholarship will be applied, but whether the work of scholars will be directed toward humane ends.

This reminder that the work of the academy ultimately must be directed toward larger, more humane ends brings me to this conclusion. I'm convinced that in the century ahead, higher education in this country has an urgent obligation to become more vigorously engaged in the issues of our day, just as the land-grant colleges helped farmers and technicians a century ago. And surely one of the most urgent issues we confront, perhaps the social crisis that is the most compelling, is the tragic plight of children.

In his inaugural address, President George Bush declared as the nation's first education goal that by the year 2000, all children in this country will come to school "ready to learn." Yet, we have more children in poverty today than we did five years ago. Today, a shocking percentage of the nation's nineteen million preschoolers are malnourished and educationally impoverished. Several years ago, when we at The Carnegie Foundation surveyed several thousand kindergarten teachers, we learned that thirty-five percent of the children who enrolled in school the year before were, according to the teachers, linguistically, emotionally, or physically deficient. One wonders how this nation can live comfortably with the fact that so many of our children are so impoverished.

These statistics may seem irrelevant in the hallowed halls of the academy or in the greater world of higher learning, yet education is a seamless web. If children do not have a good beginning, if they do not receive the nurture and support they need during the first years of life, it will be difficult, if not impossible, to compensate fully for the failure later on. My wife, a certified midwife, has convinced me that the effort has to be made not only before school, but surely before birth itself, during the time when nutrition becomes inextricably linked to the potential later on.

To start, higher education must conduct more research in child development and health care and nutrition. I do not diminish this role at all. This, too, is in service to the nation. But I wonder if universities also might take the lead in creating children's councils in the communities that surround them. The role of the university would be to help coordinate the work of public and private agencies concerned with children, preparing annually, perhaps, what I've chosen to call a "ready-to-learn" report card—a kind of environmental impact statement on the physical, social, and emotional conditions affecting children—accompanied by a cooperative plan of action that would bring academics and practitioners together. James Agee, one of my favorite twentieth-century American authors, wrote that with every child born, regardless of circumstances, the potential of the human race is born again. And with such a remarkably rich array of intellectual resources, certainly the nation's universities, through research and the scholarship of engagement, can help make it possible for more children to be "ready to learn." Perhaps universities can even help create in this country a public love of children.

As a second challenge, I'm convinced colleges and universities also must become more actively engaged with the nation's schools. We hear a lot of talk these days about how the schools have failed, and surely education must improve, but the longer the debate continues, the more I become convinced that it's not the schools that have failed, it's the partnership that's failed. Today, our nation's schools are being called upon to do what homes and churches and communities have not been able to accomplish. And if they fail anywhere along the line, we condemn them for not meeting our high-minded expectations. Yet, I've concluded that it's simply impossible to have an island of excellence in a sea of community indifference. After going to schools from coast to coast, I've also begun to wonder whether most school critics could survive one week in the classrooms they condemn. While commissioner of education, I visited an urban school with a leaky roof, broken test tubes, Bunsen burners that wouldn't work, text books ten years old, falling plaster, armed guards at the door, and then we wonder why we're not world-class in math and science, or, for that matter, in anything.

Especially troublesome is our lack of support for teachers. In the United States today, teachers spend on average $400 of their own money each year, according to our surveys, to buy essential school supplies. They're expected to teach thirty-one hours every week, with virtually no time for preparation. The average kindergarten class size in this country is twenty-seven, even though research reveals it should be seventeen. And, in one state, the average kindergarten size is forty-one. I've never taught kindergarten or first grade, but I do have several grandchildren, and when I take them to McDonald's or some other fast food spot, I come home a basket case just from keeping mustard off the floor and tracking all the orders that keep changing every thirty seconds. And I'm not even trying to cram them for the SATs. I'm just trying to keep body and soul together. Class size does matter, especially in the early years, and it correlates directly with effective learning.

About a dozen years ago, the late Bart Giomatti invited me to evaluate what was called the Yale-New Haven Teacher's Institute. I was delighted to discover that some of Yale's most distinguished scholars directed summer seminars based on curricula teachers themselves had planned. And, incidentally, teachers in that program were called Yale Fellows. I was startled to discover that they were even given parking spaces on campus, which is about the highest status symbol a university can bestow. I'm suggesting that every college and university should view surrounding schools as partners, giving teaching scholarships to gifted high school students, just as we give athletic scholarships, and offering summer institutes for teachers, who are, I'm convinced, the unsung heroes of the nation.

During my Yale visit, I dropped in on a sixth-grade classroom in New Haven. Thirty children were crowded around the teacher's desk, and I thought it was a physical attack; I almost ran to the central office for help. But then I paused and discovered they weren't there out of anger, but intense enthusiasm. They had just finished reading Charles Dickens' *Oliver Twist*, and they were vigorously debating whether little Oliver could survive in their own neighborhood, speaking of relating the great books and intellectual inquiry to the realities of life. The children concluded that while Oliver had made it in far-off London, he'd never make it in New Haven, a much tougher city. I was watching an inspired teacher at work, relating serious literature to the lives of urban youth today.

This leads me to say a word about higher education in the nation's cities. It's obvious that the problems of urban life are enormously complex; there are no simple solutions. I'm almost embarrassed to mention it as a problem because it is so enormously complex, but we live in cities. They determine the future of this country. Our children live there, too. And I find it ironic that universities which focused with such energy on rural America a century ago have never focused with equal urgency on our cities. Many universities do have projects they sponsor in urban areas such as Detroit, Buffalo, New York, Philadelphia, and Baltimore, just to name a few. But, typically, these so-called model programs limp along, supported with soft money. Especially troublesome is the fact that academics who participate are not professionally rewarded.

Higher education cannot do it all, but Ira Harkavay of the University of Pennsylvania soberly warns that our great universities simply cannot afford to remain islands of affluence, self-importance, and horticultural beauty in seas of squalor, violence, and despair. With their schools of medicine, law, and education and their public policy programs, surely higher education can help put our cities and perhaps even our nation back together.

Here, then, is my conclusion. At one level, the scholarship of engagement means connecting the rich resources of the university to our most pressing social, civic, and ethical problems, to our children, to our schools, to our teachers, and to our cities, just to name the ones I am personally in touch with most frequently.

You could name others. Campuses would be viewed by both students and professors not as isolated islands, but as staging grounds for action.

But, at a deeper level, I have this growing conviction that what's also needed is not just more programs, but a larger purpose, a larger sense of mission, a larger clarity of direction in the nation's life as we move toward century twenty-one. Increasingly, I'm convinced that ultimately, the scholarship of engagement also means creating a special climate in which the academic and civic cultures communicate more continuously and more creatively with each other, helping to enlarge what anthropologist Clifford Geertz describes as the universe of human discourse and enriching the quality of life for all of us.

Many years ago, Oscar Handlin put the challenge this way: "[A] troubled universe can no longer afford the luxury of pursuits confined to an ivory tower...[S]cholarship has to prove its worth not on its own terms, but by service to the nation and the world." This, in the end, is what the scholarship of engagement is all about.

Note: This essay is adapted from a speech delivered at the Induction Ceremony of the American Academy of Arts and Sciences, Cambridge, MA, October 11, 1995.

# Factors and Strategies that Influence Faculty Involvement in Public Service

by Barbara A. Holland

FUNDAMENTAL QUESTIONS ABOUT THE ROLE OF public service as scholarly work persist among many faculty members. Institutional leaders feel challenged in their search for effective strategies to encourage faculty involvement in public service activities. In part, mysteries remain because much of the material on public service is experiential, and has been based on individual cases or individual institutional models.

While individual experiences and campus reports can offer inspiration and good ideas for further experimentation, they often lack the compelling impact of more systematic, broad-scale research studies that may help us see patterns, or suggest answers to persistent questions. Faculty and administrators alike have resonated to recent works that take a broader view of institutional challenges and issues of implementing public service activities by considering the experiences of multiple institutions (Burack 1998; NASULGC 1999).

Since 1995, several national research and evaluation projects involving a total of thirty-two diverse institutions have provided useful evidence about the conduct of public service activities (Holland 1997,1999a, 1999b; Gelmon, Holland, and Shinnamon 1998). Each project has in common an examination of attitudes toward the role of public service from the perspective of faculty, students, community, and the institution. Because they look separately and in-depth at the actions and attitudes of each of these constituent groups, these multi-institutional studies are especially helpful in understanding individual and collective motivations, and the factors that inhibit or facilitate a decision to participate in public service activities. Patterns emerged from faculty data, and can best be presented by considering these questions about service activities:

- What motivates faculty involvement in service/outreach?

- What do faculty cite as obstacles to involvement?

- What can institutions do to facilitate faculty involvement?

## THE SOURCES OF FACULTY MOTIVATION

Most faculty who are already involved in public service and outreach report that they are motivated by personal values structures; they see mostly intrinsic rewards. Many answered this question by referring to their initiation into social activism in the 1960s. Others cited family, spiritual, community, or cultural experiences and values that have inspired their commitment to a life of service. As highly-educated individuals, they see themselves as having a responsibility to apply their knowledge toward the betterment of society. These faculty engage in both voluntary and professional service and often were found to be campus leaders in discussions about the role of outreach in the academy. They engage in service because it is the right thing to do and because it allows them to link their personal and professional lives.

Other faculty said that outreach and public service is relevant to the success of their discipline and the quality of their teaching and research agenda. These are faculty in disciplines with logical connections to external issues and audiences: social work; nursing, medicine, and other health professions; public administration; education, and so forth. In some cases, a program's accreditation may require evidence of public engagement for students and/or faculty.

Finally, motivation among faculty who more recently have become active in outreach programs often arises from their direct observation of respected institutions or colleagues, availability of incentives or rewards for participation, or evidence of the positive impact of outreach activities on organizational factors that they value, such as:

- Academic prestige of individual faculty, departments, or of the institution;

- Learning outcomes for students;

- Public and private funding including new revenues, grants and gifts; and

- Improved public image of the institution.

Faculty motivation is, therefore, found to be strongly influenced by personal experiences, individual and collective professional objectives, and evidence of positive outcomes on organizational outcomes they value. Different factors are of greater importance to different faculty and different disciplines.

## THE COMMON OBSTACLES TO FACULTY INVOLVEMENT

Obstacles cited by faculty included concern about the time it takes to create new activities, cultivate partnerships, organize the logistics of service activities, and recruit students or other participants. Resources to support new activities were sometimes a problem, though many faculty learned that some outreach efforts can be resource-generating. Time in the curriculum or in a course was also a frequent obstacle for those specifically seeking to introduce service learning into a syllabus.

Across higher education, we lack a common understanding of the language of public service. A confusing myriad of terms has arisen, and the rhetoric of public service is not clear to everyone. Faculty are often deeply concerned about the lack of clear and comparable definitions of terms such as service, public service, professional service, outreach, public engagement, community service, service learning, internships, practica, and so on. Some terms have different meanings in different campus contexts, and some may be seen locally as pejorative because of unhappy past campus experiments with outreach. Confusion over these terms was found to constrain faculty involvement and to make effective documentation and evaluation difficult.

A lack of confidence with the skills and techniques of outreach and service was cited by some faculty as an obstacle to participation. The graduate experience teaches faculty to be experts in their field and to be accomplished scholars judged by their peers. Often a discussion among faculty about what is valued by their colleagues or their department is really about faculty feeling confident and competent that they will be seen as successful. They want to pursue outreach with the same clarity of method and process they feel they have in the arena of research. Involvement in community partnerships where reciprocity and mutuality are expected can especially challenge faculty because they must learn to share the role of expert with non-academic partners. In addition, this kind of scholarly work involves collaboration including shared responsibility for outcomes and shared ownership of findings; this too is unfamiliar to many faculty and their disciplinary traditions. A companion concern was a lack of faculty experience with techniques for evaluating and documenting service activities, or a coherent campus policy regarding such documentation.

In addition, institutional mission and leadership matters to many faculty. The perception of the role of public service as a legitimate component of the institution's purposes is critically important to those faculty who do not have personal or disciplinary motivations for engagement. If a commitment to outreach is not articulated by institutional leadership and colleagues, and reflected in strategic plans and budgetary allocations, an environment of acceptance is unlikely to form for this kind of scholarly work. Not surprisingly, systems of rewards, as in promotion and tenure guidelines, were cited as obstacles to faculty involvement in outreach by junior faculty much more than senior faculty. This was related to the lack of clear procedures for documentation and evaluation, and with departmental or institutional experience with the scholarly value of public service. Formal rewards were far less important to senior faculty. Overall, faculty expressed less concern about promotion and tenure than the other obstacles mentioned in this essay.

## THE RELATIONSHIP OF MOTIVATION TO EFFECTIVE INSTITUTIONAL STRATEGIES

These findings regarding motivation and obstacles can be linked to a pattern of effective organizational strategies used at institutions that have made advances in encouraging faculty involvement in public service. The strategies involve various aspects of campus policy, philosophy, budgets, programs, and organizational structure and actions. Not all are present at every institution. Faculty and administrators made it clear that programmatic strategies must reflect each institution's mission, history, capacity, and its academic strengths and objectives. Multiple strategies were employed by most institutions in order to match the diversity of faculty motivations for involvement or their perception of obstacles to participation. The basic idea is that each institution must bring its formal and informal rhetoric about the role of public service into alignment with its policies and practices regarding faculty involvement.

**1. CLEAR MISSION** – Institutional leaders and respected faculty must articulate strong concurrence on a vision for the role of public service in the institution's mission and its relationship to individual and institutional prestige and academic excellence.

**2. INFRASTRUCTURE SUPPORT** – Public service is time and labor intensive and the institution must reflect the value it places on public service in the investment it makes in supportive infrastructure. Infrastructure can take many forms and assume many duties, according to the institution's characteristics. Generally, faculty require and expect assistance with matters of logistics, planning, evaluation, and communications.

**3. FACULTY DEVELOPMENT** – Building competence and confidence in the techniques of public service requires an investment in faculty development. Most effective were peer development activities where faculty partnered to learn from each other. A critical component of faculty development requires institutional attention to the development of a common campus language for public service activity, and specific methods of documentation and evaluation (Lynton 1995; Driscoll and Lynton 1999).

**4. INCENTIVES AND REWARDS** – Faculty were found to have different motivations and different expectations regarding recognition and rewards, so their interests in incentives and rewards were different as well. Successful institutions or departments use diverse approaches including, for example, financial incentives; recognition through publicity, awards or special titles; support for dissemination activities; or support in fund raising or grant making to support public service projects. Institutions that began a campus discussion of the role of public service by addressing the formal promotion and tenure system made little progress. It is nearly

impossible for faculty to understand the scholarly elements of public service in the abstract. Direct observation and experience lead faculty to understand how public service relates to other elements of their scholarship. Few institutions have made specific alterations in their reward systems, though some recognized faculty involvement in public service by linking it to the roles of teaching or research, depending on the nature of the activity. The best current practice is to offer many kinds of rewards, and to build a consistent framework for documenting and evaluating service.

**5. SELF SELECTION** – Not all faculty need to, want to, or are qualified to pursue public service activities. Public service does not suit all faculty or all disciplines. Understanding the diverse forms of faculty motivation helps institutions create the incentives and rewards, and the supportive systems that will attract faculty involvement. The goal is to identify areas of emphasis and importance in public service, articulate the role of public service in the overall institutional mission, and then attract sufficient numbers of the most motivated faculty to become engaged.

**6. THE ROLE OF CURRICULUM AND SERVICE LEARNING** – For many faculty, involvement in public service is unfamiliar; the relevance to their scholarly agenda is not immediately clear to them. Faculty reported that the curricular environment is an area where they feel comfortable exploring the possibilities of public service. For example, incentives that encourage faculty to create service learning components in courses gives them experience in working with community partners, observing the effects of public service, and understanding the broader relevance of public service to their overall scholarly agenda. In addition, students become advocates for institutional commitment to public service. Service learning in the curriculum is an effective learning experience for faculty as well as students, and a good approach to building faculty confidence and interest in public service (Zlotkowski 1998).

**7. COMMUNITY INVOLVEMENT AND PARTNERSHIP THEMES** – The visibility of community issues and the level of community participation in institutional planning for public service signals a level of commitment and importance for the role of public service to faculty. The degree of involvement of community representatives in advisory boards, project planning, campus-community events, and public service evaluation needs to be an accurate and balanced reflection of the institution's public service objectives. Some campuses have found it helpful to conspicuously focus on a few public service needs or themes that link academic strengths of the institution to external needs and challenges. This helps demonstrate the relevance of public service to other academic priorities and faculty roles as articulated by the institution. For example, my own institution has focused its early efforts in public engagement on urgent issues of our K-16 educational system and on economic/work force development. These priorities are reflected in recent academic program initiatives, grant proposals, and strategic objectives. In addition, we are building on our commitment to serving as an arts and cultural resource for the region by taking more events off-campus, and by partnering with new regional museum initiatives.

**8. BUDGETING AND PLANNING** – As in all organizational initiatives that represent change or new priorities, efforts to promote faculty involvement in public service require that institutional budgets must be demonstrably linked to institutional objectives. This includes making necessary investments in the elements of infrastructure, incentives and rewards, and faculty development at a level that reflects institutional aspirations and expectations. Engaging faculty from across the campus in a collective exploration of the role of public service in the campus mission can lead to strategic objectives for service activities. Administration must do its part by incorporating those objectives into financial choices.

## CONCLUSION

A coherent picture of the elements related to faculty motivations and attitudes toward public service is beginning to emerge as patterns of faculty attitudes and actions across multiple and diverse institutions become clear. Understanding the role of motivation in faculty decisions regarding public service helps point to the selection of effective strategies for creating an institutional environment that promotes and supports faculty involvement.

A good single watchword to guide the efforts of institutions to encourage faculty involvement in public service may be "consistency." Consistency across elements of mission definition, strategic priorities, budget actions, recognition and rewards, definitions of terms, internal and external communications, faculty development objectives, curricular philosophy, and community relationships sends a clear signal of the level of institutional commitment to public service. Such consistency is essential to encouraging many faculty to view service

as a legitimate and valued component of their scholarly life and work, whatever their individual source of motivation for participation.

## REFERENCES

Burack, C. A. (1998). Strengthening and sustaining faculty service. *Journal of Public Service & Outreach.* 3(2): 42–47.

Driscoll, A. and E. A. Lynton. (1999). *Making outreach visible: A guide to documenting professional service and outreach.* Washington, D.C.: American Association for Higher Education.

Gelmon, S. B., B. A. Holland, and A. F. Shinnamon. (1998). *Health professions schools in service to the nation: 1996–98 final evaluation report.* San Francisco: Community-Campus Partnerships for Health.

Holland, B. A. (1998). Analyzing institutional commitment to service. *Michigan Journal of Community Service Learning,* 4 (Fall): 30–41.

Holland, B. A. (1999a). From murky to meaningful: The role of mission in institutional change. In *Colleges and Universities as Citizens.* Edited by R. G. Bringle, R. Games, and E. A. Malloy. Boston: Allyn & Bacon.

Holland, B. A. (1999b). *Implementing urban missions project: Evaluation report.* Work-in-progress for the Council of Independent Colleges.

Lynton, E. A. (1995). *Making the case for professional service.* Washington D.C.: American Association for Higher Education.

National Association of State Universities and Land-Grant Colleges. (1999). *Returning to our roots: The engaged institution.* Report of the Kellogg Commission on the Future of State and Land-Grant Universities.

Zlotkowski, E. (1998). A service learning approach to faculty development. In *Service Learning Pedagogy and Research.* Edited by J. P. Howard and R. Rhodes. San Francisco: Jossey-Bass.

# Addressing Academic Culture:

## Service Learning, Organizations, and Faculty Work

by Kelly Ward

SERVICE IS MENTIONED IN A MAJORITY of college and university mission statements, but how its meaning translates into campus life varies considerably. For many campuses, service often means membership on committees that contribute to the institution or a faculty member's professional affiliations. On other campuses, such as Michigan State University, service tends to be defined as faculty professional outreach, such as consulting in the field in ways that call on the faculty member's scholarly expertise. On other campuses, such as Salish Kootenai College, a tribal college in Pablo, Montana, service means direct service to students and the reservation community surrounding the campus; faculty engage in efforts that benefit the community by offering their professional expertise; students participate in both curricular and co-curricular activities to meet community needs.

Clearly, these are all different interpretations of service. Now with the advent of discussions about service within the context of undergraduate education, the following new questions are being raised: What does service learning mean? Where does it fit organizationally? What implications does it have for faculty work? Responses to these questions hinge upon the culture of the institution and its faculty.

University missions are translated through symbols and systems, particularly the curriculum and faculty reward structures. The curriculum conveys what faculty identify as important to teaching and learning. The curricular integration of service learning indicates that an institution values service to the community as part of the educational experience. At Portland State University, for example, there are formalized opportunities in the curriculum for students to address the needs of the local urban community in classes ranging from art to biology. Portland State interprets service as community problem solving and sends a clear message that the university is actively involved in the life of the local community. Accordingly, at Portland State, service learning has been incorporated into faculty promotion and tenure policies.

Faculty reward structures also signal institutional values. Faculty success at the organizational level, translated as promotion and tenure, requires faculty participation in the tripartite demands of the professoriate: teaching, research, and service. These demands on faculty time vary a great deal, depending on the particular campus culture. If a campus values experiential learning and community involvement, it will value professors who utilize service learning; if it is recognized and rewarded in promotion and tenure guidelines and reviews, professors will be encouraged to incorporate service learning into their courses.

## ORGANIZATIONAL CULTURE: EXPANDING HORIZONS FOR SERVICE LEARNING

If we are to realize the ideals suggested in this issue of *New Directions for Teaching and Learning* and look to the future for more widespread use of service learning, we must consider the context within which academically based service takes place. Innovations in higher education must be assimilated into the institution or they will be short-lived (Curry, 1992). The institutionalization of service learning requires garnering support from people throughout the campus community and involves the following challenges: (1) administrative support, (2) familiarity with course-based service, (3) funding, and (4) faculty involvement. Moving service learning from the periphery to the core, and from an idea to practice, requires addressing these challenges while understanding the complexities of the organizational context and faculty work.

ADMINISTRATIVE SUPPORT. Many campuses have benefited from the involvement and support for service learning from senior administrators, particularly presidents. For example, Campus Compact, an organization of college and university presidents, is now over 600 campuses strong. The Compact's popularity among senior administrators is in part attributed to how service learning responds to many of the criticisms currently leveled against higher education, including the failure to meet public service responsibilities (Boyer, 1990; Fairweather, 1996). Presidents and other senior-level administrators look to service learning to smooth relationships with their constituencies and to better prepare students for life beyond college.

Service learning depends not only on the support of senior-level administrators, but on other administrators as well. An expanded administrative vision includes involvement of those directly and actively involved in routine academic management and policy functions (that is, provosts, deans, department chairs). These administrators can promote service learning by creating and supporting an ethos of learning that includes community service experiences. This may be accomplished by amending promotion and tenure policies to include service learning and by articulating a vision of community service to their academic units (Kuh, Douglas, Lund, and Ramin-Gyurnek, 1994).

FAMILIARITY WITH COURSE-BASED SERVICE. The reality is that much variance exists with regard to campus awareness of service learning. On some campuses service learning is a term familiar to a majority of the campus community. At Western Montana College, for example, the chancellor has been supportive of service learning by creating the Center for Service Learning and by integrating service into the campus mission statement. She has also hosted a campus-wide convocation on community service and experiential learning in addition to several faculty workshops on the topic. Service learning has also been a theme at faculty orientation for two years, and about one-third of the faculty have a service component in their courses. Faculty use service learning as a pedagogical tool and students understand that emphasis is placed on out-of-class work.

In contrast, service learning at Montana State University is still in an introductory phase. Faculty and students are increasingly involved in service learning, but interest and participation exist only in small pockets across the campus. The Office for Community Involvement is gaining visibility, but it takes time and multiple efforts to make service learning familiar campus-wide. The president, though supportive, is not actively involved in promoting service learning on campus.

FUNDING. Service learning, like all other endeavors on a campus, requires adequate funding. Financial and human resources are necessary to create and staff offices to support service learning and to support faculty efforts and service projects. Based on a review of campuses involved in Campus Compact's Project on Integrating Service with Academic Study, Morton and Troppe (1996) outline eight common steps for institutionalizing service. Among the steps they cite, five relate to funding: (1) institutional commitment of funds to ensure the development of the service learning initiative, (2) a staff person to serve as a liaison between faculty and community agencies, (3) faculty development funds to introduce faculty to service learning, (4) support of faculty travel to find out how others in their discipline and on similar campuses have implemented service learning, and (5) release time for faculty to redesign their courses to incorporate service learning.

In a series of case studies of campuses in Montana integrating service learning, faculty and administrators indicated the importance of funding of both individual projects and campus offices as reflections of institutional priorities. One mid-level administrator explained, "We can't say service learning is an important part of the college and then not put resources in to make it work." Simply put, funding allocations signify institutional priorities. An example is the creation and expansion of an office to support service learning and volunteerism. Such an office is essential to advance awareness and promote participation in curricular-based service. An actual location for service learning activities communicates to the campus that the initiative is valued. Further, a campus office is a structural means to provide information to the community, both on and off campus. Service learning administrators provide a crucial link between students, faculty, and the local community.

FACULTY INVOLVEMENT. One of the greatest challenges facing the widespread adoption of service learning is faculty involvement. Faculty are the arbiters of the curriculum, and service learning, as a curricular initiative needs both their support and their participation. Most campuses utilize a system of shared governance and make decisions via committees. Therefore, it is imperative that committees dealing with curricular issues be challenged by deans and department chairs to consider service learning and how it might be included in promotion and tenure guidelines.

The University of Utah provides an example of how faculty involvement in the advancement of service learning has been used to transform campus culture. The Lowell Bennion Community Service Center involves thousands of students in service each year. The Center has an academic senate-approved Service Learning Scholars Program for students to acknowledge their involvement in service, and several programs for faculty release time and other awards to recognize those experienced and new to service learning. Further, the faculty advisory committee that works with the Bennion Center has drafted guidelines to help departments include service learning in their promotion and tenure policies (Lowell Bennion Center, 1996).

Many factors have shaped the success of the Bennion Center. Presidential leadership was important, but perhaps even more so was the central role that faculty played in shaping policies and also reaping the benefits of such policies through reward structures. For service learning to be integrated into campus culture, as exemplified at the University of Utah, it must move from a hazy notion often perceived by faculty as additional unrewarded work to a valued and recognized endeavor.

Expanded administrative support, increasing familiarity of the campus community, funding, and faculty involvement in service learning are all crucial to the success of academic-based service on any campus. Perhaps the greatest challenge to service learning, however, is the nature of faculty work and the faculty reward structure. The challenge lies in faculty reluctance to participate in work that is not recognized and rewarded by their institution. The institutionalization of service learning cannot be addressed without discussing faculty work and rewards.

## FACULTY WORK AND REWARDS

Faculty roles are shaped by the academic department as well as by institutional culture and mission. For example, at Salish Kootenai College, service learning is a curriculum requirement and faculty are recognized for their involvement. The campus focuses on teaching and service, and faculty commitments are centered locally. Faculty are expected to serve both the campus and the local community. In contrast, at Pennsylvania State University, the mission of the institution and faculty work is centered around research and scholarship. Consequently, the vast majority of Penn State faculty devote significant portions of their time to research and writing. This is not to say that all the faculty at Salish Kootenai College are involved in service learning and none are at Penn State. The point is that differences exist between the two schools because of their reward structures. Nonetheless, some faculty at Penn State will be motivated to use service learning independent of their concerns for promotion and tenure or because they can directly tie service learning to their scholarly endeavors.

As the preceding examples illustrate, faculty work varies considerably. Faculty identify with aspects of their institutions in differing degrees. Some faculty are more focused on their department than their campus; others see their discipline as their primary affiliation; and still others see the university or college as the core unit of identification (Clark, 1987; Kuh and Whitt, 1988; Tierney and Rhoads, 1993). All of these sources of professional identity may influence one's willingness to use service learning pedagogies.

For many faculty there is increasing emphasis on research, and rewards tend disproportionately to favor excellence in research (including grant procurement) over teaching and service regardless of institutional type (Boyer,1990; Fairweather, 1993, 1996). Although service learning has the potential to enhance teaching, research, and service, it is still largely viewed by faculty as a service or instructional initiative. The faculty member who feels research is the focus of the reward structure may steer away from service learning. Consequently, specific guidelines stressing service learning as a component of promotion and tenure are needed. For example, the University of Utah provides criteria that departments can use to evaluate faculty involved in service learning. These standards offer direction to departments wanting formally to evaluate and validate involvement in service learning. The following are examples of these criteria:

- Service learning contributions must relate to the faculty member's area of scholarship.

- Service learning contributions are responsive to recognized needs of individuals and organizations within the university or local community and are seen as having lasting impact.

- The service learning activities provide a means for students to synthesize their volunteer experiences with course content (action and reflection).

Faculty participation in meaningful and academically relevant service is key to expanding involvement in community-based learning. Clearly, faculty involvement in service hinges upon being rewarded and supported for their efforts. In fact, any initiative centered around teaching or service is bound to fail if faculty are not given recognition for time they spend on these activities and time they spend with students. The campus that purports to support involvement in service learning, but then fails to recognize these efforts in faculty rewards, will not be able to attract large or even small numbers of faculty to this initiative. This is akin to the argument offered by Tierney and Bensimon (1996) when they pointed to the importance of having promotion and tenure guidelines correspond with institutional priorities.

The institution with a vision for more widespread use of service learning must consider the policies and procedures that directly influence faculty work. Institutional leaders who support service learning need to do so not only with words, but with actions as well. To be sure, presidents, provosts, vice presidents, and deans do not have absolute power. They do, however, have the ability to create offices of service learning, voice their support for faculty involvement in service, and earmark funds for faculty development and project support.

## NEGOTIATING CULTURE: OVERCOMING BARRIERS AND RESISTANCE TO CHANGE

The following strategies are suggested for faculty and administrators involved in advancing service learning on their campuses.

Make sure that all administrators—presidents, provosts, vice presidents, deans, department chairs—are familiar with campus service learning initiatives. One of the major barriers to incorporating service learning is lack of familiarity. Many people are simply unaware of academic-based service and its benefits. To garner support from all levels of the university requires familiarity within each unit.

Change takes place slowly and incrementally; try to influence culture at all levels. Service learning hinges on the involvement of all levels of the campus—students, staff, faculty, and administrators. These groups need first to be introduced to service learning and then kept apprised of strides in this area. Make the accomplishments of course-based service known to all members of the campus community

Create formal and informal faculty committees and groups to help direct the efforts of service learning. Collegial decision-making through committees and groups is the norm on most college campuses. Influencing culture requires utilizing decision-making norms to make policy about the curriculum, faculty roles, and the future of service learning on campus. A service learning committee can help create policies for service learning and can also influence other committees (for example, executive committees of the faculty senate, faculty development committees). A service learning interest group is also essential to spreading the language of service—an important cultural artifact—to all domains of campus.

Service learning is undoubtedly related to other university-based initiatives; tie into them. Higher education is facing a time in which faculty and administrators are challenged to do more with less. Service learning certainly has merits on its own, but it can also benefit by connecting with other related initiatives. For example, if an institution has an undergraduate research program, look at ways to do community-based action research to meet the goals of both service learning and research.

Work with faculty senates and curriculum committees to stress the academic side of service learning. Service learning is a component of the curriculum, and the way to influence the curriculum is through the faculty Some faculty are reluctant to acknowledge service learning as a viable academic pedagogy because words like service can conjure up images of learning that might be "soft" or "fuzzy" and perceived as tangential to the undergraduate experience. Campus members need to be educated about service learning's role in furthering academic course objectives.

Address faculty reward structures, for they mirror institutional priorities. Faculty rewards are essential to the ongoing integration and growth of service learning. Introduce the language of service learning into promotion and tenure guidelines. This may mean starting with departments that are service learning friendly and then expanding campus-wide.

Provide data about benefits of service learning. Faculty are concerned with the intellectual rigor of curricular initiatives. Influencing culture requires speaking the language, and academics tend to converse around research and evaluation. Providing research-based evidence about the benefits of service learning is useful to sway the reluctant faculty member. Research outcomes can be drawn from both national and institutional-based studies (Boss, 1994; Giles and Eyler, 1994; Markus, Howard, and King, 1993; RAND Corporation, 1996).

## INTEGRATING SERVICE LEARNING

The ideas and suggestions put forth in this chapter are meant to contribute to the institutionalization of service learning on campus. If service learning is not integrated into campus cultures through infrastructure (for example, service learning offices, institutional budgets), faculty reward structures, and curricular affairs, it is destined to be short-lived (Rhoads, 1997).

The late Ernest Boyer was one of service learning's champions. He called for a new conception of faculty work and a new vision of scholarship: "One dedicated not only to the renewal of the academy but, ultimately, to the renewal of society itself" (Boyer, 1990, p. 81). Boyer's wisdom can be honored by realizing the potential of service learning to help reshape the future of teaching and learning in higher education.

## REFERENCES

Boss, J. A. "The Effect of Community Service Work on the Moral Development of College Ethics Students." *Journal of Moral Education*, 1994, 23 (2), 183–198.

Boyer, E. *Scholarship Reconsidered: Priorities of the Professoriate.* Princeton: Carnegie Foundation for the Advancement of Teaching, 1990.

Clark, B. R. *The Academic Profession.* Berkeley: University of California Press, 1987.

Curry, B. K. *Instituting Enduring Innovations: Achieving Continuity of Change in Higher Education.* ASHE-ERIC Higher Education Report No. 7. Washington, D.C.: School of Education and Human Development, George Washington University, 1992.

Fairweather, J. S. "Academic Values and Faculty Rewards." *Review of Higher Education*, 1993, 17,43–68.

Fairweather, J. S. *Faculty Work and Public Trust: Restoring the Value of Teaching and Public Service in American Academic Life.* Needham Heights, Mass.: Allyn & Bacon, 1996.

Giles, D. E., and Eyler, J. "The Impact of a College Community Service Laboratory on Students' Personal, Social, and Cognitive Outcomes." *Journal of Adolescence*, 1994, 17, 327–339.

Kuh, G. D., Douglas, K. B., Lund. J. P., and Ramin-Gyurnek, J. *Student Learning Outside the Classroom: Transcending Artificial Boundaries.* ASHE-ERIC Higher Education Report No. 8. Washington, D.C.: George Washington University, 1994.

Kuh, G. D. and Whitt, E. J. *The Invisible Tapestry: Culture in American Colleges and Universities.* ASHE-ERIC Higher Education Report No.1. Washington, D.C.: George Washington University, 1988.

Lowell Bennion Center. *Service Learning in the Curriculum.* Salt Lake City: University of Utah, 1996.

Markus, G. B., Howard, J.P.F., and King, D. C. "Integrating Community Service and Classroom Instruction Enhances Learning: Results from an Experiment." *Educational Evaluation and Policy Analysis*, 1993, 15 (4), 410–419.

Morton, K., and Troppe, M. "From the Margin to the Mainstream: Campus Compact's Project on Integrating Service with Academic Study." In M. Troppe (ed.), *Two Cases of Institutionalizing Service Learning: How Campus Climate Affects the Change Process.* Providence, RI: Campus Compact, 1996.

RAND Corporation. *Evaluation of Learn and Serve America, Higher Education: First Year Report.* Vol. 1. Santa Monica, Calif.: RAND Corporation, 1996.

Rhoads, R. A. *Community Service and Higher Learning: Explorations of the Caring Self.* Albany: State University of New York Press, 1997.

Tierney, W. G., and Bensimon, E. M. *Promotion and Tenure: Community and Socialization in Academe.* Albany: State University of New York Press, 1996.

Tierney, W. G., and Rhoads, R. A. *Faculty Socialization as Cultural Process: A Mirror of Institutional Commitment.* ASHE-ERIC Higher Education Report No. 93–6. Washington, D.C.: George Washington University, 1993.

# Uncovering the Values in Faculty Evaluation of Service as Scholarship

by KerryAnn O'Meara

"ARCHERY IN THE DARK" (Rice, 1996, p. 31) has become a widely cited faculty complaint about problems with the tenure and promotion process. A substantial amount of research concurs that promotion and tenure are often elusive, unpredictable, and fraught with "conflicting expectations" and unwritten rules (Rice, Sorcinelli, & Austin, 2000, p. 9). Faculty struggles with promotion and tenure are attributed to ambiguous and often contradictory criteria. Conflicts between institutional rhetoric and the realities of reward structures, and the emphasis on research to the detriment of teaching and service in promotion and tenure decisions have been identified as major sources of stress and dissatisfaction in probationary faculty (Gmelch, Lovrich, & Wilkie, 1986; Rice, Sorcinelli & Austin, 2000; Sorcinelli, 1992; Tierney & Bensimon, 1996).

Women and faculty of color are the most disenchanted with the tenure process. They report lower degrees of satisfaction, fewer opportunities for professional recognition, less favorable perceptions of the academic climate, more instances of subtle discrimination, and higher degrees of stress compared to their White male counterparts (Sax, Astin, Arredondo, & Korn, 1996; Sanderson et al., 1999). A higher proportion of tenure-track women and faculty of color leave the tenure track prior to the tenure decision than their male and White counterparts (Sanderson et al., 1999). Greater dissatisfaction with the reward system has been attributed in part to the higher commitment of women and faculty of color to professional service and teaching, endeavors that are often given less weight than research in tenure reviews (Antonio, Astin, & Cress, 2000; Bellas & Toutkoushian, 1999).

The main issue addressed in this article is the influence of values and beliefs on the promotion and tenure process. Understanding the values and beliefs that influence promotion and tenure is important because these values and beliefs play a critical role in determining what kinds of faculty work are considered important and meritorious, thus conveying messages about where faculty should invest their time. Values and beliefs shape institutional direction and have consequences on the development of individual faculty careers.

With the best of intentions, colleges and universities have attempted to amend the existing tenure system (Chait, 1998). One of the most popular modifications to traditional tenure follows Ernest Boyer's (1990) suggestion that the definition of scholarship used in promotion policies be changed to include teaching, discovering, integrating, and applying knowledge. In 1994, 62% of chief academic officers in four-year institutions reported that Boyer's (1990) seminal work, *Scholarship Reconsidered,* had had a role in discussions of faculty roles and rewards (Glassick, Huber, & Maeroff, 1997). Advocates of assessing teaching as scholarship (Hutchings & Shulman, 1999) and faculty professional service as scholarship (Driscoll & Lynton, 1999; Lynton, 1995) have suggested that assessing and rewarding multiple forms of scholarship within academic reward systems encourages faculty to emphasize different kinds of work over their career and elevates the status of teaching and service to their rightful place beside research within academic culture.

However, institutions that attempt to expand their definition of scholarship for promotion and tenure take on a huge task. Just because a college changes its written definition of scholarship in promotion policies does not mean that institutional members wake up the next day with a new view of faculty work. Instead, the expanded definition of scholarship must struggle to survive in an "assumptive world" (Rice, 1996, p. 8) where specialized research published in peer-reviewed journals is central to what it means to be a valued scholar. Faculty and administrators are often "prisoners of their own thinking" (Senge, 1990, p. 27), unable to make promotion decisions based on a new definition of scholarship because they hold values about faculty roles, scholarship, and institutional identity that contradict the values inherent in the new reward structure. Research on change and innovation has shown that modifications to tenure with any hope of success must focus on the cultural realities and inner workings of institutions (ACE, 1999; Bergquist, 1992; Schein, 1992). Institutions that expand their definition of scholarship do so as part of an effort to amend or, in some cases, transform values and beliefs so that their members view faculty roles in new ways.

This study explored how values and beliefs held by faculty and administrators influenced the promotion and tenure process at four institutions that expanded their definition of scholarship in promotion policies. While expanding the definition of scholarship in promotion and tenure has implications for the assessment of teaching, integrative work, and research, this study focused on how values and beliefs influenced the promotion process in relationship to the assessment of service as scholarship.

## CONCEPTUAL FRAMEWORK

This study was guided by Schein's (1992) theory of organizational culture and Kuh and Whitt's (1988) application of cultural theory to higher education settings. Schein (1992) divided culture into a conceptual hierarchy comprised of three levels: artifacts, values and beliefs, and basic assumptions.

Artifacts are the visible products, activities, and processes that form a culture (Schein, 1992) and include reward structures, rituals, ceremonies, and insider language and terminology (ACE, 1999). Underlying assumptions are rarely questioned, taken-for-granted beliefs that reside at the inner core of organizational culture and the deepest level of institutional consciousness. This study focused on the middle layer of Schein's three levels of culture—values and beliefs.

Values are

> widely held beliefs or sentiments about the importance of certain goals, activities, relations, and feelings. Values can be (a) conscious and explicitly articulated, serving a normative or moral function guiding member behavior, (b) unconsciously expressed as themes (e.g. the tradition of collegial governance) and/or (c) symbolic interpretations of reality that give meaning to social actions and establish standards for social behavior (Kuh & Whitt, 1988, p. 23).

Values are often context bound and directly related to a college's history and wellbeing. They sometimes "surface as exhortations about what is right or wrong, what is encouraged or discouraged, and what ought to be" (Kuh & Whitt, 1988, p. 25). Espoused values are a subset of this second layer of culture. They are aspirations, or how an institution wishes to be. There are often discrepancies between the espoused values of individuals and institutions and how they actually behave. In order for a change effort to become permanent, there must be congruence between artifacts, values, and espoused values (ACE, 1999; Kuh & Whitt, 1988; Schein, 1992).

Values become "theories in use" (Argyris & Schon, 1974, qtd. in Schein, 1992, p. 22). Only when values and their effect on practice are revealed can change agents begin to transform values and modify practice. The literature on effecting successful change (ACE, 1999; Bolman & Deal, 1991; Birnbaum, 1988; Senge, 1990) and on institutional culture (Birnbaum, 1988; Bergquist, 1992; Bolman & Deal, 1994; Lindquist, 1978; Schein, 1992) is voluminous. However little research has explored the values held by faculty and administrators that influence faculty evaluation and, more specifically, the values that advance or prevent a campus from embracing a broader view of scholarship in promotion decisions.

While a broader view of scholarship was written into institution-wide evaluation policies in each of the four cases studied, I narrowed the scope of this study to values and beliefs impacting evaluation in colleges/units of education. I selected colleges of education for two reasons. First, education faculty report engaging in the greatest amount of external service of faculty in any discipline (Kirshstein, 1997). Antonio, Astin, and Cress (2000) found that faculty trained in education, along with social work and health education (considered other or service-oriented disciplines), were the most committed personally and professionally to community service. Because education faculty are routinely called upon to engage in outreach to K–12 schools and community colleges (Campoy, 1996; Viechnicki, Yanity, & Olinski, 1997), policies on how service is valued and rewarded in promotion and tenure impacts them most heavily. Second, each discipline has its own distinctive epistemology, methods, and social relations among members (Becher, 1989; Biglan, 1973). In a study of the institutionalization of Boyer's four domains of scholarship, Braxton et al. (2000) found significant differences in the amount of activity and the valuing of the scholarship of application in four academic disciplines. Isolating colleges of education reveals the values within this service-oriented discipline. The study may be replicated later in the humanities and/or sciences.

## METHODOLOGY

This study investigated the values and beliefs that influence the assessment of service as scholarship in promotion and tenure review. Its intent was to identify themes and patterns of values concerning institutional identity, the nature of scholarship, and faculty careers that influenced the promotion and tenure process. I use "promotion and tenure process" as an intentionally broad term, encompassing decisions made by promotion and tenure (personnel) committees and external factors such as voiced opinions and behavior of senior faculty, department chairs, deans, and candidates who influenced promotion decisions. I adopted a revelatory multiple case-study method to build explanations (Yin, 1994). An institution, to be eligible for this study, had to have (a) revised its promotion policies to include an expanded definition of scholarship consistent with Boyer's (1990) framework, (b) been identified by the American Association for Higher Education's Forum on Faculty Roles and Rewards and New England Resource Center for Higher Education as having made significant strides to assess service as scholarship, and (c) be accessible for research.

I sought to identify institutions with differing structures and cultures because values might vary by institutional type, and I wanted to understand the values and beliefs influencing faculty evaluation across four different types of institutions. I used the Carnegie (1976) classification system to distinguish among university types. I chose one institution in four categories (research, doctoral, master, and baccalaureate) and assigned a pseudonym to each: MidWest State University (MWSU), Patrick State University (PSU), Erin College, and St. Timothy (St. Tims).

I interviewed 12 to 15 individuals from each institution using semi-structured, open-ended question protocols. The interview protocol included questions on values and beliefs about the evolution and implementation of the new promotion policy for the purposes of defining, assessing, and rewarding service as scholarship. Academic administrators and deans of the colleges/units of education acted as primary informants and assisted me in selecting participants. I also used snowball sampling to ensure that the interview pool included faculty of each rank, both sexes, and a range of viewpoints on the assessment of service as scholarship for promotion and tenure.

Participants included education faculty who were currently on the personnel committee and/or had been within the last two years, education faculty who were and were not involved in service scholarship (tenured and untenured), and the dean, department chairs, provost, and other administrators involved in policy decisions affecting this issue. At PSU I interviewed the entire personnel committee; at the other three institutions, I interviewed 75% of the personnel committee. I taped and transcribed the interviews. I also reviewed promotion and tenure guidelines, applicant portfolios and materials, institutional reports and memoranda, meeting minutes, and descriptions of service projects. I received these documents through primary informants, at meetings with campus archivists, and from searches of electronic databases.

From the collected data, I drafted four case reports that included all of the relevant information (Yin, 1994). Out of each larger case report, I crafted a case study. I then used two three-step data-analysis processes: pattern coding, memoing, and proposition writing—first within each case and then across the four cases—to identify values that influenced the assessment of service as scholarship (Miles & Huberman, 1994). More specifically, I began data analysis by reading and rereading transcripts, noting the participants' roles, and then coding them according to categories that emerged from the data (Miles & Huberman, 1994). Coding reduced the data, allowed codes to be displayed, and facilitated drawing conclusions from patterns. I searched for, recorded, and analyzed divergent data that contradicted emerging patterns (Miles & Huberman, 1994).

## THE FOUR CASES

Organizational culture is a complex concept influenced by history and continually created and recreated by institutional mission, traditions, and experiences (Love, 1997). The values and beliefs that faculty and administrators held about faculty roles and rewards were as much embedded in how they interpreted their personal and institutional histories as they were the result of recent events and daily activities. For this reason, I briefly describe each of the four institutions and also common themes that cut across the four cases.

### Patrick State University (PSU)

PSU is a public metropolitan university located in a large northwestern city. No clear boundaries separate the campus from the city, and the faculty have always identified strongly with PSU's urban service mission. PSU is a young institution, living in the shadow of the state's flagship land-grant campus that receives greater visibility and enjoys more generous funding from the legislature. Since its founding, PSU has operated in a perpetual budget crisis. These realities have forced PSU to be entrepreneurial, to respond rapidly to change, and to innovate to meet the changing needs of its students, faculty, and city. Like other comprehensive universities, PSU has evolved from a single-purpose to a multi-purpose institution, from serving full-time to part-time students, from undergraduate to graduate focus.

### MidWest State University (MWSU)

Located in a big city, MWSU is a large, research-oriented land-grant university in the Midwest. Faculty have a reduced course load to encourage them to engage in significant scholarly research. *U.S. News and World Report* ranks at least one program in each colleges as among the top graduate programs in the United States. Like PSU, MWSU's sensitivity about being second to its state's flagship campus is a big part of the university culture.

### Erin College

Erin College is a medium-sized liberal arts/professional college in a major city in New England, founded to train women teachers. The undergraduate school remains single sex, while the graduate school is now coeducational. Erin College's name is synonymous in its region with the highest quality of teaching. Erin is a progressive place with a social action agenda. Faculty maintain a heavy workload of four courses each semester and have extensive advising and committee respon-sibilities. The culture of Erin College is student-centered, collaborative, interdisciplinary, service oriented, and committed to faculty and student interactions.

### St. Timothy (St. Tims)

St. Tims is a small, Catholic, liberal arts college in the Midwest. Students are 18 to 22 years old, and the college is mostly residential. St. Tims is 100 years old and known for excellence in teaching. The college was founded by an order of priests whose governing principle was hospitality; they "created an atmosphere that was congenial, that wasn't educationally edgy," according to one administrator. St. Tims's governing principle of hospitality nurtured a tradition of community, collegiality, and democratic decision-making. Teaching loads of three courses a semester, intensive committee work, and research mean that faculty are very busy. Budget cuts have been common yearly events and have had a significant impact on faculty and division chairs.

## THEMES

### A Tradition of Service

Since their founding, each of the four institutions in this study has had a strong, identifiable service mission. By virtue of its land-grant mission, MWSU's faculty has a long tradition of engaging in research-grounded technical assistance and community-based extension programs in agriculture, nursing, medicine, business, and education throughout the state. PSU was founded with an explicit mandate to serve its city and metropolitan area. All of its academic programs, and especially its professional schools, had established partnerships with city and nonprofit organizations. Since its early years of training women teachers, Erin College and its faculty has had a strong social justice orientation, stressing the philosophical values of serving the community and the educational benefits of service for its students. While St. Tims's service mission was not as strong as that of the other three, faculty and administrators have always viewed service as a critical extension of the college's vision of community and teaching mission. As a result, many faculty were involved in teaching-related service projects.

### Academic Recruitment and Evaluation

Another similarity among the four cases was the institutional history and context within which these institutions decided to modify their promotion and tenure policies and expand their definitions of scholarship.

Since their founding, each of the four campuses has had a history of valuing teaching and service as equal to, if not more important than, research in faculty evaluation. While the precise time of departure from this tradition differed, by the early 1980s each of the campuses had began to shift into what Rice (1996) called the "assumptive world of the academic professional" (p. 8) and which Gamson and Finnegan (1996) described as "the culture of research" (p. 172).

To different degrees, each of the four institutions wanted to increase its national standing within the academic labor market. The ability to attract graduate students and external funding and to compete with peers for national rankings rested on faculty productivity in research. As market forces brought more faculty with Ph.D.s and research backgrounds to these campuses, the campuses became more focused on traditional forms of research. By the 1990s, "scholarship" had became synonymous in these four different institutions with traditional research. Increasingly, success in tenure and/or promotion and increases in salary became closely tied with publication productivity. Promotion and tenure standards at each of these institutions began to emphasize national over local accomplishments and to value published and peer-reviewed writing over other forms of faculty work.

This shift resulted in four institutions characterized by paradox. Throughout this period of increasing research emphasis, many faculty were recruited because they believed their institutions were committed to, and rewarded, faculty service. As a result, to different degrees, each of the four institutions experienced significant difficulty in the late 1980s and early 1990s as a disconnect formed between faculty who emphasized teaching and service and reward systems that favored research. In addition, the institutional rhetoric and mission of each of the institutions remained the same; in each case, the rhetoric suggested that the institution prized and rewarded faculty teaching and service to the community. During the early to mid-1990s at each institution, some faculty who engaged primarily in teaching and service were denied promotion and tenure. Some faculty and administrators at each institution expressed dissatisfaction with inconsistencies between rhetoric and rewards.

### External Catalysts to Reform
External forces frequently force institutions to redirect institutional goals and priorities and undertake change

(Birnbaum, 1988). In the case of these four schools, external forces influenced their administrations' decision to attempt to amend the reward system. For example, PSU experienced a significant budget crisis that triggered a reexamination of the core curriculum and subsequent revision to include greater service-learning. Greater faculty involvement in service-learning triggered more faculty outreach, which encouraged faculty to push for greater alignment between their workloads and rewards. MWSU received a large grant to become a national model for how a major research-oriented land-grant university could weave service into the fabric of academic life, prompting the development of more outreach and reexamination of rewards for outreach. In the first case, a perceived crisis sparked action, in the second, a perceived opportunity.

All four institutions were involved in and influenced by the national movement toward redefining scholarship and faculty rewards that involved hundreds of campuses. Also, the national teacher education movement, which pushed for greater involvement by education faculty in professional development school partnerships, was a major reason that education faculty began to see a need for more flexibility in faculty roles and rewards.

### Internal Catalysts for Reform
The two most significant internal catalysts for reform were leadership and faculty dissatisfaction. For example, on PSU's campus, a new president who pushed for PSU to become an exemplar "urban grant university" played a major role in the decision to revise the reward system. In addition, on each of the four campuses, when faculty were denied promotion and tenure (at least in part) because they emphasized teaching or service over research, they were in disciplines with fewer publication opportunities, or were artists with nontraditional venues for dissemination of their creative work. Many faculty complained to their deans and provosts that the reward system needed to be altered. All of these issues converged in the late 1980s and early 1990s, influencing the institutions' decisions to amend faculty evaluation policies.

### Expanding the Definition of Scholarship
Each of the four campuses took different roads but arrived at the same destination: a new expanded definition of scholarship. PSU and St. Tims took the most conventional route. They held college-wide committee deliberations, circulated drafts, and received faculty

senate approval of a new definition of scholarship for promotion and tenure, which the local units then implemented. MWSU had two college-wide committees that developed criteria to assess service as scholarship; the provost requested, but did not mandate, that the individual colleges use these criteria to evaluate faculty for promotion and tenure. Erin's road to change was the least conventional. Over a ten-year period prior to 1997, the provost served in a variety of administrative positions and roles that gave him the opportunity to "sneak in various forms of clarification" and to "nudge the official promotion policies toward an expanded definition of scholarship." While not officially approved by any faculty governing body, the new definition of scholarship was written into promotion policies and used in faculty evaluation.

## VALUES AND BELIEFS

This section describes the values and beliefs that influenced the promotion process during the 1997–1998 academic year when an expanded definition of scholarship had been in place at MWSU, PSU, and Erin College less than two years and, at St. Tims, five years. Personnel committees reported using criteria to assess service as scholarship that were laid out in policy documents. These criteria included: professional/academic expertise, peer review, evidence of impact, dissemination, originality and innovation, and connection to teaching and research. While there is much to say about the apparent gap between stated criteria and actual practice, as well as the ways in which assessing service as scholarship brings existing measures of scholarship into question, this article does not address criteria unless they intersect with values and beliefs.

Love's (1997) study of campus culture describes paradoxes as aspects of a college's culture that are seemingly contradictory but which, in reality, express a truth. In each of the four cases, some actors held values and beliefs about their institution, scholarship, and faculty careers that supported the traditional definition of scholarship and Boyer's expanded definition of scholarship in promotion decisions. These perspectives resulted in colleges/ units of education that simultaneously embraced and rejected the view that service should be assessed and rewarded as scholarship. Although the same people often held these contradictory perspectives, I describe first the values and beliefs that supported the expanded definition of scholarship, then describe the values and beliefs supporting the

more traditional research paradigm, thus thwarting the intent of the modified promotion policies. Table 1 compares the values/beliefs encouraging and discouraging the assessment and rewarding of service as scholarship.

### Values/Beliefs Supporting the Assessment of Service as Scholarship

"SERVICE IS WHO WE ARE." Each of the four colleges had strong, preexisting service missions. Consequently, when the idea of multiple forms of scholarship was introduced to the college community, faculty and administrators at each institution, and especially at the colleges of education, already considered external service to be "part of who we are as a college/university." When asked about the adoption of the new way of thinking about service as scholarship, the dean of Erin's College of Education replied, "This is a comfortable place for that idea to be introduced. We are an application place here." Likewise, personnel committee members acknowledged that MWSU had always praised service as "an important piece of what people do" and stated that "service is taken very seriously here."

Faculty at each of the four institutions were regularly involved in service that Boyer would characterize as scholarship and viewed it as a critical part of their faculty roles. Faculty were most involved in professional service at PSU, then Erin, then MWSU, and then St. Tims. The involvement of Erin's faculty in service with the Center for Conflict Resolution was typical. The center received grant funding to provide partial released time for faculty to work with schools on conflict resolution programs. The director of the center said, "We've shaped the whole way of thinking about multicultural education and conflict resolution based upon the expertise of academic people here, developmental approaches to it. . . . This all comes from theoretical ideas that have been garnered by our faculty and the grass-roots efforts of community members." One education professor said, "I think it is definitely something about Erin College and this program. Service is considered part of our responsibility. A direct link with the schools is important to us." Faculty involvement in service, their widespread belief that service was a critical part of their institution's identity, and their view of their own faculty roles supported the belief that service should be assessed as scholarship for promotion/ tenure.

## Table 1: Values and Beliefs Related to Service as Scholarship

| VALUES/BELIEF TOPIC | VALUES SUPPORTING SS | VALUES AGAINST SS |
|---|---|---|
| Institutional Identity/Direction | "Service is who we are." | "Climbing the academic ladder is who we are." |
| | "We don't want our institution to be like other institutions." | "We want our institution to be like other institutions." |
| The Nature of Scholarship | "Scholarship can be teaching, integration, discovery, and application." | "Scholarship is empirical research disseminated to the academic community." |
| | "Scholarly work can be completed in collaboration with practioners." | "Scholarly work is completed apart from practioners." |
| | "The best scholarship has the most impact on students, communities, and policy issues." | "The best scholarship brings the most prestige to our positions." |
| | "Writing is scholarly because of what it is and what it does." | "Writing is scholarly because of where it is." |
| | "SS requires as much professional knowledge as other forms of scholarship." | "Traditional research requires more professional knowledge than SS." |
| Faculty Careers/Self-Interest | "The new standards reward all faculty for what they do best, which is in our self-interest." | "New faculty should have the same standards I did or the system will not be fair." |
| | "Doesn't affect me. I don't care." | "I care; if standards are perceived to be lower, my department and posisiton will be diminished." |

Not only were faculty socialized to see service as part of their institutional identity and faculty role, but they were also socialized to see service as a critical part of their identity as scholars. Even though the idea of service as a form of scholarship was new to most faculty linguistically and conceptually, the concept of "service as important work for scholars to do" was embedded in each college's culture at the time of promotion and tenure policy changes. A PSU faculty member reported: "The intellectual work of education professors is to conceptualize issues of community." It was clear that, at all of the institutions but especially at Erin College, education faculty considered a close partnership with local schools as essential to their own research and teaching. This understanding among faculty was a strong foundation from which to cultivate the idea that service should be assessed and rewarded as scholarship.

In addition, the applied and professional nature of the education discipline greatly shaped role socialization concerning service. Faculty in each case, even in the most research-oriented cultures of PSU and MWSU, valued applied knowledge and thought it would ultimately make the biggest difference in their discipline. One Erin College personnel committee member said, "I think that one of the things that Erin College tries to do is to really live the rhetoric of balancing theory and practice; and there is new knowledge to be gained in basic research and new knowledge to be gained in the domains of practice." Faculty and administrator service orientation created a fertile ground for accepting the new reward policy. "We don't want to be like other institutions." Another value that advanced the adoption of an expanded definition of scholarship was a clear message emanating from faculty and administrators:

**"WE DON'T WANT TO BE LIKE THE OTHER INSTITUTIONS."** Each of the four institutions in this study exhibited anti-isomorphism, or resistance to resembling other institutions in the environment. Like the school child who is picked last for the team and then decides he didn't want to play anyway, some might argue that anti-isomorphism was the institution's response to being less distinctive in the mainstream competition and, consequently, opting to play a different game. For example, one PSU administrator said PSU didn't have as much to lose from risktaking as other institutions because it was already "a wart on the back of higher education." By this, he meant that both research universities and liberal arts colleges would look down on PSU for its professional service focus (as opposed to research and teaching), no matter what it did. Therefore, there was no reason for the university not to "be itself." Furthermore, because of PSU's perpetual budget crises, its leaders shared the consensus that "we can't afford to do things the normal way."

By virtue of being deemed second class by one rating system or another, these institutions wanted to appear markedly different than the status quo. They wanted to stand out without being elitist and sought ways to be at odds with the established norms of higher education. For example, in the mindset of the faculty, Erin's social justice values and reputation for teaching excellence were opposite to the qualities a research university cultivates. Consequently, Erin prided itself on not being a research university.

The anti-isomorphic attitude seemed to be based on more than sour grapes. In a positive way, these institutions and their faculty seemed to have made choices to be different—even when (in certain areas) they could have been or already were first on the team, among their peers. They were proud of these choices. The belief among faculty and administrators that they personally and their institution were "an underdog," "different," and/or had "chosen the road less traveled" in higher education also paved the way for faculty to buy

in to the idea of multiple forms of scholarship. These faculty and, collectively, their institutions, enjoyed being considered a maverick in a variety of ways and were proud to be among the first institutions in the country adopting a new or different way of thinking about faculty roles and rewards.

**"WE DEFINE SCHOLARSHIP BROADLY."** By the time the amended reward policies were introduced, at least two thirds of the education faculty in this study had been exposed to Boyer's *Scholarship Reconsidered* and to the views of other higher education commentators that "scholarship" is more than traditional research. In addition, most personnel committee members had experience in assessing teaching as scholarship through teaching portfolios. Consequently, most personnel committee members approached assessing service as scholarship with at least some vague familiarity with the concept, even if they had no idea how to do it. Personnel committee members at Erin College (even before the policy change) prided themselves on Erin's openness to multiple forms of scholarship. A former personnel committee member at Erin College stated:

> I define scholarship broadly . . . as creating a musical composition . . . as art work . . . as an expression through various modes of creative thinking and critical analysis . . . much more than publishing articles in obscure journals that are read by ten people in the universe and riddled with footnotes, as if that is the sign of an impressive mind at work. One of the reasons I like working here is Erin is an environment that allows one to think outside the traditional boxes.

The history of faculty having been exposed to the idea of multiple forms of scholarship and taking for granted that they themselves had "always defined scholarship broadly," paved the way for adopting a new way of assessing faculty work for promotion and tenure.

**"NOT ALL SCHOLARSHIP APPEARS IN TIER I JOURNALS."** While standards for promotion and tenure had become more traditional on each of the campuses prior to the introduction of the new promotion policies, some faculty already viewed writing in practitioner journals, grant publications, and other less peer-reviewed venues, as scholarship. Some faculty in each institution further felt that applied writing venues were "making a bigger difference." Erin's dean of the School of Education explained that many of its faculty could publish in traditional journals but chose less traditional writing venues because they placed greater value in reaching practitioner audiences. The dean said:

> There is a more comfortable fit in this community than there was at [former research university] concerning nontraditional scholarship. I think there are a number of people who became faculty members at Erin College because of that viewpoint—not that they are opposed to writing in the narrow sense of scholarship, but they are more in the application stage, the doing. So, if they write a textbook, that is where some may feel more comfortable. I mean, that is where they would like to put their time and their energy rather than feeling as though they have to write just for refereed journals. I think there is a value part of service as scholarship. In many research universities, that would not get high marks.

Faculty at Erin College were the most comfortable, and MWSU faculty the least, with nontraditional writing venues, but all four campuses had some history of counting writing for practitioner audiences as scholarship for promotion and/or tenure. Values supporting the legitimacy of scholarship published in nonrefereed or practitioner journals were important for promotion decisions because service scholarship is often disseminated through practitioner periodicals rather than academic journals.

**"WE SHOULD BE REWARDED FOR WHAT WE DO."** There was a belief among faculty in all four cases that they personally worked hard, did good work, and deserved to be tenured and/or promoted. There was no significant difference in this self-image between traditional scholars and those faculty engaged in teaching and service scholarship, between faculty at the most research-oriented university (MWSU) or the least (St. Tims), or between younger and older faculty. Even though some faculty expressed concern over their chances for advancement, this did not diminish their own feeling of entitlement and the view that "not being rewarded for all that I do would be unfair." This belief among faculty complemented acceptance of the expanded definition of scholarship because every faculty member saw his or her work falling into this new model somewhere, even if he or she was more critical of peers.

**"DOESN'T AFFECT ME. I DON'T CARE."** William Mallon (2002) has written about faculty zones of indifference in relation to promotion and tenure, and the tendency on some campuses for faculty members to be uninterested in their institution's national reputations in disci-

plinary associations or their department's rankings. This indifference to isomorphic pressures can enable change simply by not preventing it. To a small degree, a force that supported the adoption of the modified policies was a lack of resistance from faculty members who were too involved in their own work to care if the college changed their definition of scholarship and their reward policy. These faculty were willing to accept whatever definition of scholarship was provided and did not push to maintain the traditional definition of scholarship for promotion and tenure.

### Values/Beliefs Supporting Traditional Scholarship

Values and beliefs working against the assessment of service as scholarship reflected a desire on the part of faculty, administrators, and the institution to mimic more prestigious universities than their own in emphases and rewards. This tendency has been described as isomorphism, academic ratcheting, and institutional drift.

**"OUR INSTITUTION SHOULD TRY TO CLIMB THE ACADEMIC LADDER."** Some faculty, administrators, and personnel committee members at each of the four institutions believed that their institution should try to become more like other higher education institutions and strive to climb the ladder of traditional ranking systems. Service scholarship was "nice" but would not help their institution gain higher rankings and more prestige. Therefore it was not a faculty activity they wanted to reward or "promote." For example, during the dean tenure at MWSU, the College of Education viewed itself as one of the best in the country and was eager to maintain and improve its status in *U.S. News and World Report* rankings. Because those ratings rely heavily on faculty publication productivity, and number and sums of research grants received, MWSU's personnel believed that, if its College of Education rewarded service as scholarship, there would be less traditional scholarship and the institution might slip downward in national graduate school rankings.

Self-interest also played a role. Each institution had faculty who felt that their college/university should not become too innovative, otherwise it would raise questions within the state and national system of higher education. School of Education programs, students, and faculty would not be transferable to other institutions, and their own professional standing within higher education would decrease. Considering their institution to already be too counter-cultural among their peers, they wanted it to become more mainstream, traditional. Becoming more traditional meant rejecting the expanded definition of scholarship and maintaining a hard line on research as the only form of scholarship to be assessed and rewarded.

Values concerning institutional self-image were most apparent in decisions regarding promotion to full professor. This evaluation became contested ground in a culture war between faculty who had supported the expanded definition of scholarship and those who wanted to increase the prestige of the college or unit of education and institution by hiring and promoting more traditional scholars. This phenomenon was most conspicuous at MWSU, PSU, and St. Tims to the same degree at all three and present to only a small degree at Erin College. Personnel committee members admitted that while they approved of the concept of multiple forms of scholarship—and felt good about approving "alternative career tracks" to associate professor—they felt less comfortable with teaching or service scholars being promoted to full professor. For example, when I asked a PSU personnel committee member what kind of service scholarship would lead to promotion to full professor, he answered, "The written products would have to be at a tremendous, mastery level, something of great magnitude that people could really sink their teeth into." Yet he could not imagine what these products would look like and said he doubted they existed. Senior faculty conjectured that promotion to full professor sent strong messages about institutional identity and direction. A few senior faculty at PSU noted that reward systems are "culture-building." They were not sure if they approved of the culture that would be formed under the new policy.

**"SCHOLARSHIP IS DISCOVERING THEORETICAL KNOWLEDGE WHICH SETS THE SCHOLAR APART FROM OTHERS."** Before the majority of faculty at PSU and Erin College, and many at MWSU and St. Tims, were socialized by their institutions to see service as scholarship, faculty from each institution were socialized in graduate school to believe that scholars were people who created new theoretical knowledge for the academic community and that faculty hold their positions in universities by virtue of the theoretical expertise they demonstrate in writing. Most faculty in these cases were trained to believe that scholarship is completed apart from practitioners and is scholarship only when it appears in peer-reviewed print.

Service scholarship is often the application of existing knowledge in a practical setting and/or the creation of new knowledge about practice. Faculty engage in this work in partnership with practitioners in the field so that there is "a reciprocal movement between theory and practice" (Ramaley, 1999). When this happens, faculty members facilitate the flow of knowledge and become partners in knowledge production. Some faculty, administrators, and personnel committee members saw this partnership and facilitation role as an abdication of the appropriate faculty role as expert and, therefore, as something that should not be rewarded.

Some personnel committee members commented that they did not believe a university should consist of "field people." For example, one PSU personnel committee member said, "There is some concern that we're not even sure what scholarship is anymore. Are we really changing our culture here? I mean, are we really an academic, intellectual community or are we becoming like the people we serve—you know, more field based, more practitioner?" MWSU's dean commented, "There were faculty involved in the schools who had, in many people's view, gone sort of native in terms of service; you get involved with the troops out there and you become one of them, forgetting that you are part of the university community and that role has responsibilities in a different way." The belief that expertise is exclusively demonstrated in writing, as opposed to demonstrated in practice, and that applying existing knowledge in community settings or discovering applied knowledge, especially in partnership with other community "experts," does not demonstrate that expertise worked against the acceptance and application of the new promotion policies.

**"RESEARCH IS HARDER AND REQUIRES MORE PROFESSIONAL KNOWLEDGE THAN SERVICE."** There were conscious and unconscious beliefs, even among those who advocated rewarding multiple forms of scholarship, that research is the "real hard work" of scholarship, and that it is more time-consuming and intellectual than service scholarship. Additionally, some senior faculty and personnel committee members said that, if they rewarded service as scholarship, they feared fewer faculty would choose to "carve out" time for research.

**"THEY SHOULD HAVE THE SAME STANDARDS I DID."** Some senior faculty and administrators who had been at their institutions fifteen years or more commented that, to be fair, new faculty should have to live up to the same "harder" standards they had had to endure. These faculty wanted to continue assessing scholarship the "old way" to ensure that junior faculty did not "get over" by changing research requirements. If the unspoken understanding in a particular department in 1980 was that a faculty member needed to have 10 articles in Tier I journals for tenure, some senior faculty believed junior faculty should have the same number of articles completed in 1998, regardless of service scholarship. One way this view manifested itself was in hallway conversations among senior faculty. A senior faculty member at PSU commented, "I don't know what all the fuss is about. All education faculty work with communities." She then explained that she and other senior faculty had been commenting that, when they went up for tenure, they remembered having to engage in this kind of service and meet rigid research requirements. This viewpoint shaped some personnel committee members' decisions and negatively influenced the application of new policies to promotion decisions.

**"REAL SCHOLARSHIP IS PUBLISHED IN TIER I JOURNALS."** Despite how some senior faculty remembered their own tenure reviews, there were histories, dating back a few years for some institutions and many years for others, of promotion and tenure applications with very little traditional scholarship. By the early 1990s, changes in the academic labor market had brought more traditional scholars to campus. There was a tendency by some committees to compare the scholarly portfolios of traditional and nontraditional scholars and give more praise to the traditional portfolio simply because it was different from the submissions of more "homegrown" faculty. This was most true at Erin and St. Tims but less true at MWSU and PSU. The chair of the personnel committee at Erin College commented:

> There was tension. You might think that our faculty would be the first to embrace broader ways of thinking about scholarship and teaching and service but people articulate certain things and then fall back into old frameworks when they are evaluating applicants for promotion so that even though people could articulate, "Yes, scholarship is more than that esoteric piece in that obscure journal," once the esoteric piece was in front of them, they were drooling. You know, it was like—this is real . . . This is REAL scholarship.

Faculty on personnel committees had been trained to understand that the peer review system that governed journal publications was a sanctioned indicator of quality research. These faculty had no experience dis-

cerning quality service scholarship and had no way of pointing to any existing rating system for assistance. For example, one personnel committee chair commented:

> It is harder to make the case (for service as scholarship) because we don't have the typical indicators for service that we have for research where we can search Citation Index and see how many times people cited your work and say, "You must really be hot stuff because all of these people are using your name in their work." We don't have those kinds of indicators in service.

Consequently when committee members saw research published in Tier I journals, it was hard for them not to believe that it was of greater quality than service scholarship.

**"THE BEST SCHOLARSHIP BRINGS THE MOST PRESTIGE TO THE INSTITUTION."** An important undercurrent running beneath all promotion and tenure decisions was, "What has/will this candidate do to distinguish the college and, consequently, my position?" Because service scholarship was a newer form of faculty work with fewer disciplinary and national allegiances, fewer journals, and fewer national methods of dissemination, it also had fewer opportunities than those existing in research to garner national prestige or raise the institution's national rankings. In most cases, it was very difficult for faculty members to demonstrate national impact in a medium that was structurally more local. Newspaper articles, small grants, and even national service awards were not perceived as adding anything substantial to their colleague's "positions." The belief that scholarship should help the institution climb the academic ladder disadvantaged the acceptance and application of the new policies for promotion decisions.

**"WE MUST APPEAR TO HAVE HIGH STANDARDS."** MWSU, PSU, and St. Tims's personnel committee members all reported that, in the first few months or years after expanding the definition of scholarship, they experienced pressures to appear to their colleagues as if they were doing a "rigorous assessment" when they evaluated service scholarship portfolios. Committee members said there was a "saving face" aspect of their work after policy implementation that made decisions on service-as-scholarship cases into political statements, rather than objective assessments of faculty work. They believed that promoting someone who emphasized service scholarship might seem as if they were letting "anyone pass through."

## IMPLICATIONS

These findings reveal three interesting challenges for institutions trying to strengthen their service mission, support a diverse faculty, and/or reform faculty roles and rewards.

**THE FIRST CHALLENGE IS ACKNOWLEDGING THAT REWARD SYSTEMS ARE ABOUT WHO WE VALUE AS WELL AS WHAT WE VALUE.** Increasingly, faculty are responding to calls from the public and from their institution to link their expertise to public concerns (Hollander & Hartley, 2000). Faculty in professional schools most heavily experience these expectations to engage in service scholarship and to do so despite a socialization process and reward system warning that spending time in the community may jeopardize their careers in the university (Checkoway, 2001). The faculty most heavily engaged in service scholarship are also the most marginalized within academic culture—i.e., women, faculty of color, assistant professors (Antonio, Astin & Cress, 2000; Bellas & Toutkoushian, 1999; Sax et al., 1996). In this study, 90% of the faculty who self-identified as being involved in service scholarship were women and 25% were faculty of color. These findings underscore the argument others have made (Rice, Sorcinelli & Austin 2000) that the values and beliefs sustaining traditional academic reward structures do not support the professional interests of a diverse faculty nor a diverse mission.

Antonio, Astin, and Cress (2000) concluded that, as long as service activities are practiced by marginalized faculty, they will remain marginalized in academe. This study supports these findings, further adding the conclusion that, as long as values and beliefs supporting service scholarship are held by faculty with the least status within the academy, those values and beliefs will remain marginalized in academe. For example, service scholars tend to reject the positivist paradigm that scholars are "detached" experts and instead regard community members as research partners in knowledge production (Checkoway, 2001). As long as faculty invested in the status quo shape the definitions and rewards of faculty work, newer forms of scholarship and values about its creation may not have a voice in academic culture.

My findings suggest that many faculty hold values and beliefs about service scholarship that doubt and devalue its scholarly nature, purpose, and products. Other scholars have noted an ambiguity, lack of readiness, and resistance to assessing, rewarding, and valuing teaching scholarship (Brand, 2000). Given that service and teaching are two primary scholarly interests of women and faculty of color, should we be surprised that these faculty, more than any other, experience less satisfaction with the academic workplace, endure more subtle discrimination, and have greater concerns that they are not taken seriously as scholars (Sax et al., 1999)?

Creamer (1998) argued that traditional measures of scholarly output skew productivity ratings toward White and Asian men and away from women and Blacks. Boyer's (1990) framework for expanding the definition of scholarship was an attempt to mute the trend toward valuing traditional research exclusively by making multiple forms of scholarship visible and by elevating their status within the reward system.

Ultimately, faculty who fulfill their institutions' mission of sharing and applying knowledge with their community should be rewarded. Asking faculty to do one thing and be rewarded for another is dysfunctional for individuals and for institutions (Checkoway, 2001). Faculty who commit their professional expertise to service scholarship should have the same opportunity to achieve recognition, respect, and standing in the academic hierarchy that faculty involved in other scholarly work are afforded. Institutions committed to attracting and retaining a diverse faculty might consider exploring the forms of scholarship their faculty most value and, if consistent with their mission, find ways to integrate this scholarly work, values, and commitments into their reward systems.

**A SECOND CHALLENGE POSED BY THIS STUDY IS THE NEED TO MAKE CONTRADICTIONS VISIBLE.** This study suggests that, even when official policy language includes the evaluation and reward of multiple forms of scholarship, conscious and unconscious values and beliefs held by faculty facilitating the reward system can prevent newer forms of scholarly work from being accepted and rewarded. Data from this study demonstrate the critical role that values and beliefs play in organizational culture and change.

Administrators and faculty can initiate dialogue about the values and beliefs that shape faculty work-life in several ways. One of the most effective ways to highlight the differences between espoused values and enacted values is to develop an awareness of contradictions (Love, 1997; Peterson, Cameron, Mets, Jones, & Ettington, 1986). For example, administrators can gather information about promotion and tenure cases in aggregate form and point out to personnel committees, department chairs, and faculty that their institution says it rewards service scholarship but did not award tenure to any of the applicants with strong service portfolios in the past three years, without delving into individual cases. This approach can facilitate a discussion focused on underlying values of institutional identity and direction, the nature of scholarship, and faculty careers. Values and beliefs that support and discourage the valuing of multiple forms of scholarship could be explored. Intentionally using elements of the culture to introduce dissonance about faculty roles and rewards may allow critical analyses of institutional values and philosophy (Love, 1997). By doing this, the institution and individual members might "evoke their better nature" (Burns, 1978, qtd. in Bolman and Deal, 1991, p. 314) and decide to work toward greater congruence between what they say they value and what really counts in faculty rewards.

**THE THIRD CHALLENGE IMPLIED IN THESE FINDINGS IS THE QUESTION OF FAIRNESS.** What is fair? At the heart of faculty anxiety about promotion and tenure seems to be the question, "What will my colleagues value?" The answer, of course, lies both within and outside of official faculty evaluation policy. Faculty evaluation, like education, will always be shaped by history, relations of power, values, and assumptions. Given this reality, debates about "appropriate scholarship" should be unpacked within departments before candidates are evaluated. Otherwise the discrepancy between espoused values and actual values will hurt academic careers and thwart institutional goals. Tenure and promotion are the valuing of people's professional lives. If nothing else, this process should not take place in the dark.

# REFERENCES

ACE. (1999). On change III: Taking charge of change: A Primer for colleges and universities. An occasional paper of the ACE Project on Leadership and Institutional Transformation. Washington, DC: ACE.

Antonio, A., Astin, H., & Cress, C. (2000). Community service in higher education: A look at the nation's faculty. Review of Higher Education, 23(4), 373–397.

Argyris, C., & Schon, D. A. (1974). Theory in practice: Increasing professional effectiveness. San Francisco: Jossey-Bass.

Bellas, M., & Toutkoushian, R. (1999). Faculty time allocations and research productivity: Gender, race, and family effects. Review of Higher Education, 22(4), 367–390.

Becher, T. (1989). Academic tribes and territories: Intellectual inquiry and the culture of disciplines. Buckingham, Eng.: Open University Press.

Bergquist, W. H. (1992). Four cultures of the academy. San Francisco: Jossey-Bass.

Biglan, A. (1973). The characteristics of subject matter in different academic areas. Journal of Applied Psychology, 57(3), 195–203.

Birnbaum, R. (1988). How colleges work. San Francisco: Jossey-Bass.

Bolman, L. G., & Deal, T. E. (1991). Reframing organizations: Artistry, choice and leadership. San Francisco: Jossey-Bass.

Boyer, E. (1990). Scholarship reconsidered. Princeton, NJ: Carnegie Foundation for the Advancement of Teaching.

Brand, M. (2000). Changing faculty roles in research universities: Using the pathways strategy. Change, 32(6), 42–45.

Braxton, J., Luckey, W., Helland, P., Coneal, W., & Carey, S. (2000, November). The institutionalization of Boyer's four domains of scholarship by institutional type and by academic discipline. Paper presented at the annual meeting of the American Association for the Study of Higher Education.

Burns, G. M. (1978). Leadership. New York: Harper and Row.

Campoy, R. W. (1996, March). Teacher education goes to school. American School Board Journal, 32–34.

Carnegie Council on Policy Studies in Higher Education. (1976). A classification of institutions of higher education (Rev. ed). Berkeley: University of California Press.

Chait, R. (1998). Ideas in incubation: Three possible modifications to traditional tenure policies. New Pathways Working Paper Series, Inquiry No. 9. Washington, DC: American Association for Higher Education.

Checkoway, B. (2001). Renewing the civic mission of the American research university. Journal of Higher Education, 72(2), 125–147.

Creamer, E. (1998). Assessing faculty publication productivity: Issues of equity. ASHEERIC Higher Education Report, Vol. 26, No. 2. Washington, DC: George Washington University.

Driscoll, A., & Lynton, E. A. (1999). Making outreach visible: A guide to documenting professional service and outreach. Washington, DC: American Association for Higher Education.

Gamson, Z. F., & Finnegan, D. E. (1996). Disciplinary adaptations to research culture in comprehensive institutions. Review of Higher Education, 19(2), 141–177.

Glassick, C. E., Huber, M. T., & Maeroff, G. I. (1997). *Scholarship assessed: Evaluation of the professoriate*. San Francisco: Jossey-Bass.

Gmelch, W. H., Lovrich, N. P., & Wilkie, P. K. (1986). Dimensions of stress among university faculty: Factor analysis results form a national study. *Research in Higher Education, 24*, 266–286.

Hollander, E., & Hartley, M. (2000). Civic renewal in higher education: The state of the movement and the need for a natural network. In T. Ehrlich (Ed.), *Higher education and civic responsibility*. Phoenix, AZ: Oryz Press.

Hutchings, P., & Shulman, L. S. (1999). Scholarship of teaching. *Change, 31*(5), 11–15.

Kirshstein, R. J. (1997, March). What faculty do? A look at academic work. Paper presented at the meeting of the American Educational Research Association, Chicago, IL.

Kuh, G. D., & Whitt, E. J. (1988). *The invisible tapestry: Culture in American colleges and universities*. ASHE-ERIC Higher Education Report, No. 1. Washington, D.C.: Association for the Study of Higher Education.

Lindquist, J. (1978). *Strategies for change*. Washington, DC: Council of Independent Colleges.

Love, P. (1997). Contradiction and paradox: Attempting to change the culture of sexual orientation at a small Catholic college. *Review of Higher Education, 20*(4), 381–398.

Lynton, E. A. (1995). *Making the case for professional service*. Washington, DC: American Association for Higher Education.

Mallon, W. (2002). Why is tenure one college's problem and another's solution? In R. P. Chait (Ed.), *The questions of tenure* (pp. 246–272). Cambridge, MA: Harvard University Press.

Miles, M. B., & Huberman, A. M. (1994). *Qualitative data analysis* (2nd ed.). Thousand Oaks, CA: Sage Publications.

Peterson, M. W., Cameron, K. S., Mets, L. A., Jones, P., & Ettington, D. (1986). *The organizational context for teaching and learning: A review of the research literature*. Ann Arbor, MI: National Center for Research to Improve Postsecondary Teaching and Learning.

Ramaley, J. (1999, July). Concluding plenary session: What are the priorities? What are the next steps? What have we learned. Presented at the Strategies for Renewing the Civic Mission of the American Research University, Wingspread Conference, Racine, WI.

Rice, E. (1986, January). The academic profession in transition: Toward a new social fiction. *Teaching Sociology*, 12–23.

Rice, E. (1996). *Making a place for the new American scholar*. New Pathways Working Paper Series, Inquiry No. 1.

Washington, DC: American Association for Higher Education.

Rice, E., Sorcinelli, M. D., & Austin, A. E. (2000). *Heeding new voices: Academic careers for a new generation*. New Pathways Working Paper Series, Inquiry No. 7. Washington, DC: American Association for Higher Education.

Sax, L. J., Astin, A., Arredondo, M., & Korn, W. S. (1996). *The American college teacher: National norms for the 1995–96 HERI faculty survey*. Los Angeles: Higher Education Research Institute, University of California.

Schein, E. H. (1992). *Organizational culture and leadership*. (2nd ed.). San Francisco: Jossey-Bass.

Senge, P. S. (1990). *The fifth discipline*. New York: Currency/Doubleday.

Sorcinelli, M. D. (1992). New and junior faculty stress: Research and responses. In M. D. Sorcinelli & A. E. Austin (Eds.). *Developing new and junior faculty*. New Directions for Teaching and Learning (Vol. 50, pp. 27–37). San Francisco: Jossey-Bass.

Sanderson, A., Phua, V. C., & Herda, D. (1999). *The American faculty poll: Final report*. New York: TIAA-CREF.

Tierney, W. G., & Bensimon, E. M. (1996) *Promotion and tenure: Community and socialization in academe*. Albany: State University of New York Press.

Viechnicki, K. J., Yanity, D., & Olinski, R. (1997, March). Action research in a school/university partnership. Paper presented at the annual meeting of the American Educational Research Association, Chicago, IL.

Yin, R. K. (1994). *Case study research: Design and methods*. Applied Social Research Methods Series, No. 5. Newbury Park, CA: Sage Publications.

**KERRYANN O'MEARA** is an Assistant Professor in Higher Education at the University of Massachusetts Amherst. Her scholarly efforts focus on organizational behavior and change, academic culture, and the service mission of colleges and universities. She thanks Robert Birnbaum, Cathy Burack, Cathy Trower, and two anonymous reviewers for comments on earlier drafts of this paper, which is drawn from a larger study on the process of integrating service as scholarship into academic reward systems: *Scholarship Unbound: Assessing Service as Scholarship for Promotion and Tenure* (New York: RoutledgeFalmer, 2002), part of the Studies in Higher Education Dissertation Series, edited by Philip G. Altbach. Address queries to her at the Department of Educational Policy, Research, and Administration, University of Massachusetts Amherst, Amherst, MA 01003-9308.

# Academic Culture:
## Recommended Reading

## BOOKS & CHAPTERS

Bhaerman, R., Cordell, K., & Gomez B. (1998). *The role of service-learning in educational reform*. Springfield, VA: National Society for Experiential Education.

Bok, D. (1982). *Beyond the ivory tower: Social responsibilities of the modern university*. Cambridge, MA: Harvard University Press.

Bowen, H. (1997). *Investment in learning: The individual and social value of American higher education*. Baltimore, MD: John Hopkins University Press.

Boyer, E. (1990). *Scholarship reconsidered: Priorities of the professoriate*. Lawrenceville, NJ. Princeton University Press.

Bringle, R., Games, R., & Malloy E. (1999). *Colleges and universities as citizens*. Needham, MA: Allyn and Bacon.

Burton, J., Kaplan, L., et al. (2002). Liberal arts college faculty reflect on service learning: Steps on a transformative journey. In Kenny, M.E., Simon, L.A.K., Kiley-Brabeck, K. & Lerner, R.M. (Eds.), *Learning to serve: Promoting civil society through service-learning*. Norwell, MA: Kluwer Academic Publishers

Driscoll, A., & Lynton, E. (1999). *Making outreach visible: A guide to documenting professional service outreach*. Washington, DC: American Association of Higher Education.

Ellacuria, I. (1991). Is a different university possible? In J. Hasset & H. Lacey (Eds.), *Towards a society that serves its people: The intellectual contribution of El Savador's murdered Jesuits* (pp. 208–219). Washington, DC: Georgetown University Press.

Gardner, J. (1990). *On leadership*. New York: The Free Press.

Jacoby, B. (1996). *Service-learning in higher education*. San Francisco: Jossey-Bass.

Kennedy, D. (1997). *Academic duty*. Cambridge, MA: Harvard University Press.

Kerr, C. (1995). *Uses of the university*. Cambridge, MA: Harvard University Press.

Lempert, D. (1996). *Escape from the ivory tower: Student adventures in democratic experiential education*. San Francisco: Jossey-Bass.

Lynton, E. (1995). *Making the case for professional service*. Washington, DC: American Association for Higher Education.

Martin, J. (1984). *Changing the educational landscape: Philosophy, women, and the curriculum*. New York: Routledge.

O'Banion, T. (1997). *A learning college for the 21st century*. Phoenix: American Council on Education/Oryx Press.

Rubin, S. (1990). Transforming the university through service-learning. In C.I. Delve, S.D. Mintz, & G.M. Stewart (Eds.), *Community service as values education* (pp. 111–124). San Francisco: Jossey-Bass.

Senge, P. (1990). *The fifth discipline: The art and practice of the learning organization*. New York: Currency/Doubleday.

Shor, I. (1992). *Empowering education: Critical teaching for social change*. Chicago: University of Chicago Press.

## ARTICLES & REPORTS

Astin, A.W., Keup, J.R., & Lindholm, J.A. (2002). A decade of changes in undergraduate education: A national study of system "transformation." *The Review of Higher Education*, 25 (2), 141–162.

Atkinson, M.P. (2001). The scholarship of teaching and learning: Reconceptualizing scholarship and transforming the academy. *Social Forces*, 79 (4), 1217–29.

Barber, B. (1991). A mandate for liberty: Requiring education-based community service. *The Responsive Community*, 1, 46–55.

Barr, R.B. & Tagg, J. (1995) From teaching to learning: A new paradigm for undergraduate education. *Change*, 6 (6), 12–25.

Benson, L., & Harkavy, I. (2002). Democratization over commodification! An action-oriented strategy to overcome the contradictory legacy of American higher education. *The Journal of Public Affairs*, 6 [suppl. 1], 19–38.

Boyer, E. (1991, March 9) Creating the new American college. *Chronicle of Higher Education*, A18

Bok, D. (1974). On the purposes of undergraduate education. *The Journal of the American Academy of Arts and Sciences*, 1, 159–173.

Bringle, R. & Hatcher, J. (1996). Implementing service-learning in higher education. *Journal of Higher Education*, 67 (2), 221–239.

Bringle, R. & Hatcher, J. (1997). Engaging and supporting faculty in service-learning. *Journal of Public Service and Outreach*, 2 (1), 43–51.

Franco, R.W. (2000, October). The community college conscience: Service-learning and training tomorrow's teachers. Report prepared for the Education Commission of the States, Center For Community College Policy, Denver, CO.

Franco, R.W. (2002). The civic role of community colleges: Preparing students for the work of democracy. [Supplemental issue 1: Civic engagement and higher education]. *The Journal of Public Affairs*, 6, 119–138.

Furco, A. (2001). Advancing service learning at research universities. *New Directions for Higher Education*, 114, 67–78.

Holland, B. (1997a). Analyzing institutional commitment to service: A model of key organizational factors. *Michigan Journal of Community Service Learning*, 5, 42–55.

Holland, B. (1997b). Factors and strategies that influence faculty involvement in public service. *Journal of Public Service and Outreach*, 4 (1), 37–43

Johnston, R. (1998). The university of the future: Boyer revisited. *Higher Education*, 36 (3), 253–72.

Kezar, A. & Rhoads, R.A. (2001). The dynamic tensions of service-learning in higher education: A philosophical perspective. *The Journal of Higher Education*, 72 (2), 148–71.

Kozeracki, C.A. (2000). Service-learning in the community college. *Community College Review*, 24 (4), 54–70.

Mattson, K. (1998). Can service-learning transform the modern university? A lesson from history. *Michigan Journal of Community Service Learning*, 5, 108–113.

O'Byrne, K. (2001). How professors can promote service-learning in a teaching institution. *New Directions for Higher Education*, 114, 79–87.

Prins, E.S. (2002). The relationship between institutional mission, service, and service-learning at community colleges in New York State. *Michigan Journal of Community Service Learning*, 8 (2), 35–49.

Robinson, T. (2000). Dare the school build a new social order? *Michigan Journal of Community Service Learning*, 7, 142–57.

Salthmarsh. J. (Ed.). (2002). Supplemental issue 1: Civic engagement for higher education. *The Journal of Public Affairs*.

Schall, E. (1995). Learning to love the swamp: Reshaping education for public service. *Journal of Policy Analysis and Management*, 14 (2), 202–220.

Shumer, R. (1994). Community-based learning: Humanizing education. *Journal of Adolescence*, 17, 357–367.

Ward, K. (1996). Service-learning and student volunteerism: Reflections on institutional commitments. *Michigan Journal of Community Service Learning*, 3, 55–65.

Ward, K. (1998). Addressing academic culture: Service-learning, organizations, and faculty work. *New Directions for Teaching and Learning*, 73, 73–80.

Weinberg, A. S. (2002). The university: An agent of social change? *Qualitative Sociology*, 25 (2), 263–272.

Zahorski, K.J. (2002). Scholarship in the postmodern era: New venues, new values, new visions. [special issue]. *New Directions for Teaching and Learning*, 90.

Zlotkowski, E. (1997). Service-learning and the process of academic renewal. *Journal of Public Service and Outreach*, 2 (1), 80–87.

Zlotkowski, E. (2001). Humanistic learning and service-learning at the liberal arts college. *New Directions for Higher Education*, 114, 89–96.

Zlotkowski, E. (2002). Social crises and the faculty response. *The Journal of Public Affairs*, 6 [suppl.1], 1–18.

# Promotion and Tenure

## TITLES IN THIS SECTION

Introduction

Sample Promotion and Tenure Guidelines:

- California State University-Monterey Bay

- Montclair State University

- Portland State University

Recommended Reading

## QUESTIONS FOR REFLECTION AND PLANNING

Where is/would service-learning be located in the reward structure of your institution? In which areas would service fall (e.g., scholarship, research, professional development, public outreach)?

Does your institution support community-based scholarship? How is that evidenced?

Would service enhance or impede the tenure process?

SERVICE-LEARNING EMERGED in the late 1980's as it became apparent that for service to broadly infuse academic culture and to a have a deeper cognitive and civic dimension, it would have to be closely linked to the central educational enterprise of higher education. Service-learning marked the shift from community service to service that was linked with academic study. During the early 1990's, service-learning spread across college campuses as a pedagogy of action and reflection that connected students' academic study with problem-solving experiences in local community settings. As increased numbers of faculty became involved in redesigning their curricula to incorporate service-learning, institutional issues began to emerge that challenged established institutional practices. One key issue is defined by the role service-learning can play in pushing institutions to redefine current systems of faculty roles and rewards. A significant obstacle to the growth of service-learning is the value institutions place upon nontraditional teaching and learning practices. In other words, many faculty question whether adopting service-learning impedes their promotion and tenure.

The devaluing of service-learning in the traditional academic reward structure was experienced by many early service-learning faculty and is an experience many have struggled to reconcile and understand. As Gary Hesser, a pioneering faculty member in service-learning recalls:

> This is hard to articulate, because I don't want to come down hard on the College of Wooster. They had this rather phenomenal urban service-learning program and have it to this day. But where my inclination was to work with those students when they came back to campus, the college wanted me and my colleagues to put our time into much more traditional academic matters. They wanted me to write and do research. When my tenure came up, my colleagues in urban studies were absolutely amazed that there was not a single evaluation given of my interdisciplinary urban studies work, much less living with students in the [community service] house and trying to promote it. The barrier still seemed to be that the college wanted my kind of involvement with students, but they didn't have a way to value and support people who gave that kind of energy and involvement.
>
> I don't think it's fair to point to the college and say, "That's what cost me tenure," but that would be part of it. The college during that time was still trying to become a small Princeton of the Midwest. It had image goals. When I got to Augsburg College in Minneapolis, a much more modest and humble place in both its history and resources, the faculty had thought through and affirmed the value of the external community as a resource for learning. At Wooster, there was still a very classic, traditional view of education. (Stanton, Giles and Cruz, 1999)

Kenneth Reardon, currently a full professor at Cornell University, describes his experiences with promotion and tenure at the University of Illinois at Champaign-Urbana:

> The conflict is age old, and it seems like a sore that won't heal. But if you want to institutionalize service-learning, it can't be done in student affairs. It has to be done in academic affairs. And with cuts, at least on our campus, tenure criteria are getting more conservative. Fewer people are getting approved for this kind of work. Regardless of the

rhetorical commitments of Campus Compact presidents, in places like Illinois, that just doesn't count. I still can't get tenure except in the most traditional criteria. That's a big issue. How do you provide support for folks to do this work without burning out? (Stanton, Giles and Cruz, 1999)

As these pioneering practitioners offer, while many colleges and universities across the nation are quite vocal in their support of service learning and community based pedagogy, they often undermine the efforts and sap the energy of their faculty and staff by stubbornly clinging to traditional modes of evaluation. It is critical that higher education address archaic promotion and tenure policies and explore new policies that encourage an institutional commitment to community building and civic vitality—policies that fully integrate community experiences into scholarship professional service opportunities for staff and faculty.

In the remainder of this chapter we offer examples of the ways three institutions have revised their tenure and promotion guidelines to explicitly include service-learning. These examples may serve as models for similar institutions struggling to assess the work of faculty engaged in service learning. But these examples also raise larger questions about the current systems of merit many institutions employ. Simply revising traditional policies of promotion and tenure to fit service-learning may be shortsighted. For in many ways service-learning challenges fundamental assumptions about the priorities of the academy. The search for equitable compensation and for an accurate assessment of faculty work must inevitably address the very purpose of higher education in service to the nation and the role faculty play as visionaries and stewards in guiding the university to this higher ideal.

## REFERENCE

Stanton, Timothy, Giles, Dwight Jr., and Cruz, Nadinne. *Service-Learning: A Movement's Pioneers Reflect in Its Origins, Practice, and Future.* San Francisco CA, Jossey-Bass, 1999, 199–200.

# Retention, Tenure and Promotion Policy and Process

## California State University, Monterey Bay

### PREAMBLE

THE VISION OF CALIFORNIA STATE UNIVERSITY, Monterey Bay is that of a model, pluralistic, academic community where all learn from and teach one another in an atmosphere of mutual respect and pursuit of excellence. The identity of CSU Monterey Bay is framed by substantive commitment to a multilingual, multicultural, intellectual community distinguished by partnerships with existing institutions, both public and private, and by cooperative agreements which enable students, faculty and staff to cross institutional boundaries for innovative outcomes-based instruction, broadly defined scholarly and creative activity, and coordinated community service. Faculty are expected to excel both in their respective fields and through their contributions to CSUMB and the community.

Just as institutional programs at CSU Monterey Bay strive to "value and cultivate creative and productive talents of students, faculty, and staff…"the procedures for the review and evaluation of faculty are designed to equitably assess and document the performance of individual faculty members, rewarding both excellence and diversity in contributions made to institute and university goals. In the development of these policies and procedures, the university recognizes the uniqueness of individual faculty members, the institutes of which they are a part, and of their specific fields of knowledge. To help insure the flexibility needed to reflect this diversity, the main responsibility for implementing formative and evaluative procedures will be placed in the institutes. This document outlines criteria and standards to be used until the institutes complete that work. At the same time, however, these procedures will share common commitments to fulfillment of the university's academic mission and overall vision. These shared commitments are documented below.

For the purposes of this document "institute" will refer to academic units in which faculty participate as their main assignment. In most cases, "institute" will refer to a degree-granting academic unit, but in certain cases a more flexible definition may be necessary.

### 1.0 Definitions and Examples of Scholarly Work

While the meaning of scholarship is often limited to those activities directly related to the acquisition and dissemination of knowledge, this document strives to both expand and deepen the definition to encompass all outstanding faculty work that furthers the educational goals of students, faculty, academic units, the university as a whole, and the community. This more inclusive definition allows for a greater recognition of diverse faculty activities. Faculty have a responsibility to their students, disciplines, the community, and the university, to strive for outstanding intellectual, ethical, aesthetic, and creative achievement. Such achievement in the four scholarship areas of Teaching and Learning; Discovery, Creation and Integration; Professional Application; and University Service, is an indispensable qualification for retention, tenure and promotion.

While the categorical division of faculty roles into four scholarship areas serves to clarify a complex evaluation process, it is important to remember that these divisions function primarily as tools for the assessment of faculty work. Although these areas are categorized below, it is critical to underscore that sharp distinctions between these categories do not exist and that scholarly activities should emphasize collaborative and integrative relationships. It should also be emphasized that no faculty member will be expected to commit an equal amount of time, make an equal contribution, or achieve equally in the four categories of scholarly work described hereafter.

## 1.1 Teaching and Learning

Contributions to Teaching and Learning involve facilitating student learning, critical thought, and inquiry, as well as transmitting, integrating, interpreting, and extending knowledge. In addition, teaching should reveal and develop diverse perspectives, help to facilitate creativity and life-long learning, and work to integrate various principles central to the vision of CSU Monterey Bay. The faculty member's contributions to teaching and learning will be evaluated using the Performance Evaluation Standards for scholarly achievement. Activities to consider in the evaluation of teaching and learning may include, but are not limited to, the following:

- Instructing of students including one-on-one instruction, workshops, and seminars;

- Advising, supervising, guiding, assessing and mentoring students;

- Developing learning experiences and curricula;

- Developing teaching and learning resources;

- Contributing to professional development in teaching and learning.

## 1.2  Discovery, Creation and Integration

This scholarly activity constitutes academic work that confronts the unknown, seeks new understandings, and/or offers a new perspective on knowledge, through both individual and collaborative work. The faculty member's contributions to Discovery, Creation and Integration will be evaluated using the Performance Evaluation Standards for scholarly achievement. Activities to consider in the evaluation of Discovery, Creation and Integration may include, but are not limited to, the following:

- Conducting and disseminating research;

- Involving students in discovery, creation, and integration;

- Producing creative works;

- Disseminating curriculum and pedagogical improvements;

- Editing and managing creative works;

- Leading and managing funded research and creative projects.

## 1.3 Professional Application

Faculty engaged in Professional Application use their academic training and experience to serve the public and contribute to the CSU Monterey Bay vision. The diversity of external needs, as well as faculty training and experience, leads to many different forms of Professional Application; however, Professional Application activities share all of the following distinguishing characteristics:

a. They contribute to the public welfare or the common good.

b. They call upon faculty members' academic and/or professional expertise.

c. They directly address or respond to real-world needs.

d. They support the CSUMB vision.

The faculty member's contributions to Professional Application will be evaluated using the Performance Evaluation Standards for scholarly achievement. Activities to consider in the evaluation of Professional Application may include, but are not limited to, the following:

- Contributing to applied research, creative or entrepreneurial activities and/or programs that benefit the community;

- Developing collaborative partnerships;

- Providing services to professional organizations and publications;

- Serving communities, agencies, or organizations;

- Developing, adapting, or evaluating products, practices, services, or policies in the community;

- Disseminating practical information or technology to the public.

## C.3 Professional Application

Activities to consider in the evaluation of Professional Application may include, but are not limited to the following:

### PRACTICAL APPLICATIONS:

- Making research understandable and usable in specific professional and applied settings such as in technology transfer activities;

- Developing and offering training workshops and other forums for the dissemination of teaching techniques or demonstration of novel teaching methods;

- Giving presentations or performances for the public;

- Providing services directly to the community;

- Providing extension education;

- Testifying before legislative or congressional committees;

- Writing for popular and non-academic publications, including newsletters and magazines directed to agencies, professionals, or other specialized audiences;

- Writing peer reviews for scholarly publications and funding organizations.

**PARTICIPATING IN PARTNERSHIPS WITH OTHER ORGANIZATIONS:**

- Participating in collaborative endeavors with schools, industry, or civic agencies;

- Consulting with town, city, or county governments; schools, libraries, museums parks and other public institutions; groups; or individuals;

- Participating in professional organizations.

**DEVELOPING NEW PRODUCTS, PRACTICES, PROCEDURES AND SERVICES:**

- Providing public policy analysis, program evaluation, technical briefings for local, state, national, or international governmental agencies;

- Testing concepts and processes in real-world applications;

- Contributing to university development through corporate grants, donations of equipment, and other entrepreneurial activities;

- Creating working relationships with business [and other community partners] for the purpose of generating revenue for the university;

- Participating in entrepreneurial activties.

# Criteria, Documentation and Procedures for Reappointment, Tenure and Promotion

## Office of the Provost and Vice President for Academic Affairs, Montclair State University

Candidates for reappointment, tenure or promotion are responsible for providing evidence regarding the quality of their work in each of the 4 categories listed below. For at least one of the scholarship categories (B, C or D), candidates must provide evidence of work which, following external peer review, has been selected for dissemination through normally accepted venues for academic products such as publications, conference presentations, exhibitions or performances or other equivalent forms of professional accomplishment. *The significance of the accomplishments will be judged rigorously, with disciplinary standards determining the appropriateness of the venues.* The following criteria[1] will be used to evaluate the quality of the work:

- Clarity of goals

- Adequacy of preparation

- Appropriateness of methods

- Significance of results

- Effectiveness of presentation

- Evidence of reflective critique

The promise for future productivity will be considered for reappointment, tenure or promotion.

Aspirants to higher rank are expected, as they present themselves as candidates for that rank, to have demonstrated progressively more advanced levels of professional maturity, accomplishment, and recognition extending beyond the boundaries of the university. The difference between successive ranks is primarily one of achievement. Accomplishments while in rank at other institutions can be considered if they satisfy the promotion criteria at Montclair State University. At the same time, performance in all areas while at Montclair State carries the most weight. Holders of higher rank are expected to demonstrate advanced levels of accomplishment and recognition beyond the boundaries of the university as they are considered for reappointment and tenure.

Faculty must identify their current Faculty Scholarship Incentive Program (FSIP) category and provide evidence of the products produced as a result of their participation in FSIP. Faculty who have prior participation in categories different from their current category shall include the categories and product results in their documentation.

Paid activities should be noted.

**A. TEACHING.** The category requires evidence of quality in teaching, which includes classroom, laboratory and studio instruction, as well as independent study, supervision of interns/co-op students/student teachers/student research, clinical supervision and advisement.

All faculty are expected to be more than just "good" teachers, and excellence in teaching is especially important for reappointment as or promotion to associate professor and professor.

Documentation must include a statement which communicates the candidate's views about, and strengths in, teaching. Other evidence must include student course evaluations and peer classroom evaluations as required by the contract. Candidates may, and are encouraged to, include other materials, such as syllabi and exams, that indicate content and quality as well as additional student and peer classroom evaluations and samples of student work. Evidence of the range and type of courses taught, unique teaching style and techniques, use of technology to enhance teaching/learning, participation in teaching general education courses, and interdisciplinary teaching may also be included.

Effectiveness in other on-load non-teaching responsibilities, except FSIP (if applicable), should be included in this category and considered in proportion to time spent.

**B. SCHOLARSHIP OF PEDAGOGY.** The category requires evidence of the scholarly examination of teaching. Such evidence could include documentation of attendance at workshops (both on disciplinary knowledge and pedagogical innovation); engagement in curricular revision; the coordination of mentoring activities; engagement in a major personal examination of teaching (including attending a series of professional conferences or workshops on the subject and undertaking a study documenting the effects of changes); carrying out a major programmatic curricular revision; development of novel teaching methods; laboratory experiments or other pedagogical innovations; the acquisition of significant grant or contract funding; and writing about pedagogy.

**C. SCHOLARSHIP OF DISCOVERY, INTEGRATION, OR AESTHETIC CREATION.** The category requires evidence of scholarship that adds to the field of knowledge in the discipline, makes connections among existing ideas within and across disciplines, or in the production of works of art in any medium including creative writing. Such evidence could include documentation of publications, presentations, significant grant or contract funding, performances, or exhibitions.

**D. SCHOLARSHIP OF APPLICATION.** The category requires evidence of scholarship that applies knowledge to issues of contemporary social concerns and that, in the process, yields new intellectual understanding, and could include work in, for example, the public schools, museums, social agencies, and government. Such evidence could include documentation of the service which generated position papers, reports, or other writings, and the evaluations of those who received the service; significant grant or contract funding; editorships; or holding office in regional or national professional organizations.

In this category, candidates should also report their work on campus initiatives, service on committees, as well as work in professional associations.

Faculty are expected to make contributions to their professions and to the institution. Service to Montclair State University, including contributions at the department, school/college or university level are recognized as important to the life of the scholarly community. For reappointment as or promotion to associate professor, the record must demonstrate, at a minimum, significant service at the departmental level. For reappointment as or promotion to professor, the record of service must be substantial, including contributions beyond the department level.

Department Chairs or others involved in departmental administration who receive twelve or more TCH per year to perform administrative functions may select any one of the boxes on Form B indicating the option desired as the basis for their own personnel action. Those faculty with FSIP projects must check the box on Form B indicating the FSIP scholarship category selected and show progress (current FSIP project) or results (completed FSIP project) on the form in the scholarship area(s) relating to the FSIP project(s).

## WEIGHTS TO BE ASSIGNED TO CRITERIA FOR PROMOTION DELIBERATIONS

**FSIP CATEGORY CHANGE:** A faculty member who has changed FSIP category within the five years preceding the application may choose the category of scholarship for the evaluation.

The following tables indicate the weights assigned to school/college promotions depending upon the participation of the candidate in FSIP.

### For Faculty in the FSIP Category: Teaching

| | |
|---|---|
| Teaching | 40 |
| Scholarship of Pedagogy | 20 |
| Scholarship of DIAC* | 20 |
| Scholarship of Application | 20 |

### For Faculty in the FSIP Category: Scholarship of Pedagogy

| | |
|---|---|
| Teaching | 30 |
| Scholarship of Pedagogy | 40 |
| Scholarship of DIAC | 10 |
| Scholarship of Application | 20 |

*Discovery, Integration, or Aesthetic Creation.

### For Faculty in the FSIP Category: Scholarship of Discovery, Integration, or Aesthetic Creation

| | |
|---|---|
| Teaching | 30 |
| Scholarship of Pedagogy | 10 |
| Scholarship of DIAC | 40 |
| Scholarship of Application | 20 |

### For Faculty in the FSIP Category: Scholarship of Application

| | |
|---|---|
| Teaching | 30 |
| Scholarship of Pedagogy | 20 |
| Scholarship of DIAC | 10 |
| Scholarship of Application | 40 |

### The following weights shall be assigned for Special Contributions Promotions

| | |
|---|---|
| Teaching | 30 |
| Scholarship of Pedagogy | 20 |
| Scholarship of DIAC | 10 |
| Scholarship of Application | 40 |

Revised: 1/10/03

## PROMOTION

At the time of submission of this application, information not specifically requested on these forms may be supplied. Copies of all such materials not originiating from the candidate must be supplied to the candidate.

Form A must be signed at all levels. The candidate is to receive a copy of forms C, D, E, and the summary of student data upon completion of each form.

### Steps in Processing

1. All forms are distributed to the Department Chair.

2. All candidates shall provide a broad spectrum of evidence regarding the quality of their work in each of the four required categories (A through D). All attachments shall not exceed 8 1/2" X 11". A promotion application shall consist of:

- Promotion application forms

- A curriculum vita

- Copies of published materials, creative works, and any other appropriate supporting documents and materials which the candidate wishes to submit

- Table of contents

- When an applicant submits a large number of items as evidence of contributions for a particular promotion category, the applicant will indicate the most significant items in the category; not to exceed five in number.

3. The candidate completes Form B and forwards it to the PAC Chair by the submission date listed in the Administrative Calendar.

4. The Departmental Personnel Advisory Committee evaluates candidate information Form B and completes Form C. Forms B and C are transmitted to the Department Chair with a copy of C to the candidate.

5. The Department Chair evaluates Form B, completes Form D (a copy to candidate) and transmits a complete set of forms to the Dean of the College/School. The Department Chair will insure that a summary of the completed student evaluations is forwarded to the candidate. The Chair shall send the written evaluation and recommendation to the candidate.

6. The Summary of the Student Evaluation Questionnaires must be sent to the Department Chair, Department PAC and candidate at least two days prior to the date that the PAC is to forward its report to the Chair.

   The evaluation summary is to be attached to the forms by the Department Chair.

7. The Dean evaluates Forms B, C, and D, completes Form E, and forwards the evaluation, and recommendation, and the promotion materials of all candidates to the Provost/Vice President for Academic Affairs. The Dean shall send the written evaluation and recommendation to the candidate.

8. The Provost/Vice President for Academic Affairs shall either recommend or not recommend each candidate for promotion and forward the recommendations to the President and the candidate.

9. The President will review, evaluate, make recommendations, and then forward this report to the Board of Trustees for its action. The President must inform the candidate of this recommendation.

1. Charles E. Glassic, Mary Taylor Huber, Gene I. Maeroff, *Scholarship Assessed: Evaluation of the Professoriate.* (San Francisco: Jossey-Bass Publishers, 1997), p.36.

# Policies and Procedures for the Evaluation of Faculty for Tenure, Promotion, and Merit Increases

## Portland State University

## INTRODUCTION

POLICIES AND PROCEDURES FOR THE EVALUATION OF faculty are established to provide the means whereby the performance of individual faculty members and their contributions to collective university goals may be equitably assessed and documented. In the development of these policies and procedures, the university recognizes the uniqueness of individual faculty members, of the departments of which they are a part, and of their specific disciplines; and, because of that uniqueness, the main responsibility for implementation of formative and evaluative procedures has been placed in the departments.

Departmental guidelines should set forth processes and criteria for formative and evaluative activities which are consistent with the department's academic mission. For example, departmental guidelines might identify evaluative criteria which are appropriate to the discipline, or might delineate which activities will receive greater or lesser emphasis in promotion or tenure decisions. They should also include appropriate methods for evaluating the interdisciplinary scholarly activities of departmental faculty. The deans and the provost review departmental procedures in order to ensure that faculty are evaluated equitably throughout the university.

Evaluation instruments provide a means for gathering information that can provide a basis for evaluation, but these instruments do not constitute an evaluation in themselves. Evaluation is the process whereby the information acquired by appropriate instruments is analyzed to determine the quality of performance as measured against the criteria set by the department.

Policies and procedures shall be consistent with sections 580-21-100 through 135 of the Oregon Administrative Rules of the Oregon State System of Higher Education. Approval and implementation of these poli-cies and procedures shall be consistent with the agreement between Portland State University (PSU) and the American Association of University Professors, Portland State Chapter, and with the internal governance procedures of the university. Each year the provost will establish a timeline to ensure that decision-makers at each level of review will have sufficient time to consider tenure and promotion recommendations responsibly.

## SCHOLARSHIP

### Overview of Faculty Responsibilities

The task of a university includes the promotion of learning and the discovery and extension of knowledge, enterprises, which place responsibility upon faculty members with respect to their disciplines, their students, the university, and the community. The university seeks to foster the scholarly development of its faculty and to encourage the scholarly interaction of faculty with students and with regional, national, and international communities. Faculty have a responsibility to their disciplines, their students, the university, and the community to strive for superior intellectual, aesthetic, or creative achievement. Such achievement, as evidenced in scholarly accomplishments, is an indispensable qualification for appointment and promotion and tenure in the professorial ranks. Scholarly accomplishments, suggesting continuing growth and high potential, can be demonstrated through a variety of activities:

- Research, including creative activities

- Teaching, including delivery of instruction, mentoring, and curricular activities

- Community outreach

All faculty members should keep abreast of developments in their fields and remain professionally active throughout their careers.

At PSU, individual faculty are part of a larger mosaic of faculty talent. The richness of faculty talent should be celebrated, not restricted. Research, teaching, and community outreach are accomplished in an environment that draws on the combined intellectual vitality of the department and of the university. Department faculty may take on responsibilities of research, teaching, and community outreach in differing proportions and emphases. Irrespective of the emphasis assigned to differing activities, it is important that the quality of faculty contributions be rigorously evaluated and that the individual contributions of the faculty, when considered in aggregate, advance the goals of the department and of the university.

All faculty have a responsibility to conduct scholarly work in research, teaching, or community outreach in order to contribute to the body of knowledge in their field(s). Effectiveness in teaching, research, or community outreach must meet an acceptable standard when it is part of a faculty member's responsibilities. Finally, each faculty member is expected to contribute to the governance and professionally-related service activities of the university.

## Scholarly Agenda

**INDIVIDUAL FACULTY RESPONSIBILITY.** The process of developing and articulating one's own scholarly agenda is an essential first step for newly appointed faculty and is a continuing responsibility as faculty seek advancement. Each faculty member, regardless of rank, has the primary responsibility for planning his or her own career and for articulating his or her own evolving scholarly agenda.

The purpose of a scholarly agenda is not to limit a faculty member's freedom nor to constrain his or her scholarship, but, primarily, to provide a means for individuals to articulate their programs of scholarly effort. The scholarly agenda needs to be specific enough to provide a general outline of a faculty member's goals, priorities, and activities, but it is not a detailed recitation of tasks or a set of detailed, prescribed outcomes. A scholarly agenda accomplishes the following:

- Articulates the set of serious intellectual, aesthetic, or creative questions, issues, or problems, which engage and enrich an individual scholar.

- Describes an individual's accomplished and proposed contributions to knowledge, providing an overview of scholarship, including long term goals and purposes

- Clarifies general responsibilities and emphases placed by the individual upon research, teaching, community outreach, or governance.

- Articulates the manner in which the scholar's activities relate to the departmental mission and programmatic goals.

As a faculty member grows and develops, his or her scholarly agenda may evolve over the years. New scholarly agendas may reflect changes in the set of questions, issues, or problems, which engage the scholar, or in the individual's relative emphases on teaching, research, community outreach, and governance. The process of developing or redefining a scholarly agenda also encourages the individual scholar to interact with and draw upon the shared expertise of his or her departmental peers. This process promotes both individual and departmental development, and contributes to the intellectual, aesthetic, and creative climate of the department and of the university.

**DEPARTMENTAL, SCHOOL, AND COLLEGE RESPONSIBILITIES.** The development of a scholarly agenda supports a collective process of departmental planning and decision-making which determines the deployment of faculty talent in support of departmental and university missions. Departments, schools, and colleges have the primary responsibility for establishing their respective missions and programmatic goals within the context of the university's mission and disciplines as a whole. Recognizing that departments often accomplish such wide-ranging missions by encouraging faculty to take on diverse scholarly agendas, departments and individual faculty members are expected to engage in joint career development activities throughout each faculty member's career. Such activities must serve certain purposes:

- Recognize the individuals career development needs.

- Respect the diversity of individual faculty interests and talents.

- Advance the departmental mission and programmatic goals.

Departments shall develop processes for establishing, discussing, agreeing upon, and revising a scholarly agenda that are consistent with the focus upon individual career development and collective responsibilities and shall establish regular methods for resolving conflicts which may arise in the process of agreeing upon scholarly agendas. Finally, departmental processes shall include periodic occasions for collective discussion of the overall picture resulting from the combination of the scholarly agendas of individual faculty members.

**THE USES OF A SCHOLARLY AGENDA.** The primary use of a scholarly agenda is developmental, not evaluative. An individual's contributions to knowledge should be evaluated in the context of the quality and significance of the scholarship displayed. An individual may include a previously agreed upon scholarly agenda in his or her promotion and tenure documentation, but it is not required. A scholarly agenda is separate from such essentially evaluation-driven practices as letters of offer, annual review of tenure-track faculty, and institutional career support-peer review of tenured faculty, and from the consideration of individuals for merit awards.

## Expressions of Scholarship

The term scholar implies superior intellectual, aesthetic, or creative attainment. A scholar engages at the highest levels of lifelong learning and inquiry. The character of a scholar is demonstrated by academic achievement and rigorous academic practice. Over time, an active learner usually moves fluidly among different expressions of scholarship. However, it also is quite common and appropriate for scholars to prefer one expression over another. The following four expressions of scholarship apply equally to research, teaching, and community outreach.

**DISCOVERY.** Discovery is the rigorous testing of researchable questions suggested by theory or models of how phenomena may operate. It is active experimentation, or exploration, with the primary goal of adding to the cumulative knowledge in a substantive way and of enhancing future prediction of the phenomena. Discovery also may involve original creation in writing, as well as creation, performance, or production in the performing arts, fine arts, architecture, graphic design, cinema, and broadcast media or related technologies.

**INTEGRATION.** Integration places isolated knowledge or observations in perspective. Integrating activities make connections across disciplines, theories, or models. Integration illuminates information, artistic creations in the literary and performing arts, or original work in a revealing way. It brings divergent knowledge together or creates and/or extends new theory.

**INTERPRETATION.** Interpretation is the process of revealing, explaining, and making knowledge and creative processes clear to others or of interpreting the creative works of others. In essence, interpretation involves communicating knowledge and instilling skills and understanding that others may build upon and apply.

**APPLICATION.** Application involves asking how state-of-the-art knowledge can be responsibly applied to significant problems. Application primarily concerns assessing the efficacy of knowledge or creative activities within a particular context, refining its implications, assessing its generalizability and using it to implement changes.

## Quality and Significance of Scholarship

Quality and significance of scholarship are the primary criteria for determining faculty promotion and tenure. Quality and significance of scholarship are overarching, integrative concepts that apply equally to the expressions of scholarship as they may appear in various disciplines and to faculty accomplishments resulting from research, teaching, and community outreach.

A consistently high quality of scholarship, and its promise for future exemplary scholarship, is more important than the quantity of the work done. The criteria for evaluating the quality and significance of scholarly accomplishments include the following.

**CLARITY AND RELEVANCE OF GOALS.** A scholar should clearly define objectives of scholarly work and clearly state basic questions of inquiry. Clarity of purpose provides a critical context for evaluating scholarly work.

- Research or community outreach projects should address substantive intellectual, aesthetic, or creative problems or issues within one's chosen discipline or interdisciplinary field. Clear objectives are necessary for fair evaluation.

- Teaching activities are usually related to learning objectives that are appropriate within the context of curricular goals and the state of knowledge in the subject matter.

**MASTERY OF EXISTING KNOWLEDGE.** A scholar must be well-prepared and knowledgeable about developments in his or her field. The ability to educate others, conduct meaningful research, and provide high quality assistance through community outreach depends upon mastering existing knowledge.

- As researchers and problem solvers, scholars propose methodologies, measures, and interventions that reflect relevant theory, conceptualizations, and cumulative wisdom.

- As teachers, scholars demonstrate a command of resources and exhibit a depth, breadth, and understanding of subject matter allowing them to respond adequately to student learning needs and to evaluate teaching and curricular innovation.

APPROPRIATE USE OF METHODOLOGY AND RESOURCES. A scholar should address goals with carefully constructed logic and methodology.

- Rigorous research and applied problem solving require well-constructed methodology that allows one to determine the efficacy of the tested hypotheses or chosen intervention.

- As teachers, scholars apply appropriate pedagogy and instructional techniques to maximize student learning and use appropriate methodology to evaluate the effectiveness of curricular activities.

EFFECTIVENESS OF COMMUNICATION. Scholars should possess effective oral and written communication skills that enable them to convert knowledge into language that a public audience beyond the classroom, research laboratory, or field site can understand.

- As researchers and problem solvers, scholars make formal oral presentations and write effective manuscripts or reports or create original artistic works that meet the professional standards of the intended audience.

- As teachers, scholars communicate in ways that build positive student rapport and clarify new knowledge so as to facilitate learning. They also should be able to disseminate the results of their curricular innovations to their teaching peers.

Scholars should communicate with appropriate audiences and subject their ideas to critical inquiry and independent review. Usually the results of scholarship are communicated widely through publications (e.g., journal articles and books), performances, exhibits, and/or presentations at conferences and workshops.

SIGNIFICANCE OF RESULTS. Scholars should evaluate whether or not they achieve their goals and whether or not this achievement had an important impact on and is used by others. Customarily, peers and other multiple and credible sources (e.g., students, community participants, and subject matter experts) evaluate the significance of results.

- As researchers, teachers, and problem solvers, scholars widely disseminate their work in order to invite scrutiny and to measure varying degrees of critical acclaim. They must consider more than direct user satisfaction when evaluating the quality and significance of an intellectual contribution.

- Faculty engaged in community outreach can make a difference in their communities and beyond by defining or resolving relevant social problems or issues, by facilitating organizational development, by improving existing practices or programs, and by enriching the cultural life of the community. Scholars should widely disseminate the knowledge gained in a community-based project in order to share its significance with those who do not benefit directly from the project.

- As teachers, scholars can make a difference in their students' lives by raising student motivation to learn, by developing students' lifelong learning skills, and by contributing to students' knowledge, skills, and abilities. Teaching scholars also can make a significant scholarly contribution by communicating pedagogical innovations and curricular developments to peers who adopt the approaches.

CONSISTENT ETHICAL BEHAVIOR. Scholars should conduct their work with honesty, integrity, and objectivity. They should foster a respectful relationship with students, community participants, peers, and others who participate in or benefit from their work. Faculty standards for academic integrity represent a code of ethical behavior. For example, ethical behavior includes following the human subject review process in conducting research projects and properly crediting sources of information in writing reports, articles, and books.

### Evaluation of Scholarship

Scholarly accomplishments in the areas of research, teaching, and community outreach all enter into the evaluation of faculty performance. Scholarly profiles will vary depending on individual faculty members' areas of emphasis. The weight to be given factors relevant to the determination of promotion, tenure, and merit necessarily varies with the individual faculty member's assigned role and from one academic field to another. However, one should recognize that research, teaching, and community outreach often overlap. For example, a service-learning project may reflect both teaching and community outreach. Some research projects may involve both research and community outreach. Pedagogical research may involve both research and teaching. When a faculty member evaluates his or her individual intellectual, aesthetic, or creative accomplishments, it is more important to focus on the general criteria of the quality and significance of the work than to categorize the work. Peers also should focus on the quality and significance of work rather than on categories of work when evaluating an individual's achievements.

The following discussion is intended to assist faculty in formative planning of a scholarly agenda and to provide examples of the characteristics to consider when evaluating scholarly accomplishments.

DOCUMENTATION. The accomplishments of a candidate for promotion or tenure must be documented in order to be evaluated. Documentation and evaluation of scholarship should focus on the quality and significance of scholarship rather than on a recitation of tasks and projects. Each department should judge the quality and significance of scholarly contributions to knowledge as well as the quantity.

In addition to contributions to knowledge, the effectiveness of teaching, research, or community outreach must meet an acceptable standard when it is part of a faculty member's responsibilities. Documentation should be sufficient to outline a faculty member's agreed-upon responsibilities and to support an evaluation of effectiveness.

Documentation for promotion and tenure normally includes several items:

- Self-appraisal of scholarly agenda and accomplishments including: 1) a discussion of the scholarly agenda that describes the long-term goals and purposes of a scholarly line of work, explains how the agenda fits into a larger endeavor and field of work, and demonstrates how scholarly accomplishments to date have advanced the agenda; 2) a description of how the agenda relates to the departmental academic mission, within the context of the university mission

and the discipline as a whole; 3) an evaluation of the quality and significance of scholarly work; 4) an evaluation of the effectiveness of teaching, research, or community outreach when it is part of a faculty member's responsibilities.

- A curriculum vitae including a comprehensive list of significant accomplishments.

- A representative sample of an individual's most scholarly work rather than an exhaustive portfolio. However, a department may establish guidelines requiring review of all scholarly activities that are central to a faculty member's scholarly agenda over a recent period of time.

- Evaluations of accomplishments by peers and other multiple and credible sources (e.g., students, community participants, and subject matter experts). Peers include authoritative representatives from the candidate's scholarly field(s).

RESEARCH AND OTHER CREATIVE ACTIVITIES. A significant factor in determining a faculty member's merit for promotion is the individual's accomplishments in research and published contributions to knowledge in the appropriate field(s) and other professional or creative activities that are consistent with the faculty member's responsibilities. Contributions to knowledge in the area of research and other creative activities should be evaluated using the criteria for quality and significance of scholarship. It is strongly recommended that the following items be considered in evaluating research and other creative activities:

- Research may be evaluated on the quality and significance of publication of scholarly books, monographs, articles, presentations, and reviews in journals, and grant proposal submissions and awards. An evaluation should consider whether the individual's contributions reflect continuous engagement in research and whether these contributions demonstrate future promise. Additionally, the evaluation should consider whether publications are refereed (an important form of peer review) as an important factor. In some fields, evidence of citation or use of the faculty member's research or creative contributions by other scholars is appropriate.

- The development and publication of software should be judged in the context of its involvement of state-of-the-art knowledge and its impact on peers and others.

- In certain fields such as writing, literature, performing arts, fine arts, architecture, graphic design, cinema, and broadcast media or related fields, distinguished creation should receive consideration equivalent to that accorded to distinction attained in scientific and technical research. In evaluating artistic creativity, an attempt should be made to define the candidate's merit in the light of such criteria as originality, scope, richness, and depth of creative expression. It should be recognized that in music and drama, distinguished performance, including conducting and directing, is evidence of a candidate's creativity. Creative works often are evaluated by the quality and significance of publication, exhibiting, and/or performance of original works or by the direction or performance of significant works. Instruments that include external peer review should be used or developed to evaluate artistic creation and performance. Including critical reviews, where available, can augment the departmental evaluations. The evaluation should include a chronological list of creative works, exhibitions, or performances.

- Contributions to the development of collaborative, interdisciplinary, or interinstitutional research programs are highly valued. Mechanisms for evaluating such contributions may be employed. Evaluating collaborative research might involve addressing both individual contributions (e.g., quality of work, completion of assigned responsibilities) and contributions to the successful participation of others (e.g., skills in teamwork, group problem solving).

- Honors and awards represent recognition of stature in the field when they recognize active engagement in research or creative activities at regional, national, or international levels.

- Effective participation in disciplinary or interdisciplinary organizations' activities should be evaluated in the context of their involvement of state-of-the-art knowledge and impact on peers and others. For example, this participation might include serving as editor of journals or other learned publications, serving on an editorial board, chairing a program committee for a regional, national, or international meeting, or providing scholarly leadership as an officer of a major professional organization.

**TEACHING, MENTORING, AND CURRICULAR ACTIVITIES.** A significant factor in determining a faculty member's merit for promotion is the individual's accomplishments in teaching, mentoring, and curricular activities, consistent with the faculty member's responsibilities. Teaching activities are scholarly functions that directly serve learners within or outside the university. Scholars who teach must be intellectually engaged and must demonstrate mastery of the knowledge in their field(s). The ability to lecture and lead discussions, to create a variety of learning opportunities, to draw out students and arouse curiosity in beginners, to stimulate advanced students to engage in creative work, to organize logically, to evaluate critically the materials related to one's field of specialization, to assess student performance, and to excite students to extend learning beyond a particular course and understand its contribution to a body of knowledge are all recognized as essential to excellence in teaching.

Teaching scholars often study pedagogical methods that improve student learning. Evaluation of performance in this area thus should consider creative and effective use of innovative teaching methods, curricular innovations, and software development. Scholars who teach also should disseminate promising curricular innovations to appropriate audiences and subject their work to critical review. PSU encourages publishing in pedagogical journals or making educationally-focused presentations at disciplinary and interdisciplinary meetings that advance the scholarship of teaching and curricular innovations or practice.

Evaluation of teaching and curricular contributions should not be limited to classroom activities. It also should focus on a faculty member's contributions to larger curricular goals (for example, the role of a course in laying foundations for other courses and its contribution to majors or contributions to broad aspects of general education or interdisciplinary components of the curriculum). In addition, PSU recognizes that student mentoring, academic advising, thesis advising, and dissertation advising are important departmental functions. Faculty may take on differential mentoring responsibilities as part of their personal scholarly agenda.

To ensure valid evaluations, departments should appoint a departmental committee to devise formal methods for evaluating teaching and curriculum-related performance. All members of the department should be involved in selecting these formal methods. The department chair has the responsibility for seeing that these methods for evaluation are implemented.

Contributions to knowledge in the area of teaching, mentoring, and curricular activities should be evaluated using the criteria for quality and significance of scholarship. It is strongly recommended that the following items be considered in the evaluation of teaching and curricular accomplishments:

- Contributions to courses or curriculum development

- Outlines, syllabi, and other materials developed for use in courses

- The results of creative approaches to teaching methods and techniques, including the development of software and other technologies that advance student learning

- The results of assessments of student learning

- Formal student evaluations

- Peer review of teaching, mentoring, and curricular activities

- Accessibility to students

- Ability to relate to a wide variety of students for purposes of advising

- Mentoring and guiding students toward the achievement of curricular goals

- The results of supervision of student research or other creative activities including theses and field advising

- The results of supervision of service-learning experiences in the community

- Contributions to, and participation in, the achievement of departmental goals, such as achieving reasonable retention of students

- Contributions to the development and delivery of collaborative, interdisciplinary, university studies, extended studies, and interinstitutional educational programs

- Teaching and mentoring students and others in how to obtain access to information resources so as to further student, faculty, and community research and learning

- Grant proposals and grants for the development of curriculum or teaching methods and techniques

- Professional development as related to instruction; e.g., attendance at professional meetings related to a faculty member's areas of instructional expertise

## Honors and Awards for Teaching

COMMUNITY OUTREACH. A significant factor in determining a faculty member's advancement is the individual's accomplishments in community outreach when such activities are part of a faculty member's responsibilities. Scholars can draw on their professional expertise to engage in a wide array of community outreach. Such activities can include defining or resolving relevant local, national, or international problems or issues. Community outreach also includes planning literary or artistic festivals or celebrations. PSU highly values quality community outreach as part of faculty roles and responsibilities.

The setting of Portland State University affords faculty many opportunities to make their expertise useful to the community outside the university. Community-based activities are those which are tied directly to one's special field of knowledge. Such activities may involve a cohesive series of activities contributing to the definition or resolution of problems or issues in society. These activities also include aesthetic and celebratory projects. Scholars who engage in community outreach also should disseminate promising innovations to appropriate audiences and subject their work to critical review.

Departments and individual faculty members can use the following guidelines when developing appropriate community outreach. Important community outreach can:

- Contribute to the definition or resolution of a relevant social problem or issue

- Use state-of-the-art knowledge to facilitate change in organizations or institutions

- Use disciplinary or interdisciplinary expertise to help groups conceptualize and solve problems

- Set up intervention programs to prevent, ameliorate, or remediate persistent negative outcomes for individuals or groups or to optimize positive outcomes.

- Contribute to the evaluation of existing practices or programs

- Make substantive contributions to public policy

- Create schedules and choose or hire participants in community events such as festivals

- Offer professional services such as consulting (consistent with the policy on outside employment), serving as an expert witness, providing clinical services, and participating on boards and commissions outside the university

Faculty and departments should evaluate a faculty member's community outreach accomplishments creatively and thoughtfully. It is strongly recommended that the evaluation consider the following indicators of quality and significance:

- Publication in journals or presentations at disciplinary or interdisciplinary meetings that advance the scholarship of community outreach

- Honors, awards, and other forms of special recognition received for community outreach

- Adoption of the faculty member's models for problem resolution, intervention programs, instruments, or processes by others who seek solutions to similar problems

- Substantial contributions to public policy or influence upon professional practice

- Models that enrich the artistic and cultural life of the community

- Evaluative statements from clients and peers regarding the quality and significance of documents or performances produced by the faculty member

**GOVERNANCE AND OTHER PROFESSIONALLY RELATED SERVICE.** In addition to contributions to knowledge as a result of scholarly activities, each faculty member is expected to contribute to the governance and professionally related service activities of the university. Governance and professionally related service create an environment that supports scholarly excellence and the achievement of the university mission. Governance and professionally related service actives include the following:

- Committee service. Service on university, school or college, and department or program committees is an important part of running the university. Department chairs may request a committee chair to evaluate the value a faculty member's contributions to that committee. Such service also may include involvement in peer review of scholarly accomplishments.

- University community. Faculty are expected to participate in activities devoted to enriching the artistic, cultural, and social life of the university, such as attending commencement or serving as adviser to student groups.

- Community or professional service. Faculty may engage in professionally related service to a discipline or interdisciplinary field, or to the external community, that does not engage an individual's scholarship. For example, a faculty member may serve the discipline by organizing facilities for a professional meeting or by serving as treasurer of an organization.

## COMMUNITY OUTREACH PORTFOLIO
### PORTLAND STATE UNIVERSITY

Note: The material presented here is taken from the work of Amy Driscoll and Ernest Lynton. *Making Outreach Visible: A Guide to Documenting Professional Service and Outreach* (AAHE, 1999), edited by Driscoll and Lynton, provides chapters offering rationale, lessons learned, good practice, administrator perspective, and a campus action agenda.

Documentation of an individual's scholarship manifested in a community outreach project should provide information about the following principal elements, using an appropriate combination of narrative and illustrative materials, and whatever sequence and format is appropriate to the specific activity.

### The Purpose: Defining the Task
The documentation needs to describe and explain:

- The nature and context of the project;

- Its responsiveness to the needs and priorities of the external client, its consistency with institutional and departmental mission, and its appropriateness to the individual's development;

- The utilization of the complementary expertise and experiences of the individual and external partners;

- The diagnostic steps taken to understand the principal characteristics of the situation, as well as to identify the situation-specific aspects requiring adaptation of commonly used approaches and the available and potential resources.

No matter how these elements are presented and where they occur within the overall documentation, they should give the reader of the portfolio an understanding of the activity's context and circumstances, of the applicable knowledge base as well as situation-specific aspects, and of the needs and expectations of the several stake holders.

### The Process: Carrying It Out

The elements listed under "Purpose" must be used to describe and explain the rationale for the design of the project, i.e., the reasoned, situation-pertinent choice of attainable goals and appropriate method. The documentation must in addition describe the reflective delivery or implementation—how it was monitored and what adaptations were made in an ongoing design. The principal elements of process are:

- Attainable goals

- Appropriate method

- Continuous reflection

- Ongoing adaptation

### The Outcomes: Impact of the Activity

The outcomes of a community outreach project include these four elements:

- The impact on the external partner, including (1) how the specific goals were met in terms of responding to the partner's immediate needs and expectations; and (2) how the activity enhanced the partner's understanding and capability of dealing with similar situations in the future.

- The impact on the individual (faculty member), including (1) what was learned from the project by the individual and how this enhanced his/her own capability of undertaking similar projects in the future; (2) how the activity enriched the individual's teaching; and (3) how it influenced her/his research or scholarship.

- The impact on the institution and department including (1) how the activity contributed to the institutional and departmental missions and priorities; (2) how it influenced the curriculum and the teaching of colleagues; (3) how it provided direct or indirect opportunities for student involvement; and (4) how it reinforced collective research programs and the research of colleagues.

- The impact on the knowledge base of the individual's discipline including (1) how the activity contributed to existing principles and/or methodology, and (2) how these contributions were communicated to fellow specialists, as well as to others engaged in similar activities, including external stake holders.

The importance of the above items will vary from discipline to discipline, and depend on the particular nature of the project. Furthermore, the list is not necessarily complete, and may need to include additional items. Remember, the portfolio should tell a coherent story through a combination of narrative and illustrative material. Community outreach projects are often carried out in a non-linear fashion, starting at different points with continuous reflection, ongoing collaboration with external partners, and multiple feedback. Projects are often begun by a trial or pilot phase which implies flexibility in the development of the framework. Likewise, the guidelines provided here should be subject to the same flexibility in the development of a Community Outreach Portfolio.

## BOOKS & CHAPTERS

Arreola, R.A. (1995). *Developing a comprehensive faculty evaluation system.* Bolton, MA: Anker Publishing.

Bowker, L.H., Mauksch, H., Keating, B. & McSeveney, D. (1992). *The role of the department chair.* Washington DC: American Sociological Association Teaching Resources Center.

Boyer, E.L., (1990). *Scholarship reconsidered: Priorities for the professoriate.* Princeton, NJ: Carnegie Foundation for the Advancement of Teaching.

Braskamp, L. & Ory, J. (1994). *Assessing faculty work.* San Francisco: Jossey-Bass.

Centra, J. (1994). *Reflective faculty evaluation.* San Francisco: Jossey-Bass.

Cleary, C. (Ed.) (n.d.). *Service-learning faculty manual.* Fort Collins, CO: Office of Community Services, Colorado State University.

Cochran, L.H. (1992). *Publish or perish: The wrong issue.* Cape Girardeau, MO: StepUp Publications.

Diamond R.M., & Bronwyn, A. (1995a). *The disciplines speak: Rewarding the scholarly, professional, and creative work of faculty.* Washington, DC: American Association for Higher Education.

Diamond R.M., & Bronwyn, A. (1995b). *The disciplines speak II: More statements on rewarding the scholarly, professional, and creative work of faculty.* Washington, DC: American Association for Higher Education.

Driscoll, A., et al. (1997). *Assessing the impact of service-learning: A workbook of strategies and methods.* Portland, OR: Center for Academic Excellence, Portland State University.

Driscoll A., & Lynton, E. (1999). *Making outreach visible: A guide to documenting professional service and outreach.* Washington, DC: American Association for Higher Education.

Elman, S.E., & Smock, S.M. (1985). *Professional service and faculty rewards: Toward an integrated structure.* Washington, DC: National Association of State Universities and Land-Grant Colleges.

Fairweather, J.S. (1996). *Faculty work and public trust: Restoring the value of teaching and public service in American academic life.* Needham Heights, MA: Allyn and Bacon.

Farmer, J.A., & Schomberg, S.F. (1993). *A faculty guide for relating public service to the promotion and tenure review process.* Champaign, IL: Office of Continuing Education and Public Service, University of Illinois at Urbana-Champaign.

Glassick, C.E., Huber, M.T., & Maeroff, G. (1997). *Scholarship assessed: Evaluation of the professoriate* (A special report of the Carnegie Foundation for the Advancement of Teaching). San Francisco: Jossey-Bass.

Hutchings, P. (1996). *Making teaching community property: A menu for peer collaboration and peer review.* Washington, DC: American Association for Higher Education.

Jacoby, B., et al. (1996). *Service-learning in higher education.* San Francisco: Jossey-Bass.

Licata, C., & Morreale, J. (Eds.). (2002). *Post-tenure faculty review and renewal: Experienced voices.* Washington, DC: American Association for Higher Education.

Lynton, E. (1995). *Making the case for professional service.* Washington, DC: American Association for Higher Education.

Singleton, S., Hirsch, D., & Burack, C. (1999). Organization structures for community engagement. In R.G. Bringle, R. Games, & E.A. Malloy (Eds.), *Colleges and universities as citizens* (pp.121–140). Needham Heights, MA: Allyn and Bacon.

University of Maryland. (1999). *Faculty handbook for service-learning.* College Park, MD: Office of Commuter Affairs and Community Service, University of Maryland.

University of Utah. (1996). *Evaluating service-learning as a component of teaching in the tenure process.* Salt Lake City, UT: Lowell Bennion Community Service Center, University of Utah.

Wergin, J.F., & Swingen, J.N. (2000). *Departmental assessment: How some campuses are effectively evaluating the collective work of faculty.* Washington, DC: American Association for Higher Education.

## ARTICLES & REPORTS

Abes, E.S., Jackson, G., & Jones, S.R. (2002). Factors that motivate and deter faculty use of service-learning. *Michigan Journal of Community Service Learning, 9* (1), 5–17.

Amy, L., & Crow, A. (2000). Shaping the imaginary domain: Strategies for tenure and promotion at one institution. *Computers and Composition, 17* (1), 57–68.

Checkoway, B. (2002). Renewing the civic mission of the American research university. *Journal of Public Affairs, 6* [suppl. 1], 295–314.

Crasson, P.H. (1985). *Public service in higher education: Practices and priorities* (ASHE-ERIC higher education report no. 2). Washington, DC: ERIC Clearinghouse on Higher Education.

Favero, M. (2002). Linking administrative behavior and student learning: The learning centered academic unit. *PJE: Peabody Journal of Education, 77* (3), 60-84.

Gelmon, S., & Agre-Kippenhan, S. (2002). A developmental framework for supporting evolving faculty roles for community engagement. *Journal of Public Affairs, 6* [suppl. 1], 161–182.

Holland, B. (1997). Analyzing institutional commitment to service: A model of key organizational factors. *Michigan Journal of Community Service Learning, 4,* 30–41.

Knight, P.T., & Trowler, P.R. (2000). Department-level cultures and the improvement of teaching and learning. *Studies in Higher Education, 25* (1), 69–83.

Lidstone, J.E., Hacker, P.E., & Owen, F. (1996). Where the rubber meets the road: Revising promotion and tenure standards according to Boyer. *Quest, 48* (2),100.

O'Meara, K.A. (1997). *Rewarding faculty professional service* (Working Paper #19). Boston: New England Resource Center for Higher Education (NERCHE).

Schomberg, S.F., & Farmer, J., Jr. (1994). The evolving concept of public service and implications for rewarding faculty. *Continuing Higher Education Review, 58* (3).

University of Maryland. (n.d.) Policy on appointment, promotion and tenure of faculty. www.faculty.umd.edu/policies/policy.htm

# Great Books:

## Further reading on the foundations of service-learning, civic education, and engagement

Addams, J. (1893). *Philanthropy and social progress*. New York: Thomas Y. Crowell and Co.

Addams, J. (1910, 1981). *Twenty years at Hull House*. New York: Macmillan.

Addams, J. (1985). *On education*. New York: Teachers College Press.

Arendt, H. (1958). *The human condition*. Chicago, IL: University of Chicago Press.

Arendt, H. (1977). *The life of the mind*. New York: Viking Press.

Arendt, H. (1968). *Men in dark times*. New York: Harcourt, Brace and World.

Ayers, W., & Miller, J. (Eds.) (1998). *A light in dark times: Maxine Greene and the unfinished conversation*. New York: Teachers College Press.

Berry, W. (1996). *The unsettling of America: Culture and agriculture*. Third Edition. San Francisco, CA: Sierra Club Books.

Canada, G. (1995). *Fist stick knife gun*. Boston: Beacon Press.

Coles, R. (1993). *The call of service*. New York: Houghton-Mifflin.

Coles, R. (1989). *The call of stories*. New York: Houghton Mifflin.

Daloz, L.P., Keen, C., Keen, J., & Parks. S.D. (1996). *Common fire: Lives of commitment in a complex world*. Boston: Beacon Press.

Dewey, J. (1938). *Experience and education*. New York: Collier Press.

Dewey, J. (1946). *The public and its problems*. Chicago: Gateway Press.

Dewey, J. (1976). *Democracy and education*. Vol. 9 of The Middle Works of John Dewey. Carbondale: Southern Illinois University Press. (Originally published 1916).

Emerson, R. W. (1837, August). "The American Scholar." (An oration delivered before the Phi Beta Kappa Society at Cambridge, August 31, 1837).

Erickson, E. H. (1969). *Gandhi's truth: On the origins of militant non-violence*. First Edition, New York: Norton.

Feinstein Institute for Public Service. (1996). *Community service in higher education: A decade of development*. Providence, RI: Providence College.

Freire, P. (1973). *Pedagogy of the oppressed*. New York: Continuum.

Gardner, H. (1991). *The unschooled mind*. New York: Basic Books.

Goldman, E. (1934). *Living my life*. Garden City: Garden City Publishing Co.

Greene, M. (1995). *Releasing the imagination: Essays on education, the arts, and social change*. San Francisco, CA: Jossey-Bass.

Greenleaf, R. (1977). *Servant leadership*. New York: Paulist Press.

Hadot, P. (1998). *The inner citadel: The meditations of Marcus Aurelius*. (Translated by Michael Chase.) Cambridge, MA: Harvard University Press.

Hilfiker, D. (1994). *Not all of us are saints: A doctor's journey with the poor*. New York: Hill and Wang.

Hooks, B. (1994). *Teaching to transgress: Education as the practice of freedom*. New York: Routledge.

Horton, M. (1990). *The long haul*. New York: Doubleday.

Horton, M., & Freire, P. (1990). *We make the road by walking: Conversations on education and social change*. Philadelphia, PA: Temple.

Ignatieff, M. (1986). *The needs of strangers: An essay on privacy, solidarity, and the politics of being human*. New York: Penguin.

James, W. (1984). *The moral equivalent of war*. In Wilshire, B. (Ed.) *William James: The essential writings*. Albany, NY: State University of New York Press.

King, M. L. (1986). *Letter from Birmingham city jail*. In Melvin, J. (Ed.) *A testament of hope: The essential writings of Martin Luther King, Jr*. New York: Harper and Row.

Kozol, J. (1995). *Amazing Grace*. New York: Random House.

Lasch, C. (Ed.) (1965). *The social thought of Jane Addams*. Indianapolis, IN: Bobbs-Merril.

Levi, C. (1947, 1963). *Christ stopped at Eboli*. New York: Farrar, Straus and Co.

Lipset, S. M. & Altbach, P. (1969). *Students in revolt*. Boston, MA: Houghton Mifflin Company.

Lubove, R. (1973). *The professional altruist: The emergence of social work as a career, 1880-1930*. New York: Athenaeum.

Noddings, N. (1984). *Caring: A feminine approach to ethics and moral education*. Berkeley, CA: University of California Press.

Parks, S. (1986). *The critical years: The young adult search for a faith to live by*. San Francisco, CA: Harper and Row.

Putnam, R. (2000). *Bowling alone: The collapse and revival of American community*. New York: Simon & Schuster.

Rhorty, R. (1998). *Achieving our country*. Cambridge, MA: Harvard University Press.

Ross, E. D. (1942). *Democracy's college: The land grant movement in the formative stages*. Ames, IA: The Iowa State College Press.

Ryan, A. (1998). *Liberal anxieties and liberal education*. New York: Hill and Wang.

Sennett, R. (1977). *The fall of public man*. Boston, MA: Faber and Faber.

Slim, H., & Thomson, P. (1995). (Bennett O. and Cross, N. contributing editors). *Listening for a change: Oral testimony and community development*. Philadelphia, PA: New Society Publishers.

Sigmon, R. (1996). *Journey to service learning: Experiences from independent, liberal arts colleges and universities*. Washington, DC: Council of Independent Colleges.

Stanton, T., Giles, Jr, D. E., & Cruz, N. (1999). *Service-learning: A movement's pioneers reflect on its origins, practice and future*. San Francisco, CA: Jossey-Bass.

Weil, S. (1987). *A modern pilgrimage*. Reading, MA: Addison-Wesley.

Williams, W. C. (1984). *The doctor's stories*. New York: New Directions Press.

Williams, W. C. (1975). *The knack of survival in America*. New Brunswick, NJ: Rutgers University Press.

Wills, G. (1999). *A necessary evil: A history of American distrust of government*. New York: Simon and Schuster.